War and economic development

War and economic development

Essays in memory of David Joslin

edited by

J. M. WINTER

Lecturer in Social History, University of Warwick

Cambridge University Press

Cambridge
London · New York · Melbourne

Published by the Syndics of the Cambridge University Press
The Pitt Building, Trumpington Street, Cambridge CB2 1RP
Bentley House, 200 Euston Road, London NW1 2DB
32 East 57th Street, New York, NY 10022, USA
296 Beaconsfield Parade, Middle Park, Melbourne 3206, Australia

Library of Congress catalogue card number: 74-82219

ISBN: 0 521 20535 2

First published 1975

Printed in Great Britain
at the University Printing House, Cambridge
(Euan Phillips, University Printer)

Contents

Preface: David Joslin
H. J. HABAKKUK, *Jesus College, Oxford*   *page* vii

Introduction: The economic and social history of war   1
J. M. WINTER, *University of Warwick*

1 War, taxation and the English economy in the late thirteenth
and early fourteenth centuries   11
EDWARD MILLER, *Master of Fitzwilliam College,*
Cambridge University

2 Taxation for war and peace in early-Tudor England   33
G. R. ELTON, *Professor of English Constitutional History and*
Fellow of Clare College, Cambridge University

3 War and economic change: the economic costs of the Dutch
Revolt   49
GEOFFREY PARKER, *Lecturer in History, St Andrews University*

4 Swords and ploughshares: the armed forces, medicine and
public health in the late eighteenth century   73
PETER MATHIAS, *Chichele Professor of Economic History and*
Fellow of All Souls College, Oxford University

5 War and industrialisation   91
PHYLLIS DEANE, *Reader in Economic History and Fellow of*
Newnham College, Cambridge University

6 The exigencies of war and the politics of taxation in the
Netherlands 1795–1810   103
SIMON SCHAMA, *Fellow of Christ's College, Cambridge University*

7 War and the failure of industrial mobilisation: 1899 and 1914   139
CLIVE TREBILCOCK, *Lecturer in History and Fellow of Pembroke*
College, Cambridge University

8   War and economic development: government and the optical
    industry in Britain, 1914–18   *page* 165
    ROY AND KAY MACLEOD, *History and Social Studies of Science,*
    Sussex University

9   War demand and industrial supply: the 'Dope Scandal', 1915–19   205
    D. C. COLEMAN, *Professor of Economic History and Fellow of*
    Pembroke College, Cambridge University

10 Administrators and agriculture: aspects of German agricultural
    policy in the First World War   229
    JOE LEE, *Professor of Modern History, University College, Cork*

11 Social planning in war-time: some aspects of the
    Beveridge Report   239
    JOSÉ HARRIS, *Lecturer in Social Science and Administration,*
    the London School of Economics

Select bibliography of works on war and economic development   257
    J. M. WINTER

Index   293

Preface: David Joslin

David Maelgwyn Joslin was born in 1925 in Barry, a seaport in South Wales. His surname was English and his paternal forebears came originally from Somerset. But in temperament, upbringing and background he was Welsh. Both his parents were teachers and from an early age he had an ambition, common among the children of Welsh teachers, to excel in intellectual activity. He attended the local elementary school and the Barry County School and, after three years in the Royal Navy during the war in which he acquired a knowledge of Japanese, he went up to St John's College, Cambridge, in 1946. He was placed in the First Class of Parts I and II of the Historical Tripos in 1947 and 1948, and in 1951 he was elected Fellow and Tutor in History at Pembroke College; in 1954 he was appointed University Lecturer and in 1965 he succeeded Professor Postan in the chair of Economic History. He died in 1970 as the result of a heart attack.

In Part II of the Tripos David took Professor Postan's Special Subject on the British Economy between 1886 and 1938 and when he decided to undertake research he naturally looked to economic history. His first intention was to investigate English country banking in the eighteenth century, particularly in East Anglia, and he collected a good deal of material on this subject. But he was diverted by the great richness and fascination of the records of Child's Bank, Hoares and Gosling's to explore the activities of the London private bankers in the eighteenth century, and these were the subject of his first article, which was published in 1954. He continued his publications in this field with a contribution to the *Festschrift* for Professor T. S. Ashton, a scholar who greatly influenced David's work on the eighteenth century and for whom David had immense admiration. The subject was full of potentialities, the sources were abundant and in due course David's work in this field would have resulted in a major work. But in 1956 he was invited by the Board of Directors of the Bank of London and South America to write the history of the banks which had gone to the making of that institution, as a commemoration of the centenary of the oldest of them. David was well-equipped for the task, not only by his mastery of banking history but by the knowledge of Spanish he had acquired at school; and the invitation and the extensive tour of South America he undertook in 1957 enormously enlarged the range of his interests. The work appeared in 1963 and is a major contribution to the history of the role of the British in the economic development of Latin America, and for the rest of his life this area remained one of his main interests.

In his academic work, David liked getting a complicated subject straight and setting it in its proper proportions; he had an orderly, logical and analytical mind and was circumspect and judicious in his use of evidence. Only rarely, as for example in his portrait of Colonel John North, the nitrate king, was his passionate interest in people given rein on the printed page. But the personality which became evident in his human relations was, to an exceptional degree, exuberant, warm and spontaneous; he was fascinated by human foibles and by the tactics of human situations; and he had a keen sense of person and place, and a skill as a raconteur which would have made him a brilliant historian of politics. He liked few things better than talking with friends and for them he peopled the world with characters which, if sometimes larger than life, were always vivid and exciting. Affection for his friends was linked with another characteristic, a strong sense of loyalty to the institutions to which he belonged. This was in part the result of a desire to be in the thick of things, a delight in having his finger on the pulse; but more fundamentally it was due to a sense of obligation which arose from his religious convictions, for he had been brought up as a keen churchman. Because he was evidently a capable and sagacious administrator and an excellent committee man, the institutions to which he belonged made full use of his services. He was Senior Tutor of Pembroke; he was a member of the General Board at Cambridge; and for many years he gave devoted service to the *Economic History Review* as assistant editor. He was one of the moving spirits behind the South American Centre in Cambridge and was editor of the *Journal of Latin American Studies* and of *Cambridge Latin American Studies*. And he was above all, and this remained his primary obligation, a devoted and stimulating teacher and lecturer. He took endless pains with his pupils and, in the best traditions of College life, had a wide and varied circle of friends among undergraduates.

When he died he was at the height of his powers; his main historical interests were settled, his marriage had given him new strength and purpose, and a life of dedicated scholarship seemed to lie before him. This was not to be; but that his influence as a scholar, teacher and friend remains bright and vigorous the essays in this volume testify.

H. J. HABAKKUK

Introduction

The economic and social history of war

J. M. Winter

'We are as ignorant about war as the physicist is of the true nature of matter.'[1] With this characteristic flourish, Fernand Braudel launched his discussion of the 'forms of warfare' in the Mediterranean world in the sixteenth and seventeenth centuries.[2] His discussion of privateering, of brigandage and piracy, of the financial, logistic, and technological problems of wars, both declared and undeclared, has illuminated many aspects of the interaction of armed conflict and social change.[3] It is no surprise that the historian of 'la longue durée' has rejected the legalistic view, which has passed into colloquial language, that there are chronological limits to wars, and that there is an exact moment when a state of war between social groups ends and a state of peace begins.[4] By studying war as part of a spectrum of group conflict, Braudel, like Clausewitz and Marx, has suggested that war cannot be understood if abstracted from non-military developments, which both affect and are affected by it.[5]

The leading historian of the *Annales* school has not been alone in his effort to foster the study of the economic and social history of war. Indeed, R. H. Tawney anticipated Braudel's argument in his inaugural address of 1932, when he called on students to turn their attention to 'the most neglected factor in social development, the institution of war' and to the ways that wars and other non-economic forces 'twist and divert' economic activity. Any account of past economic life which ignored these forces, Tawney believed, was bound to remain 'abstract and artificial'.[6] More recently the American historian F. C. Lane also called upon historians to pay closer attention to the topic of war. 'Economic theorists', he wrote in 1958, 'have generally traditionally defined their subject so as to exclude analysis of the use of violence. One of the tasks of economic history is to overcome the exclusion.'[7] In a number of studies of the history of Venice and of European commerce in general, he took as first priority the need to 'distinguish those uses of force that contributed to economic development and those that did not'.[8]

The shadow of the Second World War reinforced the sense of the urgency of the task of relating war and economic development. A glance at the *Economic History Review* for the war years will suffice to show the influence of events on historians' choices of subjects for study.[9] In the post-war decades, however, research largely returned to less disturbed, and less disturbing, aspects of economic development. In France after the end of the Second World War, a number of scholars attempted to break down the divisions between military, economic, and social history and to found a new social science of war, or 'polémologie'.[10] But such movements were isolated and the old compartmentalisation between the disciplines of military and economic history easily withstood the challenge.

There are numerous exceptions to this rule, as the bibliography which is appended to this book shows. Many military and political historians have written extensively about economic problems of recruitment and supply. Still, there have been relatively few comparative studies of the war economies of belligerents or of the consequences of different wars for any country or region.[11] G. N. Clark's classic work on war and society in seventeenth-century Europe,[12] J. H. Clapham's essay on 'Europe after the Great Wars, 1816 and 1920',[13] and A. S. Milward's valuable studies of the German, French, and Norwegian economies during the Second World War[14] are examples of the kind of work that remains to be done.

The reticence of economic historians on the subject of war is surely related to the intractability of the problems that it raises. To write about the effects of war is to come up against the difficulty, as Professor Postan has put it, of distinguishing 'the action of war from the action of mere time'.[15] To write on the economic preconditions and causes of war is to face a different set of problems. It is to enter the ideological debate about imperialism opened by Hobson, Hilferding, Lenin and Rosa Luxemburg, that still engages the energies of some Marxists and anti-Marxists.[16] Others face the further, and in many cases decisive, barrier of the scantiness or non-existence of appropriate evidence about wars in earlier centuries.

If historians were to turn to economic theory for assistance, they would find many observations and tangential comments on war as an 'exogenous variable' but no fully worked-out analysis open to empirical testing.[17] The sociological literature, in contrast, presents almost the opposite case. There is a large and growing body of statements about 'the war-phenomenon',[18] and its effects on social stratification.[19] Many of these studies are ambitious in scope and in claims of predictive value, but there is at least some question about their usefulness to students of particular wars. More concrete work has been done by psychologists in the analysis of the burdens borne by soldiers in combat and in its aftermath. The problem of civilian stress in war-time has received less attention. Here too collaboration among scholars is required for a fuller understanding of war.

It is not the purpose of this collection of essays to examine the validity of any theoretical statement about war and social or economic change. It is rather to show both the similarities and the differences in the ways societies have prepared for war, have met its economic demands, and have coped with its economic consequences. Professor Braudel has put the point well when he wrote that 'Every age constructs its own war, its own types of war.'[20] Every generation also has its own vision of war, its own sense of what war meant to those who lived through it and to those who lived in its aftermath. Economic and social historians have an important part to play in shaping that interpretation. This book is intended in part as a contribution to such an effort.

The subject of war and economic development is among those which occupy what Professor Coleman has called 'the border-country between economic and political history: a region remarkably neglected by economic historians'.[21] Those who have ventured into this field have written about war for many different purposes and from many different viewpoints. There are, however, a number of approaches which many writers, including the contributors to this book, have shared.

One way that historians have studied war is by writing what may be termed the 'internal history' of armed conflicts. These scholars have focused on war itself, and they have discussed both the mobilisation of resources which precede it and the ways in which economic activity and policy have been altered by what G. N. Clark has called 'the multifarious abnormalities of war'.[22]

The greatest incentive to research along this line has undoubtedly been the experience of the two world wars. In Britain, the twelve-volume Official History of the Ministry of Munitions, published in 1922, was a pioneering attempt to chart the development of war production. An even more ambitious project was launched in the early days of the First World War, when the Carnegie Endowment for International Peace decided to sponsor 'an historical survey' which would 'attempt to measure the economic cost of the war and the displacement it was causing in the process of civilisation'. The sense of the urgency of this task deepened the longer the war went on and the more it released

complex forces of national life not only for the vast process of destruction, but also for the stimulation of new capacities for production. This new economic activity, which under normal conditions of peace might have been a gain to society, and the surprising capacity exhibited by the belligerent nations for enduring long and increasing loss – often while presenting the outward semblance of new prosperity – made necessary a reconsideration of the whole field of war economics.[23]

The outcome was the 134-volume Economic and Social History of the World War. Some of the strengths and many of the weaknesses of this monumental effort are a result of the fact, as J. T. Shotwell, its editor-in-chief, put it, that 'this greatest of all co-operative histories was not a task for historians. Its authors had to be those who held office in wartime from which they could watch how things actually were done.'[24] The organisers of the project in Europe were distinguished men who had unique first-hand knowledge of their subject. Among them were Beveridge in Britain, Pirenne in Belgium, Charles Gide in France, and Einaudi in Italy. But the very fact of the authors' personal involvement in the war inevitably led to studies which Shotwell himself said were 'best described as about half-way between memoirs and blue books'.[25] These 'autobiographical overtones', one later critic suggested, were 'at times inimical to the critical appraisal of effort, failure and achievement'.[26]

This judgement was made by the man who organised the first historians' economic history of war, Professor (now Sir) Keith Hancock, editor of the British Civil History of the Second World War. Like the Carnegie Series, his project was launched in the midst of war, but this time with the full consent and cooperation of a war-time government. That historians were asked to study the war effort while it was in progress, Hancock wrote, was an indication of how widespread was the recognition that 'the fighting services are no more than "the cutting edge" of the nation at war'[27] and that therefore, any account of the military effort must be accompanied by studies of the economy and the medical services in wartime. The thirty-one volumes of the Civil Series which have appeared fulfil Hancock's aim of providing a 'comprehensive and precise understanding of the economic, social, and administrative problems of a twentieth-century nation at war'.[28] Not all the disadvantages of 'official history' were avoided, though, and now that the appropriate papers are open to research, the documentary record on which these studies rested without citation can be scrutinised afresh.

A second approach to the study of the non-military side of war has been adopted by other historians. These scholars have been concerned to evaluate the way war may deflect or accelerate trends in motion long before the outbreak of hostilities. Others have chosen a similarly long-term perspective to examine the effect of economic and social change on the waging of war and its destructiveness.

One of the men whose writing stimulated debate about the consequences of war was Werner Sombart, professor of sociology and national economy at the University of Berlin from 1917 until his death in 1941. His first major work was a study of capitalism which appeared in 1902 and in which he followed Weber's challenge to Marxist economic history.[29] Eleven years later he published a book, the stated purpose of which was to free the problem of war and capitalism from 'the clutches of historical materialism' by asking not whether war was an inevitable outcome of capitalism, but rather whether capitalism was an outcome of war.[30] Sombart's affirmative answer to this latter question rested on his contention that war and only war was able to fulfil many preconditions of capitalist development in Europe. Armed conflict provided the means to instil in the masses the discipline so central to the capitalist spirit and the incentive to create large-scale enter-prises to meet the demand for food, clothing, and above all, for arms.[31] To satisfy the requirements of the military, Sombart argued, businessmen were forced to rationalise their methods of production and exchange and to develop industries, such as heavy metals and shipbuilding, which were essentially 'children of war'.[32] The impoverishment of many by war taxation was undeniable, but there were others whose gains during war financed nascent capitalist industry and trade. In sum, war was not the offspring of economic structures, but rather their progenitor.

The attack on Sombart's thesis has been led by the American scholar J. U. Nef. By the time Nef had begun his series of rebuttals of Sombart, the latter had become an ardent supporter of Hitler.[33] This fact convinced Nef that the author of *Krieg und Kapitalismus* was not only profoundly mis-taken, but that his book was also an expression of elements in German intellectual life which helped prepare the way for the Nazis. Writing in 1942, Nef was not surprised that the 'constructive' side of war had struck 'espe-cially an historian of the Reich, because his country during the past eighty years had been busy invading foreign territory, without the more disagreeable experience of finding enemy armies spreading havoc in Germany itself'.[34] Furthermore, Sombart's argument was 'of little service to truth' because it examined only 'the economic consequences of the production of the instru-ments of war as if this could be kept separate from the economic consequences of their use'.[35] As Nef put it, 'With one hand, the continental war lords and their marching armies created a need for large new establishments to furnish war materials. With the other, they interfered with the progress of large new establishments designed to cater to peacetime markets.'[36] Indeed it was precisely England's avoidance of continental wars in the century 1540–1640 to which much of her economic progress in those years must be ascribed. Conversely, Nef considered her more bellicose behaviour in the following century as one of the causes of the retardation in British economic growth between his 'early industrial revolution' and the eighteenth-century one.[37] For these reasons he concluded that war in Europe has been 'less a cause for industrialism . . . than its nemesis'.[38]

Nef's views have not been universally accepted,[39] but they have not been subject to the scathing criticism which Sombart's thesis has received. For example, T. S. Ashton made clear his position in his inaugural lecture of 1946 by chastising those 'who so confuse Economics with Technology as to think that, because wars sometimes lead to inventions, those who make wars are to be given a place among the pioneers of social development'.[40]

A similarly sceptical approach was taken by Professor M. M. Postan in an article which appeared in the same issue of the *Economic History Review* in which Nef's first broadside appeared. Attributing to Sombart the view that 'it is in the nature of war to revolutionise economic processes', Postan set out to examine the evidence relating to the Hundred Years' War.[41] His conclusion was definitely anti-Sombart. 'In the machinery of social change', he wrote,

the War was not so much the mainspring as a make-weight. Wherever its actions ran counter to the economic tendencies of the age, as in the development of financial capitalism or the movement of land values, it was on the whole ineffective. Only at points at which changes were taking place anyhow was its influence great and irrevocable enough to deserve the attention not only of the chronicler but also of the social historian.[42]

This argument about the formative influence of the Hundred Years' War was taken up in 1962, when K. B. McFarlane challenged Postan's interpretation. His main complaint was that too many historians were blinded by 'the dogmatic belief, inherited from the nineteenth century, that wars can never be anything but damaging to every society involved in them'.[43] To correct this mistaken idea, he re-examined the costs of the war in terms of the profits raked in by men like Sir John Fastolf in the course of the 'systematic exploitation' of occupied provinces, which 'increased the wealth of England . . . swollen still further by tribute from the European mainland in the form of taxation on exported wool'.[44] In addition, 'the ways in which the noble captains spent their winnings set up eddies in other parts of the economy' which, McFarlane argued, must be counted among the war's consequences.[45] A rebuttal by Postan two years later did not narrow the gap between their positions.[46]

Certainly Sombart's thesis has been neither the sole inspiration nor the guiding force behind much research into the problem of war and economic development. Numerous scholars have written, without any reference to Sombart or Nef, about the possibility that military or naval requirements may have been more productive of large-scale enterprise than those in the private sector. For example, John Ehrman in his study of the British Navy in the later seventeenth century, has pointed out that in 1688, the Navy was 'the most comprehensive, and in some respects the largest industry in the country'.[47] A. H. John has considered some of the ways that government demand for war supplies in the early eighteenth century favourably affected the heavy metal and capital goods industries without any corresponding contraction in investment in other forms of economic activity. John did not make the same claim for the Napoleonic wars which, in his opinion, produced 'counterbalancing forces' which 'probably negatived the advances of war.'[48] The research of Professors Ashton, Rostow, and Crouzet has tended to support this conclusion with reference both to Britain and the continent.[49]

This brief survey of some of the literature on war and economic development illustrates the historiographical background against which the essays in this book must be set. Six of the contributors have followed the 'internal' approach to war in their studies of war production, war finance, and the overall guidance of the economy during war. In different ways, C. Trebilcock and D. C. Coleman illustrate the problem faced by British businessmen who produced goods essential to the war effort and by the public officials who had to see that the necessary orders were met. E. Miller and S. Schama discuss in very different settings the sources of war taxation, the protests at such exactions, and the effects on government finance and economic activity as a whole. The traditional association of taxation and war is highlighted by G. Elton's discussion of how much of an innovation was the Tudor claim of the right to tax for purposes other than war. J. Lee examines aspects of the formation and consequences of agricultural policy in Germany during the First World War.

The other essays in this book examine the effects of war on long-term patterns of economic and social development. The impact of the Napoleonic wars on the process of industrialisation in Britain and of the revolt of the Netherlands on the Low Countries and Spain are examined by P. Deane and G. Parker respectively. P. Mathias discusses the contribution of military and naval doctors in eighteenth-century Britain to preventive medicine and improvements in standards of public health. R. and K. MacLeod present a case-study of the effects of government intervention during the First World War on science-based industry and on the development of scientific and technical education for industry as a whole. J. Harris places the Beveridge Report in the context of the pre-war and war-time debates on British social policy.

No comprehensive treatment of the economic implications of war is possible in a single volume. The effects of war on population growth, on patterns of consumer demand, on agricultural productivity, on banking, on the housing and working conditions of labour, on family structure: there is room for work on these and many other subjects not treated here. What a book of this kind can do is to point the way to further research and interchange between scholars who are working on different aspects of this complex historical problem.

The contributors to this volume have in common an association as colleagues, students, and friends of the late Professor of Economic History in the University of Cambridge, David Joslin. After his death in 1970, this book of essays on but one of his historical interests was begun. As a reminder of his influence on the study of history at Cambridge and of his learning, his generosity, and the kindness we all knew, we dedicate this book to his memory.

NOTES

1 F. Braudel, *The Mediterranean and the Mediterranean World in the Age of Philip II*, trans. S. Reynolds (2 vols, London, 1972–3), vol. 2, p. 836.

2 *Ibid.* ch. 7 et passim.

3 *Ibid.* p. 837 for a brief statement of his thesis: 'no sooner was regular war suspended than a subterranean, unofficial conflict took its place – privateering on sea and brigandage on land – forms of war which had existed all along but which now increased to fill the gap like second growth and brushwood replacing a fallen forest. There are different 'levels' of warfare then, and it is only by studying the contrasts between them that sociologists and historians will make progress towards explaining them. The dialectic is essential.'

4 Braudel, 'Historie et sciences sociales: La longue durée', *Annales: économies, sociétés, civilisations* (Oct.–Dec. 1958), pp. 725–53.

5 On the problem of the definitions of war, see Q. Wright, *A Study of History*, 2nd edn (Chicago, 1965), ch. 1.

6 R. H. Tawney, 'The Study of Economic History', *Economica*, XIII (Feb. 1933), p. 15.

7 F. C. Lane, 'Economic Consequences of Organised Violence', *Journal of Economic History*, XVIII (1958), p. 402, reprinted in *Venice and History: The Collected Papers of Frederic C. Lane* (Baltimore, 1966).

8 Lane, 'Force and Enterprise in the Creation of Oceanic Commerce', *Jnl. Econ. Hist.*, X (1950) supplt, p. 28, reprinted in *Venice and History*.

9 Among the articles published are: J. U. Nef, 'War and Economic Progress, 1540–1640', XII (1942); B. Pearce, 'Elizabethan Food Policy and the Armed Forces', XII (1942); M. M. Postan, 'Some Social Consequences of the Hundred Years' War', XII (1942); R. H. Tawney, 'The Abolition of Economic Controls, 1918–1921', XIII (1943); W. O. Henderson, 'The War Economy of German East Africa 1914–1917', XIII (1943); J. Hurstfield, 'The Control of British Raw Material Supplies, 1919–1939', XIV (1944); and D. Hay, 'The Official History of the Ministry of Munitions 1915–1919', XIV (1944).

10 G. Bouthoul has written extensively on the subject. See his *Cent millions de morts* (Paris, 1946); 'Guerres et population', *Revue de défense nationale* (Oct. 1946), pp. 453–67; *Le Phénomène-guerre, méthodes de la polémologie, morphologie des guerres, leur infrastructures (technique, démographique, économique* (Paris, 1962); and the journal *Etudes polémologiques*.

11 A group of patriotic German economists did make an attempt in the 1930s to formulate principles of *Wehrwirtschaft* by drawing on recent historical experience. These studies of 'War Economic Research and Training' published in Hamburg from 1935 to 1938 were inspired by a desire to contribute to the buildup of Germany's war machine. See: W. M. Stern, '*Wehrwirtschaft*: A German Contribution to Economics', *Economic History Review*, 2nd ser., XIII (1960–1), pp. 270–81.

12 *War and Society in the Seventeenth Century* (Cambridge, 1958); *The Dutch Alliance and the War against Dutch Trade* (1923); *Science and Social Welfare in the Age of Newton* (Oxford, 1937).

13 *Economic Journal*, XXXI (Dec. 1920).

14 *German Economy at War* (London, 1965); *The New Order and the French Economy* (Oxford, 1970); *The Fascist Economy in Norway* (Oxford, 1972).

15 M. M. Postan, 'Some Social Consequences of the Hundred Years' War', *Econ. Hist. Rev.*, XII (1942), p. 4.

16 In the recent *Festschrift* for Raymond Aron, *Science et conscience de la société* (2 vols, Paris, 1971), there are two essays which illustrate well the ongoing debate about the economic causes of war. They are: P. Wiles, 'War and Economic Systems', vol. 2, pp. 271–97; and B. Brodie, 'Theories on the Causes of War', vol. 2, pp. 369–84.

17 See: E. Silberner, *La guerre dans la pensée économique de 16ᵉ au 18ᵉ siècle* (Paris, 1939), and the same author's *The Problem of War in Nineteenth Century Economic Thought*, trans. A. H. Krappe (Princeton, 1946). Silberner's careful studies raise doubts about Quincy Wright's claim that 'Economists have not discussed war very much.' *A Study of War*, 2nd edn (Chicago, 1965), p. 708. Equally open to debate is Wright's claim (p. 1565) in the introduction to the second edition of his book that 'I did not consider economics a primary approach to the study of war in 1942', when the first edition was published, 'and it has not been so considered since either by economists or by [statisticians]'.

18 The phrase is Gaston Bouthoul's. See note 10.

19 S. Andreski, *Military Organization and Society* (London, 1954); P. A. Sorokin, *Man and Society in Calamity* (New York, 1942); Sorokin, *Social and Cultural Dynamics* (4 vols, New York, 1937) vol. 3, pp. 259–380. L. Bramson and G. W. Goethals (eds), *War: Studies from Psychology, Sociology, Anthropology* (New York, 1964). Quincy Wright's *magnum opus* provides the fullest bibliography of the sociology of war.

20 Braudel, *The Mediterranean*, vol. 2, p. 891.

21 D. C. Coleman, *What Has Happened to Economic History?* (Cambridge, 1972), p. 29.

22 G. N. Clark, 'War Trade and Trade War, 1701–1713', *Econ. Hist. Rev.*, I (1927–8), p. 263.

23 From the editor's preface which appeared in each vollume, p. v.

24 J. T. Shotwell, *The Autobiography of James T. Shotwell* (New York, 1961), p. 371.

25 Shotwell, Editor's Preface, p. viii.

26 Sir Keith Hancock, 'British Civil Histories of the Second World War', in R. Higham (ed.), *Official Histories: Essays and Bibliographies from Around the World* (Manhattan, Kan., 1970), p. 518.

27 *Ibid.* Here the phrase is attributed to General Ismay. In another memoir, it is voiced by Sir Edward Bridges, Secretary of the War Cabinet. Cf. Hancock, *Country and Calling* (London, 1954), pp. 196–7, and D. Hay, 'British Historians and the Beginnings of the Civil History of the Second World War', in M. R. D. Foot (ed.), *War and Society* (London, 1973), pp. 39–56.

28 Hancock, 'British Civil Histories', p. 521.

29 W. Sombart, *Der Moderne Kapitalismus* (Munich, 1902).

30 Sombart, *Studien zur Entwicklungsgeschichte des Modernen Kapitalismus, II. Krieg und Kapitalismus* (Munich, 1913), p. 3.

31 *Ibid.*, pp. 14, 70, 84.

32 *Ibid.*, pt III, et passim.

33 See Sombart, *A New Social Philosophy*, trans. by K. F. Geiser (Princeton, 1937), in which he claims to be 'not in the least ... indifferent or unfriendly to the Hitler government' (p. ix) and offers some suggestions to help 'free ourselves from the Jewish spirit' including stripping Jews of civil rights (pp. 176–9).

34 J. U. Nef, 'War and Economic Progress, 1540–1640', *Econ. Hist. Rev.*, XII (1942), p. 21.

35 Nef, *War and Human Progress* (Cambridge, Mass., 1950), p. 65.

36 Nef, 'War and Economic Progress', p. 25.

37 Nef, *War and Human Progress*, chs 12–15; cf. Nef, 'La Guerre', *Proceedings of the Ninth International Congress of Historical Sciences* (Paris, 1950), p. 603.

38 Nef, *Cultural Foundations of Industrial Civilisation* (Cambridge, 1948), p. 66.

39 Cf. J. Hale, 'War and Public Opinion in the Fifteenth and Sixteenth Centuries', *Past & Present*, 22 (1962), p. 21: 'if the art of war prompted no vital physical

or chemical research, it broadened the interest in applied mathematics and so
helped contribute to the changed atmosphere in which real scientific advance
became possible'. R. Bean, 'War and the Birth of the Modern State', *Journal
of Economic History*, xxxiii (1973), p. 205 in which it is argued that changes in
military technology or in administrative technique altered the 'range of optimum
sizes of the state' and H. Kamen, *The Iron Century: Social Change in Europe
1550–1660* (London, 1971), pp. 123–5, in which he discusses 'how the practice
of war came to be an integral feature of early modern capitalism'.

40 T. S. Ashton, 'The Relation of Economic History to Economic Theory', *Economica*, n.s. xiii (1946), p. 84.

41 M. M. Postan, 'Some Social Consequences of the Hundred Years' War',
passim.

42 *Ibid.* p. 12.

43 K. B. McFarlane, 'War, the Economy and Social Change: England and the
Hundred Years War', *Past & Present*, 22 (1962), p. 3.

44 *Ibid.* pp. 10–11.

45 *Ibid.* p. 11.

46 Postan, 'The Costs of the Hundred Years' War', *Past & Present*, 27 (1964).

47 J. Ehrman, *The Navy in the War of William III, 1689–1697* (Cambridge, 1953),
p. 174.

48 A. H. John, 'War and the English Economy, 1700–1763', *Econ. Hist. Rev.*, 2nd
ser., vii (1954–5) pp. 330–4.

49 Ashton, *An Economic History of England: the 18th Century* (London, 1955), pp.
126–7 and his *Iron and Steel in the Industrial Revolution* (Manchester, 1924), p.
152: W. W. Rostow, 'War and Economic Change: the British Experience', in
The Process of Economic Growth (New York, 1952), p. 158, and his article, 'The
Beginnings of Modern Growth in Europe: an Essay in Synthesis', *Jnl. Econ.
Hist.*, xxxiii (1973), pp. 550–3; F. Crouzet, 'Wars, Blockades, and Economic
Change in Europe, 1792–1815', *Jnl. Econ. Hist.*, xxiv (1964), pp. 567–88; 'Bilan de
l'économie britannique pendant les guerres de la Révolution et de l'Empire',
Revue Historique, ccxxxiv (1965) pp. 71–110; and *L'Économie britannique et le
blocus continental, 1806–15* (2 vols, Paris, 1958). It is some comfort to those
who write 'traditional' economic history that two practitioners of the 'new
economic history' have recently published articles which reach diametrically
opposite conclusions about the effects of the Napoleonic wars. For the optimist's
view, see J. L. Anderson's 'counterfactual analysis': 'Aspects of the Effects on
the British Economy of the Wars against France, 1789–1815, *Australian Journal
of Economic History*, xii (1972), pp. 1–16. For the pessimist's view, see G.
Hueckel's 'General Equilibrium Analysis: War and the British Economy
1793–1815', *Explorations in Economic History*, xi (1973), pp. 1–17.

1 War, taxation and the English economy in the late thirteenth and early fourteenth centuries

Edward Miller

In the middle ages, as in later times, war was a great consumer of revenues, calling for taxation of more than customary severity and of greater than customary frequency. The fact, too, that the normal range of government expenditure was narrower in the middle ages than in more modern times made wider the gap between revenues adequate for peacetime and those demanded by war. Almost automatically, therefore, war taxation provoked criticism of its effect upon private fortunes, and also of the peremptoriness with which it was apt to be exacted. There is, in fact, a close correlation between periods of war taxation and 'constitutional movements'; and the effectiveness of taxation in generating political action may suggest that taxes had a sharp and immediate economic impact. How sharp that impact was is a proper subject of enquiry. If it is followed, moreover, it is not easy to dissociate the way in which taxation affected groups and individuals from the more difficult problem of the influence taxation may have had on economic development in general. Questions of this sort, given the nature of the evidence available, are unlikely to be answered with certainties; but they remain questions worth asking.

I

From this point of view, a particularly important episode was the controversy over war taxation in the years 1296–7, because some of the participants in that debate were unusually specific about the effects of taxes upon their fortunes. This crisis over taxation came at the end of a period during which Edward I had maintained for much of the time armies in Gascony, Scotland and Wales; and in 1297 he planned to mount another campaign against the French from Flanders. These armies consisted for the most part of paid soldiers; they had to be supplied; and Edward also built a grand alliance of western princes against the French mainly by paying them cash subsidies. To meet these costs the English laity were subjected to annual direct taxes from 1294; annual taxes were also demanded of the clergy, beginning with a monstrous half of their incomes in 1294; and the export duty on wool was

[11]

raised six-fold by the *maltote* imposed on merchants in 1294. Further, foodstuffs were requisitioned on a massive scale to supply the armies; plans were made to seize the wool clip for state trading ventures in 1294 and 1297; and a large forced loan in wool was ordered in July 1297. 'Prises' of wool and army supplies, as well as taxes of the more conventional sort, raised the temperature of political controversy in 1296 and 1297.[1]

The clergy (not unreasonably, for they were taxed more heavily than the laity) were the first to rebel. Vouching to warranty the bull *Clericis laicos* late in 1296 and early in 1297, they refused to grant further taxes without the Pope's permission having been obtained. A sentence of outlawry was required to persuade them of the virtues of tax-paying. In 1297, however, the laity joined the fight under the leadership of the Constable and Marshal of England. When faced by a demand for military service in Flanders the dissidents dealt most circumstantially with the effects of Edward's war taxation in the *Monstraunces*, drawn up by the earls and their followers in the summer of 1297.[2] The burden of aids and tallages, they alleged, and of prises taken without a penny paid, was such that they could not afford to serve the king in his armies. More than that, their poverty precluded them for paying taxes either; for, after the taxes they had paid and the prises they had suffered, they had barely enough to sustain themselves, many having no sustenance and being unable to cultivate their lands. There was also the special grievance of the *maltote* on wool exported. It was too heavy a charge and a grievous burden, for wool approached a half, and the tax on wool a fifth, of the total value of the land. It is rare for English earls to wax statistical, and the rarity of the occasion justifies our dwelling upon it.

At the same time the years 1294–7 were merely a dramatic interlude in a longer period of change in the financial basis of the English government. Edward I had already, in 1275, added to the regular revenue available to him an export duty on wool; he had obtained occasional taxes from the laity in support of his Welsh wars and to enable him to pay his debts; and the clergy had contributed to crusading tenths, of which Edward appropriated some part even though he never again went crusading. In the years before 1294, in fact, Edward's average revenue was probably about £40,000 yearly, a good deal higher than that which Henry III had enjoyed; and this figure rose to around £75,000 between 1294 and 1307.[3] This result was achieved by augmenting and diversifying taxes on trade, and by securing direct taxes sometimes every year and certainly every three or four years. The precedents set by Edward I, moreover, were followed by his son and exploited still more ruthlessly by his grandson. Taxation during these generations became a normal charge upon the community, a fact which makes it all the more desirable to test the assertions about its insupportability made by the Constable and Marshal in 1297.

II

It is simplest to begin with the *maltote*, although at once a problem must be faced. Wool, said the earls, approached half the 'value of the land'; but how can we estimate what the value of the land, presumably the total of incomes from land, really was? The answer to that question must be that any estimate can be little more than guesswork. Extrapolation from the value placed by papal assessors upon clerical incomes in 1291 possibly suggests that the total of incomes from land was in the region of £1m. Despite the wailings of the clergy, however, that this last thirteenth-century assessment of church incomes *usque ad ossa excoriat*, there is evidence that its severity was exaggerated,[4] and in any case all assessments of income probably underrated the considerable proportion of produce that was consumed in kind. On the other hand, this very rough estimate does bear comparison with Dr Prestwich's calculation that 'it seems unlikely that there was ever more than £1m current coin circulating at any time [in the reign of Edward I]; the figure of £800,000 is probably nearer the mark'.[5] It may well represent, therefore, the order of magnitude of the pool of cash resources from which the Edwardian war taxes were paid.

On this assumption it is clear that the barons were not averse to exaggerating the impact of the *maltote*. In 1297 Edward's officials estimated that a levy of 8,000 sacks of wool was required to raise a sum of £50,000 in Flanders to finance the invasion force.[6] Provided that estimate was reasonably grounded the very considerable proportion of England's wool clip which was then being exported, averaging around 30,000 sacks yearly, can have been worth under £200,000 to English growers.[7] Whatever allowance is made for wool used by England's native industry, which was only beginning to emerge from its thirteenth-century depression,[8] there is every indication that wool was a good less than half the value of the land. At the same time, when all necessary qualifications have been made, the effects of the *maltote* should not be minimised unduly. First, between 1294 and September 1297 it probably yielded around £116,000.[9] Secondly, the average receipts of about £40,000 annually were about four times the average revenue from the customs in the years before the French war began, indicating how sharply fiscal exploitation of trade increased. Thirdly, total receipts increased less than the rate per sack, indicating a fall in annual exports, as was to be expected when privateers were at large in the North Sea. Further, the regular course of merchandise was interrupted by royal requisitioning of wool and by Edward's use of an embryonic staple policy as part of his European diplomacy.[10] The trade in wool, therefore, was affected both by the heavy duties and by fluctuating markets. In these circumstances, merchants tried to buy cheaper in order to offset the higher customs; they sometimes found difficulty in raising cash to pay customs at the new rates; and, in any case, in uncertain times growers could not always easily find buyers. Producer prices, in consequence, were driven sharply down to levels lower than at any time since the mid-thirteenth century.[11]

This trend of wool prices is significant precisely because wool was a cash crop par excellence of many of the greatest landowners. The Earl Marshal himself, one of the leaders of the dissidents in 1297, was numbered amongst the sheep farmers. Even on his Irish lands he had 850 or more ewes and wethers at Old Ross in the 1280s, and there were also considerable flocks on a number of his English manors. In September 1296, despite the ravages of disease in 1294–5, he had 324 sheep and lambs at Weston (Herts), 485 at Kennet (Cambs), and in Suffolk 115 at Peasenhall, 211 at Staverton and 171 at Dunningworth. Some of these flocks had at one time been larger (Weston 563, Kennet 557 and Peasenhall 163); and in 1297 the Earl's flocks at Sloughton in Sussex numbered 634.[12] On these manors the sale of wool represented some 8 per cent of the gross revenues derived from them during the 1290s. The contribution of this item to the total revenue received by the Earl Marshal was, of course, considerably less than that, for he had many manors on which there were few or no sheep; but at the very least he and his advisers could speak from direct knowledge about the profits of sheep farming. They also had direct experience of the consequences of the *maltote*. At Weston the sale price of wool dropped from 2s 6d–2s 8d to 1s 6d–1s 10d per stone;[13] and at Peasenhall the price per pound fell from around 4d to as low as $1\frac{1}{2}$d.[14] On a number of manors, too, wool accumulated unsold. At Staverton and Dunningworth the 1295 clip waited for sale until 1296,[15] and at Sloughton in 1298 wool from two or three past years was despatched along with that of 1298 to the receiver of Bosham.[16] The trouble may have been a lack of buyers in a troubled market; or the Earl's officials may have refrained from selling in the hope that prices would improve. Whatever the explanation, manorial revenue was reduced for the time being, so that the Earl had cause to feel 'oppressed by the tax on wools, which is too heavy'. If we look at the evidence for England as a whole, moreover, the annual mean price of wool fell during the years 1294–7 by just over 1s per stone, or by about 24 per cent.[17] Falling wool prices alone could have clipped perhaps £40,000 a year from landowners' incomes. This is a sufficient sum to justify some sense of oppression.

III

The taxation of wool exports, however, was by no means the only grievance in 1297. Since 1294 Edward I's direct taxes had amounted to about £150,000 from the laity and £100,000 from the clergy.[18] The sums were large by contemporary standards and there was no precedent for the frequency of these imposts. The war taxes, too, followed hard upon other recent taxes. A lay subsidy in 1290 has yielded the very high return of £116,000;[19] the church had conceded a tax on spiritualities in that year, incomplete returns for which total £6,650;[20] and it had also been subjected to papal mandatory tenths between 1292 and 1294, of which some £53,000 was collected by 1296.[21] For the church especially, and to a lesser degree for the laity, the recurrent taxes of 1294–7 continued the story of previous exactions.

The burden of these taxes, particularly for lay landlords, has sometimes been minimised. The Earl of Cornwall, it has been pointed out, paid towards the twelfth of 1296 in respect of his manor at Berkhamsted £2 6s 8d only in a year when his receipts there were over £160.[22] The juxtaposition is not quite a fair one, for it is reasonable to relate the amount paid in taxes to net rather than gross revenue (i.e. to receipts of £109 rather than £160). Even so the tax burden amounted to only 2.2 per cent of that year's revenue. It is even more important to note, however, that in this year the Earl's total tax bill was a mere £10 or so; and this charge only fell upon eight manors of his vast estate at an average rate of just under 2 per cent of his income from those eight manors.[23] As a proportion of his total revenue, which in gross amounted to some £4,700, his tax payments were minimal. The Earl Marshal was somewhat more heavily burdened, although it would be hard to make his burden crippling. At least eighteen of his English manors contributed to taxes between 1294 and 1297. The aggregate net income from these manors was around £900; they paid at most about £41 in taxes on any occasion, or about 4½ per cent of revenue.[24] Five years earlier five of the Earl's manors were assessed to the fifteenth of 1290 at a much higher rate of around 10 per cent of net annual income;[25] but the weight of this charge was lessened by the fact that payment was made in half-yearly instalments over a period of two years.[26] In other words, annual contributions to the fifteenth of 1290 were not significantly heavier than payments of the successive war taxes in the years following the outbreak of war with France.

At the same time these examples of the weight of taxation must be kept in perspective. Even on very large estates its incidence varied very considerably. Taxes were as low as 1–2 per cent of net revenue on the Earl Marshal's manors of Hollesley and Staverton, but reached 10 per cent at Dovercourt and nearly 28 per cent at Thorney (Sussex).[27] There is some correlation between these different rates and the proportion of the Earl's manorial income deriving from sales of agricultural produce. Where that figure was relatively high, as at Thorney (63 per cent), the rate of taxation was relatively high; where it was low, as at Staverton (26 per cent), the rate of taxation was low.[28] A similar correlation is evident on the manors of the earldom of Cornwall in 1296–7 (Table 1). Perhaps it might be added that at Glatton the Earl was prepared to withdraw altogether from the direct demesne cultivation, and his steward was instructed to lease the manor if he could.[29] In other words, progress towards a rentier regime was apt to be reflected in low levels of taxation. There is nothing surprising in that fact, since the assessment of contributions to lay subsidies was principally based upon valuation of a man's agricultural crops and livestock.[30] The system clearly favoured lords whose income derived in large part from rents and the profits of lordship; and it favoured above all some amongst the greatest of them who, like the earls of Cornwall, derived only a small proportion of their revenues (little more than 10 per cent) from sales of agricultural produce.

Table 1

Manor	Taxation as percentage of net income	Percentage of gross manorial receipts	
		From agricultural sales	From other sources
Sundon	9.8	58	42
Iver	10.8	58	42
Berkhamsted	2.2	30	70
Newport (Essex)	0.9	27	73
Glatton	0.6	9	91

At the same time we would do well to avoid measuring the weight of taxes upon the landed classes by reference solely to Berkhamsted, or even to such notables as the Earl Marshal or the Earl of Cornwall. In the first place we must remember that no small part of the land of England was in the church's lordship; that taxation of the church took the form of a tax on income, however inadequately measured; and that churchmen paid taxes more frequently and taxes that relatively were heavier than those the laity paid in the years leading up to 1297. Three mandatory papal tenths were paid between 1291 and 1294; the clergy were bullied into the payment of half their incomes in 1294 and a further tenth in 1295; and they were coerced by outlawry into concession of a fifth in 1297. It is hardly surprising that churchmen were rebellious and grasped at the protection of *Clericis laicos*. There is specific evidence to indicate how sharply and how immediately ecclesiastical communities were affected by these successive taxes which, as the accounts of Bolton Priory show, came annually from 1292 to 1298, and which, in the black year of 1294–5, absorbed 29 per cent of the priory's net revenue.[31] At St Mary's, York, the bread ration of the monks was reduced in direct response to the half of 1294; and at Dunstable priory not only was the table less well served but some revenues were anticipated. Tithes were leased for a rent paid three years in advance and corrodies were sold for a lump sum down.[32] It is clear that even relatively wealthy establishments had few reserves which were easily mobilised. In the face of heavy taxes they were compelled to mortgage future resources in order to meet present emergencies.

If the sufferings of the clergy were by no means all imaginary, neither should the laity's burden be judged only by reference to the incidence of taxes upon a few great men. A detailed analysis of the surviving lay subsidy rolls of the 1290s has yet to be undertaken; but some rough computations from one or two of them are not without interest. In Northumberland the proportion of the lay subsidy granted in 1295 that was paid by manorial lords ranged from 19 per cent in West Coquetdale ward to 29 per cent in Castle ward, and averaged 24 per cent in the county as a whole.[33] It reached this level, moreover, without contributions from the demesnes of great churches like Tynemouth, Brinkburn and Newminster, which were not rated to this tax. Similarly, the roll for three Bedfordshire hundreds in 1297 shows that, while the peasantry paid 65 per cent of the tax, lay and ecclesiastical lords contributed 35 per cent. These proportions are virtually identical with the division of land between demesnes and peasant tenures in the Bedfordshire hundreds surveyed in the 1279 Hundred Rolls.[34] In these instances, at least, taxes paid corresponded roughly to the amount of land cultivated respectively by lords and tenants. If they are not wholly exceptional, taxation may have been somewhat less inequitable than has sometimes been supposed. Inequities, of course, remained. The poorest inhabitants of town and country were exempt;[35] but thereafter the rate of taxation was the same for the most wealthy and the least wealthy. Further, even though the burden of taxation bore a rough relationship to the amount of land cultivated by different classes, peasant tenures were liable for seignorial and ecclesiastical dues which might in aggregate amount to as much as half the product of the land.[36] For that reason alone the peasant's contribution to direct taxation must obviously have been heavier, and often very much heavier, than the contribution of his lord.

It is another matter to put a figure on this burden. The economics of the peasant household are virtually unknowable. We are seldom if ever in a position to establish, at any given moment, how many mouths a holding had to feed, how much was added to it or subtracted from it by inter-peasant leases, and what ancillary sources of income were available to the family.[37] Differences in circumstances such as these may help to explain why men with apparently equal resources were anything but equal as taxpayers. The *bondi* of Middle Chirton in Northumberland were each said to hold thirty-six acres in 1295, but their contributions to the Prior of Tynemouth's tallage in 1294 ranged from nothing (*quia pauper*) to 13s 4d; and those of them who paid the eleventh granted to the king in 1295 were assessed for sums ranging from 2s 9¾d to 4s 1½d.[38] These differences between individuals are likely to remain beyond our powers of explanation. At best taxation records indicate the order of magnitude of tax burdens on the broad band of the middling and upper peasantry.

The peasantry, like their betters, grumbled about taxation; but in connection with Lincolnshire in 1298, we are told 'there is no complaint that the taxes are being levied too frequently, or that the assessments are too high'.[39] Men's grievances were rather about the extortions and rapacities of the tax collectors. These facts are not altogether surprising. The justices perambulating the counties in that year were commissioned to enquire into administrative abuses, not to give ear to political grievances. For that reason poems like the contemporary *Song of the Husbandman* may provide fuller evidence than the court rolls about the way taxes affected the peasant.[40] The poet, like the Lincolnshire jurors, was certainly concerned about the way royal officials cheated and bullied, hunting the poor man as hounds hunt a hare on the hill. He was concerned that great lords and their bailiffs, as well as the king's minions, picked the poor full clean. He was also concerned, however, that in one way or another every fourth penny earned must go to the king, compelling the husbandman to spend whatever he had saved, and to sell his mare, his corn crop in the field, even his seed corn for the following year. So his land lay fallow and learned to sleep, with the corollary that there would be less to eat for the husbandman and his family in succeeding years. A fall in living standards consequent upon tax paying was likely to be even more marked in peasant cottages than in the refectories of Dunstable Priory or St Mary's Abbey. In this context we also need to keep in mind the purchasing power of some of the apparently puny sums charged to peasant taxpayers. Alice, the clerk's widow of Goldington, was only just above the exemption limit when she was assessed at 12¼d to the ninth of 1297; but at the prices prevailing in that year this amount would have bought more than one and a half bushels of wheat or three bushels of oats. Similarly, when her fellow villager, Nicholas atte Hurne, paid 2s 6½d he was foregoing, in effect, four bushels of wheat or eight bushels of oats.[41] The nature of that sacrifice can be appreciated by reference to the levels of agricultural wages in the later thirteenth century. Full-time labourers, like ploughmen, shepherds or carters, commonly received each week a cash wage of 1½d to 1d together with a livery in kind, normally of mixed grains, of two-thirds to one bushel.[42] Within this context even the widow Alice's shilling tax was an impost that might hurt. The hurt was the harder to bear because so many peasant families lived so close to the margin of subsistence.

IV

We must, therefore, not discount too much the impact of medieval taxes upon all ranks of society; and reluctance to pay, together with strenuous efforts at evasion, are some testimony to the resentment they aroused. The Constable of Colchester seized twenty-two cattle from the Earl Marshal's manor at Dovercourt in 1296 to encourage the Earl to pay his contribution to the eleventh, and the next year the arrest of oxen speeded the reeve of

Kennet into seeking money from the Constable of Framlingham to pay taxes.[43] Payments of expenses to the collectors and payments, in cash or kind, *pro favore habendo* may well have lightened the tax burden. The valuation of the Earl Marshal's manor at Weston shrank from £52 to £32 between 1295 and 1296 for a modest expenditure of 12s in the one year and 7s 2d in the other. Here there is no question that the Earl was the net gainer in the form of reduced outgoings.[44] The advantage gained by the Fellows of Merton at Cuxham in 1296 is a little more problematical. They affected a reduction in the tax paid by this manor from £6 2s 2d towards the tenth of 1295 to £1 1s 6d towards the twelfth of 1296. The cost, however, was high: 'entertainment' involved expenditure of £1 2s 8¼d in cash together with 101 bushels of wheat, a pig, ten hens and two cheeses.[45] Taking the values on these comestibles into account payments in 1296 were probably almost as high as in the preceding year. What was probably at least as important, however, was the precedent established for a very low valuation of the manor as a point of departure for bargaining in future years.

The *maltote* and the taxes taken from layfolk and clergy were the most obvious ways in which royal needs and royal policies affected the generality of Englishmen in the war years of the 1290s. For that reason they bulk largest in the spate of political argument in 1296–7. Even then, however, they did not stand alone. There was also concern about 'prises' – the seizure of wool in 1294 and 1297, and the much more frequent requisitioning of supplies for armies.[46] Wool prises, except in so far as they disorganised markets, probably mainly affected merchants; and some of them awaited recompense for what was in effect a forced loan in kind for very many years.[47] The requisitioning of army supplies was both more frequent and affected more people. The Lincolnshire men from whom Nigel Chapman purveyed a single sheep have all the appearance of peasants; and the purveyors of grain there, at least in some instances, appear to have levied specified amounts from vills collectively.[48] In 1296–7, moreover, prises were taken in virtually every county, and in some more than once.[49] The victim might be affected in two ways. Firstly, payment might be deferred. Even the Earl Marshal suffered such unpaid bills. In 1296–7 ten quarters of wheat, three quarters of barley and ten quarters of oats were taken for the king's prise without either payment or tally given on his Hertfordshire manor at Weston, and ten quarters of wheat and ten quarters of barley were similarly taken at Kennet in Cambridgeshire the following year.[50] It is hardly to be supposed that lesser men found it easier to secure payment on the nail. Secondly, since the king's procedures amounted to requisitioning, his purveyors had some powers to fix an artificially low price.[51] In either event, men who were being taxed more heavily than they had been in the past were also being deprived of some of their means to pay those taxes. It is hardly surprising that prises also figure amongst the grievances of 1297.

There were other, and doubtless at the time less obvious consequences of these years of crisis. In particular, between 1294 and 1297, Edward I had to support armies in Gascony and Flanders, and at the same time build up a coalition of European princes whose support he bought for cash. The fact that he broke with his principal bankers, the Riccardi, in 1294[52] limited his capacity to finance his military operations and diplomacy by overseas borrowing. In Gascony, it is true, Bayonne and Bordeaux merchants and others advanced at least £50,000; but in Flanders only some £15,000 could be borrowed from the Frescobaldi, English merchants trading there and a few other lenders. Yet the Gascon campaign cost some £400,000 by 1298; at least £165,000 was paid in subsidies to allies; and a further £50,000 was needed for the Flanders campaign in 1297–8.[53] To meet these charges, therefore, Edward had to export cash in very considerable quantities.[54] Edward's taxation, in other words, represented raids on the domestic money supply at a time when new issues from the mint were running at a low level.[55] If the estimate[56] that some £350,000 was exported from England in cash during the war years is of the right order of magnitude, the net loss of currency stocks was clearly considerable. It was probably sufficient to have a depressing effect on prices, although this may have been partly offset by an influx into England of lighter currency from the continent (those pollards and crockards which were finally demonetised during the recoinage of 1299–1301). That recoinage, and the continuing activity of the mints from that time down into the reign of Edward II, may also have been timely enough to prevent the effects of reduced currency supply upon price levels becoming fully effective.

The multiple effects of war taxes during the years 1294–7 makes the reaction to them the more comprehensive. That reaction was conditioned by the fact that men of all degrees tended to live up to their incomes, whether that meant living in a nobleman's relative luxury or, as so many of the peasantry did, somewhere near the margin of subsistence. Men did not hold reserves from which to pay taxes, for taxes in the past had been so infrequent that a need to provide against them had not yet become a dictate of prudence. Edward I's financial measures, therefore, affected immediately men's ability to satisfy their consumption expectations. Their response might go no further than a passive resistance like the clergy's appeal to *Clericis laicos* as a protection against taxation of church incomes. It might take the form of judicious payments to the taxors *pro favore habendo*, which almost certainly contributed to a steady fall in the valuations of goods assessed to lay subsidies.[57] In the end, however, taxes were a central issue in the political crisis of the summer of 1297 which destroyed the whole basis of Edward I's foreign policy, turned his Flanders campaign into a fiasco, and forced from him concessions of principle which narrowed his range of fiscal options for the rest of his reign. In that sense the confirmation of the Charters in the autumn of 1297 may be taken as something of a turning point.

V

That episode has indeed been so taken by some scholars. After 1297 or at the latest after 1301, it has been argued, Edward I decided that 'it was politically safer to incur heavy debts than to levy oppressive taxes and to seize private property'.[58] In many respects, of course, this judgement is soundly based. After the ninth he got for confirming the Charters in the autumn of 1297, Edward took only two more lay subsidies during his reign: the fifteenth of 1301 and the thirtieth of 1306. Despite the fact that these were years of almost continuous fighting in Scotland, he made do with three levies yielding under £120,000 over the course of a decade. By comparison, £150,000 or thereabouts had been wrung from the lay subsidies granted during the three years 1294–6.[59] Not surprisingly, Edward's unpaid debt escalated during the last years of the reign to a figure far beyond Tout's estimate of £60,000, and he may have owed as much as £200,000 by 1307.[60] Clearly his surrender of initiative in 1297 had been a real one; and the concessions he had to make[61] to secure the 1301 subsidy did not encourage him to repeat such negotiations.

At the same time the change of direction after 1297 must not be exaggerated. Even three lay subsidies in a decade constituted more frequent taxation than in Edward's earlier days or in the days of his predecessors; and churchmen were less impressed than laymen by a moderation of fiscal pressure. They paid taxes in nineteen out of the twenty-four years between 1291 and 1315, even if at less onerous rates than their complaints suggest (amounting to 4.4 per cent of the expenditure of Bolton Priory down to 1305 and 3 per cent thereafter).[62] Following on earlier extortions, the clergy made grants towards meeting the Scottish threat to the north in the autumn of 1297; the fifteenth of 1301 was finally extended to their possessions;[63] and from 1301 onwards churchmen paid tenths by papal mandate in most of the years down to 1307, much of the proceeds of which found their way into the royal coffers.[64] Perhaps not surprisingly one chronicler diagnosed a great dropsy of avarice as the common ailment of pope and king.[65]

Nor were churchmen the sole contributors to the king's needs. The *maltote* had to be given up in 1297, but some recompense was obtained in 1303 when Edward persuaded foreign merchants trading in England to accept increased export duties and new import duties.[66] English merchants gave short shrift to Edward's disingenuous suggestion that they, too, were willing to pay these new charges;[67] but alien traders were sufficiently important in the commerce of England for the customs in the last years of the reign, helped by a high level of wool exports, to produce not far short of double their yield before 1294.[68] Finally, and by no means least, Edward did not entirely keep his hands from private property. He continued to supply his armies and garrisons in Scotland with grain and other foodstuffs requisitioned on a massive scale in eastern Ireland and most English counties. The consequence was that some men still had to wait for payment or were paid less than they would have got for their crop in a free market.[69]

There is no question, then, of the intensification of fiscal pressure being totally reversed after 1297. Nor was the situation altered by Edward I's death. His principal bequest to his successors was a monstrous debt and the Anglo-Scottish war which continued at intervals for much of the fourteenth century. The Anglo-French tensions, which came to the surface in the 1290s, also persisted and led to the war of Saint-Sardos in 1323–5 and ultimately to a major international conflict of 1337. Military needs, therefore, continued to determine fiscal policies and Edward I's methods of sustaining warfare were perpetuated. Whenever English forces were put into the field, within Britain or without, supplies were requisitioned for them.[70] After some vicissitudes in Edward II's time the additional customs duties negotiated in 1303 became the basis for a permanent differential between the rates paid by denizen and alien merchants; the wool custom was again steeply increased to help in financing the Hundred Years' War; and by the mid-century English merchants had been persuaded to pay duties on cloth exported and tunnage and poundage on imports.[71] Finally, direct taxation was levied with a regularity unknown before 1294. Edward II reigned less than twenty full years; but in that time he collected seven lay subsidies totalling over £260,000[72] and a variety of clerical grants and mandatory taxes may have provided him with nearly a further £200,000.[73] Then, in the first decade of Edward III's reign, four lay subsidies yielded around £130,000 and clerical taxation possibly another £100,000,[74] before the outbreak of war with France drove up government expenditure, and what was extracted from the country, to figures which were astronomical in medieval terms.

The basic contrast would seem to lie, therefore, between the post-1294 epoch and all the preceding time. From that time forward periodic Anglo-French and Anglo-Scottish warfare meant that private fortunes were fairly regularly raided by taxes, and duties on trade became a principal recourse of a hungry exchequer. These developments were accentuated by the fact that, from very early in Edward I's reign, the conduct of government had come to depend upon regular borrowing from merchant bankers, helping to establish a fiscal pattern which lasted until the 1340s. Kings borrowed for their day-to-day needs, repaying routine advances from the customs and larger debts from direct taxes.[75] Even in peace-time, therefore, taxation became regular and recurrent; and to that extent it exercised a continuous influence on economic development.

VI

In one particular the nature of this influence is a matter of common agreement. After 1337 English governments taxed wool exports heavily and cloth exports lightly, if at all. The unintended result was that England's developing cloth industry was given a protective cover. This stimulus to home industry probably dates back in some measure to the beginning of the wool custom in 1275, for even that modest charge was likely to raise somewhat the cost of English wool in Flanders. For that reason, the original duty and subsequent additions to it probably helped English producers to capture much of the home market by the 1330s and at the same time to break into export markets overseas.[76] It is also possible that the customs exercised an equally unintended influence in another direction. Edward I's failure in 1303 to extend the new custom to English merchants opened a period during which aliens normally paid duties at higher rates than denizens. When cloth exports were taxed in 1347, the tariff for foreign merchants was higher than that for Englishmen, and the same was normally true of the wool custom from 1322.[77] These differential rates were clearly advantageous to English merchants; and it is not unreasonable to see in them one, although not necessarily the only, influence which gave native merchants a growing share in England's trade. The evidence relating to wool exports is less than complete, but what there is of it suggests a falling off of alien shipments and an increase of native traffic between 1300 and the 1330s.[78] At the same time, the developing export trade in cloth was mainly in English hands;[79] and by Edward III's early years English merchants had captured from Gascons the lion's share of the Bordeaux wine trade to England.[80]

Taxation of overseas trade, therefore, probably improved the prospects of clothworkers and served the competitive interests of English merchants. At the same time the duties on wool exports, particularly when they reached extravagant levels in the 1290s and after 1337, encouraged merchants to defend their margins by depressing producer prices. English weavers might again benefit from a reduction in the price of their raw material; but any adverse influence on the selling price of a major cash crop was hardly advantageous to the agricultural interest. At the same time, the wool custom was probably not the sole influence at work. A downward trend in wool prices appeared before the reimposition of very high duties in order to finance the French war, and at a time when exports were also running at a high level.[81] Nor was the trend in wool prices by any means unique, for it can also be observed in the prices of other agricultural staples.[82] The fortunes of agriculturalists, in other words, seem to have been governed by a general deflationary tendency and not solely by the depression of wool prices under the influence of export taxes.

The explanation of that tendency is a matter of some debate. There is an influential school of thought which sees the decisive factor as a change in the direction of the demographic curve after the famines of the second decade of the century.[83] Certainly, we would be rash to underrate the mortality during those years of dearth;[84] and the tendency of wages to rise after 1320 might also be indicative of a falling population.[85] On the other hand, not all prices fell; and some actually rose.[86] This suggests that a complex interplay of influences determined the way in which the prices of particular commodities behaved. Amongst those influences monetary factors possibly should not be totally excluded. That a famine of bullion was a significant force in determining price levels has been denied,[87] but during the later middle ages men very commonly suffered from the illusion that currency supplies were inadequate. The possibility that this illusion may have corresponded to reality in the 1320s and 1330s is not quite out of the question since in these decades mint output fell below even the very meagre levels of the 1290s.[88]

Why minting virtually ceased, and what the effects of that cessation were, are questions not easily answered. The reduction of output may have reflected an unfavourable trade balance, since imported silver seems to have been the main sources of new issues.[89] Whatever the explanation, there is likely to have been some loss of currency over this period from wear, hoarding and possibly export.[90] Thus, with a very low rate of replacement, currency stocks are likely to have been running down, a situation which may well have contributed to a fall in prices, although once again (since not all prices fell) it was not the sole influence at work. The outbreak of war in 1337 may also have intensified this effect. True, Edward III did not (like Edward I) export currency on any large scale to finance armies or purchase allies;[91] but heavy taxation once again diverted a good deal of the money supply from normal exchanges. The king's council and subjects alike were convinced of a great lack of money in the realm of England.[92] If they were right, that lack could have contributed to sagging prices until the recoinages initiated in 1343 and 1351 increased the money supply and considerably lightened the current coin. By 1351, of course, the catastrophe of the Black Death had altered the whole context; but both before and after 1349 money supply may have played some part in determining the levels of prices.[93]

However the trend of producer prices for many agricultural commodities is explained, it was on the whole one adverse to agriculturalists. Larger producers were the more seriously affected because contemporaneously wage rates were rising;[94] and there is little sign of any great fall in rents and other charges which might have compensated the peasant. In these circumstances, increasingly regular taxation of country folk was both a grievance and, possibly, a source of genuine economic difficulties. Evidence of these difficulties does not disappear after 1297. In place after place, in the course of his visitation of 1304, Archbishop Corbridge of York found religious houses alleging impoverishment *propter taxaciones et extorsiones varias hiis diebus impositas*.[95] Fiscal burdens might likewise explain some of the ills of south-western monasteries a generation later, which Bishop Grandisson of Exeter attributed solely to maladministration.[96] Prior Henry of Eastry of Christchurch, Canterbury, was after all an able administrator; but he too found papal and royal taxes a heavy charge on the resources of his church. The total he paid under these heads during thirty-seven years of his priorate was nearly £6,000, or some £160 yearly on average. This annual charge is not far short of what he spent on repairs and improvements in the manor of Monkton throughout his time; and the total was one and a half times as great as all his expenditure on building, repairs and manuring on all the manors of the priory.[97] The effects of papal and royal imposts can be looked at from another angle at Bolton Priory. There between 1291 and 1315 taxes accounted for between 3 and 4½ per cent of that church's expenditure. The burden may appear light in absolute terms and in terms of its theoretical relationship to income; but as a regular charge against receipts it was both novel and severe.[98]

Particularly on church estates, therefore, and to some extent on all estates, taxes represented a not inconsiderable outgoing from the 1290s onwards; and particularly after about 1320, when the relationship of producer prices to costs was unfavourable, it is likely to have influenced the direction of economic change. Signs of retrenchment appear to multiply: a cutting back in the scale of demesne enterprise, the abandonment of some of the less fertile arable, a reduction in the rate of capital investment in repairs and improvements. These signs became manifest sometimes earlier and sometimes later. On the Winchester estate arable under crops began to shrink after about 1270 and had been reduced by almost 40 per cent before 1330 in a process which was cumulative on five manors out of six.[99] On the Clare estates, by contrast, a period of considerable economic activity only ended in the 1320.[100] In many places, moreover, a retreat of demesne enterprise was not balanced by a comparable advance of peasant economic activity. On the contrary, although the peasantry took up some of the land shed by demesnes (even when it was *debilis*) they did not take up by any means all of it.[101] Further, it seems clear that in 1341 a good deal of peasant land was uncultivated (in some cases possibly temporarily) in regions other than those subjected to Scottish raiding and fenland flooding.[102] The scale of this recession may have been marginal; some regions, like parts of the southwest,[103] may have escaped it; but the long term advance of economic activity in most of England had been decisively checked well before 1349.

VII

The part which fiscal causes played in this change of economic direction cannot, of course, be measured or allotted a place in the scale of influences at work. It seems clear enough, however, that the customs duties offered advantages to English clothworkers and English merchants, and probably contributed to a reduction in the returns from agricultural production. Those returns, further narrowed by rising labour costs after about 1320, were also raided with fair regularity for contributions to direct taxation from 1294 onwards. The response of landowners to this situation is excellently illustrated by the financial records of Bolton priory during the forty years or so after 1286.[104] Like most other landlords the canons of Bolton lived from year to year, so that when famine came in 1316–17, in the absence of any reserves, consumption had to be drastically cut. Good years, on the other hand, encouraged them to increase the number of their servants and the lavishness of hospitality. The canons lived up to their income; and if that income fell below what was required to keep them in their accustomed state, if they were able they borrowed or they anticipated future income to enable that state to be maintained. The response to taxation by men with these attitudes was inevitably resentment and a willingness to cut back investment in order to preserve an acceptable standard of living. More than that, the lord who gave up demesne production and drew the greater part of his income from rents was likely to reduce his liability to lay subsidies; and the more marginal his demesne land was, as costs rose and prices fell after 1320, the more likely he was to see advantage in such a course. The fiscal measures of governments in this way reinforced other influences at work making for a reduction in the scale of seignorial enterprise.

Taxes, however, affected tenants as well as lords; indeed, they probably affected tenants more as their lords became to an increasing extent receivers of rents. Moreover, when from 1334 lay subsidies ceased to be re-assessed on each occasion, contributions were sometimes demanded from poorer men who might earlier have been exempt.[105] When the returns of the ninth of 1341 offered explanations of the fact that some tenant land lay uncultivated in so many English counties, they spoke of shortage of seed corn following upon a poor harvest and of the poverty of tenants. Once again, though at a very different level of subsistence, the picture is of men who live from hand to mouth, with few or no resources in reserve. Sometimes, however, the poverty of tenants is directly attributed to recurrent taxes;[106] and once again poets as well as politicians were critical of the burdens heaped by governments upon poor folk. Around 1339 one versifier denounced the fifteenths and the wool prises levied by Edward III on the ground that they compelled men to sell their cattle and their goods; and he drew a picture of a countryside in which, for lack of money in men's pockets, markets were virtually idle. He concluded with a veiled threat of possible rebellion and with an admonition to the government to make the rich pay.[107] Doubtless, like all good pamphleteers, the poet exaggerated; but his version of the consequences of taxing the peasantry is not altogether at variance with that contained in the sober taxation records of 1341.

Once again, in the years after 1336, questions of taxation became major political issues in a nation at war, when what had become customary imposts were increased both in their frequency and in their severity. The response to these fiscal measures, in the 1290s and in the 1330s and 1340s, was not altogether out of proportion, since their immediate effect was probably a good deal sharper than has sometimes been assumed. The yield of medieval taxation appears puny to our eyes, but its impact upon the subsistence standards of medieval men could be direct and even severe. At the same time, these years of acute military crisis also had the effect of establishing both direct and indirect taxes as normal requirements for the conduct of government; and regular taxation exercised a cumulative influence upon economic developments in the generation or two preceding the Black Death. The precise part played by government financial measures in generating economic change cannot be accurately measured; but it may well be that those measures were as significant in the economic field as they were in instigating those constitutional developments which made the reigns of the first three Edwards a watershed in English history.

NOTES

The following abbreviations are used in the notes: *Econ. Hist. Rev.* (*Economic History Review*); *EHR* (*English Historical Review*); PRO (Public Record Office).

1 J. G. Edwards ' *Confirmatio Cartarum* and Baronial Grievances in 1297', *EHR*, LVIII (1943), pp. 147–72, 273–300; M. Prestwich, *War, Politics and Finance under Edward I* (1972), pp. 177ff. The author wishes to express his special indebtedness to Dr Prestwich's study of this period, and also to Professor Edmund Fryde for his advice after reading a draft of this essay.

2 The best modern text is that printed by Edwards, ' *Confirmatio Cartarum*', pp. 170–2; and see *Cronica Walteri de Gyseburne*, ed. H. Rothwell, Camden 3rd ser., LXXXIX (1957), pp. 292–3.

3 Prestwich, *War, Politics and Finance*, pp. 177–203.

4 *Liber Memorandorum Ecclesie de Bernewelle* (1907), ed. J. W. Clark, p. 191; W. E. Lunt, *Financial Relations of the Papacy with England to 1327* (1939), pp. 346–65; R. Graham, *English Ecclesiastical Studies* (1929), pp. 271–301.

5 Prestwich, *War, Politics and Finance*, p. 195; and see his 'Edward I's Monetary Policies and their Consequences', *Econ. Hist. Rev.*, 2nd ser., XXII (1969), pp. 406–16.

6 *Parliamentary Writs*, I (1827), pp. 394–5.

7 See E. M. Carus-Wilson and O. Coleman, *England's Export Trade, 1275–1547* (1963), p. 1n where the value of exports is put at £150,000–£180,000, and pp. 36–9 for the volume of exports at this time. The return of producers was, of course, lower than the price obtained by the merchants overseas.

8 E. Miller, 'Fortunes of the English Textile Industry during the Thirteenth Century', *Econ. Hist. Rev.*, 2nd ser., XVIII (1965), pp. 64–82.

9 Prestwich, *War, Politics and Finance*, p. 197.

10 J. de Sturler, *Les Relations politiques et échanges commerciaux entre le duché de Brabant et l'Angleterre au moyen âge* (1936), pp. 180–220.

11 T. H. Lloyd, *The Movement of Wool Prices in Medieval England* (*Econ. Hist. Rev.* Supplt, no. 6, 1973), pp. 16–17; and for the difficulty experienced by merchants in raising cash, PRO E159/68, m. 82d (1294); E159/70, m. 5 (1296).

12 P. H. Hore, *History of the Town and Country of Wexford: Old and New Ross* (1900), pp. 11, 33; PRO, SC6, Bdles 768/16, 18; 873/17, 19; 995/22; 1003/17, 20; 1005/17; 1030/20.

13 SC6, Bdles 873/14–17.

14 SC6, Bdles 1003/17–19.

15 SC6, Bdles 995/22, 1005/17.

16 SC6, Bdle 1030/20.

17 Lloyd, *The Movement of Wool Prices*, Table i.

18 Prestwich, *War, Politics and Finance*, p. 189.

19 J. F. Willard, *Parliamentary Taxes on Personal Property* (1934), p. 343. At least one commentator denounced it as a heavier charge than any Edward's predecessors had imposed: 'Annales de Osneia', *Annales Monastici*, ed. H. R. Luard, iv (1869), p. 326.

20 H. S. Deighton, 'Clerical Taxation by Consent', *EHR*, lxviii (1953), p. 171.

21 Lunt, *Financial Relations of the Papacy*, pp. 356–7; some additional arrears were subsequently extracted from the recalcitrant, but the amount was not significant.

22 Prestwich, *War, Politics and Finance*, p. 192.

23 *Earldom of Cornwall Accounts, 1296–1297*, ed. L. M. Midgley (Camden Soc., 3rd ser., lxvi and lxviii, 1942 and 1945), i, pp. 9, 21, 29, 36, 46, 51, 88; ii, p. 181.

24 SC6, Bdles 768/18, 840/9, 873/17–19, 932/25, 935/35, 937/3, 938/9, 944/31, 995/22, 997/11, 998/29, 999/15, 1003/20, 1004/11, 1005/17, 1006/3, 1030/20, 1030/30, 1031/1.

25 SC6, Bdles 768/15, 934/31, 937/1, 995/5, 1003/15.

26 *Parliamentary Writs*, i, p. 24.

27 SC6, Bdles 840/9, 998/29, 1005/17, 1030/30.

28 These figures relate to gross manorial income since any attempt to apportion expenditure between agricultural and other costs raises formidable difficulties. For the present purpose, in any case, gross income from agricultural sales and from other sources is probably sufficiently indicative.

29 *Earldom of Cornwall Accounts*, ed. Midgley, ii, p. 185.

30 For the basis of taxation in rural areas, see generally Willard, *Parliamentary Taxes*, pp. 73–5; and for representative assessment rolls, *The Taxation of 1297*, ed. A. T. Gaydon, Bedfordshire Hist. Record Soc., xxxix (1958) and the rather later Buckinghamshire assessments in *Early Taxation Returns*, ed. A. C. Chibnall, Buckinghamshire Record Soc., xiv (1966), pp. 2–88 (1332), 119–39 (1327).

31 I. Kershaw, *Bolton Priory* (1973), pp. 167, 189.

32 *Chronicle of St Mary's Abbey, York*, eds H. H. E. Craster and M. E. Thornton, Surtees Soc., cxlviii (1934), p. 25; 'Annales de Dunstaplia', *Annales Monastici*, ed. H. R. Luard, iii (1866), p. 387.

33 *The Northumberland Lay Subsidy Roll of 1296*, ed. C. M. Fraser (1968).

34 *The Taxation of 1297*, ed. A. T. Gaydon, p. xxv; and cf. the review of this text by A. Tompkinson, *Econ. Hist. Rev.*, 2nd ser., xii (1960), p. 469 and E. A. Kosminsky, *Studies in the Agrarian History of England* (1956), p. 90.

35 For the criteria, see Willard, *Parliamentary Taxes*, pp. 87–92.

36 M. M. Postan (ed.), *Cambridge Economic History*, i (2nd edn, 1966), p. 603.

37 *Carte Nativorum*, eds C. N. L. Brooke and M. M. Postan, Northants Rec. Soc., xx (1960), pp. lii–liii; and see also M. M. Postan, *Medieval Agriculture and General Problems of the Medieval Economy* (1973), pp. 135–7.
38 *Northumberland County History*, viii, ed. H. H. E. Craster (1907), pp. 330–1. It should be added that the order of tallage payers does not correspond to the order of taxpayers save that the poor man, Henry son of Wyot, pays nothing to either tallage or tax.
39 *A Lincolnshire Assize Roll for 1298*, ed. W. S. Thomson, Lincoln Rec. Soc., xxxvi, (1944), p. li.
40 *Political Songs of England*, ed. T. Wright, Camden O.S., vi (1839), pp. 149–52.
41 *The Taxation of 1297*, ed. Gaydon, p. 4.
42 Based upon data from: Tiddenham (Glos), SC6, Bdle 859/24; Crondal (Hants), *Crondal Records*, ed. F. J. Baignent, i, Hants Rec. Soc. (1891), p. 78; Sundon (Beds), Berkhamsted and Iver (Bucks), and Howden (Yorks), *Earldom of Cornwall Accounts*, ed. Midgley, i, pp. 8, 10, 20, 24, 29–30; ii, p. 211; Seven-hampton (Wilts), *Accounts and Surveys of the Wiltshire Lands of Adam of Stratton*, ed. M. W. Farr, Wilts Arch. Soc. Records Branch, xiv, (1959), p. 181; Oakington, Kennet and Soham (Cambs), F. M. Page, *Estates of Crowland Abbey*, p. 225 and SC6, Bdles 768/7, 770/1; and the Ramsey manors, J. A. Raftis, *Estates of Ramsey Abbey* (1957), p. 205.
43 SC6, Bdles 768/19, 840/9.
44 SC6, Bdles 873/17–18. Similar payments are made on a number of his other manors, but they are generally modest in amount.
45 P. D. A. Harvey, *A Medieval Oxfordshire Village* (1965), p. 106.
46 Prestwich, *War, Politics and Finance*, 114–36; *Lincolnshire Assize Roll of 1298*, ed. Thompson, pp. lii–lxxxviii.
47 Some men, though this may be exceptional, still awaited payment in 1307 for wool taken in 1297: *Cal. Close Rolls*, 1302–7, pp. 504–5.
48 *A Lincolnshire Assize Roll*, ed. Thomson, pp. 9–10 (nos 31–2), 72 (no. 315), 77 (no. 332).
49 *Ibid.*, pp. lxxii–lxxiv.
50 SC6, Bdles 768/19, 873/18.
51 Prestwich, *War, Politics and Finance*, p. 135 cites instances of household officials securing a better price than others from whom corn was requisitioned.
52 R. W. Kaeuper, *Bankers to the Crown: the Riccardi of Lucca and Edward I* (1973), pp. 209–27.
53 Prestwich, *War, Politics and Finance*, pp. 171–5, 209.
54 E. B. Fryde, 'Financial Resources of Edward I in the Netherlands', *Revue Belge de Philologie et d'Histoire*, xl (1962), esp. pp. 1185–7.
55 The average issues for the quinquennia 1294–8 and 1289–93 were £5,316 and £6,123 respectively per year, compared with an annual average of around £44,000 in 1284–8: J. Craig, *The Mint* (1953), p. 410.
56 By M. Prestwich in *Econ. Hist. Rev.*, 2nd ser., xxii (1969), p. 411.
57 See Willard, *Parliamentary Taxes*, pp. 343–4 for the falling yield of taxes during these years, reflecting a fall in the valuation of chattels assessed to less than a half of the 1294 figure.
58 Prestwich, *War, Politics and Finance*, p. 270.
59 See above, p. 14.
60 Prestwich, *War, Politics and Finance*, p. 221.
61 H. Rothwell, 'Edward I and the Struggle for the Charters', *Essays in Medieval History presented to F. M. Powicke* (1948), pp. 319–32.

62 I. Kershaw, *Bolton Priory*, p. 167.
63 Collection was ordered in 1303 after many changes of mind: *Registrum Roberti de Winchelsey*, ed. R. Graham, II (1956), pp. 641–3, 757–8, 760–1; *Cal. Close Rolls*, 1296–1302, p. 579; *Cal. Fine Rolls*, I, pp. 474–5, 479.
64 A triennial tenth was granted in 1301 and a further biennial tenth in 1306: Lunt, *Financial Relations of the Papacy*, pp. 366–84, 608.
65 *Flores Historiarum*, ed. H. R. Luard, III (1890), p. 110.
66 For the text of the *Carta Mercatoria* recording the agreement, see N. S. B. Gras, *The Early English Customs System* (1918), pp. 259–64.
67 *Parliamentary Writs*, I, p. 135; *Cal. Close Rolls*, 1302–7, p. 89.
68 The customs were averaging about £18,000 in 1303–7 (Prestwich, *War, Politics and Finance*, p. 199) compared with an average of about £10,000, after the allowance of expenses, between 1286 and 1294 (figures from the Pipe Rolls kindly communicated to the author by Professor E. B. Fryde).
69 Between 1296 and 1307 Yorkshire contributed to thirteen, and Lincolnshire, Cambridgeshire and Essex to twelve prises: Prestwich, *War, Politics and Finance*, p. 133.
70 *The English Government at Work, 1327–36*, I (1940), ed. J. F. Willard and W. A. Morris, pp. 367–70 (prises for armies in Scotland); H. J. Hewitt, *Organization of War under Edward III, 1338–1362* (1966), pp. 50–63 (prises for armies in France).
71 Gras, *Early English Customs System*, pp. 72–3, 81–5.
72 Willard, *Parliamentary Taxes*, pp. 344–5.
73 The figure is that of J. H. Ramsay, *A History of the Revenues of the Kings of England, 1066–1399* (2 vols, 1925), II, p. 148 and may be on the high side; but mandatory taxes alone appear to have produced over £120,000: Lunt, *Financial Relations of the Papacy*, pp. 381–412, 609.
74 Ramsay, *Revenues of the Kings of England*, II, p. 294; *The English Government at Work*, II (1947), ed. W. A. Morris and J. R. Strayer, p. 226.
75 E. B. Fryde, in *Cambridge Economic History*, III (1965), pp. 454–9.
76 E. M. Carus-Wilson, *Medieval Merchant Venturers* (1954), pp. 242–5; Miller, 'Fortunes of the English textile Industry', pp. 78–82.
77 Gras, *Early English Customs System*, pp. 72, 79–80. An exception to these generalisations was the privileged position ultimately achieved by Hanseatic merchants who, by the beginning of the fifteenth century, paid at rates lower than Englishmen: *Studies in English Trade in the Fifteenth Century* (1933), ed. M. M. Postan and E. Power, p. 98.
78 Carus-Wilson and Coleman, *England's Export Trade*, graph on p. 122.
79 Carus-Wilson, *Medieval Merchant Venturers*, diagram facing p. xviii.
80 M. K. James, *Studies in the Medieval Wine Trade* (1971), pp. 13–15.
81 Lloyd, *Movement of Wool Prices*, pp. 18, 63 (especially in the years 1328–35).
82 On the Winchester estates wheat prices were 11 per cent lower in 1320–39 than in 1300–19: M. M. Postan, *Essays on Medieval Agriculture and the General Problems of the Medieval Economy* (1973), p. 191; and the prices of all grains, sheep and wool in the period 1331–50 were lower than in the period 1261–1310 (a comparison which avoids the distorting effect of famine prices during the second and third decades of the fourteenth century): D. G. Watts, 'A Model for the Early Fourteenth Century', *Econ. Hist. Rev.*, 2nd ser., XX (1967), p. 545.
83 Postan, *Essays on Medieval Agriculture*, pp. 186–213 and *Econ. Hist. Rev.*, 2nd ser., XII (1959), pp. 77–82.

84 Postan, *Essays on Medieval Agriculture*, p. 169; I. Kershaw, 'The Great Famine and Agrarian Crisis in England', *Past & Present*, 59 (1973), pp. 3–50.

85 A seemingly general upward trend in wages is not easily explained by local competition for labour from the still infant cloth industry, as suggested by Barbara Harvey: 'The Population Trend in England between 1300 and 1348', *Trans. Royal Historical Society*, 5th ser., XVI (1966), pp. 29.

86 D. G. Watts, 'A Model for the Early Fourteenth Century', p. 545.

87 e.g. by M. M. Postan, *Essays on Medieval Agriculture*, pp. 7–10.

88 Craig, *The Mint*, pp. 410–11.

89 A. E. Feaveryear, *The Pound Sterling* (1931), pp. 12–13; and cf. H. A. Miskimin, 'Monetary Movements in Fourteenth and Fifteenth Century England, *Journal of Econ. Hist.*, XXIV (1964), p. 477.

90 Export was prohibited in 1335 following upon a petition in 1334 which attributed to this cause the great lack of money in the land: *Statutes of the Realm*, I, p. 273; *Rotuli Parliamentorum Anglie hactenus Inediti*, ed. H. G. Richardson and G. O. Sayles (Camden 3rd ser., LI, 1935), p. 237.

91 E. B. Fryde, 'Financial Resources of Edward III in the Netherlands, 1337–40', *Revue Belge de Philologie et d'Histoire*, XLV (1967), p. 1143.

92 *Rotuli Parliamentorum*, II, p. 137 (1343).

93 Miskimin, 'Monetary Movements', pp. 476–90.

94 Postan, *Essays on Medieval Agriculture*, p. 191.

95 *Register of Thomas Corbridge*, ed. W. Brown and A. Hamilton Thompson, Surtees Soc., CXXXVIII (1925), I, nos 227, 250, 742; and cf. no. 788 for St Mary's, York, in 1301.

96 H. P. R. Finberg, *Tavistock Abbey* (1951), pp. 261–2.

97 D. Knowles, *Religious Orders in England*, I (1948), pp. 324–5.

98 Kershaw, *Bolton Priory*, pp. 163, 167.

99 J. Z. Titow, *English Rural Society, 1200–1350* (1969), p. 53 and *Winchester Yields* (1972), pp. 136–44.

100 G. A. Holmes, *The Estates of the Higher Nobility in Fourteenth-Century England* (1957), pp. 88–90.

101 M. M. Postan, in *Cambridge Economic History*, I (2nd edn, 1966), p. 558.

102 A. R. H. Baker, 'Evidence in the *Nonarum Inquisitiones* of Contracting Arable Land in England', *Econ. Hist. Rev.*, 2nd ser., XIX (1966), pp. 518–32.

103 J. Hatcher, *Rural Economy and Society in the Duchy of Cornwall* (1970), pp. 80–101.

104 Kershaw, *Bolton Priory*, pp. 144–8, 173.

105 E. B. Fryde, 'Parliament and the French War, 1336–40', *Essays in Medieval History presented to Bertie Wilkinson* (1969), ed. T. A. Sandquist and M. R. Powicke, p. 256.

106 A. R. H. Baker, 'Evidence in the *Nonarum Inquisitiones*', p. 258.

107 *Anglo–Norman Political Songs*, ed. I. S. T. Aspin (Anglo–Norman Text Society, XI, 1953), pp. 105–15; and for the date see E. B. Fryde in *Essays in Medieval History presented to Bertie Wilkinson*, pp. 263–4. Professor Fryde's essay is an excellent study of the reaction to Edward III's war taxation between 1336 and 1340.

2 Taxation for war and peace in early-Tudor England

G. R. Elton

The effect of war upon any country's economy always poses difficult problems for the historian, but in early-sixteenth-century England one point immediately stands out. War was the time of taxation: direct taxes were imposed on the nation only when war or the likely prospect of it could justify such exceptional burdens. It was, indeed, something very like a constitutional principle that the king had no right to call for special supply on any other grounds; extraordinary revenue – that is, revenue granted in parliament – could be refused unless it were demanded by the purposes of war. Quite possibly this principle had a less ancient history behind it than was once supposed,[1] but it clearly existed by the reign of Edward IV. Henry VII's taxation observed it faithfully.[2] So did Henry VIII's in the first half of his reign. Every one of the seven parliaments that met between 1510 and 1523 was called to grant money, and every grant of a fifteenth and tenth, or of the new subsidy, explained in its preamble that it arose from the special needs of war, even though on occasion the money was required to cover martial expenses already incurred.[3] Even the life-grant of tonnage and poundage in 1510 was (as convention dictated) 'for the defence of this your said realm and in especial for the safeguard and keeping of the sea'.[4] At times the preambles amounted to quite a lengthy historical exposition of foreign affairs, as when parliament was made to inform the king in 1511 and 1512 how well it knew the recent machinations of France – encouraging the duke of Gueldres against the king's ally, the prince of Castile, or organising a schism in the Universal Church. The preamble of the Subsidy Act of 1523 reviewed the international scene from the war of 1513 onwards. Evidently great care was taken to make sure that the Crown's extraordinary claims should rest securely on grounds conventionally accepted as proper.

Thus down to the meeting of the Reformation Parliament war always affected the national purse in the most direct and obvious manner, and conversely the economic consequences of national taxation were felt only in times of actual or impending war. No other aspect of government policy had any comparable effect upon the economy. Yet one of the side-effects of the major reorganisation which began in the 1530s was to end this simple correlation. As the king pulled together the national identity of his dominions, his subjects were to discover that they would in future find themselves more regularly called upon to contribute to the cost of government. Very soon, attempts were made to secure supply in times of peace, and new justifications emerged for these unpopular calls on people's pockets. The government managers thus found it necessary to frame a different formula to explain the demand for direct taxation and conciliate opinion in parliament.[5]

The parliament of 1529 was called for several reasons, but financial need played its part, too. Immediately, however, no one felt able to attempt a new taxation, especially since that of 1523, when actual war had provided a legitimate excuse, had met sufficient resistance. All that the king secured in the first session was a cancellation of the repayment of money raised by means of forced loans.[6] In effect, this act constituted a concealed and retrospective grant, and it is interesting to note that it was justified – in highly coloured and rather emotional language – on the grounds that the king had incurred great expenses in helping to stamp out disunity in Christ's Church and in preserving the realm in safety. Although there had been no war and none looked likely to come, the preamble almost managed to suggest that English armies had taken the field against heretics and schismatics: it is among the most specious and insincere statements to be found even in the preambles of Tudor taxation statutes. But by that very fact it demonstrates that so far the Crown remained anxious to preserve the constitutional principle which governed the granting of taxes.

However, the needs of government even in times of peace could hardly any longer be covered by 'the king's own', and the diplomatic proceedings touching the Divorce were exceptionally expensive. The need to conciliate France if the emperor should turn actively hostile put the French pension (renewed in 1526) in jeopardy; though in fact it was duly paid down to 1534, planning had to proceed on the assumption that it would cease. The fall of Wolsey and the rise of Cromwell were accompanied by signs that the ordinary sources of revenue would be more energetically exploited,[7] but these would never yield enough and certainly were not sufficiently elastic. From 1531 the government turned to the wealth of the church, but the first attack – the *praemunire* fine of £118,000 of which less than two-thirds were ever collected – secured only an unrepeatable windfall. Before Cromwell obtained a more permanent addition to the king's income by means of the transfer, in 1534, of the clerical first fruits and tenths, he was thus driven to consider the possibility of parliamentary taxation to fill empty coffers at a time of likely national crisis. National crisis, yes, but not the crisis of a war: for the whole success of the break with Rome depended on avoiding war. If war came, supply could be demanded; but if war came, or was even officially admitted to threaten, the chance of establishing the royal supremacy without major internal disruption would be gone. The simple fact was that Tudor government had reached the point where traditional financing would no longer do, and so Cromwell was driven to finding a way of imposing taxation at a time when the maintenance of peace was one of the government's most effective propaganda claims. The resort to specious pretences about war, as employed in 1529, was out from 1532 onwards.

If the imperial ambassador was correctly informed (and in this case there is no reason why he should not have been) an attempt was made, and the difficulties were brought home, in 1532. It appears that the Crown tried for a fifteenth and tenth on the grounds that the Scots were threatening an attack, an unconvincing allegation at the time and exposed in the Commons where some bold men pointed out that all danger from the Scots could be avoided if the king would stop pursuing his present policy and thus remove all occasion of trouble. The ambassador heard that the allegedly subservient House had nevertheless agreed to the grant, but here he was wrong; nothing came of these negotiations, and Cromwell had to make do without direct taxation at this stage.[8] (1532 was the last session in which he was not yet the king's leading councillor.) He next tried in 1534, by which time parliament had been more firmly subjected to his managerial influence and the drastic new policy had fully proclaimed itself, and this time he succeeded in getting an act whose preamble discovered quite a new line of justification.[9]

Certainly, the grounds on which this grant rested were in part traditional. They spoke of the late wars against Scotland, which could hardly mean real war but only border skirmishing since no war had been fought since 1513 while the manoeuvres of 1522 had already done duty in the money bills of 1523 and 1529. They mentioned the present troubles in Ireland which had unquestionably involved reinforcing the garrison there. References to expenses incurred in building defence works – especially repairs at Calais and Dover – might just be accepted as falling within the traditional categories of reasons. But the main justification was put first: the king 'by the space of twenty-five years' has so effectively governed and guarded the realm and kept it 'in wealth, unity, rest and quietness, to the high pleasure of Almighty God, the great glory praise honour and merit of our said sovereign lord the King', that his most loving subjects felt obliged to assist. This was the first time that the Almighty made his appearance as the backer of a subsidy bill. A very fulsome paragraph committed the parliament to a fruitful love and admiration for this most marvellous of monarchs; more, it explained that in making the grant the Commons had considered not only past burdens but also the great national benefits to be gained in the future from the repair of Dover and Calais (not by any means yet completed, after all) and 'the reformation of the said land of Ireland'. The whole lengthy preamble, very different from the sober and precise factual recitals that characterised Wolsey's subsidy acts, breathed a new spirit: a commitment of the nation to the national policy of the Crown and its readiness to support government with money now and in future. Such actual occasions of expense as were cited were turned into examples of a general policy, and the extraordinary start, acknowledging the splendour of twenty-five years of Henry's rule as grounds for taxation, coloured all the detail that followed.

Cromwell knew that he was innovating, and moreover doing so on exceptionally touchy territory. After all, he had sat in the House of Commons which proved so refractory to Wolsey's demands in 1523 and had himself there delivered a powerful speech in which he had attacked the kind of foreign policy habitually used to justify taxation.[10] Moreover, there are signs that in 1534 he was not primarily interested in raising money. The details of the act which concerned its administration were loosely drafted,[11] and the sum asked for was modest – one fifteenth and tenth and one subsidy rated on the wealthier members of the nation only. Even so it proved hard to raise; collectors met with quite unusual resistance and underassessment.[12] As a money-raiser, the act was not a patch on the subsidy acts promoted by Wolsey between 1512 and 1523. It looks as though the reluctant taxpayers recognised Cromwell's real purpose, a purpose plain from three things. This was taxation in peace-time, and effectively admitted to be so. It introduced the principle that national government needed financial support for extraordinary expenses not incurred by war. And the lavish gratitude to the king expressed in the preamble, together with two technical points – the royal assent was given in the 'public act' formula *le roi le veult*, and the commissioners for the subsidy were to be appointed by letters patent, not as hitherto in parliament – underlined Cromwell's conviction that the king should be entitled to call for such contributions however little tradition sanctioned them.

However, from the purely financial point of view this first step towards reorganising the royal finances on the basis of national, and possibly regular, taxation proved rather a failure, and Cromwell fell back on the expropriation of the church. The parliament of 1536 encountered no request for supply. In 1539, however, Cromwell felt both able and compelled to try again. The suppression of the rebellions in the north had been expensive, and the cost of modernising the country's defences, a task which he comprehensively tackled from 1538 onwards, threatened ruin to the exchequer. (The king's mania for building did not help, but this could hardly be used as an argument in public.) It looks as though Cromwell tried for a subsidy in the 1539 session, though none was granted. On 20 May 1539, the twelfth day of the session, his enemy the duke of Norfolk delivered a curious speech in the House of Lords the inwardness of which cannot be wholly explained but from which it appears that proposals for raising a tax may by that date have reached the Upper House from the Lower.[13] Norfolk agreed that the king's expenses and labours had been very great and hoped that their lordships would give serious consideration to them: no doubt each man would wish to give according to his ability. However, pressure of time made it impossible to do anything about this just then, and he therefore moved for a petition to the king that, inasmuch as parliament was about to be prorogued, the decision on supply might be deferred to that later time. This representation was debated in the privy council on the same day, and on the 23rd the House was prorogued for a week;[14] but though it sat thereafter for another four weeks, the question of supply never came up again. Instead, the debates over the Six Articles took precedence in the Lords. It looks very much as though Norfolk, who had been a firm supporter of that reactionary measure from the start, may have used the prorogation to clear the road for his preferred subject by ending discussion of a subsidy. In that way he would score a double victory over Cromwell: he forced on a settlement of religion deeply distasteful to the Lord Privy Seal, and he lowered the minister's credit as the man who could get money from parliament.

It is in fact apparent that Norfolk throughout this session outmanoeuvred Cromwell who was in an impossible position. On 5 May, a committee consisting of Cromwell and a mixture of radical and conservative bishops had been appointed to consider the problem of diversity in religion. The vicegerent in spirituals could hardly avoid appointment to it, but since he was saddled with irreconcilable opponents and knew that the king would accept only a solution repulsive to himself he was sure to lose face and credit. He tried to save something by inaction, but here, too, Norfolk got the better of him. On the 16th, the duke, protesting at the committee's failure to achieve anything, himself introduced the Six Articles (agreed with the king) as a basis for a definition of the faith and asked for a penal act.[15] Possibly Cromwell blocked him for a few days by getting the money bill brought up from the Commons. However, as we have seen, on the 20th the duke intervened to stop that debate, his private knowledge of the forthcoming prorogation and evident assurance that a postponement of supply would not be resented showing where at this point the ascendancy in the council lay. And the Whitsun prorogation does seem to have been decisive: on reassembling the Lords at once received a royal message supporting the demand for a penal statute on religion, and thereafter the Six Articles Act took shape while no more was heard of money.

Before this parliament met for its third session in the spring of 1540, Cromwell had recovered much ground, and he made very careful preparations to secure the subsidy upon which his political standing now depended. Fortunately some important evidence survives to show the workings of his mind. He was engaged upon the act by February 1540, and on the eve of the session (which opened on 12 April) he reminded himself to inform the king 'what hath been done touching the grant to be made in the Parliament'.[16] This was to be unmistakably *his* subsidy bill. In the drafting he paid particular heed to the arguments used to justify the demand. A long roll was compiled giving a very detailed list of reasons to be advanced: the costs of suppressing the northern rebellions; the expenses of reorganising the local councils in the north, the Welsh marches and the west (advertised as offering swifter justice and greater safety to the people); the charges for putting the navy on a war footing during the previous year's invasion scare; the garrisoning of towns and fortresses in the Pale of Calais and against Scotland, as well as the heavy building programme of forts around the south and south-east coasts; the repairing of Dover harbour which had turned out to be unexpectedly expensive; the maintenance of an army in Ireland; general rearmament (casting of guns, stockpiling of bows, arrows, gunpowder and so forth); repairs to Westminster Hall; and the unbelievable costs sustained by the king in carrying through the break with Rome and the Reformation which had meant such a saving to the nation.[17] All these points, except the minor ones touching rearmament and Westminster Hall, appeared concisely stated in the preamble of the statute, except also that the last point was here put first.[18]

The statute in fact followed the precedent of 1534 by first of all reminding the nation of the excellent government they had enjoyed since 1509 and then enlarged upon this by particularising. Special gratitude was owed to the king for bringing his people 'out of all blindness and ignorance into the true and perfect knowledge of Almighty God'. This point was made separately from the more practical reminder that the abolition of papal authority had saved the nation such vast sums of money in payments to Rome, and it needs a closer look. To the drafters of the act it was a serious point, not a mere flourish: they really wished to emphasise the Reformation as the basis of all that the government had done. This becomes clear in an alternative preamble, ready drafted but in the end not used.[19] This concentrated exclusively on the glories of the Reformation in discussing which it adopted quite an exalted tone. The Commons are made to describe themselves as 'members of the same Church [of England], men selected to utter and express the voices and minds of the whole realm'. They have before their eyes 'the manifest commodities and high benefits that it hath pleased Almighty God to pour on us through the opening and showing of his most holy Word to the salvation of our souls, the prosperity and wealth of our bodies, and the most high advancement and benefit of the common wealth of this our most dear and beloved country'. They remember the 'errors and blindness that we and our forefathers have long slept in', deceived by 'the subtle serpent, the bishop of Rome – enemy to Christ and his gospel'. They therefore think it right 'to bestow not only our goods and all that we have but also to spend our lives' in protecting the reform and destroying the old evil. The preamble deviates into Scripture, citing Christ's promise to those who will leave all to follow him. True Christians (it goes on) have ever suffered persecution; wherefore they 'look for none other but for the extreme persecution and devilish hatred of the bishop of Rome and his adherents'. True, they trust in God's protection: 'yet we ought to put our aiding hands to our power in the defence of our wives, children and proper persons'. It is necessary, in fact, to prepare for the defence of the realm, an expensive business. The Commons, 'having perfect confidence and affiance in the said pardon of our Saviour, most heartily and above all things desiring to be partakers thereof', determined to show that they have fully renounced the papacy, and also resolved 'to prefer, set forth and glorify Christ and his gospel', therefore offer the necessary money.

This passionate preamble would certainly have looked pretty odd on the statute book, and it is no wonder that in the event it was replaced by a more convenientional statement of needs. However, it remains highly significant. The language is that usual in the circle of humanist and reformist common-wealth-men who surrounded Cromwell; but the language also reflects the minister's own convictions concerning the nature of the reforms he had carried through, the rule of Scripture, and the social regeneration involved in the Reformation.[20] The document is in a hand that may well be Ralph Sadler's (Cromwell's confidential secretary), and Cromwell showed that he had read it by endorsing its purpose on it; it represents a considered, not a cranky, view of what taxation should be justified by. It was Cromwell's point that the renewal of the common weal was the financial business of the nation. He took up the hints of 1534: the nation owes such special benefits to the king's rule that it must do all it can to respond to his call for money. There had been no war nor, by the time that the subsidy bill was introduced, could anyone any longer pretend that the danger of war existed; Cardinal Pole's mission of 1539 had clearly collapsed, and there was no immediate threat.[21] Nor does the preamble try to present a case based on war. The most it can say is that papal hostility will continue and demand future in-vestment in defence. Its real purpose is to commit parliament to the achieve-ments of Cromwell's decade and express a free willingness to support the Reformation by paying taxes.

In the event, these sentiments were boiled down into a perfectly sober recognition of the gains made – spiritually and materially – in the wake of the rejection of the papacy, and care was taken to append the other more usual justifications listed in the resumé prepared beforehand. Cromwell indicated his order of priorities when he took the benefits of good govern-ment from the end of the list and put them at the head. The other grounds may indeed have been more usual, but they were still unusual enough. Certainly much play was made with the costs of military preparedness, but no one suggested that there had been a war or was going to be one. Pre-Cromwellian subsidy acts had always been able to tie even mere preparations to proven bellicose events. Items like the benefits of local councils or the repair of Dover harbour (for trade) did not even profess to be linked to the possibilities of war, and the repetition of the general gratitude for the king's now thirty-one years of rule plainly restated the fact that taxation could be demanded to support government in general, not only the extraordinary expenses incurred through war.

What is more, Cromwell took care to have these novel ideas pressed home in the House. Himself unable to speak there, he used Richard Morison, a member of his secretariat for whom he had obtained a seat in 1539 explicitly that he might act as a government spokesman.[22] Morison's draft of the speech which (presumably) he delivered survives, with some interesting corrections by Cromwell.[23]

Significantly the speech opens with a sonorous passage stressing the king's charges but saying not a word of war:

Forasmuch as reason, honesty and duty bind all subjects that will be counted loving both oft to consider the manifold benefits that they receive of their prince's politic governance, and also the excessive charges that those princes are called unto, which pass little of money where either the wealth or safety of their subjects require the expense of it, we assembled here in Parliament, men chosen to utter the voice, to express the mind, of the whole realm, have thought it our bounden duties, whereas the King's majesty's charges have been of late wonderful great and are now like to be greater than ever they have been in his highness' time, to show unto his majesty, though we be not able fully to satisfy his grace's innumerable benefits towards us his loving subjects, that yet according to the true profession of obedient subjects we are body, soul and goods all whole at his grace's commendment.

The king, says Morison, has found us ready to aid him in times past; the issues are greater than ever (still no word of war), and should we refuse now to prove our good will to his grace 'and this our most dear country'? He admits that there have been payments before: but look how well they were spent, and you will have to think rather we gave too little. 'His highness well declareth that a private person had it not of us, but one that remembereth still both in what place God hath set him and also for what purpose God hath given him more than a great many, which would serve his highness if the tender love he beareth to this his empire, to us his subjects, did not enforce him daily to new charges.' In 1540, after all, any talk of taxation was bound to encounter the obvious argument: the king's revenues had of late been so much augmented that a demand for more subsidies seemed thoroughly unjustified. Morison foresaw and blocked that line of thought. He went on to elaborate on the costs of military preparations, with an impassioned reference to Pole's mission but again with no pretence that there might still be any danger of war. All Morison can say is that the parliament must do everything possible to forestall any move that might restore the pope in England – and the papists, he warns, 'care not what charges they be at, so usurped power may run again'. There follows an appeal for support for the Reformation, rather along the lines of the discarded preamble which altogether had left its mark on this speech. If the enemy will risk their all to advance 'error and idolatry', are we to refuse to give our property or even our lives 'for the defence of God's Word, for the maintenance of his glory, for the keeping with us rightly restored religion'? Victory depends on God, but he will only help those who prove their worth by helping themselves. The women of ancient Rome are called in to aid, for sacrificing their jewels ('which, ye know, women love little worse than life') to defend their country. A merchant travelling in a tempest-tossed ship would rightly be thought mad if he refused to cast overboard his merchandise at the behest of the master, and thus to save some piece of property be fully cast away. Morison goes to some lengths to paint the horrors of papal rule.

This tyrant of Rome is not content with the thraldom of bodies except souls brought from light and liberty be hurled into the deep dungels of errors. The Turk compelling no man to forsake his faith, this tyrant resteth not while Christ be forsaken and his baggage in Christ's place taken.

Dangers like these cannot be dealt with afterwards: they must be provided against beforehand. And the king is doing just that. Here Morison takes up the points of the preamble and drives them home rhetorically. Any of you who used to know Calais or Guisnes should see them now! The charges the king has incurred at Dover! Ireland, the maintenance of Berwick and Carlisle – you have no idea how expensive it all is! The king cannot for ever pay for all this himself, and when his money runs out where shall we be?

Lastly the speaker turned to argue that the nation could well afford to tighten its belt – if indeed to do so was necessary for a people given to indulging themselves. We live much too well in England: 'might we not think honesty would we left the love of our bellies for a season and gave that we foolishly spend in our exceeding fare to our country, being in need of it?'

Let us lay up our sweet lips for a three or four months, giving the overplus of our accustomed monthly charges to the present necessity of the commonwealth, to the maintenance of Christ's religion and pure doctrine, to the utter confusion of our enemies and perpetual establishment of God's honour. Let us spend it thus awhile, and if any man think it evil spent so he may imagine it is spent in belly cheer, as it was wont to be. After this sort we shall not only highly serve God, maintain the prosperous wealth of our country, abash the brags of our utter enemies, without the abating of our bags and coffers, but also hereby much enrich ourselves and make our bodies, which commonly now are with superfluities of meat in danger of many diseases, very lusty and healthy. More might be said, but where they will not serve, of like more would little move.

A powerful speech, though Morison's draft did not entirely satisfy his master. Some of Cromwell's corrections remind one of his attested concern for the English language, though it is of interest to note that, being an older man, he disapproved on occasion of Morison's modernised spelling.[24] Most of his changes make the devotion to Henry even more fulsome. In the last passage quoted, Cromwell added several phrases to give greater weight to the good prospects to be expected from the use of the tax-money; after his revision it read:

giving with good will not only the overplus of our accustomed monthly charges to the present necessity of the commonwealth, to the maintenance of Christ's religion and pure doctrine, but also liberally and with good heart to depart with our goods worldly, lent to us but for a time, to our good King and protector, which shall be spent to the utter confusion of our enemies, the assurance of ourselves and posterity, and the perpetual establishment of God's honour.

We see how anxious he was to emphasise the general purposes of taxation and the general need for it. Two of his corrections, however, display a careful realism. The dangerous, because obviously nonsensical, phrase 'without the abating of our bags and coffers' he crossed out: he was not fool enough to pretend to the House of Commons that paying taxes left people as well off as they had been. And Morison's 'three or four months' during which self-restraint should be applied became 'years': the burden on the country of the money asked for – four fifteenths and tenths and a subsidy spread over two years – would be heavier than Morison's airy phrase pretended.

In Morison's speech, therefore, we hear the voice of Cromwell. And once again in 1540, the arguments put forward for raising a tax concentrated on the general benefits of government and the particular benefits of the reform in the church. It is to support these and to protect them from possible (but so far by no means actual) attack that the nation is to pay. The preliminary memorial, the preamble of the act itself, this supporting speech in the House all revolve around the same complex of ideas. The act of 1540 abandoned some of the less fortunate features of its predecessor. The formula of assent returned to tradition inasmuch as the parliament once again formally presented the grant and the king thanked his loyal subjects for their generosity.[25] It is just possible that the failure to observe these ancient forms had been an oversight in 1534, but there could also have been purpose behind it – the purpose of stressing some sort of right to tax possessed by the Crown. The 1540 act, nicely constitutional in this respect, nevertheless preserved the new principle that commissioners for the subsidy were not appointed by parliament; it empowered a council committee to see to this. The important clauses dealing with assessment and collection were much more carefully drafted. This time Cromwell really wanted money quite as much as he needed to assert his novel principle, and indeed, the country was to pay much more readily and completely than it had done in 1535–6. But 1540 was very careful to continue the real innovation of 1534, namely that extraordinary contributions could be levied for reasons other than war.

It should be emphasised what it was that Cromwell really wanted. There is no sign at all that he either meant to free taxation from the need for parliamentary consent or to make parliamentary supply a regular feature of every session. The first could not be contemplated by a government which always operated within the confines of law and custom; the second, which, thanks to all those wars, had been virtually achieved in the first half of Henry's reign, was both less necessary and less desirable in these later days of political upheaval when crown revenue had gained so much from the church. Cromwell's point was rather that the whole concept of extraordinary expenditure needed enlarging. No doubt there had been a time when only war demanded outlays from the crown for which its customary and prerogative revenues were insufficient. The money grants of Henry VII's day and Wolsey's had accepted that principle: Henry VII had managed his government satisfactorily inside it, but by Wolsey's time inflation and the consequences of an active policy had rendered it highly doubtful. The great expansion of government activity since 1529, and especially since 1533, had really brought its inadequacy into the open. There had, of course, been particular expenses like those occasioned by the northern rebellions or the Irish unrest, but most of the arguments but forward centred on the making good of past neglect, and on the general reform of church and commonwealth. Thomas Cromwell conceived himself to be presiding, under the king, over a national government engaged upon the reconstruction of the polity, a government which could fairly demand support for all its work when this involved so much beneficial innovation and reconstruction. His attitude is revealed in every aspect of his work; not surprisingly it also comes out in his readiness to tax in peace-time and in the justifications he offered for doing so.

The renewal of war soon after Cromwell's fall allowed the new principle to retreat. Henry VIII secured two more grants, in 1543 and 1545.[26] The first could point to the victorious war against Scotland and explain how the king's lawful claim to that crown had led to hostilities; the second referred to the unhappy necessity of war imposed on a peaceful king by those 'ancient enemies', Scotland and France. The basic justification thus reverted to traditional grounds. However, Cromwell's work left important residue behind. The acts continued to appeal to memories of the king's prosperous reign, in the formula first introduced in 1534. That of 1543 made the bad mistake of interpreting the Cromwellian principle much too crudely:

And forasmuch as among other considerations and respects the civil and politic bodies ought to have in all commonwealths they should most principally and specially regard study and devise for the conservation and increase of the royal estate honour and dignity and estimation of their chief head and sovereign lord by whom they be stayed and governed, and for the preservation and surety of his person and of his succession, and with all their powers might and substance to resist and stand against all such which by violence force fraud deceit or otherwise would attempt to decrease diminish appair or hurt the same, in body dignity title or honour: We therefore . . .

Here the king was claiming financial support as of right, by virtue of his kingship. Where Cromwell had alleged that royal government, being for the good of the nation, could rightly call for support when policy could be shown to be yielding benefit, his successors tried to assert that every call for money from the Crown demanded loyal obedience as a matter of course. This extravagant and dangerous idea had disappeared by 1545 when the preamble turned quite exceptionally humble, even smarmy, with absurd touches which one may be well advised in ascribing to Henry himself, but said nothing about a generalised duty to pay.[27] The Byzantinism of these later acts was assuredly initiated in Cromwell's preambles which, anxious to hammer home feelings of gratitude and duty convenient in smoothing acceptance of a new and disconcerting principle in taxation, had deserted the factual sobriety of earlier drafting. But Cromwell was not responsible for the absurdities to which this sort of thing came to descend after his time. He was responsible for successfully reminding the nation that even without war government now cost more money than the personal revenue of the king could support, and when war again came to make the justifying of taxes easier that reminder survived in the phrasing of preambles.

The initiative of Cromwell's day was not forgotten when again it became desirable to raise money in peace-time. Edward VI's sole tax-grant, obtained in 1552, did refer to the financial consequences of the Protector Somerset's disastrous war policy, but the tax was justified on grounds of ordinary government: gratitude for the preservation of the realm in peace, gratitude for the restoration of a decayed commonwealth (a likely story), gratitude for the establishment of the true religion, and desire to demonstrate a proper loyalty to the king.[28] Mary also raised money only once, in 1555, before she got involved in the Habsburg-Valois wars; her statute is peculiar in that the grant came jointly from both Houses instead of being moved by the Commons alone, and in that the preamble abruptly returned to concise brevity.[29] The grounds stated were exclusively of the new type: appreciation for the general benefits of the queen's rule, the great debts she had inherited from the previous reign, and the large present burdens of government. This act in a way consummated the changes introduced by Cromwell: not a word about war or even preparation for defence, nor any attempt to make the brief statement of motives more convincing or more palatable by elaboration. Peace-time taxation had become accepted.

The crunch came in the reign of Elizabeth – the first reign in English history in which money was asked for and granted in every session of parliament, whether the sessions came at long intervals or more closely together. Indeed, it looks very much as though the queen called parliament only when she wanted money, a fact which made the rarity of meetings a matter of propagandist pride to her. Despite the political developments in parliament during those forty-five years, Elizabeth's insistence on supply is likely to have evoked a general appreciation for her kindness in calling so few. Nor did she make any bones about the justification of taxation. In 1559, 1563, 1571 and 1576 the grounds stated circle around such non-extraordinary needs as the crown's penury, thanks for the restoration of a protestant church, the preservation of peace, and the restoration of the coinage.[30] Even in 1563 when she had just been involved in a species of warlike operations in Scotland, with undoubted military expenditure, the Subsidy Act alluded delicately to a 'provident and seasonable enterprise' successful in preventing war. Instead of thankfully accepting the chance of using the ancient grounds, she deliberately pretended that none such existed. The act of 1566 is a singular exception in the century: its preamble was drafted in and by the Commons. That session witnessed a major political battle between the queen and a patriotic opposition, and the latter, much to her fury, succeeded in forcing a preamble into the Subsidy Act which offered money in return for her alleged promise to marry and settle the succession.[31] She never again allowed parliament any such paper victory.

War, however, was not permanently avoided in the reign, and the later subsidy acts reflected the fact. The three grants of 1581–7, using a virtually standardised formula, spoke of rebellion in Ireland and threats from Rome.[32] The last four grants were made after the outbreak of war with Spain, and all of them naturally stressed that event in justifying themselves.[33] Even so, the last two spread themselves on the general splendour and beneficial virtue of the Queen's long rule and do not use the war alone to explain the need for money. As in her father's reign so in Elizabeth's, the renewal of war brought heavier taxation which not surprisingly was claimed to be necessary to pay for the war. But even as Henry VIII's later acts spoke of other general grounds as well, so did his daughter's. In any case, the practice of the years 1555–76 had settled it: the crown could now legitimately claim to tax in peace-time, for purposes other than war or the threat of war. From 1534 it became accepted that government finance would at all times depend in part at least on direct taxation and parliament from that time forward made grants of a kind that had been neither necessary nor strictly constitutional in the first half-century of Tudor rule.

Thanks to Cromwell, therefore, constitutional theory had by mid-century caught up with the inescapable facts of the situation: in an age of inflation and increasing commitments, the crown could no longer live of its own. Until 1601 at least, the crown nevertheless managed to maintain independence. It retained control of the administration of tax money; until 1624, there was no return to pre-Yorkist practices of parliamentary supervision (which had never worked well). Subsidy bills were regularly introduced early in the session: thus the famous notion of redress of grievances before granting of supply did not become part of the English constitution,[34] although it had long been established in other parliaments, especially the Cortes of Aragon, and although it was brought up in the remarkable session of 1566. But that one occasion when the Commons used supply to exert political pressure upon government proved a flash in the pan because Elizabeth showed that she could learn lessons in management. However, the comfortable situation in which the crown could hope to obtain parliamentary assistance in the financing of government without having to concede anything to parliamentary opposition, would not necessarily endure, as events were soon to prove under the Stuarts. Probably Elizabeth avoided her successor's troubles in this respect because she used her rights sparingly and her explanations rang true. Taxation in peace-time had come to stay, but political sense suggested that it should not be too frequent or too obviously unproductive of benefit to the realm. As it turned out, the taxation most vocally resented in the queen's reign was that of the 1590s, even though that could appeal to the full force of traditional justifications – resented because it was so heavy, not because it was thought wrong in principle. No parliament after 1534 questioned the Crown's right to ask for supply on whatever grounds of need could be put forward.

The historian concerned to understand the effects of war upon the economy in the sixteenth century therefore needs to be careful in the use of his most obvious indicator. Down to 1529, he can treat all taxation (and its effects) as the product of war; thereafter he needs to distinguish. It then becomes desirable to follow up the collection of revenue by an investigation of expenditure, in order to ascertain whether the impact of government on the economy through direct taxation may be ascribed to actual war, impending war, or much more ordinary peace-time needs. That task waits to be done.

NOTES

1 Cf. B. P. Wolffe, *The Royal Demesne in English History* (London, 1971), pp. 40ff. He argues that the English Crown financed its work mainly from taxation until the notion that the King should 'live of his own' emerged in the fourteenth century.
2 7 Henry VII, c. 11; 11 Henry VII, c. 10; 12 Henry VII, c. 12.
3 3 Henry VIII, c. 22; 4 Henry VIII, c. 19; 5 Henry VIII, c. 17; 6 Henry VIII, c. 26; 7 Henry VIII, c. 9; 14 & 15 Henry VIII, c. 16.
4 1 Henry VIII, c. 20.
5 For the general setting of the problems here treated cf. R. S. Schofield, 'Parliamentary Lay Taxation 1485–1547' (unpublished Ph.D. dissertation, Cambridge, 1963). I am grateful to Dr Schofield, who kindly commented on this paper, for many discussions on the subject.
6 21 Henry VIII, c. 24.
7 Cf. G. R. Elton, *The Tudor Revolution in Government* (Cambridge, 1953), pp. 145–7.
8 *L[etters and] P[apers of Henry VIII]*, v, nos 762, 941, 989.
9 26 Henry VIII, c. 19.
10 R. B. Merriman, *Life and Letters of Thomas Cromwell* (Oxford, 1902), I, pp. 30–44.

11 Schofield, 'Lay Taxation', p. 215.
12 *Ibid.* pp. 328–9.
13 *Journals of the House of Lords* [hereafter *LJ*], ı, 111a.
14 *Ibid.* ı, 111b, 112b.
15 *Ibid.* ı, 105b, 109a.
16 *LP* xv, nos 195, 332, 438.
17 Public Record Office, SP 1/159, fos 37–46 (*LP* xv, no 502[2]).
18 32 Henry VIII, c. 50.
19 Public Record Office, SP 1/159, fos 33–36 (*LP* xv, no. 501[1]), endorsed by Cromwell 'for a subsidy'.
20 Cf. G. R. Elton, *Reform and Renewal: Thomas Cromwell and the Common Weal* (Cambridge, 1973).
21 The bill reached the Lords on 3 May, the twelfth day of the session (*LJ* ı, 134b). The foreign threat that started with the Truce of Nice of June 1538 had led to an apparent danger of invasion in the spring of 1539, but by April that year Charles V had plainly abandoned all such purposes. In February 1540, Norfolk's embassy to France announced that normal relations with that country had been resumed.
22 Merriman, *Life and Letters*, ıı, p. 199.
23 British Museum, Cotton MSS, Titus B, ı, fos 109–16 (*LP* xıv, ı, no. 869). The *LP* dating to 1539 is purely conjectural; 1540 answers much better. The document is a speech drafted for delivery, not (as *LP* has it) a memorial: this becomes plain in the reading of it.
24 Cf. my *Reform and Renewal*, p. 10. Morison wrote that 'reason, honesty and duty bind all subjects'; Cromwell changed this to 'bindeth'. His insertion of 'duty' into 'benevolence, gratitude and love' no doubt makes a substantive point but also achieves a more sonorous balance. Where Morison spelled fetched 'fecched', Cromwell substituted the old-fashioned 'fett'. Morison's 'leaue' becomes 'leue'. Morison's 'what charges hath his grace been at Dover' rightly seemed to Cromwell to lack an 'in' before 'Dover'. Evidently the great man could be a pedant at times.
25 Schofield, 'Lay Taxation', p. 58.
26 34 & 35 Henry VIII, c. 27; 37 Henry VIII, c. 25.
27 Despite the storms of war, Englishmen, like 'small fishes of the sea' who in tempests hide under rocks and banks, had, thanks to the king, lived in peace; it is hoped that the king will accept the Commons' poor gift, 'as it pleased the great King Alexander to receive thankfully a cup of water of a poor man by the highway-side'. Ugh.
28 7 Edward VI, c. 12.
29 2 & 3 Philip and Mary, c. 23.
30 1 Eliz. I, c. 21; 5 Eliz. I, c. 31; 13 Eliz. I, c. 27; 18 Eliz. I, c. 23.
31 8 Eliz. I, c. 18; cf. J. E. Neale, *Elizabeth and her Parliaments 1559–1581* (London, 1953), pp. 161–4.
32 23 Eliz. I, c. 15; 27 Eliz. I, c. 29; 29 Eliz. I, c. 8.
33 31 Eliz. I, c. 15; 35 Eliz. I, c. 13; 39 Eliz. I, c. 27; 43 Eliz. I, c. 18.
34 Though 'everybody knows' that the principle existed in the medieval history of the English parliament, it is in fact hard to discover it there. It could operate in practice, as apparently it did in Henry IV's reign, and it was certainly affirmed in the *Modus tenendi parliamentum* (cf. K. B. McFarlane, *Lancastrian Kings and Lollard Knights* [Oxford, 1972], pp. 96–7). However, Henry himself successfully refused to admit that any such principle existed, and the *Modus* notoriously

embodied the views of a radical reformer, not the constitutional practice of the realm. Of course, the idea of using the power of the purse to put pressure on governments that failed to please was too obvious never to occur; what matters is that it was never established as a parliamentary right and that taxation was usually passed early in the session. In the middle ages, the Commons did not try to force legislative concessions from the Crown by threatening to withhold supply: they confined themselves to asking that the money be spent on the purpose for which it had been granted (A. Rogers, 'Henry IV, the Commons and Taxation', *Medieval Studies*, 31 (1969), 44–70, esp. pp. 49, 68). Even in the early Stuart period, when the difficulties between king and Commons brought the alleged principle back again, it did not operate: thus the very disturbed sessions of 1621 witnessed the passing of subsidy acts and nothing else, a manifest indication that grievances did not have to be satisfied before money was granted.

3 War and economic change: the economic costs of the Dutch Revolt[1]

Geoffrey Parker

In 1580 the States-General of France commissioned a royal official, Nicolas Froumenteau, to ascertain the costs of the civil and religious wars fought since 1559. Froumenteau scanned the civil, ecclesiastical and judicial records of each diocese of France in search of statistics, and his report – which took up 591 closely printed pages – even included an estimate of the total number of French women raped between 1559 and 1580 (no less than 12,300 of them). Froumenteau's was a remarkable achievement. It was also unique: nothing else quite like it was composed in early modern times. For other wars in other areas historians have had to do their own sums.

Unfortunately, since the volume of surviving archival and literary material is so vast, there have been many studies published on individual communities or areas but few syntheses or general surveys. Generalisation is hampered by the fact that the experience of each community tends to be unique, some registering total dislocation, others only a slight disturbance. A recent survey of the economic consequences of the Thirty Years' War in Germany, for example, counted ten local studies published between 1910 and 1943 which suggested that Germany was in decline before the war began as against twenty-four which supported the view that the war dealt a catastrophic blow to a previously booming economy. The discussion remains open.[2] The debate over the economic consequences of the Dutch war of liberation (1568–1648) has followed much the same course. The view has been advanced by some scholars that the economy of the South Netherlands was permanently crippled and that of the North decisively stimulated by the conflict; others hold that the war was not nearly so influential, that Holland gained less and 'Belgium' lost less than had been supposed. A number of regional and local studies have been produced to support each interpretation.[3]

The aim of the present essay is to examine and correlate the various sources which bear on this question and to consider the effects of the war upon some of the numerous participants. The Eighty Years' War was, *par excellence*, a war of intervention. Throughout early modern times the Netherlands were the 'cockpit of Europe' and almost every European state became involved in the Dutch struggle for independence at some time. Several German princes sent occasional subsidies; Elizabeth of England sent at least 15m florins to the Low Countries between 1585 and 1603; and Henry IV of France sent 12m florins between 1598 and 1610. These sums were considerable, but they could hardly compare with Habsburg Spain which often sent as much as that in a single year, and sometimes more. Then there were manpower costs. England, France, the German states, Spain and Italy as well as the Netherlands provided a steady supply of troops and the cumulative loss of life, civilian and military, must have been considerable – although not, perhaps, as high as the estimate of the Spanish writer Quevedo who, through the mouth of an imaginary Dutch sea captain informing the ignorant Indians of Chile about the Revolt, wrote:

The harsh spirit [*ánimo severo*] of Philip II placed the bloody punishment of the two noblemen [Egmont and Hoorn] above the retention of all those provinces and lordships. . . . In wars lasting sixty years and more we have sacrified more than two million men to those two lives, for the campaigns and sieges of the Netherlands have become the universal sepulchre of Europe.[4]

It is with the Netherlands as a 'sepulchre', of money, material and morale as well as of men, that this essay is concerned; and inevitably, therefore, attention will be focused primarily upon the three areas which were most affected, economically speaking, by the Dutch Revolt: modern Belgium, the Iberian peninsula, and the Dutch Republic.

I

Perhaps the least disputable economic consequence of the Dutch Revolt was a catastrophic fall in the population of the South Netherlands.[5] We have a relatively large amount of information concerning the demographic decline of 'Belgium' between 1572 (the outbreak of continuous fighting) and 1609 (the Twelve Years' Truce), and with scarcely an exception there is clear evidence that almost every community in Flanders and Brabant lost between a half and two-thirds of its inhabitants. Moreover this long-term development, illustrated in figure 1, in most cases masks an even sharper fall in the decade 1578–88. The demographic experience of the small Flemish village of Evergem – the subject of figure 2 – appears to have been all too typical. Rural areas suffered particularly severely. In southern Flanders it has been estimated that only 1 per cent of the farming population remained on their land throughout the crisis decade of the 1580s, while further north, around Ghent, the area under cultivation fell by 92 per cent over the ten years. It was the same story in Brabant where farms were destroyed, crops burned and entire families of peasants murdered by the soldiers and freebooters.[6] Only the provinces which defected to Spain without a blow in 1577–9 – Artois, Hainaut and French Flanders – appear to have escaped the devastation.

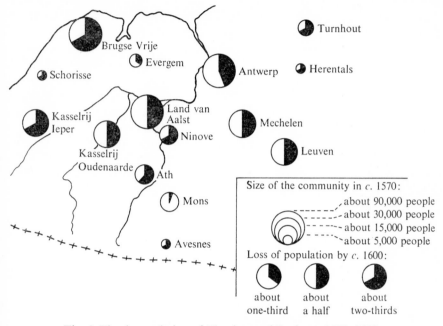

Fig. 1 The depopulation of Flanders and Brabant, 1570–1600.
(For sources see appendix.)

The proximity of heavy fighting also had an adverse effect on industrial production. Heavy capital equipment was wantonly destroyed by the troops of both sides. The clothworks of Hondschoote, far and away the largest in the Netherlands, changed hands six times between 1578 and 1582, when they were burnt to the ground by French soldiers. The town's population fell from 18,000 in the 1560s to 385 in 1584. Figure 3 (below) shows the severe slump in its production. Other textile centres virtually ceased to produce during the 1580s and some of them never recovered.[7]

Thus far, therefore, the traditional picture appears correct. Flanders and Brabant, the ancient heart of the Low Countries, formerly the most prosperous provinces, were totally ruined. In 1585 and 1586 it proved impossible even to sow crops in many areas through shortage of labour.[8] However the South Netherlands did not remain at this low level for long. After about 1600 the character of the war in the Low Countries changed. The battle-line was dramatically shortened by the victories of Maurice of Nassau in the 1590s and hostilities were gradually limited by the system of 'contributions' (whereby a community paid protection money to the enemy in return for a guarantee that it would not be molested) and 'convoy and licence money' (dues paid to the Dutch to allow ships to sail to Antwerp). These conventions,

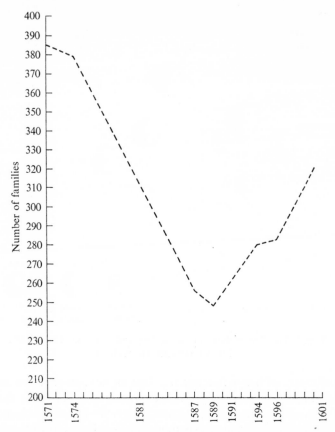

Fig. 2 The population of the village of Evergem (just north of Ghent), 1571–1601. (Source: A. de Vos, 'Dertig jaar bevolkingsevolutie to Evergem (1571–1601)', *Handelingen der Maatschappij voor Geschiedenis en Oudheidkunde te Gent*, XIV (1960), p. 122.)

although deplored by many professional soldiers on the Spanish side, did create the conditions of security which were the essential prerequisite of any economic recovery. Gradually, the population increased anew. The parish registers of the southern towns reveal a substantial increase in the number of baptisms recorded between the 1590s and the 1640s: over 90 per cent up at Lier and Leuven, 82 per cent up at Mechelen, and 76 per cent up at Ghent.[9] The former metropolis of Antwerp, whose population fell from almost 84,000 in 1582 to 42,000 in 1589, had recovered to about 54,000 in 1612. Antwerp merchants began to trade again with Italy and Spain and even with the Spanish and Portuguese overseas empires.[10] Almost 600 South Netherlands merchants are known to have traded with the Iberian powers

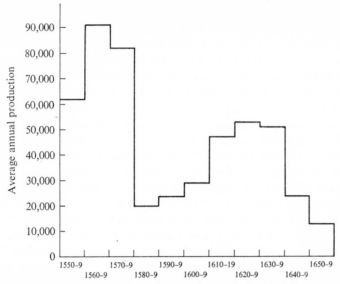

Fig. 3 Hondschoote: production of serge cloths for export. (Source: E. Coornaert, *Un centre industriel d'autrefois. La draperie-sayetterie d'Hondschoote (XIVe–XVIIIe siècles)* (Paris, 1930) – based upon the statistical appendix at the end.)

and their empires between 1598 and 1648. Silk, sugar and other 'colonial' goods flowed into Antwerp in considerable quantities after 1589, while the vast sums spent by the king of Spain on his army in the Netherlands, most of it sent from Castile, also brought prosperity to some bankers, sutlers and military contractors in the 'obedient provinces'.[11] There was considerable industrial recovery too. As figure 3 shows, even Hondschoote produced almost as many broad-cloths in the 1620s as in the 1550s: almost 60,000 were turned out in some years, most of them exported to Spain through Oostende and Dunkirk. Ghent too produced large quantities and many varieties of textiles in the first half of the seventeenth century: 29,000 linen cloths were brought to market in 1636, of which 20,000 were exported to Spain.[12] In many towns new activities grew up to compensate for the demise of the old – silk, lace, tapestries, glass-making, jewellery, diamond-cutting and printing – while in general there was a shift of emphasis from quantity to quality. The profits made from these enterprises are reflected to this day in the rich town houses of Antwerp, Ghent, Brussels, Berghes and elsewhere constructed between 1600 and 1670. One-eighth of Ghent – 1,260 houses – was rebuilt or refaced in stone during this period.[13] In the countryside, too, there was recovery. The improvements in farming methods became legendary and an English observer, Sir Richard Weston, wrote in 1644–5 that between Dunkirk and Bruges 'I saw as rich a countrie as ever my eies beheld, stokt with goodly wheat and barlie, and excellent meadow and pasture'.[14] Rural Flanders had come a long way since 1586.

Yet neither the degree nor the duration of the recovery must be exaggerated. The war continued to take its toll. Taxes were required in ever-increasing quantities to finance the war – about 4m florins a year between 1600 and 1640 – diverting capital from productive investment and impoverishing the taxpayers. The 70,000 and more troops who regularly fought for Spain in the South Netherlands, mainly foreigners, were expensive in other ways too: quite apart from the malicious damage they so often committed, the soldiers all had to be fed and lodged in billets at the Netherlanders' expense. The areas near to the theatre of military operations therefore recovered very slowly. Some relatively sheltered areas also failed to thrive. The population of the rural areas around Ieper, for instance, declined steadily throughout the period of the Twelve Years' Truce, while the cloth works at Dixmuide, Eecke, Menin, Poperinghe and other lesser centres never fully recovered from the destruction of the 1580s. Farther south, the city of Mons, which had weathered the storms of the later sixteenth century with relatively little loss, began to decline fairly rapidly after 1600. Its population in 1593 was 17,239, but it had fallen to 13,944 by 1625. For Mons and the other large towns along the southern border, the war which broke out between Spain and France in 1635 brought widespread devastation and industrial collapse.[15]

Thus, if it is possible to overestimate the 'crisis' caused by the Eighty Years' War in the South Netherlands, it is equally easy to exaggerate the recovery. The southern provinces never fulfilled the promising destiny which seemed to beckon during the reign of Charles V. They remained an economic backwater from 1572 until the coal and steel boom of the early nineteenth century made Belgium the first continental country to experience an industrial revolution.

II

If the costs of the Dutch Revolt to the South Netherlands were severe, they were scarcely less deleterious for the other dominions of the king of Spain. In the opinion of Don Fernando Girón, an experienced councillor of Philip IV, 'The war in the Netherlands has been the total ruin of this monarchy'.[16] This view was echoed in the highest quarters. In 1604, for example, Philip III succinctly summarised the effects of the Low Countries' wars upon Spain as follows:

My uncle [the Archduke Albert, ruler of the Netherlands] is well aware of the extent to which my kingdoms [of Spain] resent the continuation of such great provisions as he has been sent, seeing that all the money which arrives from the Indies goes into them, and that since this does not suffice the people of Spain have always to pay extraordinary taxes; these are the fruits of the war that they see, together with the absence of their sons, brothers, dependents and relatives, who either die or return wounded, without arms, sight or legs, totally useless; and having yielded the promise of their lives there, their parents, brothers and relatives have to support them here.[17]

Spain sacrificed an unacceptably large number of her young men upon the altar of the Netherlands war. Recruiting for the Spanish army removed perhaps 8,000 men a year from Castile when Spain was at war: they went to defend the African garrisons, Italy and the Netherlands and to man the Mediterranean and Atlantic fleets. Between 1567 and 1574, some 42,875 soldiers actually left Spain to fight in Italy and the Netherlands alone – an average of over 5,000 a year even though none left in 1569 and 1570 because of the war of Granada. In the period 1631–9 over 30,000 Castilians were sent to the army of Flanders alone: over 3,000 a year.[18] This military drain of manpower was far more important than, for example, the emigration to the New World, at least in quantitative terms, although of course not all the troops sent to the army were permanently lost: as the king pointed out, many returned when they were unfit for further service, 'wounded, without arms, sight or legs, totally useless'. The human waste associated with the war in 'Flanders' also revolted a man of letters like Quevedo, who found fault with a popular saying of Golden Age Spain: *No hay más Flandes* ('There's no place like Flanders'): 'We condemn those who in some light conversation say *No hay más Flandes* in praise of some pleasure ... because up to now we have seen nothing worthy of note to come from that country except eyes torn out or squint, or broken arms and legs.'[19]

Overshadowing these 'social costs' of the war, however, was the far more debilitating haemorrhage of Spanish treasure and the virtual destruction of the Castilian economy in order to finance the war against the Dutch. Figure 4 illustrates the two great 'waves' of Spanish spending in the Netherlands, the first stretching from 1586 until the truce in 1607, the second from 1621 until 1640. They corresponded to the two massive thrusts of Spanish imperialism in Europe under Philip II and under Olivares. But this flexing of Spain's imperial muscles was only achieved at a terrible cost. Philip III was quite correct to claim that more was sent to the Netherlands than arrived legally on the New World treasure fleets. His father, Philip II, had voiced exactly the same complaint, with equal justice, in 1578:

[The war has] consumed the money and substance which has come from the Indies, while the collection and raising of revenues in these kingdoms has only been done with great difficulty because of the dearth of specie in them (since so much is exported) and because of the damage which this does and causes to the commerce and trade on which the yield of our taxes depends.[20]

There was no exaggeration in this amazing claim. Between 1571 and 1575 the total 'royal' receipts from the Indies came to 3.9m ducats; over the same quinquennium the paymaster-general of the army of Flanders received some

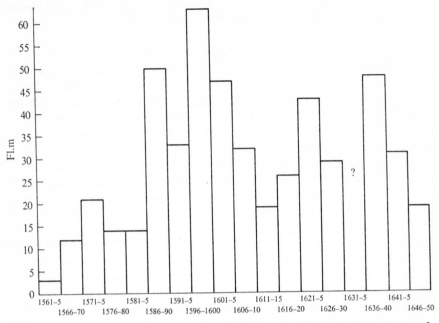

Fig. 4 Money received from Castile by the Paymaster-General of the Army of Flanders. (Source: G. Parker, *The Army of Flanders and the Spanish Road* (Cambridge, 1972), pp. 293–5.)

9m ducats from Castile. In the same period, the paymaster-general of the Mediterranean fleet received a further 5m ducats, bringing Philip II's total outlay on 'imperialism' to around 14m. This pattern was repeated in subsequent years: the crown regularly spent more in the Netherlands than it received from the Indies. Between 1566 and 1654, the Military Treasury in the Netherlands received a minimum of 218m ducats from Castile, while the crown received only 121m ducats from the Indies. This vast shortfall, together with the rest of the government's needs, was made up in the end by the Castilian taxpayers. As one outraged delegate in the *Cortes* of Castile expostulated in 1586: 'However much money comes [from the Indies], this kingdom has less!'[21]

The Spanish Habsburgs left virtually no stone unturned in their efforts to finance the subjugation of the Dutch. Taxes were increased repeatedly and it was generally agreed by travellers in the early modern period that the population of Castile was taxed more heavily than any other people in Europe. Modern calculations have shown that while prices in the sixteenth century rose three-fold between 1500 and 1590 in Castile, taxation rose more than five-fold, so that by 1590 one-third of the average peasant's income in a good year was consumed in tax. In the last decade of the century new taxes were imposed (above all the *millones*, a new excise tax) and harvest yields fell, so that taxation bit even deeper into the economy.[22]

Yet even the most savage and onerous fiscal measures could not make current income match expenditure. To bridge the deficit caused by Habsburg imperialism the government was compelled to borrow on a grand scale. In 1557, at Philip II's accession, the Castilian national debt stood at 36m ducats; in 1598, when the king died, it stood at 85m. Two years after Philip IV's accession, in 1623, the total public debt had risen to 112m ducats – the equivalent of at least ten years' revenue; two years after his death, in 1667, the debt stood at 180m. This five-fold increase in a little over a century was caused in large measure by Spain's insistence on heavy military spending in the Low Countries: the periods of fastest increase in the debt corresponded with the periods of greatest expenditure in the Netherlands.

These costs of the war in 'Flanders' were felt by all (or almost all) parts of the Habsburg empire, but there were two areas which suffered especially heavy damage: Old Castile and Portugal. *Castilla la Vieja*, more or less the Duero basin, was famous in the early sixteenth century for its wool. Some of it was made into cloth locally, mainly at Segovia, but most – often two-thirds – was exported via Burgos, Santander and Bilbao to northern Europe, especially to the Netherlands. This trade was crippled by the Dutch Revolt. In 1570, some 17,000 sacks of wool were exported through Santander; by 1622 this total had fallen to 605 sacks. It was the same story in Bilbao: the port insurance registers reveal that shipments to the Netherlands, having risen steadily throughout the earlier sixteenth century, ceased abruptly in 1572–3 when the Sea Beggars closed the Scheldt to Spanish shipping. The entire economy of Old Castile, which had centred for so long on the wool trade, was seriously dislocated. Wealth and population drifted to the south on an increasing scale. By the 1590s Old Castile, the ancient heart of Spain, was in full decline.[23]

As Professor C. R. Boxer has written, the struggle between Spain and the Dutch in many ways deserves to be called the 'First World War' since it was fought out in Africa, America and Asia as well as in many parts of Europe. From the 1590s onwards the Dutch organised expeditions of trade, war or piracy to many parts of the Iberian empires overseas. Regular trade was carried on with the Guinea Coast after 1592 and with the Caribbean after 1594; in all, perhaps 150 ships were involved annually. In 1615 the first Dutch fleet entered the Pacific and ravaged the west coast of Mexico and Peru before sailing on to attack the Philippines. Later expeditions followed, coordinated after 1621 by the Dutch West India Company. This upsurge of hostilities on the high seas around America inevitably led to an increase in Spanish defence spending there. Heavier (and more expensive) escorts were needed for the fleets and costly fortifications were required on land. Already in 1624 the viceroy of Peru spent 200,000 *pesos* on defence; in 1643 he spent 948,000 (the *peso* was worth a little more than a ducat). It was the same in Mexico. The government there sent 1,500,595 *pesos* to Spain in the four years 1618–21, but it sent 1,653,253 to the Philippines to pay for the islands' defence.[24] This was all money which could otherwise have been shipped back to Spain (and used to finance military operations in the Netherlands).

But at least the Castilian seaborne empire lost little of its overseas territory; just a few small islands in the Caribbean. Portugal and her empire suffered far greater losses. The first Dutch attacks on Portuguese possessions came in 1598–9 when the islands of Príncipe and São Tomé in the gulf of Guinea were raided by a fleet of seventy-two Dutch ships. In 1605, ten years after their first expedition to the Far East, the Dutch captured some of the major spice islands; in 1612 they took their first stronghold in West Africa (Fort Nassau); and in 1624 they invaded Brazil. Despite setbacks and defeats, the Dutch consolidated and extended their bases on all three continents and by the 1650s Portugal had lost for good her control of Asia and Africa and only held on to Brazil thanks to a revolt by the native Catholic population (Indian and Negro) against the Calvinist invaders. The costs of this dogged, global struggle were enormous: an ever-increasing burden of taxation was laid upon the inhabitants of Portugal and her colonies, while the need to organise convoys, escorts and fortresses for the defence of trade tended to strangle the commerce they were meant to protect. Although no doubt the Dutch would sooner or later have come into conflict with the Portuguese over the right to trade in the Indian Ocean, there can be little doubt that Philip II's war with the Dutch caused the struggle to break out earlier than it might otherwise have done.[25]

III

These impressive Dutch conquests overseas, like the capture of innumerable towns and villages in Gelderland, Limburg, Brabant and Flanders, were not achieved at all cheaply. On the contrary, the need to finance operations at home and abroad, on land and sea, represented an enormous, continual and constantly rising charge on the North Netherlands. In the first place there was defensive expenditure: garrisons, militia and, above all, fortifications. A comparison of the detailed maps made of many Dutch towns by Jacob van Deventer in the 1550s with those made by Johan Blaeu a century later reveals a total transformation: the defences of almost every town, large and small, had been totally rebuilt to conform to the latest standards and refinements of military science. The cost must have been enormous.[26] Then there was the need to finance operations against the enemy. From 3.2m florins in 1591, the first year in which the Dutch mounted an offensive campaign, the annual cost of the republic's armed forces rose to 8.8m florins in 1607, 13.4m in 1622, and 18.8m in 1640.[27] Prolonged military expenditure on this scale compelled the Dutch government to impose heavy taxes on its subjects – far more onerous than the duke of Alva's 'Tenth Penny' which had done so much to start the Revolt! – and to create a large public debt. In 1651 the debt of the province of Holland alone stood at 153m florins. Fortunately for Dutch trade, throughout the seventeenth century there was enough capital in Amsterdam alone to float government loans and finance trade and industry without pushing up interest rates. The government was able to borrow at 10 per cent in the 1600s, at 5 per cent in the 1640s and at 4 per cent after 1655.[28]

There is no doubt that a substantial part of this capital seeking investment was provided by merchants exiled from the South Netherlands who sought refuge in the North. Of the 320 largest depositors in the Amsterdam Exchange Bank in 1611, over half were southern refugees. Surviving tax registers from 1631 reveal that about one-third of the richest Amsterdammers were of southern origin. Some 27 per cent of the shareholders of the Amsterdam chamber of the Dutch East India Company in 1602, including the three largest subscribers, were Walloon or Flemish exiles, and they provided almost 40 per cent of the company's total capital. It was the same story in the West India Company later on: at least half of the sixty-six directors who ran the company between 1622 and 1636 are known to have come from the South Netherlands.[29]

The refugees from the south were important for their numbers as well as for their wealth. 1,283 persons from the southern provinces – 780 from Antwerp alone – became citizens of Amsterdam between 1580 and 1606. Most of them were heads of households who may have brought their families with them. Many other southern exiles came to the city and either did not need or could not afford to purchase citizenship. An analysis of marriages celebrated at Amsterdam between 1586 and 1601 reveals that 1,478 bridegrooms, 16 per cent of all men married in the city in those years, came from the south (and 788 of these came from Antwerp).[30] The stream of refugees, mainly but not entirely from the south, was an important factor in the growth of the towns of Holland and Zeeland: Amsterdam grew from almost 31,000 people in 1585 to 120,000 in 1632 and Leiden, with its famous clothworks, rose from not quite 13,000 in 1574 to 65,000 in the 1640s. But very few parts of the Dutch republic underwent a demographic boom on this scale during the Eighty Years' War. Even in Holland, the population of the northern areas appears to have increased less rapidly after 1569 than before. The military operations and political upheavals of 1572–9 took a heavy toll, and the picture was much worse in the eastern provinces of the republic which were involved in the fighting for far longer. In Overijssel a large number of farms were laid waste and up to 20 per cent of the agricultural

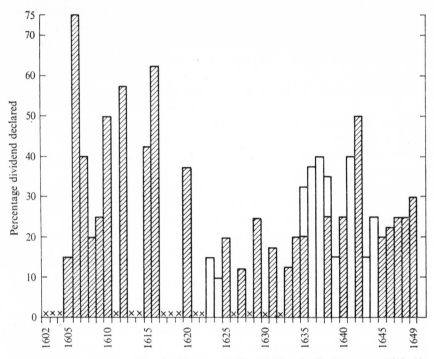

Fig. 5 Dividends paid to shareholders by the Dutch East India Company 1602–49. Open columns represent dividends paid in spices; hatched columns represent dividends paid in cash. (Source: For 1602–19, O. van Rees, *Geschiedenis der staatshuishoudkunde in Nederland tot het einde der 18e eeuw*, II (Utrecht, 1868), pp. 146–7. For 1619–49, G. C. Klerk de Reus, *Geschichtlicher Ueberblick der administrativen, rechtlichen und finanziellen Entwiklung der Niederländisch Ost-Indischen Compagnie* (The Hague–Batavia, 1894), Beilage VI).

land was abandoned. In the Veluwe, south-west of Overijssel, the population does not appear to have grown at all, while further south in the town and 'meierij' (district) of 's Hertogenbosch there was a marked decline.[31]

Yet despite the decay in the landward provinces, seen from Holland – and particularly from Amsterdam – it was hard to resist the impression that the war with Spain had made a decisive contribution towards the unparalleled prosperity of the republic in the seventeenth century. The Amsterdam magistrate, C. P. Hooft (1547–1626), was quite explicit in his claims that the 'war of Liberation' had had a beneficial effect on the economy of his country. 'It is known to all the world', he wrote, 'that whereas it is generally the nature of war to ruin the land and people, these countries on the contrary have been notably improved thereby.'[32] Naturally, Hooft had in mind the newly burgeoning trade with the East and West Indies which was based on Amsterdam. Many men besides him were captivated by the rich cargoes of

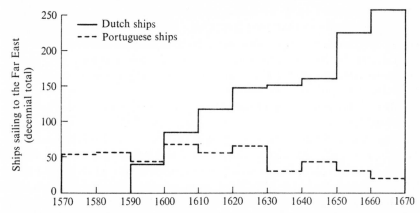

Fig. 6 Dutch and Portuguese ships sailing to the East Indies 1570–1670. It must, of course, be remembered that not all the ships sailing to the East were the same size; nevertheless the trend of the trade of both nations emerges clearly enough. (Source: For Dutch shipping, R. Bijlsma, 'De archieven van de Compagnieën op Oost-Indië, 1594–1603', *Verslagen omtrent 's Rijks Oude Archieven, xlix,* I (1926), pp. 173–225; Algemeen Rijksarchief, 's Gravenhage, *Kolonialische Archief* 4389, 'Uitloopboekje van Scheepen van 1603 tot 1700'. For Portuguese shipping, C. R. Boxer, *The Portuguese Seaborne Empire, 1415–1825* (London, 1969), 379.

spices brought from Asia and the sugar brought from Brazil. In particular the return of the 'second voyage' to the East Indies under Jacob van Neck in 1599 created a tremendous impression. 'So long as Holland has been Holland' wrote one contemporary, 'never have such richly laden ships been seen here'. The profit on the venture was some 400 per cent. Undoubtedly the economic gains from breaking the Spanish and Portuguese monopolies on extra-European trade were great, but they must not be overestimated or antedated. Although the gains were often spectacular, for many years they were also sporadic. As figure 5 shows, between 1611 and 1632 (a period of twenty-two years), the Dutch East India company declared only ten dividends. Large dividends were only paid regularly after 1634. Likewise, as figure 6 demonstrates, the largest increase in the outward-bound shipping from the Netherlands to the East Indies only occurred after the signing of a final peace with Spain in 1648. Dutch commerce with other areas outside Europe was even less successful. Trade with the West Indies (sc. America), although it started earlier, never really got off the ground at all. Although between 1599 and 1605 almost 800 ships arrived off Punta de Araya in Venezuela to collect salt, there were heavy losses in 1605 at the hands of the Spanish navy and the erection of a fort by the Spaniards in 1622 prevented further activity. After 1622 all Dutch trade to America was controlled by a special trading and para-military organisation, the West India Company.

Major fleets, heavily armed, were sent to the Caribbean from 1623 onwards and to Brazil after 1624. In 1628 the company's fleet captured the treasure fleet of New Spain in Matanzas Bay, Cuba, and some 12m florins (3,300,000 *pesos*) of silver and merchandise were brought back to Holland. The company declared a bumper dividend of 75 per cent and its stock rose from 115 points to 206, but in the event this was practically the only dividend the West India Company ever issued! At all other times the profits it made, whether from the lucrative Guinea slave trade or from the even more lucrative Brazilian sugar trade were immediately absorbed by the costs of conquering and defending its strongholds in Brazil. In 1647 the company estimated it made 400,000 florins profit from Brazil, but spent 1,100,000 florins on its defence. Operations there even required regular contributions from the States-General: 1,200,000m were provided between 1623 and 1626 and 700,000 florins annually from 1631 until 1644, when the sum had to be increased still further on account of the revolt of the native population of Brazil. By 1640 the West India Company's debt stood at 18m florins and in September of that same year the last of its large trading fleets sent to the Caribbean was destroyed by the Spaniards off Cuba. Dutch Brazil was steadily lost between 1645 and 1654 and the company's stock fell from 100 points in 1642 to 14¼ in 1650. After 1660 it stood at just three points until the unhappy company was liquidated in 1674. Those who had invested in this branch of Dutch imperialism lost their money.[33]

It is therefore hard to substantiate the numerous extravagant claims about the importance to the Republic of the trade with the East and West Indies, the only sector of the Dutch economy which clearly developed from the war with Spain. Undoubtedly some influential and voluble Amsterdammers were enriched, and undoubtedly Amsterdam became able to corner the supply of many exotic products, thus increasing its importance as a commercial centre. But this is no reason to believe the special pleading of the directors of the two chartered companies to the effect that their enterprises were 'the foremost source ... of the prosperity of an incalculable number of inhabitants of our Republic'.[34] Impartial observers all agreed that the soul of Dutch trade in the seventeenth century was in reality the seaborne commerce with the Baltic, normally referred to as the 'mother trade' of the Dutch economy because it gave birth to so many other activities. A survey of Dutch shipping in 1634 gives an unmistakable picture:[35]

The fishing fleet	2,250 boats
Trade with the Mediterranean and Baltic	1,750 boats
Trade with the East and West Indies and Guinea	300 boats
Total	4,300 boats

The relatively small part of the Republic's shipping resources devoted to extra-European trade – 7 per cent of the total – seems even smaller when one recalls that a round trip to the East Indies took two years, often with a ballast or bullion cargo on the way out, while ships bound for the Baltic could make two, three or four voyages a year. Only ten to twenty ships sailed to the Far East every year, compared with between 1,000 and 2,000 annually passing through the Sound into the Baltic and out again to Spain and southern Europe. 'The importance and magnitude of the trade [with the Baltic] is so great that it alone is the soul of business affairs, upon which all other trades and dealings depend' observed the States of Holland in 1646, and there is a wealth of evidence to support them. It occupied many hands; it supplied grain to feed a large part of the Dutch population; it supplied domestic industries with vital raw materials; and it provided a strong incentive to build more and bigger ships.[36]

However, to a considerable extent this vast and important trade depended on the re-export of Baltic goods, and especially grain and timber, to Spain and Portugal, in return for the purchase of Iberian salt which was required by both Holland and the Baltic states. Of 1,068 ships which left Amsterdam between 1591 and 1602 declaring that they were bound for Spain or Portugal, 434 also declared that they intended to sail straight from there to the Baltic. 314 of these ships were going south for salt which they would carry direct to the ports of North Germany and Poland. Spain and Portugal were crucial to the health of Dutch trade to the Baltic. It is therefore pertinent to enquire how far this 'mother trade' of the Dutch economy was helped by the war with Spain. The answer is clear: hardly at all. After 1572 the growing contacts between North Netherlands merchants and Spain ceased abruptly. Although there was some clandestine recovery after a year or so, the commerce of Holland, Zeeland and Friesland with the Iberian peninsula was frequently disrupted by Spain's periodic decisions to prohibit all trade with the 'rebels' (1585–6, 1595–6, 1599, 1601, 1603–4 . . .) or by the hostility of the Inquisition towards the Dutch, which often led to confiscations and imprisonment.[37] These difficulties naturally favoured the merchants of other countries who could offer more or less the same services as the Dutch. Thus the 'obedient provinces' gained to some extent – even though they were obliged to pay 'convoy and licence money' to the Dutch in order to use the port of Antwerp – and many Antwerp firms continued to deal with Spain, Portugal, Italy and the overseas colonies (cf. pp. 52–3 above). The English too developed a lively trade with Spain during the reign of James I and in the 1630s, as did the French (Amiens sent vast quantities of cloth to Seville between 1600 and 1635); but above all it was the Hanseatic merchants, especially the men of Hamburg, who profited.[38] From the 1580s onwards their ships made the 'Westfahrt' in ever-increasing numbers and from the 1590s they too began to trade direct with Brazil and the Canaries. About 100 ships from Hamburg alone sailed to the Iberian peninsula annually in the 1590s. It was all trade lost by the Dutch.[39]

The war hampered Dutch trade in other ways. The formation of a war fleet in Dunkirk after its recapture by Spanish forces in 1583 constituted a serious menace to Dutch shipping. There were perhaps fifty privateers based on the port during the 1590s and they took a regular toll of Dutch ships. In the 1620s and 1630s, some fifty to sixty privateers (half of them government owned) were the scourge of shipping in the North Sea and no less than 1,835 vessels, mainly Dutch, were captured or sunk between 1626 and 1634. (By way of comparison, between 1623 and 1636 the Dutch West India Company captured or destroyed only 547 Spanish or allied ships.) The cost to the Dutch in higher rates of insurance, in convoy and escort charges, and in direct loss was considerable. Further south, the Spanish squadrons which patrolled the Mediterranean also claimed a number of prizes.[40]

A brief survey of Dutch commerce during the period of the war with Spain thus supports the verdict of Dr F. Snapper, that until 1627 at least 'war brought more loss than profit to Holland's seaborne trade'.[41] The growth of the republic's overseas commerce was substantial between 1572 and 1635, it is true; but there is every reason to suppose that it would have been greater still if a permanent peace with Spain had been arranged. It was not until France declared war on Spain in 1635, diverting the formidable resources of the Hispanic empire away from the North Netherlands, that Dutch trade could prosper and develop untrammelled by the fortunes (and misfortunes) of war.

IV

It is tempting to suppose that all these losses must have produced some gains for the participants elsewhere – after all it seems fairly clear that in the seventeenth century at least conflicting economic aspirations were the main reason for the continuance of the war.[42] However, apart from the towns of Holland, which drew immense benefit from the influx of men and money from the south, and apart from the handful of *hoofdparticipanten* (major share-holders) in the East India Company, it is hard to point to any single group even in the Dutch republic who made substantial profits *which they would not have made without the war*. True, there were the numerous generals and administrators in Spanish service who were given a landed estate in the Netherlands as a reward for their services, and the sutlers, arms manufacturers and financiers on both sides who served the military machine and made a profit from it. But any enumeration of individuals can only be misleading, as a perceptive French writer observed at the time, since: 'For every two soldiers who find wealth in the wars, there are fifty who acquire only injuries or incurable illnesses. To win favour in the sight of their sovereign they squander all their money.' Even the duke of Alva, who did so much to precipitate the revolt of 1572, plunged his estates deep in debt by assuming command of the Army of Flanders.[43]

It must be admitted that most of the money and resources which the various combatants poured into the war in the Netherlands were, in economic terms, entirely unproductive. There was little or no technological spin-off; the men paid to fight were men lost to agriculture and industry; the taxes raised to pay for the armies yielded little return (at least to the belligerent states) in the shape of increased demand for goods and services. The war was, in many ways, conspicuous expenditure on a monstrous scale by the various governments of Europe.

As so often in war, it was the neutrals who made the real gains. England, Sweden and Germany in particular acquired trade, export markets and skilled refugees which they would otherwise not have had. The bankers of Genoa and Portugal who financed the war for Spain made a fortune at the expense of the Castilian taxpayers. The independent principality of Liège, an enclave in the Spanish Netherlands, burgeoned after 1572 as local armourers and industrialists met the rising demand of both sides in the war for powder, arms and artillery. The prosperity of individual towns like Frankfurt-am-Main, whose community of 600 Dutch refugees included most of the wealthiest citizens, owed much to the Netherlanders who brought their capital and expertise into exile with them. It was on the periphery of the great conflict, not in Spain or the Netherlands, that the true economic beneficiaries of the Eighty Years' War were to be found.[44]

The participants' 'gains', if we may call them that, were not really economic at all. Spain was fighting in the sixteenth century to preserve the absolute authority of the king and the religious monopoly of the Roman Catholic Church in the Netherlands. In the end she succeeded in ten out of the seventeen provinces inherited by Philip II. In the seventeenth century it seems that Spain fought more to save her overseas empire from falling into the hands of the Dutch, and here too there was partial success. Although in 1640 Portugal had been lost as well as most of her empire, in 1648 the Peace of Münster stipulated that the Dutch would not 'journey to or trade in the harbours and places' which belonged to the king of Spain (clause six). This was a major victory, albeit tempered by the fact that by 1648 the Indies no longer produced the treasure nor required the European goods which had made them such a priceless trading partner in the sixteenth century. The Dutch West India Company was giving up relatively little. The only tangible gains which Spain made from the war were therefore political and religious.

One can say almost the same for the Dutch. They too had fought for the right to govern themselves and to worship in the Calvinist manner, and in both these aims they succeeded, although it must be remembered that the benefits were only shared by a minority of the Dutch population. On the political plane, only the provinces which sent representatives to the States-General had a share in the decision-making processes of the Republic, and the citizens of North Brabant, North Flanders and Limburg were therefore

3

unfranchised. And even in the provinces which had States of their own, power rested securely in the hands of the 2,000 or so families who formed the town oligarchies (the 'regent class'). The major gain of the oligarchs from the 'war of liberation' was that control by the central government was removed; after the revolt, each provincial and municipal administration became its own master. The religious 'gains' of the Dutch were also far from being universally shared: they were enjoyed only by the 2,000 or so ministers and the congregations of the 'Reformed religion' which even in 1650 still unquestionably constituted a minority of the total population, outnumbered by the combined forces of Roman Catholics and Anabaptists.

No historian is really entitled or qualified to measure in economic terms whether such intangible achievements in the end vindicated the human and material sacrifices. There is no doubt that the Spanish and Dutch leaders fully realised the economic costs of their policies and considered them justified. But there is equally little doubt about the scale of the sacrifice. While one must not – to adapt an aphorism of Professor Postan – ascribe to the war what was due to the eighty years, it seems clear that the prolonged conflict generated by the Revolt of the Netherlands served to retard the growth of the northern republic (and particularly of its landward provinces), to inflict permanent damage on the economy of large areas of the Spanish empire, and to ruin for two centuries the prosperity of 'Belgium'. These were the harsh material consequences of the *ánimo severo* of Philip II. They must not be forgotten in assessing the significance of the Dutch Revolt. It was not perhaps entirely in the spirit of cant and humbug that those who drafted the Peace of Münster in 1647–8 began their preamble:

Let all persons know that, after a long succession of bloody wars which for many years have oppressed the peoples, subjects, kingdoms and lands which are under the obedience of the Lords King of Spain and States-General of the United Netherlands, the aforesaid Lords, the King and the States, moved by Christian piety, desire to end the general misery and prevent the dreadful consequences, calamity, harm and danger which the further continuation of the aforesaid wars in the Low Countries would bring in their train. . . . They invite and call upon other princes and potentates to allow themselves to be moved by the same pity and to avert the mishaps, destruction and disorders which the heavy plague of war has made men suffer for so long and so heavily.[45]

APPENDIX

The sources for Figure 1 are as follows:

Antwerp: R. Boumans, 'La dépeuplement d'Anvers, 1575–1600', *Revue du Nord*, XXIX (1947), pp. 181–94.
Ath and Avesnes: M. A. Arnould, 'Ath et Avesnes en 1594. Etat démographique de deux villes hennuyères à la fin du XVIᵉ siècle', *Annales du cercle royale d'archéologie d'Ath*, XXVII (1941), pp. 89–101.

Brugse Vrije (Franc de Bruges): K. Maddens, 'Het uitzicht van het Brugse Vrije op het einde van de XVIE eeuw', *Annales de la société d'emulation de Bruges*, XCVII (1960), pp. 31–73.
Evergem: A. de Vos, 'Dertig jaar bevolkingsevolutie te Evergem (1571–1601)', *Handelingen der Maatschappij voor Geschiedenis en Oudheidkunde te Gent*, XIV (1960), pp. 117–29.
Herentals: H. van der Wee, *The Growth of the Antwerp Market and the European Economy* (3 vols, the Hague, 1963), II, p. 262.
Kasselrij Ieper (châtellenie d'Ypres): K. Maddens, 'De krisis op het einde van de XVIE eeuw in de kasselrij Ieper', *Revue Belge de Philologie et d'Histoire*, XXXIX (1961), pp. 365–90.
Kasselrij Oudenaarde (châtellenie d'Audenarde): J. de Brouwere, 'Les dénombrements de la châtellenie d'Audenarde, 1469–1801', *Bulletin de la Commission royale d'Histoire*, CIII (1938), pp. 513–46.
Land van Aalst (Pays d'Alost): J. de Brouwere, *Demografisches evolutie van het Land van Aalst, 1570–1800* (Brussels, 1968), p. 111.
Leuven (Louvain): H. van der Wee, *The Growth of the Antwerp Market*, II, p. 262.
Mechelen (Malines): J. Verbeemen, 'De demografisches evolutie van Mechelen, 1370–1800', *Bulletin de la cercle archéologique de Malines*, LVII (1953), pp. 63–97.
Mons: J. Verbeemen, 'L'évolution démographique d'une ville wallonne: Mons (1283–1766)', *L'intermédiaire des généalogistes*, LV (1955), pp. 23–5.
Ninove: H. Vangassen, 'De honger van Ninove', *Het Land van Aalst*, V (1953), pp. 213–32.
Schorisse: C. de Rammelaere, 'De bevolkingscijfer in het Land van Schorisse (1569–1796)', *Handelingen der Maatschappij voor Geschiedenis en Oudheidkunde te Gent*, XIII (1959), pp. 53–98.
Turnhout: H. van der Wee, *The Growth of the Antwerp Market*, II, p. 262.

NOTES

1 I am very grateful to Mrs A. M. Parker, Dr R. M. Price, Dr H. Soly, Professor Charles Wilson and Dr J. M. Winter for supplying me with helpful suggestions and comments about this paper.
2 N. Froumenteau, *Le secret des finances de France* (Paris, 1581); T. K. Rabb, 'The effects of the Thirty Years' War on the German economy', *Journal of Modern History*, XXXIV (1962), pp. 40–51.
3 For Holland: F. Snapper, *Oorlogsinvloeden op de overzeese handel van Holland, 1551–1719* (Amsterdam, 1959). For 'Belgium': C. Verlinden, 'En Flandre sous Philippe II: durée de la crise économique', *Annales E.S.C.*, VII (1952), pp. 21–30, and J. A. van Houtte, 'Onze 17e eeuw 'Ongelukseeuw''?', *Mededelingen van de Koninklijke Vlaamse Akademie*, XV (1953), no. 8.
4 Francisco Gómez de Quevedo y Villegas, *La Hora de Todos*, ch. 36 (written in 1635–6). Cf. *Biblioteca de Autores Españoles*, XXIII, p. 409.
5 Although even here there have been some doubting voices: cf. S. H. Steinberg, *The Thirty Years War and the Conflict for European Hegemony* (London, 1967), p. 107 – 'None of the campaigns fought on its ['Belgium's'] soil between the arrival of Alva and the departure of Marlborough had any appreciable effect on the steady growth of its towns.'
6 Abundant details are to be found in H. van der Wee, *The Growth of the Antwerp Market and the European Economy*, II, pp. 245–62 and 269–80.

7 H. E. de Sagher, *et al.*, *Receuil de documents relatifs à l'histoire de l'industrie drapière en Flandres*, 2e partie, II (Brussels, 1961), pp. 244–5 (collapse of Dixmuide's production), pp. 271–2 (Eecke); III (Brussels, 1966), *sub art.* Menin, Neuve Eglise et Poperinghe. It was the same story with the linen industry: E. Sabbe, *De Belgische vlasnijverheid* (Bruges, 1943), pp. 300–17.

8 Archivo General de Simancas, *Estado* 589 fo. 120, Alexander Farnese, duke of Parma, to Philip II, 31 December 1585 ('no haviendo sembrado ni en Brabante ni en Flandes'), and Archives Générales du Royaume, Brussels, *Audience*, 189 ff. 85–91, Parma to Philip II, 12 January 1587.

9 J. Verbeemen, 'De werking van economische factoren op de stedelijke demografie der XVIIe en der XVIIIe eeuw in de Zuidelijke Nederlanden', *Revue Belge de Philologie et d'Histoire*, XXXIV (1956), pp. 680–700 and 1021–55; on p. 695.

10 On the remarkable recovery of Antwerp, cf. the rich and perceptive article of W. Brulez, 'Anvers de 1585 à 1650', *Vierteljahrschrift für Sozial- und Wirtschaftsgeschichte*, LIV (1967), pp. 75–99. Cf. also F. J. Smolar, 'Resiliency of enterprise: economic crises and recovery in the Spanish Netherlands in the early seventeenth century', in *From the Renaissance to the Counter-Reformation*, ed. C. H. Carter (London, 1965), pp. 247–68.

11 E. Stols, *De Spaanse Brabanders, of de Handelsbetrekkingen der Zuiderlijke Nederlanden met de Iberische wereld, 1598–1648* (Brussels, 1971), bijlage I; W. Brulez, *De firma Della Faille en de internationale handel van Vlaamse firma's in de 16e eeuw* (Brussels, 1959), pt II, cf. p. 574; H. Pohl, 'Die Zuckereinfuhr nach Antwerpen, durch Portugiesische Kaufleute während des 80-jährige Krieges', *Jahrbuch für Geschichte von Staat, Wirtschaft und Gesellschaft Lateinamerikas*, IV (1967), pp. 347–73.

12 J. Craeybeckx, 'Les industries d'exportation dans les villes flamandes au XVIIe siècle, particulièrement à Gand et à Bruges', *Studi in onore di Amintore Fanfani*, IV (Milan, 1962), pp. 411–67; J. Bastin, 'De Gentse lijnwaadmarkt en linnenhandel in de 17e eeuw', *Handelingen der Maatschappij voor Geschiedenis en Oudheidkunde te Gent*, XXI (1967), pp. 131–62; E. Coornaert, *Un centre industriel d'autrefois. La draperie-sayetterie d'Hondschoote, XIVe–XVIIIe siècles* (Paris, 1930).

13 D. van Rijssel, *De Gentse Huishuren tussen 1500 en 1795* (Brussels, 1967), pp. 56–7 and 73–95.

14 R. Weston, *A discours of husbandrie used in Brabant and Flanders, showing wonderful improvement of Land there* (London, 1650), p. 2.

15 Cf. G. Parker, *The Army of Flanders and the Spanish Road (1567–1659)* (Cambridge, 1972), pp. 143–5 for the financial cost of the Spanish Army to the Netherlands; for population loss in the south, cf. J. de Smet, 'Les dénombrements de la population dans la châtellenie d'Ypres (1610 et 1615 à 1620)', *Bulletin de la commission royale d'histoire*, XCVI (1932), pp. 255–332, and J. Verbeemen, 'L'évolution démographique d'une ville wallonne: Mons (1283–1766)', *L'intermédiaire des généalogistes*, LV (1955), pp. 23–5.

16 Archivo General de Simancas, *Estado* 2037 fo. 11, *consulta* of the Council of State, 14 April 1623, *voto* of Don Fernando Girón.

17 Archivo General de Simancas, *Estado* 634 fo. 19, Instruction of Philip III for Don Rodrigo Niño y Lasso, envoy to the Netherlands, spring 1604.

18 I. A. A. Thompson, 'War and administrative devolution: the military government of Spain in the reign of Philip II' (Cambridge University Ph.D. thesis, 1965), pp. 184–5 estimated annual recruiting at 8,000 men per year in wartime;

for some detailed figures cf. G. Parker, *The Army of Flanders*, pp. 42–3 and 278–9. Of course the burden of recruiting grew heavier as the population of Castile declined (from c. 1600 onwards).

19 Quoted by M. Herrero García, *Ideas de los Españoles del siglo XVII* (2nd edn, Madrid, 1966), p. 420.

20 Archivo General de Simancas, *Estado* 575 fo. 134, Philip II to Don John of Austria, 16 March 1578 (minute).

21 Clearly the financial provisions sent to the Army of Flanders were an important channel by which the treasure of the Spanish Indies was transferred to northern Europe. Treasure figures from J. H. Elliott, *Imperial Spain (1469–1716)* (London, 1963), p. 175 (the original figures of E. J. Hamilton converted into ducats); expenditure in the Netherlands from G. Parker, *The Army of Flanders*, pp. 293–6; expenditure in the Mediterranean from Archivo General de Simancas, *Contaduría Mayor de Cuentas 2a época* 814 (account of Paymaster-General Juan Morales de Torre).

22 J. Vicens Vives, 'The decline of Spain in the 17th century', in *The Economic Decline of Empires*, ed. C. M. Cipolla (London, 1970), p. 154; N. Salomon, *La campagne de Nouvelle Castille à la fin du XVIe siècle d'après les 'Relaciones topográficas'* (Paris, 1964), pp. 234–5 and 250–1.

23 J. Vicens Vives, 'The decline of Spain in the 17th century', pp. 149–50; F. Braudel, *La Méditerranée et le monde méditerranéen à l'époque de Philippe II* (2nd edn, Paris, 1966), I, p. 449 note 6; A. Castillo, 'Population et richesse en Castille, 1550–1600', *Annales E.S.C.*, XX (1965), pp. 710–33. Although some Castilian wool continued to be exported to Italy and to England after 1572, the quantities were not sufficient to offset the lost market of the Low Countries.

24 J. Lynch, *Spain under the Habsburgs*, II (Oxford, 1969), p. 182; P. Bakewell, *Silver Mining and Society in Colonial Mexico, Zacatecas 1546–1700* (Cambridge, 1971), p. 232.

25 C. R. Boxer, *The Portuguese Seaborne Empire, 1415–1825* (London, 1969), ch. 5; F. Mauro, *Le Portugal et l'Atlantique au XVIIe siècle, 1570–1670. Etude économique* (Paris, 1960), pp. 440–55.

26 Compare the maps of van Deventer printed by R. Fruin, *Nederlandsche steden in den 16e eeuw. Plattegronden van Jacob van Deventer* (Hague, 1916–23 – facsimiles of 111 maps) with J. Blaeu, *Tooneel der steden van de Vereenighde Nederlanden met hare beschrijvingen* [Amsterdam, 1649]. Of course, exactly the same process had taken place in the South Netherlands, as a comparison of the same two sources shows: cf. C. Ruelens, *Atlas des villes de la Belgique au XVIe siècle* (2 vols, Brussels, 1884) and J. Blaeu, *Toonneel der steden van 's Konings Nederlanden met hare beschrijvingen* [Amsterdam, 1649].

27 Figures taken from the *Staten van Oorlog* of the Dutch Republic, summarised conveniently in Algemeen Rijksarchief, the Hague, *Raad van State*, 1499 and 1500.

28 G. Parker, *The Emergence of Modern Finance in Europe, 1500–1730* (London, 1974), pp. 50–1.

29 J. G. van Dillen, 'Amsterdam in Bredero's tijd', *De Gids*, XCIX (1935), part II, p. 311; van Dillen, *Bronnen tot de Geschiedenis van het Bedrijfsleven en het Gildewezen van Amsterdam* I, (the Hague, 1929), pp. xvii and xxxvi; van Dillen, *Het oudste aandeelhoudersregister van de Kamer Amsterdam der Oost-Indische Compagnie* (Hague, 1958), pp. 60–1; W. J. van Hoboken, 'The Dutch West India Company; the political background of its rise and decline', in J. S. Bromley and E. H. Kossmann, *Britain and the Netherlands*, I (1960), pp. 41–61.

30 van Dillen, *Bronnen*, I, pp. xxxii-xxxvi; L. van Nierop, 'De bruidegoms van Amsterdam van 1578 tot 1601', *Tijdschrift voor Geschiedenis*, XLVIII (1933), pp. 337–59, XLIX (1934), pp. 136–60 and pp. 329–44. Cf. p. 154.

31 Faber *et al.*, 'Population changes and economic developments in the Netherlands: a historical survey', *Afdeling Agrarische Geschiedenis Bijdragen*, XII (1965), pp. 47–113, esp. 53, 75–6, 93–4, and 105.

32 Quoted by P. Geyl, *The Revolt of the Netherlands, 1559–1609* (2nd edn, London, 1958), p. 233. Hooft's writing often harped upon the 'gains' which the war had brought to Holland; cf. *Memoriën en Adviezen van Cornelis Pieterszoon Hooft*, I (Utrecht, 1871), p. 186 (from 1617) and pp. 383–4 (1619), and II (Utrecht, 1925), p. 73 (from 1598), pp. 223 (from 1611) and 340 and 345 (from 1616–17). For corroboration from an English source of 1664 (*The Dutch Drawn to the Life*), cf. the quotation in C. Wilson, *Queen Elizabeth and the revolt of the Netherlands* (London, 1970), p. 19.

33 W. J. van Hoboken, 'The Dutch West India Company'; C. C. Goslinga, *The Dutch in the Caribbean and on the Wild Coast 1580–1680* (Assen, 1971), pp. 323, 328, 509; S. P. L'Honoré Naber & I. A. Wright, *Piet Heyn en de Zilvervloot* (Utrecht, 1928), pp. *9–*11; I. A. Wright, *Nederlandsche Zeevaarders op de Eilanden in de Caraibische Zee en aan de kust van Columbia en Venezuela gedurende de jaren 1621–1649*, I (Utrecht, 1934), pp. *36–*46.

34 Quoted by I. J. Brugmans, 'De Oost-Indische Compagnie en de welvaart in de Republiek', *Tijdschrift voor Geschiedenis*, LXI (1948), pp. 225–31. Although this actual quotation comes from 1785 it epitomises a long tradition of similar argument which originated – as far as I can see – in the 1607–9 truce talks. Although he does not wholly accept the Brugmans thesis, Professor C. R. Boxer furnishes a number of quotations and references which suggest that the importance of Dutch colonial trade in the seventeenth and eighteenth century has been overrated: cf. Boxer, *The Dutch Seaborne Empire* (London, 1965), pp. 86 and 278–81.

35 J. E. Elias, *Het voorspel van den eersten Engelschen oorlog*, I (Hague, 1920), pp. 61–2. Elias dismisses as exaggerated a calculation of 1636 used subsequently by Professor Brugmans in the article cited above.

36 Evidence of the predominance of Baltic trade in the Dutch economy is abundant. Cf., for a sample, A. E. Christensen, *Dutch Trade to the Baltic about 1600* (Copenhagen, 1941); J. G. van Dillen, 'Amsterdam's rôle in seventeenth-century Dutch politics and its economic background', in J. S. Bromley & E. H. Kossmann, *Britain and the Netherlands*, II (Groningen, 1964), pp. 133–47; and J. A. Faber, 'The decline of the Baltic grain trade in the second half of the seventeenth century', *Acta Historiae Neerlandicae*, I (Leiden, 1966), pp. 108–31.

37 For full details cf. J. H. Kernkamp, *Der handel op den vijand, 1572–1609* (2 vols, Utrecht, 1931).

38 This was precisely what Philip II had intended. Cf. his letter explaining the purpose of the embargo, Archivo General de Simancas, *Estado* 2218 fo. 32, Philip II to Parma, 29 December 1585.

39 For German trade: H. Kellenbenz, *Unternehmerkräfte im Hamburger Portugal- und Spanienhandel, 1590–1625* (Hamburg, 1954), e.g. pp. 106 and 335; F. Mauro, *Portugal et l'Atlantique*, 494. For French trade: P. Deyon, *Amiens – capitale provinciale. Etude sur la société urbaine au 17e siècle* (Paris, 1967), pp. 156–63. For English trade: F. J. Fisher, 'England's export trade in the early seventeenth century', *Economic History Review*, III (1950), pp. 151–61; H. Taylor, 'Price revolution or price revision? The English and Spanish trade after 1604', *Renaissance*

and modern studies, XII (1968), pp. 5–32, and 'Trade, neutrality and the 'English Road', 1630–1648', *Economic History Review*, XXV (1972), pp. 236–60.

40 H. Malo, *Les corsaires: les corsaires dunquerquois et Jean Bart*, I (Paris, 1913), pp. 333–5; F. Mauro, *Le Portugal et l'Atlantique*, p. 449.

41 F. Snapper, *Oorlogsinvloeden op de overzeese handel van Holland, 1551–1719* (Amsterdam, 1959), p. 76. Cf. also the views even of Amsterdam merchants that the Truce had been a golden age of profits: J. G. van Dillen, 'De West-Indische Compagnie, het Calvinisme en de politiek', *Tijdschrift voor Geschiedenis*, LXXIV (1961), pp. 145–71.

42 A close analysis of why Spain and the Dutch made a truce confined to Europe in 1609 instead of a general peace, of why the truce was not renewed in 1621 and of why no cease-fire was arranged at the peace conferences of 1627–9 and 1632–3 reveals that in each case the stumbling block was trade with the East and West Indies. The Dutch would not abandon their trading posts there and the Spaniards would not relinquish their claim to monopoly status. I shall discuss this point in detail in part III of my forthcoming book, *The Dutch Revolt*.

43 G. Parker, *The Army of Flanders*, pp. 119 and 120 n, quoting E. Crucé, *Le nouveau Cynée*, (Paris, 1623), p. 13.

44 For the prosperity of Liège, cf. J. Lejeune, *La formation du capitalisme moderne dans la principauté de Liège au XVIe siècle* (Paris–Liège, 1939), and J. Yerneaux, *La métallurgie liégeoise et son expansion au XVIIe siècle* (Liège, 1939). For the 'gains' of Frankfurt, R. van Roosbroeck, *Emigranten. Nederlandse vluchtelingen in Duitsland, 1550–1600* (Leuven, 1968,) pp. 308–17. Of course many other German towns also gained from the arrival of the Dutch refugees, cf. *ibid.* pp. 318–46.

45 H. H. Rowen, *The Low Countries in early modern times* (New York, 1972), pp. 179. For Professor Postan's views on war and economic 'gains' cf. his brilliant article 'The costs of the Hundred Years' War', *Past & Present*, 27 (1964), pp. 34–53.

4 Swords and ploughshares: the armed forces, medicine and public health in the late eighteenth century

Peter Mathias

Many of the interrelationships between the armed forces and economic and social change in Britain generally during the eighteenth century have yet to be explored in depth. The impact of military spending and war upon industrial expansion, technical innovations, shipbuilding, the balance of payments, for example, deserve more systematic investigation than they have yet received. Military spending, the claims it made upon resources and the economic effects of the activities promoted by such spending, was inescapably important, if only because of the immense scale upon which such transfers were being conducted during the eighteenth century. During war-time military expenditure rose to between two-thirds and three-quarters (occasionally exceeding three-quarters) of net public expenditure; while peacetime levels of spending on the armed forces absorbed at least half of total central government outlays on trend after the 1730s. The level of military spending was running at a rate of £5–6m per year of war in the early eighteenth century and to no less than £40m per year of war by its end. Discounting for the effects of monetary inflation this represents at least a five-fold increase in the level of real expenditure. When judged against the expansion of the economy, which enabled such a massive increase to be sustained, military spending represented roughly 5 per cent of national income at the close of the Marlborough wars and probably above 15 per cent of national income in the closing years of the French Revolutionary wars in 1801.[1] These figures, which show the broad dimensions of the financial significance which the army and navy had for the economy in the eighteenth century, set the framework within which more specialised enquiries have to be pursued. It is the scale, above all, which creates the potential importance, and this has been largely unacknowledged by economic historians.

The present paper explores the links between one area of military commitment and developing knowledge, skills and innovations which were not without effect in the country more widely, though with certain time-lags: the relations between the armed forces, medicine and public health in the later eighteenth century. It deserves to be documented more systematically than space allows in the present volume, if only because historians of naval and army medicine have not considered these wider effects of the development they have recorded, while economic and social historians, in this case no less than in many others, have not given the army and navy in the eighteenth century the attention which their importance deserves.

The numbers of professional medical men in the armed services, when mobilised for war after 1793, suggest the scale of the commitment within which these influences have to be considered. By 1794–5 there were 500 naval surgeons and hospitals at all five of the main naval ports, and over 700 by 1800. Forty-five ships in the channel fleet carried surgeons (thirty-two ships of the line, eight frigates and five lesser vessels) with a hospital ship. Over sixty physicians served the army and the position of surgeons was, if anything, on a greater scale than for the navy with every regiment of over 500 men being attended by a surgeon and two assistants (with the 'completest equipment of medicines and hospital bedding'). The artillery had a separate medical establishment. In the navy most medical regulations had been within the authority of individual physicians to the fleet, acting under the authority of the admirals of different squadrons who had appointed them, as Rodney had appointed Gilbert Blane, his personal physician, to be physician to the West Indies squadron in 1780. However, in 1797 the Admiralty established a medical board under the first Sea Lord with Blane and Dr Robert Blair as Physicians to the Fleet. General Admiralty orders then gave more centralised, generalised authority for imposing medical standards throughout the navy, as general orders had required the universal distribution of specific anti-scorbutics for the first time in 1795 (see below).

This large establishment and its progressive institutionalisation within the armed services conditioned the influence of the professional medical personnel within it. The sense of professional identification and status became much enhanced by the growing presence of doctors within the armed services: their presence in a formally organised hierarchical society with precise allocations of seniority, authority, status and reward meant that their interests, as a professional group, were determined in all these respects. Not accidentally much discussion took place during the Napoleonic wars, as before, on these matters, with demand for professional equality in status and pay for doctors in the navy compared with the army. Thomas Trotter, the most obdurate spokesman for naval surgeons, on much lower *per diem* payments and with much lower degrees of entitlement to half pay, argued always in terms of the professional importance of the surgeons to naval strength. 'A medical establishment,' he wrote, 'can alone prescribe those means of prevention from sickness which has often, and may again, unnerve the naval arm.' Naval doctors served 'the vital part of the machine that is our glory.'[2] His own publications represent, for a serving officer subject to the orders of the commander in chief and the Admiralty, astonishingly outspoken claims for the professional authority of medically qualified practitioners in all that had to do with the health of seamen – and earned him savage rebuke from St Vincent, for example, who accused Trotter of suborning his authority and threatening his strategic plans by ordering captains not to put to sea before taking on their full complement of anti-scorbutics.[3] Trotter also demanded that the physicians of all naval hospitals should be fully qualified, university MDs in accordance with expected professional standards.

The connections between military medicine and the wider national context existed at various levels. The transference of doctors between the army and navy (as the East India Company ships) and civilian practice is the most obvious, and must have been amongst the most significant, given the numbers involved, in time of peace. With skills embodied, above all, in the persons of practitioners this link brought interrelationships in a two-way traffic. It was particularly important in a field which this paper does not consider – surgery. In the eyes of naval doctors, army physicians had a great advantage. The army doctor could live in towns with 'polished society' taking advantage of the 'gay manner of life peculiar to the army' which kept him in touch with advances in civilian medicine and his prospective clientele, while the naval doctor was isolated, away from books and civilian preferment. 'Many of the Physicians in London and other great towns of England', commented Trotter, 'began the practice of Medicine in the army . . . but there are few of the navy list that have been so fortunate in their career.'[4]

The effectiveness of the services as a training ground for preventive medicine owed much to the greater premium given to health in this specialised environment as well as to the greater medical hazards faced by troops and seamen. In civilian life physical effectiveness was not of such immediate concern to government or employers, save in the rare communal emergencies imposed by plague or equivalent catastrophe, which could invoke dramatic public response. As long as epidemic disease was accepted as inevitable, its visitations unpredictable, its causes unknown (or interpreted as divine retribution upon the wicked), and treatment ineffectual there was little likelihood of public resources being mobilised against it. Public costs stood in the way of private benefits as long as no immediate public gain could be captured. The political imperatives of a 'minimum' state in the eighteenth century also stood against public action. City councils and merchant interests in England, for example, stood out against effective quarantine laws in municipal action against plague because the siege economy this entailed imposed high costs, with authoritarian controls, and interrupted trade. Continental countries, where such local libertarian principles did not obtain, could implement *cordons sanitaires* more effectively.[5]

These constraints lost much of their influence when countered by the urgency of improving the effectiveness of the armed forces in the emergencies of war, where sanctions were much greater. One of the central dynamics of the nation – its ability to win wars in a bellicose world – was put at risk by such a failure. The increase in the scale of warfare, with larger communities of men living at close quarters in barracks, encampments, naval ports and fleets increased the hazards of disease. Colonial expansion (particularly in the West Indies and India), which kept fleets and troops in hot climates, added a further dimension to medical risks. And, from the mid-seventeenth century, naval strategy had become much dependent upon how long a fleet could stay at sea. This, in turn, depended very much upon the number of seamen in good health. As levels of incapacity in troops and seamen from sickness became major constraints upon military effectiveness, in that measure were incentives for medical improvements enhanced. It is noticeable, for example, that little attention was paid to discovering counter measures against scurvy in the merchant marine (where it certainly existed in the more distant trades) or in the civilian population, where the disease was said to be rife in the seventeenth century.[6] In those contexts, the structure of incentives for devoting resources to its cure was absent. In contrast two of the most celebrated, or notorious, military and naval expeditions of the period tell their own story: 1,051 out of 1,955 seamen died during Anson's navigation of the globe in 1740–1, mainly from scurvy; while the 'Walcheren fever' (malaria, dysentery, typhoid and typhus) incapacitated over half the troops on this fatal venture and killed forty times more men than the enemy. The context in which these disasters befell was such that very energetic enquiries were held to investigate the matter, followed by urgent demands for action and the mobilisation of resources and effort to effect it.[7]

If incentives and sanctions within the armed forces were more effective in promoting investigations into infectious and deficiency diseases than in civilian life, the institutional conditions of the army and navy greatly helped the physicians in charge of them. Financial resources which could be mobilised for investigation and experiment were not limited by the prospects of short-term profitability in a commercial context. The whole concept of 'cost-effectiveness' in a military context is not evaluated in commercial terms. Because of the incentives to discover a cure for the scurvy the Admiralty put much effort into commissioning research. A long sequence of experiments was conducted into producing a beer concentrate which could provide an easily stored antidote for ships' crews long on foreign station. Cook's circumnavigation of the globe was, in effect, a multi-purpose scientific expedition, with high priority given to an experimental search for antidotes against scurvy. Malt, 'sourkrout', salted cabbage, 'saloup' (a conserve of oranges and lemons), 'portable broth', mustard, 'marmalade of carrots', and spruce beer were tried out, with systematic testing in the fleets during the war of American independence.[8]

Circumstances allowed much greater scope for comparative testing and experimenting under controlled conditions than in civilian medicine. The army and navy (particularly ships' companies when afloat) were very tightly controlled authoritarian communities. The same was true of military hospitals ashore, to a greater extent than civilian hospitals. Other authoritarian communities such as orphanages, schools, prisons and poor houses were not so concerned with medical innovations. The influential naval doctors took full advantage of these opportunities. James Lind, whom Trotter called the 'father of nautical medicine', demonstrated conclusively that scurvy was a specific deficiency disease responding most effectively to oranges and lemons by undertaking a controlled clinical trial of comparative diets, conducted by rational observation and experiment. 'Several medicines [were] tried at sea in this disease', he reported, 'on purpose to discover what might promise the most certain protection ... The following are the experiments. On the 20th May 1747 I took twelve patients in the scurvy on board the *Salisbury* at sea. Their cases were as similar as I could have them.' He then administered different diets and medicaments to these seamen, in pairs: a quart of cider, elixir of vitriol, vinegar, sea water, oranges and lemons and other mixtures. His conclusion: 'the consequence was that the most sudden and visible good effects were perceived from the use of the oranges and lemons.'

He worked within assumptions that were deliberately and articulatedly committed to empirical, comparative, experimental, controlled, observations. 'The true causes of the disease' were to be determined 'from observations made upon it.'[9] Thomas Trotter, as its Physician, deliberately used the Channel Fleet as his laboratory after 1793. Ships' surgeons were required to report observations regularly on diet, clothing, the incidence of infection and incapacity. 'The operations of a large Fleet in Channel service offer a field for observation of the first importance to the medical enquirer', he wrote, and he backed up his demands to the Admiralty for regular distributions of fresh meat, fresh 'sallad', oranges and lemons and vegetables against scurvy with the systematic reporting of observations from ships' surgeons and captains – 'this immense field for observation which the Channel Fleet has afforded.' Scurvy was now (at long last) conquered. The stock of facts about it were great beyond all precedent; prevention and cure had been brought to such a certainty by recent experiments 'as to suspend the utility of future investigations'. General Admiralty orders to all ships for issuing oranges and lemons in 1795 (issued on the authority of Sir Gilbert Blane) meant that no general outbreak occurred again.[10]

Typhus was the next problem and Trotter held great hopes of preventive measures being worked out 'from the advantage of having attended an immense number of cases in very diversified situations'.[11] He also proposed a systematic vaccination campaign for all seamen as ships successively arrived in port, once convinced of the efficacy of Jenner's new method.[12]

Efforts to utilise the opportunities afforded for experiment in authoritarian communities depended, not only upon the incentives to achieve results, but also upon this prior and associated belief in the efficacy of the scientific method. Lind was praised for ignoring as irrelevant and unscientific the intellectual authority of ancient authors. Sir Gilbert Blane and Sir John Pringle, the most prestigious of military medical authorities, both argued forcibly for the experimental method.[13] Sir Gilbert Blane praised Bacon as 'the great author and leader in the employment of inductive reasoning': he held that medicine advanced by ascertaining the agencies of nature 'by observation and experiment'. 'By the former,' he wrote, 'we may be said to listen to nature, by the latter to interrogate her.'[14]

Paradoxically the advocacy of preventive measures in personal and public hygiene did not spring from any exact awareness of the intrinsic nature of the main infectious diseases involved or their carriers. No bacilli or viruses were identified during the eighteenth century, and even in the case of scurvy and smallpox, where specific medical remedies had been evolved, this was without benefit of scientific knowledge. The essence of the matter was scientific method, rather than formal scientific knowledge, a scientific procedure of systematic observation and experiment. Such empiricism, without formal scientific knowledge, greatly widened the area of awareness in associating infectious diseases with their habitat, of what associations increased the likely incidence and what measures reduced it. It was much more effective in preventive action than in proposing cures, once a disease had been caught, because effective cures depended rather more specifically upon (or the probability of discovering a cure was increased by) formal knowledge about the intrinsic nature of the disease. The chapters in Pringle, Blane and Trotter analysing the medical causes of infectious fevers and their formal transfer mechanisms are still almost medieval, as are the remedies proposed for those having caught the diseases.

Fevers are not separately identified in a scientific way. Typhus, typhoid and malaria, for example, are not distinguished by their different modes of infection: the vocabulary remains that of distempers, fluxes, remitting, continued and intermittent fevers, although dysentery has its modern connotation. 'Putrid exhalations' and variants of the 'miasmic' theory of infection dominated views of infective mechanisms, with a heavy medieval overlay. For example, Pringle's analysis of the incidence of hospital and gaol fevers made shrewd remarks about the predispositions of infection – the 'quantity of the contagious matter, the closeness of the air and crowds of people' – but he identified the mechanism of infection as 'corruption of the air . . . deprived of its elastic parts . . . vitiated with the perspirable matter, which, as it is the most volatile part of the humours, is also the most putrescent'. Similarly, the symptoms of the diseases are accurately described, being immediately responsive to observation, but the medical therapy directed at the infected patients was essentially medieval: vomiting agents, bleeding, purging and blistering.[15] References to Galen, Hippocrates, other less famous classical commentators and medieval writings are made up into a witch's brew of explanation.

Blane was very clear about the medical ignorance of curing, as distinct from preventing, fevers and the other main infectious diseases. It was a moot point, he wrote, 'whether recoveries have been effected by *virtue* of medicine or in *spite* of it . . . we must frequently run the risk of congratulating ourselves on a great *cure* where there may have only been a happy escape'.[16] This was, in effect, the continuance of the medieval and immediately post-medieval pattern of the response to plague. Preventive measures, based upon observation were rational and effective as far as they went: the isolation of victims, fumigation and cleansing of infected premises, destruction of the clothing, etc. of those infected, the attempt to isolate the plague-ridden communities by a *cordon sanitaire*. But this was combined with ignorance of the medical nature of plague, with its carriers, and virtually irrelevant medications for its victims.[17] Medical ignorance, of course, blunted the edge of preventive measures, as well as preventing cures; but the observed association between diseases and their environment did lead to much greater rationality in prevention if not in cures, despite the ignorance of carriers and vector mechanisms.[18]

The experimental method itself, advocated so vigorously by those eighteenth-century doctors concerned with preventing the spread of infectious diseases, embodied a motivational structure, a mentality, itself encouraging activism in the search for new knowledge and new measures. The assumption was that the secrets of nature would yield to the efforts of man through observation and experiment and that control over nature could be enhanced by such deliberate efforts. This was true despite the scientific ignorance about the main diseases which prevailed well into the nineteenth century until the development of the new science of bacteriology – with the carriers of typhus and typhoid separately identified only in 1861, the cholera bacillus discovered in 1883 and that of plague in 1894.[19]

In this sense generalisations concerning the relations between scientific knowledge and innovations in medicine fit into a wider tradition. Even though it may be argued that formal scientific knowledge did not provide a main stimulus to innovation in Western Europe until well into the nineteenth century, scientific attitudes and the experimental tradition, reflecting a changing intellectual consciousness, had an influence of their own.[20] When the incidence of disease was mysterious, or taken as the hand of divine providence striking the dissolute, public effort would be less engaged in diagnosing a more material explanation or devising appropriate preventive measures (particularly where the dissolute in question happened to be of the lower income groups). In the army and navy the premium upon improvements, as well as the intensity of the problem, was greater, particularly in time of war, but a call for action was created in much more insistent terms by evidence explaining scurvy as a specific deficiency disease than by older traditions of explanation embodied in Cockburn's *Sea Diseases* (1696, 3rd edn 1736) which provided the main rationale up to that point, where scurvy was put down to congenital laziness, bad air and indigestible food. They were doubtless more a response to medical ignorance than its cause, as the reactions to plague had been five centuries earlier (and a rational psychological response to such ignorance), but such a response in turn reinforced the structural logic of the intellectual world of which that scientific ignorance was a part. When the historian investigates disease, the investigation is not into an autonomous medical problem. Disease is a medical phenomenon given significance (even medical significance) by its environment and by the contemporary consciousness of the disease and its environment, because human reactions are conditioned by such consciousness.[21]

Hospital practice and preventive medicine were two important areas where military example led innovations and strongly influenced national practice (although interactions also moved in the other direction). There was no question about the work of naval and military doctors feeding a common pool of professional knowledge and skills. Sir Gilbert Blane became Physician of St Thomas's Hospital, after the peace of 1783, one of the most prestigious and influential medical posts in the country, where he energetically implemented the practices and standards he proposed for naval hospitals. He then attained the senior medical post in the navy, as Physician to the Fleet, after the outbreak of war once more in 1793 – a sequence which symbolises the links between military and civil practice at the highest level. Sir John Pringle, the leading army physician, attained the eminence of being president of the Royal Society. Their writings were of justified renown in their professional world, military and civilian, in specialised periodicals and independent publications. Thomas Trotter's declared intention was that his writings should translate knowledge from the naval service 'to medical readers in general'.[22] The fame of such men as Lind, Blane, Pringle, Robert Blair, Robert Robertson, William Farr and Thomas Trotter ensured a wide professional audience for their publications. Sir John Pringle's *Observations on the Diseases of the Army*, first published in 1752 had reached its fifth – cumulatively revised – edition by 1815. The essence of the work had appeared in the *Philosophical Transactions* in 1750, gaining a wider currency from there in the *Gentleman's Magazine* in the following year.[23] A similar transmission belt brought the experiments of James Lind and James Cook from a professional to a wider audience. By the early nineteenth century specialised medical journals, such as *Medico-Chirurgical Transactions* (1809–) were supplementing general scientific journals in London, quickly followed by equivalent periodicals in the main provincial centres.

Knowledge of preventive measures was transferable from naval and military experience over infectious and deficiency diseases to a wider context because the worst medical problems faced by the fighting services were exactly those of the urban poor; although experienced in an intensified form through the greater intensity of conditions facing seamen and soldiers. Moreover improvements in medical practice concerning hygiene were demonstrable. Although mortality rates for the navy during the Napoleonic Wars were twice that of comparable civilian age-groups, over time the gain was substantial. Sick rates fell from 1 man in 2.45 of those serving in 1779 to 1 in 10.75 by 1813 and death rates fell over the same period from 1 in 42 to 1 in 143. Blane saw these improvements adding one-third to the effective naval manpower.[24] Trotter argued that not less than 100,000 seamen had been saved from death by scurvy during the wars since 1795, comparing the rate of mortality from the disease in the preceding war with the total numbers of seamen in 1795–1814.[25] This came primarily from the success of preventive rather than curative measures. Only scurvy and smallpox had been eliminated (or could be eliminated) by specifically medical therapy: none of the epidemic fevers was yet responsive to effective medication.

Hospital practice had the most direct parallels with civil experience – and Sir John Pringle prefaced his main book with the mordant observation 'Among the chief causes of sickness and death in an army, the reader will little expect that I should rank, what is intended for its health and preservation, the Hospitals themselves.' The principal aim of his book was to show how to prevent infection, 'the common and fatal consequences of a large and crowded hospital'.[26] Coupled with this were conditions of overcrowding, privation, lack of ventilation and warmth, dirt, insanitary habits, inadequate (or unbalanced) diets, filthy clothing and bedding, bad water supplies, and the other conditions which were more generally the lot of the poor throughout the land, and more particularly the lot of the urban poor. Sir John Pringle explicitly projected the relevance of his treatise on 'hospital and jayl-fevers' from military to civilian hospitals, and from hospitals to the fevers 'more frequent in large and populous cities than elsewhere', and Trotter also drew attention to the links between typhus in ships and 'in great towns, among poor people in low, dirty, ill-aired and damp houses towards the fall of the year and particularly in times of scarcity or during long and rigorous winters'.[27] Blane emphasised repeatedly the predisposing conditions for fevers and enteric diseases: 'circumstances of personal filth and want of ventilation, frequently combined with hardships and privation'.[28]

The importance of the preventive measures advocated by these famous military doctors is exactly that they spoke for the poor as a whole, and it was no accident that their main research into preventive measures against infectious diseases should have been initiated from the very specialised

environment of ships, army camps and hospitals. Their efforts were particularly aimed at mitigating 'crowd' diseases, even though they were made
without specific knowledge of the intrinsic nature of these diseases, or their
carriers, and despite the fact that contemporary curative medicine was
largely irrelevant. Collectively, these diseases were the worst demographic
killers of the eighteenth century, and their incidence was not alone amongst
urban dwellers, although the intensive living conditions of insanitary towns
provided the best context for their propagation. The 'dismal' peaks of the
crude death rates curve, occurring every few years, occasioned by epidemic
disease, particularly fevers and enteritis, were an important demographic
phenomenon. It was just this range of infections which contemporary doctors
thought preventive measures might check. The measures they proposed –
which appear enlightened commonsense for the most part to our later view
– were not specific to the diseases, none of the principal vectors or carriers
being known, apart from the special cases of scurvy and smallpox. Perhaps
because of that, paradoxically, they could have a wider effect upon improving
health and survival rates. A consequence of holding a generalised rather than
specific view of the nature of infectiveness of different diseases was that the
preventive measures proposed were also generalised, and could be of wider
effect than specific prophylactics. Rationality was to be judged by results
even if not by the test of formal knowledge.

The measures advocated in chorus by this group of eminent military and
naval doctors, and implemented wherever the emergencies of active campaigning did not prevent it, amounted to a systematic programme of social medicine – ranging from public health measures to household hygiene, from
personal hygiene to questions of diet and clothing. They were aimed at
specific problems of their specialised constituencies – communities of adult
men for the most part, healthy, sick and wounded, in conditions of privation
but not, in normal circumstances, of deprivation of the essentials of food,
clothing, warmth and shelter. The range of issues and the range of diseases,
which received their attention were limited, for this reason, and did not
touch important branches of family medicine, midwifery, the care of babies
and infants directly (although much of their work became of indirect relevance). Thus, in matters of public, domestic and personal hygiene their
influence was complementary to the work of such famous civilian doctors as
William Buchanan and his influential *Domestic Medicine* (1769) which had
gone into twenty-two editions by 1826.[29]

The centre of the military doctors' concern lay with public health measures
for community health in densely occupied institutions, particularly hospitals.
All wards in naval and military hospitals were to be whitewashed, scrubbed,
and fumigated regularly. All dirt, and particularly excrement, had to be
cleared away, privies had to be kept clean, bedpans washed and water supplies

isolated from pollution. Thomas Trotter's rigorous visitation and report on conditions in the Haslar Naval Hospital (with the subsequent regime imposed with his new authority as Physician to the Fleet) went beyond these measures. He ordered that 'W.C.'s . . . should be in a separate building so as not to endanger the drinking water.' He refused to allow visitors to the fever wards and segregated patients with infectious fevers. Dispensers, apothecaries and physicians were required to *end* their rounds with the smallpox and fever wards, to reduce the spread of infection.[30] For army camps Pringle advised the sterilisation of faeces (as a main source of infection), placing privies on the leeward side of camps, covering them daily with earth, clearing all rotting straw from tents and the like. Blane brought iron bedsteads into St Thomas's on hygienic grounds.

All put very great emphasis on ventilation. Hospitals were to have airy rooms of good height, with windows and doors opened daily in strict routine. Barrack rooms and wards were to have open chimneys and fires rather than enclosed stoves: the ventilation caused by the fire was more important than the warmth created. Blane, in particular, believed that much infection arose from want of fuel and warmth in the winter, which led the poor to close up their windows and remove all sources of ventilation. He thought that the greater availability and cheapness of fuel, by increasing both warmth and (of necessity) ventilation in open fires, very important indeed in reducing infections and mortality in the populace at large.[31] Captain Cook had ventilated the lower decks of HMS Resolution by lighting 'portable fires' to create draughts.[32]

A logical progression took the analysis forward from institutional measures to questions of personal hygiene, clothing and diet. When Blane was appointed Physician at St Thomas's in 1783 he took immediate measures to improve hygiene, quoting the tag about cleanliness being next to godliness. Patients were washed regularly and had regular changes of clean clothes. Their hair was cut. Dirty clothing (particularly that of infected patients) was to be burned or fumigated.[33] Equivalent measures were advocated by Pringle, Lind, and Trotter as part of the regime to ensure good health and low mortality rates.[34] The health regime established by Captain Cook in his circumnavigation of the globe, which recommended 'close attention to cleanliness', fresh water and regular washing was widely reported.[35]

A similar point was made about clothing: it should be adequate for warmth in winter but, more particularly, undergarments should be of cotton and linen so that they could be washed and changed regularly. Trotter gave full publicity to a disagreement he had had with the traditionalist martinet Admiral Earl St Vincent, over clothing. St Vincent had issued a general memorandum to the fleet, without reference to his Physician (there had been earlier rows over diet and scurvy), requiring all captains to enforce the wearing of flannel shirts or waistcoats 'next the skin' and ordering pursers to provide them. Trotter delivered a furious rebuttal to his commander in chief, whom he accused of turning seamen, without the possibility of changing their clothes regularly, into 'walking stink-pots'. 'If British seamen are to wear flannel next the skin,' he wrote with the full force of professional authority, 'they . . . must soon lose the hardihood of constitution that fits them for duty. Clothe them as warm as you please but in the name of cleanliness give them linen or cotton next the skin.'[36] Such sustained advocacy of soap and water, cotton and linen garments (regularly washed) began in the mid-eighteenth century, but there is good reason to doubt whether cotton cloth became a commodity in mass demand at home until after 1780. What percentage of the nation wore linen, or clothes of cotton mixes, which could be (and were) washed regularly remains a matter of speculation.

Scurvy had shown one specific association between diet deficiencies and disease. In the search for antidotes much useful dietary advice had been proposed, with particular emphasis on fresh (rather than salt) meat, salad and green vegetables. Pringle, Blane and Trotter all noted the importance of vegetables in diet from continuous observations reported from ships and army camps; and both Blane and Pringle argued that considerable improvements had taken place in this respect in the feeding habits of the nation during the eighteenth century.[37] Blane, in common with Adam Smith and many other non-medical observers, praised potatoes particularly as an 'invaluable auxiliary' item of diet.[38] In general terms the fact that the mortality rate from many diseases (as distinct from the rate of infection) was strongly influenced by the nutritional standards of those infected was quite clear to these contemporaries, although compounded with other attributes of the lives led by their potential patients – overcrowded, poor housing, insanitary conditions.[39] Enteric diseases, with lethal fevers, were directly associated with bad harvests, high food prices, and the poor eating bad food by these contemporaries as well as by modern scholars.

It is not easy to assess the wider significance of the new knowledge and improved practices being developed by military doctors in the late eighteenth century. Other influences upon changes have to be acknowledged. Advances in knowledge have to be distinguished from its implementation. The implementation of improved practice has to be considered according to the scale of change. To use the terminology more familiar in discussions of innovations in technology: invention has to be distinguished from innovation; increases in the capital stock of knowledge follow a different logic to the incentives which determine the putting into practice of selections from that stock of knowledge. The diffusion of innovations, and the incentives which govern the choices of technique within a known technology, requires a different analysis from that concerned to understand advances at the frontiers of technology. The extent of diffusion of new techniques, the time-lags involved with the process of diffusion, the distribution between 'best practice' technology and traditional technology in an industry all govern the significance of an innovation.

Space permits only a general consideration of some of these issues here, but all of them, where operative, imply a certain narrowing of the general significance to be afforded to the work of these military doctors, whether judged in the context of the social groups directly influenced by them, or the period in which their influence has to be judged. It is difficult to come to anything more than subjective conclusions when seeking to judge the long-term indirect effects of their professional contribution or to place it in an order of priority with other influences.

Their work has to be seen in terms of a contribution to knowledge as much as to improved practice in the first instance – although, in larger perspective, advances in the first conditioned progress in the latter. In these terms, the special conditions prevailing in the institutional context in which they worked created particularly effective incentives for the advancement of knowledge and the deployment of improved knowledge – as earlier pages have sought to argue. The army and navy were not the only institutions promoting the development and professionalisation of medicine in eighteenth-century England, of course, nor was England unique in Europe in this regard. The most comprehensive schema of social medicine published in the eighteenth century, for example, is that of Johann Peter Frank, the great Austrian doctor.[40] But the contributions to advances in knowledge of the association between diseases and environment made by doctors in the armed forces has not been sufficiently acknowledged.

Within their own world these advances in medicine (particularly the conquest of scurvy) were not without effect. As we have seen, Sir Gilbert Blane and Thomas Trotter believed that the gains in the effectiveness of seamen from improved health could be quantified. Blane was also proud of the fact that the regime he introduced into St Thomas's Hospital after 1783 considerably reduced cross-infection and mortality there, death-rates for in-patients falling from 1 in 14 in 1773–83 to 1 in 16.2 by 1803–13.[41] But the practical success of the measures proposed presupposed, in many cases, an authoritarian community, whether that of a ship, barracks, army camp or hospital, and could not be applied to the institutional conditions of the populace at large. One petty, but important, regulation proposed by Sir John Pringle for the layout and use of privies in an army camp is evidence enough: 'let there be some slight penalty, but strictly inflicted', he ordered, 'upon every man that shall ease himself anywhere about the camp but on the privies.'[42]

Much of the success of the measures advocated depended upon an authoritarian regime required to enforce them: very precise instructions laid down for all controllers of hospital wards; regular inspections and systems of report to ensure compliance; general orders imposed upon all subordinate commanders (as when Blane, on his appointment as a commissioner, made lemon and orange juice a compulsory general issue to all ships, whereas it had depended upon more individual initiative up to that time) and like measures. Even here practice could fall well short of advocacy, particularly in the emergencies of campaigning, as the disasters of the Walcheren expedition and the initial circumstances of the Crimean War revealed. No equivalent controls were possible over the civilian population, whether by magistrates, civil servants or doctors, although local government regulations by city ordinance evidently did embody rising standards of expectations to a degree during the eighteenth century. The gap between knowledge and effective, compulsory action remained very wide, with local authorities resisting centralising forces and the authoritarian pressure of professional opinion, as Edwin Chadwick found to his cost forty years into the nineteenth century.

When considering improvements in mortality more generally, during the eighteenth century (which he certainly assumed) Gilbert Blane listed many of these general measures: 'the use of linen and soap, the greater facility of procuring fuel and the more ample supply of water', less filth accumulating in London streets in the eighteenth century compared with the seventeenth ('the improved state of agriculture having rendered it very valuable as manure'), wider streets and brick houses, more effective statutory control in providing common sewers in London. He argued, on the evidence of the bills of mortality, that infant mortality had almost halved between 1728–50 and 1800–20, putting this down partly to specific measures against smallpox, but more generally to 'ventilation and cleanliness and more judicious management . . . such as greater warmth in appartments and clothing and the correction of the vulgar error that the exposure of children to the open air at all seasons is salutary'. 'It is a question', he concluded, 'how far improved medical treatment has had any share in it.'[43]

Even though these assertions remain unquantifiable, much of this contemporary optimism has to be discounted, at least for eighteenth-century conditions. Blane had London principally in mind when he spoke of improvements in paving and street cleansing (but not when he was considering the benefits of cheaper fuel, because he singled out Lancashire for comment) and with only 10 per cent of the total population in the metropolis this was clearly an unrepresentative sample, both for certain improvements in hygiene and because the spread of high density living in urban conditions increased mortality for many of the main causes of death. The increase in the proportion of population living in towns intensified the problems of sanitation, sewerage and public health down to the mid-nineteenth century in a context where the administrative framework for coping with a mass urban society had yet to be evolved (if the relative death rates between large towns and country districts be a guide). Equally, certain other improvements noticed by contemporaries, such as the increased use of healthier cotton clothing, spread more slowly down the social pyramid than contemporaries assumed. Rational responses by individuals, in questions of personal hygiene, and effective family response for household hygiene, were always dependent to a degree upon income levels – a minimum critical level of incomes set a threshold to adopting many of even the most elemental improvements in diet, clothing, shelter, warmth and cleanliness – whereas some of the most important attributes of hygiene, such as sanitation and water supplies, in practice lay beyond the power of rational action by individual families in rapidly growing towns.

The general preventive measures rather than specific medical therapy (save in the case of scurvy) advocated by military and naval doctors probably had the greatest potential significance. These were promoted in the light of a general awareness of the association between the context (personal, household and environmental) and disease rather than from specific medical knowledge. But carriers of many main infectious diseases – whether lice, fleas or contaminated food and water – would have had their effect removed or reduced by the adoption of such hygienic standards.

It may also be argued that only a demographically insignificant percentage of the population ever saw the inside of an institution to which the standards of public health and hygiene being propounded by military doctors were applied – whether ship, army camp or hospital – which were most unrepresentative habitats for the population at large. But this is not the whole point. Much of the new knowledge, and the measures, born within these highly specialised habitats, where mortality was intense and the premiums on reducing it very high, were of more general applicability. Personal hygiene, a better balanced diet and cleaner clothes had universal relevance; so did household and family hygiene with cleaner water, better heated and ventilated rooms. Overcrowded, ill-ventilated, unsanitary accommodation was the universal lot of poor families, not just those living in towns. Equally, even if most improvements depended upon access to higher family earnings, not all did; while the attainment of higher purchasing power does not, of itself, ensure the allocation of extra resources to promote healthier living without change in habits and patterns of spending. Some improvements required only changed practice on the basis of new knowledge and advocacy; others presumed changes in priorities of spending rather than incremental purchasing. It is demonstrable, at the other end of the social scale, that adopting a healthier life-style was not simply a function of a minimum critical level of income. New knowledge, new priorities, new fashions were influential determinants of cultural change for the upper classes, who also adopted higher standards in these respects during the eighteenth and nineteenth centuries. It is also salutary to remember how dramatically certain cultural changes could spread down the social scale during the eighteenth century, without changes in living standards always being a critical variable – fashion in clothing, inoculation after 1750, the potato and tea drinking amongst them.

The influences which combine to affect levels of health, morbidity and mortality (quite apart from fertility) are manifold and their interactions still largely unravelled and certainly unquantified. However during the nineteenth century, improvements in public health, hygiene, preventive measures (particularly against infectious diseases), improved diet and clothing are considered collectively to be principal agents in the decline in national death rates. The contributions of doctors in British fleets and armies in the eighteenth century form one of those influences and have a place in the interactions. Their full effect came much later than in the lifetimes of the individuals whose work has been considered here. But to study that work is to stand in the hills observing streams from which great rivers were eventually sustained.

NOTES

1 These rough estimates are drawn from B. R. Mitchell, *Abstract of British Historical Statistics* (1962), pp. 389–91; P. M. Deane, 'The Industrial Revolution and Economic Growth: the evidence of the early British National Income Estimates', *Economic Development and Cultural Change*, v (1957), pp. 159–74; 'The Implications of Early National Income Estimates for the Measurement of Long-Term Growth in the United Kingdom', *Ibid.* iv (1955), pp. 3–38; P. Mathias, *The First Industrial Nation* (1969), pp. 41, 43–6, 463.

2 T. Trotter, *Medicina Nautica* iii (1801), pp. 37–8.

3 *Ibid.* pp. 74–5.

4 T. Trotter, *Medicina Nautica* ii (1797), p. 14.

5 Of course, the fact that Britain was an island reduced the need for such measures. See C. M. Cipolla, *Cristophano and the Plague* (1972) and 'Origine et developpement des bureaux de santé en Italie', *Medicina Economia e Societa nell'Esperienza Storica* (Pavia, 1974); G. E. Rothenberg, 'The Austrian Sanitary Cordon and the Control of Bubonic Plague, 1710–1871', *Journal of the History of Medicine and Allied Sciences* xxviii (1973). The effectiveness of these measures was another matter.

6 G. Blane, *Select Dissertations* (1822), p. 121.

7 C. Lloyd and J. L. S. Coulter, *Medicine and the Navy* (1961), iii, ch. 18; R. M. Feibel, 'What happened at Walcheren: the Primary Medical Sources', *Bulletin of the History of Medicine* xlii (1968), with full bibliography. Detailed evidence on medical organisation in the Walcheren expeditionary force is given in *Parl. Papers* (1810) vii, i.

8 See PRO/Adm. papers and other authorities listed in P. Mathias, *The Brewing Industry in England, 1700–1830* (1959), pp. 204–9; J. Cook, *A Voyage towards the South Pole* (1777), J. Cook, *Phil. Trans.* dxvi (No. xxii), p. 402; A. Sparrman, *Voyage round the world* (1953 edn), pp. 26, 112.

9 J. Lind, *A Treatise on the Scurvy* (1753), pp. 118, 119–23.

10 The dramatic resurgence of the disease in 1794 had provoked a 'crisis' administrative response which determined the definitive preventive measures.

11 T. Trotter, *Medicina Nautica* i (1797), pp. 405, 426; ii (1797), pp. 304.

12 *Ibid.* III (1801), p. 78.
13 Blane became Physician to St Thomas's Hospital and Pringle president of the Royal Society. See below p. 80.
14 G. Blane, *Elements in Medical Logic* (1821), pp. 17–18.
15 Sir J. Pringle, *Observations on the Nature and Cure of Hospital and Jayl Fevers* (1750), pp. 2, 4, 8–33; *Observations on the Diseases of the Army* (5th edn, 1815), 126ff. 149–56, 183–5.
16 G. Blane, *Select Dissertations* (1822), p. 147.
17 L. F. Hirst, *The Conquest of Plague* (1953); C. Cipolla, *Cristophano and the Plague* (1973).
18 Examples of medical ignorance countering the effectiveness of preventive measures are manifold: amongst them the 'shutting up' of houses against plague, where the infected were isolated with the uninfected; the general absence of 'isolation' wards or 'isolation hospitals' for infectious diseases; Lind advocating the near-boiling of citrus fruits to produce a 'rob' for taking against scurvy; Chadwick flushing out sewers into rivers (a main source of drinking water) to clear 'miasmas' in the cholera epidemic of 1848.
19 See W. Budd, *Typhoid Fever* (1861); L. F. Hirst, *The Conquest of Plague* (1953); M. Greenwood, *Epidemics and Crowd-Diseases* (1935).
20 The debate is summarised in P. Mathias, 'Who Unbound Prometheus?' in P. Mathias (ed.) *Science and Society, 1600–1900* (1972).
21 This is the essential point of Charles Rosenberg's study of the reactions to cholera epidemics in the nineteenth century. He remarks: 'A disease is no absolute physical entity but a complex intellectual construct, an amalgam of biological state and social definition'. *The Cholera Years* (1962), note to p. 5.
22 T. Trotter, *Medicina Nautica* II (1797), p. 2.
23 *Phil. Trans. Royal Society* XLVI (1750); *Gentleman's Magazine* XXI (1751).
24 C. Lloyd and J. L. S. Coulter, *Medicine and the Navy*, pp. 183–4.
25 T. Trotter, *A Practical Plan for Manning the Royal Navy without Impressment* (1819), pp. 26, 45.
26 Sir John Pringle, *Observations on the Diseases of the Army* (1752), preface.
27 Sir John Pringle, *Observations on the Nature and Cure of Hospital and Jayl-Fevers* (1750), p. 51; T. Trotter, *Medicina Nautica* I (1797), pp. 252–3.
28 G. Blane, *Elements in Medical Logic* (1821), p. 209.
29 See T. C. Smout, *A History of the Scottish People, 1560–1830* (1969), pp. 257–9.
30 T. Trotter, *Medicina Nautica* I (1797), pp. 27–34.
31 J. Pringle, *Observations on the Nature and Cure of Hospital and Jayl-Fevers* (1750), pp. 33, 46–51; *Observations on the Diseases of the Army* (1752, 1815 edn), pp. 84–5, 96–7, 101–3, 107–9; G. Blane, *Select Dissertations* (1822), pp. 91, 125, 127, 137–40, 172–3; *Elements in Medical Logic* (1821), p. 209.
32 J. Pringle, *Discourse upon some late Improvements . . .* (1776), p. 28.
33 G. Blane, *Select Dissertations* (1822), pp. 122, 125–6, 136–7, 140, 172–3.
34 J. Pringle, *Observations on the Nature and Cure of Hospital and Jayl-Fevers* (1750), pp. 46ff.; *Discourse upon some late Improvements of the Means for Preserving the Health of Mariners* (1776); J. Lind, *An essay on the most Efficient Means of Preserving the Health of Seamen* (1757); *Two Papers on Fevers and Infection* (1763); T. Trotter, *Observations on the Scurvy* (1786).
35 J. Cook, *Methods taken for preserving the Health of the Crew of H.M.S. Resolution* (read to the Royal Society in 1776).
36 T. Trotter, *Medicina Nautica* III (1801), pp. 93–4. See also T. C. Smout, *A History of the Scottish People*, p. 258.

37 J. Pringle, *Observations on the Diseases of the Army*, 1752 (5th edn, 1815), p. 111; *Discourse upon some late Improvements of the Means for Preserving the Health of Mariners* (1776), pp. 11–13; G. Blane, *Select Dissertations* (1822), pp. 121–2; T. Trotter, *Medicina Nautica* I (1797), pp. 405–25; III (1808), pp. 74–6, 387–402. For a Scottish parallel see T. C. Smout, *A History of the Scottish People* (1969), pp. 250–2.

38 G. Blane, *Select Dissertations*, pp. 161–2. He added 'but by no means as a staple article, far less as an exclusive constituent of national subsistence'.

39 N. Greenwood, *Epidemics and Crowd-Diseases* (1935), pp. 139, 175, 178–9.

40 J. Peter Frank, *System einer vollständigen medicinischen Polizey* (Vienna, 1784).

41 G. Blane, *Select Dissertations* (1822), p. 141. He was very aware, in recording these improvements, that improved medical techniques did not necessarily reduce death rates, but extended the range of patients being treated. 'The comparative mortality of different hospitals', he commented, 'is a most fallacious test of the success of practice, unless the nature and intensity of the several diseases are taken into account. A large mortality may even be considered as a presumption of a hospital being well conducted, in as far as it indicates that the most severe disorders had been admitted.' (*Ibid.* p. 140.)

42 J. Pringle, *Observations on the Diseases of the Army* (5th edn 1815), p. 101.

43 G. Blane, *Select Dissertations* (1822), pp. 122–3, 126–8.

5 War and industrialisation

Phyllis Deane

The origins of modern economic growth, i.e. of that sustained increase in income per head which is associated with an industrial revolution, can be traced back to eighteenth-century England. Yet this was a period when England was more often at war than at peace. Over the one and a quarter centuries that elapsed between the 'glorious revolution' and Waterloo, England was involved in major wars for roughly seventy years. Did the process of industrialisation begin to gather momentum in this stormy period because of, or in spite of, the incidence of war?

Clearly, it is impossible to generalise usefully about the impact of war on the economic progress of nations for it has depended on the special circumstances of particular wars and of the countries concerned. To the extent that war involves: (1) physical destruction of real capital; (2) diversion of scarce labour, capital and raw material resources from productive to unproductive uses; and (3) an increase in the risks and uncertainties of mercantile or manufacturing enterprise, it must have a retardative effect on economic development. To the extent that the demands of war: (1) draw into productive use under-employed factors; (2) stimulate output in industries whose expansion reduces costs or creates opportunities for other branches of industry; and (3) precipitate fiscal or financial or organisational developments which redistribute incomes or opportunities in favour of innovating enterprise, its effects are more likely to be growth-promoting than growth-retarding. For the countries concerned, success or failure in war may further affect industrialisation by enlarging or diminishing either their international markets for domestic produce or their access to crucial raw materials or other resources.

There have been differences too in the nature of warfare through time which have conditioned its economic consequences. For Western Europe, the limited balance-of-power, or trade-protection, confrontations which characterised the seventeenth and eighteenth centuries were evidently less disturbing to national economies than either the earlier religious or the later ideological conflicts.[1] War became more institutionalised, less unpredictable and more contained. The rise of standing armies, the increase in the importance of naval warfare and the tendencies towards centralisation of supplies and standardisation of weapons, all contributed to stabilise levels of economic activity by creating a persistent demand for defence equipment and stores, e.g. barrack accommodation and ordnance stores, ships and ships' stores, uniforms, rations, etc., which was expanded or contracted by the outbreak of hostilities or the advent of peace, but never completely disappeared. In England public expenditure on defence constituted an increasing counter-weight to the recurrent peace-time variations in national economic activity due to harvest or trade fluctuations.[2] On the continent of Europe, and particularly in France, according to Professor Nef, the growth in the standing defence commitment over the period 1640–1713 was responsible for a con-siderable extension of state authority over economic enterprise and for an improvement in the social position of the mercantile classes – though that was not a period in which the progress of industrialisation was at all im-pressive.[3]

For Britain in the period 1700–63, the evidence assembled by Professor John suggests a positively beneficial impact of war on industrial development – not merely through its influence on expanding the level of demand for industrial goods generally, but in stimulating technological progress in certain capital goods industries which were of importance in the early stages of the English industrial revolution.[4] In drawing up the balance sheet he finds, on the one hand, no evidence that the war-inflated demands of government forced a significant contraction on other branches of economic activity, and, on the other hand, a good deal of evidence to suggest that government demand induced an expansion of output and encouraged technical advance in the shipbuilding and metal industries (notably iron and copper) and through these in coal, steampower and transport facilities. However the wars of the later eighteenth century were different again and he suggests that there were then 'considerable counterbalancing factors to the war-time expansion of industry, which, on the whole, probably negatived the advances of war. During the years 1776–83, for example, the financing of government demand was balanced by a contraction of investment on other branches of activity: and there was also a fall in employment in the export industries, particularly those supplying the North American market.'[5] Certainly the statistics of overseas trade lend support to the view that the American war exerted a brake on the progress of the British economy. Even leaving aside the lucrative North American trade, which fell away almost to vanishing point, British imports and exports declined over the period of the American war: and the spectacular upsurge in the international trade figures which dates from the end of the war further emphasises the wartime recession. Nevertheless, the indicators of industrial output not heavily dependent on the import or export trades (and even some that were, e.g. raw cotton imports), scanty though they are, do not all tell the same story of stagnation or decline:[6]

and it may be that the American war was less positively inimical to industrial progress, even in the shortrun, than the evidence of the relatively abundant overseas trade figures might lead one to suppose.

However the really intriguing questions centre on the lengthy period of the French and Napoleonic wars which began in 1793 and finally ended in 1815. For the impact of that conflict on the British economy was evidently more disturbing than any other eighteenth or nineteenth century war: and it fell in a period which on any interpretation (take-off or not) represented a significant phase in the English industrial revolution.

First of all then, we can assess the relative weight of the war-inflated central government expenditures – relative that is to ordinary peace-time levels of public expenditure and to the overall level of the nation's economic activity. The extent of the war-time fluctuation in public expenditure is plain enough. Thanks to a painstaking analysis of Treasury records for the period 1688–1869, made by a chief exchequer clerk in the middle of the nineteenth century, there exists an annual series of balancing public income and expenditure accounts running back to the late seventeenth century.[7] True, there is a break in the series at 1801 when the basic accounting procedure was shifted to a new basis in which many items previously netted out (e.g. costs of revenue collection) began to be included in total public expenditure: and unfortunately the compiler of the historical series made no attempt to provide an overlap between his tables of net income and expenditure for Great Britain ending in 1801 and the gross accounts for the United Kingdom beginning in the year 1801/2. However, the accounts show that net public expenditure, which had averaged £10.2m in the pre-war quinquennium 1770/4, reached its war-time peak towards the end of the American war (i.e. in 1782) when the total exceeded £29m and fell back to a peace-time low of less than £15½m in 1787, before creeping up again to a pre-war peak of nearly £18m in 1791. The upward creep in peace-time expenditure in the brief interval between the American and French wars was itself largely a result of preparation for war, for four-fifths of the £2½m increase in net public expenditure between 1787 and 1791 was attributable to increased defence expenditure (largely naval defence). By the second half of the 1790s when the French wars were well under way, net public expenditures were running at more than two and a half times their level in the corresponding quinquennium a decade previously.[8] Even after deflating to allow for the price inflation which characterised this period (and was largely a consequence of the war expenditure) net public expenditure in 1795/9 was averaging more than three times the 1770/4 level and twice the 1785/9 level.[9]

So in terms of its recent peace-time levels public expenditure soared to unprecedented heights soon after the 1793 outbreak of war. It is not as easy to measure its importance in relation to overall national economic activity for the national income estimates available for the period are discontinuous and at best impressionistic. However, estimates of total national expenditures at market prices suggest an amount of between £250m and £260m for Great Britain, circa 1801, when net public expenditure was in the region of £51m (1800/1) and gross public expenditure about £65½m (1801/2). Gross public expenditure would thus appear to have amounted to over a quarter of total national expenditure at market prices, which was not a negligible proportion.[10]

Since the absolute national expenditure estimates are of dubious value, however, it is worth trying to check the hypothesis that central government expenditure had become a substantial element in total national expenditure by reference to the evidence on some other component in the total. The only other major form of expenditure for which we have usable statistics is export demand. The statistics of overseas trade are, like the fiscal data, available annually from the end of the seventeenth century and are amongst the most comprehensive quantitative data available for the period. Here again, however, there are problems of interpretation arising out of a break in the series as between the eighteenth and nineteenth centuries. Until 1796 for domestic exports and 1854 for imports or re-exports, commodities entering into international trade were recorded at constant (so-called 'official') values rather than at market prices. After 1796 domestic exports were recorded at current (generally declared) values and for the period 1796–1853 Professor Imlah has constructed annual estimates of the current values of re-exports as well as of imports.[11] Table 1 compares total gross public expenditures (estimated for the period 1781–1800 when *net* expenditures are shown in the public accounts) with corresponding estimates of export demand arrived at by adding current values of domestic exports to one-fifth of the current values of re-exports.

The estimates in Table 1 then suggest that government demand was a larger component of total national expenditure than was export demand over the whole period 1781–1830, except for a brief span during the late 1780s. For a few years before the French wars began to dominate the economy exports may have weighed more heavily than government expenditure. But for the rest of the period public expenditure, inflated in peace-time by a heavy burden of war-created debt service charges, was significantly larger. Whether these weighty expenditures stimulated or retarded the process of industrialisation which was evidently gathering momentum in the later decades of the eighteenth century must have depended, of course, on how they were financed and how they were spent.

A very broad indication of the sources of war finance can be obtained from the public income accounts. When Pitt took over in 1784 as Chancellor of the Exchequer he found himself saddled with the legacy of the American war in the form of a still substantial budget deficit, at a time when the main source of public revenue (about 70 per cent of the net public income of Great Britain) was an inefficient hotch-potch of customs and excise and stamp duties. He succeeded in raising the yield of these duties, mainly by a process of rationalisation, and also began a deliberate development, of what came to be known as the 'assessed' taxes – a group of taxes which represented the rudimentary beginnings of a progressive direct tax on incomes or wealth. They included taxes on the 'establishment' maintained by the upper income groups (e.g. on male servants or on horses and carriages) and also the window tax and the inhabited house duty (both aimed at taxing relatively wealthy householders). By 1787 Pitt had turned the budget deficit into a surplus

Table 1. *Estimated public and international components of total expenditure at current prices 1781–1830*

Annual averages	Total gross public expenditure (£m)	Total value domestic exports plus $\frac{1}{5}$ re-exports (£m)
1781–5	30.8	15.0
1786–90	19.6	21.0
1791–5	29.4	27.1
1796–1800	59.0	35.0
1801–5	61.5	42.2
1806–10	77.5	44.3
1811–15	101.1	45.8
1816–20	60.7	42.5
1821–5	55.8	38.9
1826–30	54.2	37.2

SOURCES. Basic public expenditures and export data from Mitchell and Deane, *Abstract of Historical Statistics*. Estimates of market value re-exports 1796–1830 from A. H. Imlah, *Economic Elements in the Pax Britannica*. Gross public expenditure 1781–1800 based on notional addition of 20 per cent to net public expenditure figures. Estimates of market value of exports and re-exports 1781–95 based on relationship between official and market values for domestic exports and re-exports respectively over average of period 1796–1800.

and set up a sinking fund for systematically reducing the national debt. By 1792 total net public income was 40 per cent above its 1784 level, there was a budget surplus of over £1½m and the amount of the national debt was steadily falling.

Then came the war and by 1796 the budget deficit was larger than net public income and still rising. The assessed taxes, based in principle on 'ability to pay' seemed to offer the most promising prospects for expansion in this inflationary context, but attempts to raise their yield proved disappointing and Pitt turned in the end to a more direct approach to the taxation of personal incomes. The income and property tax was introduced in 1799 and had been elaborated to something approaching its modern form by 1803 when it was levied in five schedules – Schedule A being a tax on rents, Schedule B on farmers' profits (also based on rents), Schedule C on interest in the funds, Schedule D on incomes from trade, commerce and professions and Schedule E on incomes from offices, pensions and stipends.

Table 2. *Principal sources of government finance 1781–1830*

	Budget deficit	Customs duties	Excise duties	Income, assessed and land taxes
As percentages of:	%	%	%	%
Net public expenditure G.B.				
1781–5	46.7	12.6	23.7	10.2
1786–90	—	23.3	43.8	18.0
1791–5	24.2	15.8	35.7	12.1
1796–1800	46.7	10.6	21.7	9.2
Gross public expenditure U.K.				
1801–5	24.9	17.2	31.4	14.8
1806–10	13.4	17.3	34.1	26.0
1811–15	26.2	13.9	27.7	21.8
1816–20	—	21.2	43.7	18.1
1821–15	—	25.8	49.2	12.0
1826–30	—	36.0	38.4	9.6

SOURCE. Based on public income and expenditure accounts summarised in Mitchell and Deane, *Abstract of Historical Statistics*. Since Irish customs and excise duties were not separately returned for the period 1801–6 (though they are included in gross public income) they have been estimated for this table by analogy with their proportion to the corresponding British totals for the period 1807–10.

Table 2 illustrates the changing pattern of government finance over this period by showing the main sources of finance as a percentage of total public expenditure.[12] The introduction of the income tax helped to keep an escalating budget deficit under control but even after 1800 it was still the customs and excise duties, particularly the latter, which carried most of the extra burden of war expenditure. Considering the war years (1793–1815) as a unit it would appear that about 27 per cent of public expenditure was met by borrowing (budget deficit), 29 per cent by excise duties, 15 per cent by customs duties, 9 per cent by land and assessed taxes and 9 per cent by the income tax. Dividing the war period into two parts we find that in the years 1793–1800 the budget deficit accounted for 44 per cent of public expenditure and in 1800–15 for 22 per cent. In the second and longer period income tax met about 12 per cent of gross public expenditure and excise duties about 31 per cent.

Without a more detailed analysis of the incidence of taxation than the available data permit, it is not possible to draw firm, quantifiable, conclusions concerning the extent to which the financing of the war effort may have retarded or promoted the process of industrialisation. To the extent that it was financed by borrowing, or out of industrial or commercial profits, it must have diverted investment funds from other and possibly more productive uses. However the bulk of the increased indirect taxation necessitated by war seems to have been borne by consumers rather than producers and the new direct taxes touched the mercantile and manufacturing classes relatively lightly. Of the 9 per cent of gross public expenditure financed by the income tax during the years 1803–15, for example, only 2 per cent was met from Schedule D assessments, compared with nearly 5 per cent drawn mainly from the agricultural community under Schedules A and B. Indeed, a striking feature of the income tax returns is the fact that the Schedule D assessments, which had risen to £3½m in 1806 never exceeded £4m, in spite of the fast rate of inflation. On the other hand the Schedule C and E assessments (the easiest to assess and collect) rose from under £2.9m in 1806 to £6.2m in 1815 while the Schedule A and B assessments (the tax commissioners had a long experience of assessing rent, particularly land rents) rose from £6.4m to £8.1m over the same period.[13]

On balance then, although some of the excise duties (e.g. the paper and glass duties) may have retarded industrial expansion, the evidence does not suggest that actually financing the war effort involved a significant redistribution of incomes away from the groups which were actively financing the process of industrialisation. The agricultural sector seems to have carried a disproportionately heavier share of the war effort than the mercantile and manufacturing sectors; rentiers (fund holders) and upper income employees a higher relative proportion than capitalist entrepreneurs; and consumers a bigger share, overall, than producers.

On the other side of the public accounts, the increasing war expenditures generated a greatly expanded and sustained demand for the products of the iron industry at a time when it was going through a costly process of technological change. It was in the first decade of the nineteenth century that the British iron industry escaped from its dependence on imported bar iron, so that the bulk of its wrought iron, as well as its cast iron output was produced from British ore processed by British coal. The other major direct effect of the war-expenditures lay in activating labour and land resources which had hitherto been under-employed. In 1801 over 350,000 men were voted for the army, navy and ordnance departments: in 1811 the corresponding total was over 514,000 representing between 9 and 10 per cent of the total British labour force in the latter year, even before allowing for the increased numbers of civilian employees of government in public departments, dockyards, etc. These numbers were not large enough to make labour scarce in industry generally, nor to eliminate unemployment in years when the continental

4

blockade and the closure of American ports to British shipping forced a recession in the export trades: but they must have made the average level of employment significantly higher during the war years than in either the pre-war or the post-war period.

At the same time government expenditure on food for the armed forces, plus the war-time restrictions on imports of food, ensured a strong and expanding demand for the products of agriculture, even in months when harvest failures drove up grain prices to levels that were prohibitive for private households. The result was a marked acceleration in the rate at which waste land and under-employed common fields or pastures were brought into intensive use. Over the whole period 1793–1816 more than 3m acres were subject to parliamentary enclosure acts and an unknown further acreage enclosed by private arrangement.[14] The rate of enclosure at this period was higher than for any other period in British history and the estimated increase in the share of agriculture in the British national product between 1801 and 1811 was associated with taking up much of the slack in under-employed agricultural labour and land.[15] It is thus not surprising that the agricultural sector was able to carry so much of the financial burden of the war effort. More important, however, for the long-term development prospects of the British economy than the absolute war-time expansion of agricultural output, was the increase in potential productivity in agriculture which enclosure permitted.

On the face of it then, it would appear that public expenditure on the 1793–1815 war effort was at least as likely to have had a growth-promoting as a growth-retarding effect on the British economy. What one needs to be able to do, of course, to assess the impact of the war on the process of indus-trialisation, is to calculate the rate of growth of investment or output for major or key industries. Unfortunately the data do not exist that would permit a reasonably comprehensive assessment. The excise and trade returns give an indication of output trends (or partial output trends) for a limited range of industries but they are too sketchy and too few to carry much weight of analysis. Any attempt to combine them into an overall total (e.g. as in the famous Hoffman production index) depends on applying an arbi-trary set of weights to an incomplete collection of indicators whose individual coverage and reliability are incalculable. Table 3 lists the results of trying to derive growth rates for a selection of the more useful production indicators, distinguishing the pre-war and post-war periods and two war sub-periods – one lasting until the short peace of 1802 and the other running through to the year of Waterloo.

For what they are worth, most of these industrial indicators suggest some retardation during the war period, a deceleration in some cases more marked in the second war sub-period than in the first. Were we to extend the range of production indicators by drawing more freely on the trade returns the further deceleration in the second sub-period would show up more strongly. For the overseas trade sector was characterised by (1) a vigorous rebound 1783–93 from the artificially depressed levels caused by the American war; (2) a continued upsurge 1793–1802 when Britain's main commercial rivals were heavily disadvantaged by war conditions; (3) a subsequent tightening of the restrictions on British trade culminating in 1806–13 with the continental blockade and in some years a closing of North American ports to British shipping, and (4) a modest recovery in the post-war period when the

Table 3. *Selected industrial growth rates*

Compound rates per cent per annum calculated between quinquennial averages centred on years specified.

	1783–93 (%)	1793–1802 (%)	1802–15 (%)	1815–25 (%)
Glass	3.7	0.4	decline	2.9
Bricks	n.a.	decline	0.6	6.4
Paper	2.8	1.6	2.3	2.9
White tin	2.7	decline	decline	6.2
Tallow candles	1.6	1.5	1.2	3.3
Beer	1.5	decline	0.3	1.1
British spirits	9.2	decline	1.8	3.3
Soap	2.1	1.6	2.3	3.4
Hides and skins	1.1	0.3	1.3	1.3
Scottish linens	2.0	0.2	1.9	n.a.
Yorkshire woollens	4.0	3.1	1.6	6.9
Printed goods	6.9	7.2	3.9	5.3
Raw cotton imports	8.7	8.9	2.9	6.9

SOURCE. Basic quantity data from Mitchell and Deane, *Abstract of Historical Statistics*. Most of these relate to excise returns and some are based on weighted averages of the original data. Net raw cotton imports exclude re-exports.

war-time restrictions on trade were lifted but British virtual monopoly of the Atlantic carrying trade was lost. These movements are reflected in the overall rate of growth of British overseas trade (measured in terms of the volume of total imports plus domestic exports) which averaged 4.6 per cent in the first period distinguished in Table 3 (i.e. 1781/5–1791/5), 4.5 per cent in the second (1791/5–1800/4), 2 per cent in the third (1800/4–1813/17) and 2.4 per cent in the post-war period 1813/17–1823/27). Most output indicators derived from, or heavily dependent on, the movements in international trade exhibit this pattern of rebound, continued upsurge, deceleration and modest recovery.[16] It is significant, however, that even in the period of relative deceleration, i.e. in the second war sub-period, the rate of growth of British overseas trade, measured in real terms (i.e. at constant prices) was proceeding faster than the rate of growth of British population. So too, so far as one can judge, was the rate of growth of total GNP.

Whether the overall pace of industrial growth would have been appreciably faster had there been no war it is impossible to say. It seems likely that the industries for which export demand was an important stimulus to output and technical change (e.g. cotton textiles) benefited from the first phase of the war and were retarded by the second. However there were other industries (e.g. iron) where direct government demand for war purposes was a major factor in stimulating a more rapid development than would have been possible in normal peace-time conditions. There may also have been other industries (e.g. consumer goods produced primarily for the home market) where the maintenance of a high average level of employment kept demand generally above peace-time norms: just as there must have been industries where plans to expand investment were inhibited by the high cost of money or of producers' goods (e.g. bricks, coal, timber) associated with the inflationary environment of war.

The war also had implications for Britain's competitive position in world markets. To the extent that it became harder for other Western European countries – more severely shocked by the physical losses and recurrent real costs of combat fought on home soil – to follow the British example, it may have enabled this country to widen its technological lead. On the other hand to the extent that it disrupted the normal channels of trade with the USA it may have stimulated that country to develop import substitutes for manufactures which it might have gone on buying longer from British sources. The counterfactual propositions concerning what might have happened had there been no war lead on, however, to some unanswerable questions. How can one judge, for example, what might have been the situation of British industry by the early years of the nineteenth century had there been no war in Europe, and had the freeing of trade which began so hopefully with the French Treaty of 1786 been allowed to run an unimpeded course and possibly even been extended to other western European countries?

In the end, however, it must be admitted that although a full and accurate reckoning of the costs and benefits might tip the balance of the account one way or another, the accessible evidence taken as a whole does not support the view that the war of 1793–1815 exerted a serious brake on British industrial progress. Even in years when public defence expenditure depended most heavily on loan finance (e.g. in the second half of the 1790s) there seem to have been adequate investment funds available to the private sector to maintain an unprecedentedly fast rate of capital accumulation in the leading industries of the industrial revolution (particularly cotton and iron) and in the transport facilities (e.g. canals, docks and harbours) which constituted the essential overhead capital needed for sustained industrialisation. When in the second phase of the war the expansion of overseas trade was restricted by the way the conflict developed, British merchants still found it possible to find new markets for and sources of raw materials and the increase in public expenditure was more than enough to maintain a high level of domestic demand for British industry. In the last analysis, and leaving aside the intractable hypothetical questions, it would appear that the war of 1793–1815, prolonged and expensive though it was, does not seem to have caused more than superficial fluctuations in the pace and content of the British industrial revolution.

NOTES

1 Cf. E. Robson, 'The Armed Forces and the Art of War', *New Cambridge Modern History* (1957), VII, p. 165: 'In theory and in practice, eighteenth century wars were wars of limited liability – about something concrete, rather than the earlier wars of righteousness and moral purpose – clashes between rulers, between dynastic States in limited wars fought with limited means for limited objectives, which ended with the drawing up of a balance sheet.'

2 E. B. Schumpeter, 'English Prices and Public Finance, 1660–1822', *Review of Economics and Statistics*, XX (Feb. 1938), p. 28, gives a table of central government expenditures for selected years of peace with relatively low expenditures and of war with peak expenditures. In 1754, a year of peace, direct war expenditures plus interest and management charges on the national debt (which can be regarded as mainly indirect war expenditures) amounted to almost £5m compared with £2½m in 1700. It is unlikely that total national product increased by more than about 50 per cent between the same two dates.

3 J. U. Nef, *War and Human Progress* (1950), pp. 218–9.

4 A. H. John, 'War and the English Economy, 1700–1763', *Economic History Review*, 2nd ser., VII (1954–5).

5 *Ibid.* p. 344.

6 There were substantial increases as between 1774–5 and 1782–3 (average of two years in each case) for British spirits consumed, West Riding woollens, paper and soap charged to duty, for example, and a lesser, but nonetheless distinct increase for beer.

7 The results (which involved a twelve-year research project) were published in parliamentary papers in 1869, *Sessional Papers* 1868/9 vol. XXXV, and have been reprinted in summary form in B. R. Mitchell and Phyllis Deane, *Abstract of British Historical Statistics* (1962).

8 Net public expenditures averaged £46.8m annually 1795/9, compared with £18.1m in 1785/9 and £10.2m in 1770/4.

9 The Gilboy-Schumpeter index (taking an arithmetic average of producers goods plus consumer goods excluding cereals) suggests a 12 per cent increase between 1770/4 and 1785/9 and a further 22 per cent between then and 1795/9.

10 See Phyllis Deane and W. A. Cole, *British Economic Growth 1688–1959* (1962), p. 161 for an estimate of £232m for British national income at factor cost 1801. This has been converted to an estimate of national expenditure at market prices by adding indirect taxes and deducting subsidies.

11 A. H. Imlah, *Economic Elements in the Pax Britannica* (1958), pp. 37–8.

12 The figures relate to net public expenditure of Great Britain up to 1800 and gross public expenditure of the United Kingdom thereafter.

13 *Sessional Papers*, 1870, xx summarises the duty assessed by Schedules over the years 1803–15 inclusive.

14 Cf. A. H. John, 'Farming in Wartime: 1793–1815' in *Land, Labour and Population in the Industrial Revolution*, ed. E. L. Jones and G. E. Mingay (1967), p. 31. 'Wartime developments virtually closed the frontier of cultivation in this country, so marking a stage in our agricultural history.'

15 See Phyllis Deane and W. A. Cole, *British Economic Growth, 1688–1959*, p. 161 for estimates of value-added in agriculture rising from £75½m in 1801 (32½ per cent of British national product at factor cost) to £107½m (35½ per cent of national product) in 1811.

16 Given the relative abundance of statistics derived from the overseas trade records and the scarcity of evidence on the home trade it is only too easy to exaggerate their importance in trying to assess trends in total industrial activity.

6 The exigencies of war and the politics of taxation in the Netherlands 1795–1810

Simon Schama

If not exactly an 'aberration of nature' the public finances of the eighteenth-century Netherlands were, according to George Crawfurd, an Anglo-Rotterdammer businessman, a bewildering 'exception to the general rule that the prosperity of a nation is reflected in its revenue'.[1] Indeed it was difficult to be unimpressed by the contrast between the still considerable private and commercial affluence and the makeshift penury of the Republic's treasury. Foreign commentators from Gregory King to Adam Smith were agreed that, even in peace-time, the unfortunate Dutch were the most heavily taxed people in Europe.[2] The effects of war could be calamitous. In 1713 it was calculated that the wars of the Spanish Succession had cost the Republic in the neighbourhood of 128m guilders.[3] As a result the interest on the public debt of the province of Holland had almost doubled between the peace of Nijmegen and the peace of Utrecht, from fl.7,107,128 to fl.13,475,029.[4] Given relatively stagnant demographic and economic resources Dutch statesmen had no option but to learn the lesson that, as Professor Wilson has succinctly put it, 'war was a luxury the Netherlands could no longer afford'.[5] But a policy of prudent neutrality brought its rewards. Interest on the debt was contained; the Dutch took a healthy slice of the French carrying trade, and despite sharp fluctuations on the money market, their government was able to borrow at the low rate of $2\frac{1}{2}$ per cent.[6] Unhappily the years of benign torpor did not last. The temptation to profit from British discomfort in America; nervousness concerning the Habsburgs' intentions at Ostend and the Scheldt, and the general anxiety to avoid the fate of a Poland of the west combined to persuade the Dutch to seek their security from the protection of a powerfully ally. Depending on whether Orangist or Patriot forces held the upper hand within the Republic itself, foreign policy oscillated between the British and French connections – with equally disastrous results.[7] By 1793 war had become not a luxury but a necessity. And it was then that the painful question, held at bay for most of the eighteenth century, finally caught up with the Dutch. Just how expensive was the price of independence, and could a nation of less than two million, its major sources of livelihood crippled by a pan-European war, afford to foot the bill indefinitely?

In less acute terms, the problem of finding the wherewithal to defend national integrity was common to every eighteenth-century state. As L. P. van de Spiegel, one of the shrewder Dutch statesmen, observed, his country was a casualty of the habit of more grandiose powers of living well beyond their means.[8] Accustomed to regard war as a legitimate extension of diplomacy and unconcerned by, or ignorant of, the real cost, the princes of Europe left it to their servants to provide, as and when needs commanded. These in turn relied on the versatility of private financiers, usually in consortium; on the farming of indirect revenue, and the brutal and inefficient extortion of direct taxes, for the most part from those sections of their subjects least able to pay them. Rarely, if ever, were the requirements of foreign policy determined by an awareness of fiscal resources. Rarely, indeed, was the information to hand. Necker remains notorious, despite his later confession of the French debt (and after his own manner) for having scraped through the American war on a variety of expedients as lucrative to the creditors of the crown as they were damaging to its long-term solvency. Only at the eleventh hour was a forward policy in the United Provinces overruled by Brienne's warnings of an imminent bankruptcy.[9] But if rulers never shrank from the call of *realpolitik* for the sake of pinching the odd penny, it is equally true that the exorbitant costs of war directed the attention of the more inventive and conscientious of their officials to the need to provide systematic and accountable methods of finance, to transform, in Dr Bosher's phrase, 'business into bureaucracy'.[10] Not only in France, but in Vienna, Potsdam and the petty German principalities the exponents of *kameralwissenschaft* devoted themselves to the task of finding the rational means to supply even the most capricious and greedy prince with a steady sufficiency of revenue. It was, perhaps, a measure of the universality of the problem that Europe's first chair of political economy was established at Naples.

The ingenuity of both political economists proper and the more empirical practitioners of political arithmetic was, however, often matched by their political myopia. If there were few more pressing needs for the sovereigns of the old regimes than the reform of their finances, neither was there (with perhaps the exception of relations between church and state) any subject which was more popularly emotive. Taxation may have been the necessary auxiliary of absolutism, but it was also the trigger of rebellion. Where the proposals of physiocrats like Turgot were applied in practice they ran headlong into incensed resistance. However unreal their community of interest the imposition of a new tax, and above all a new direct tax was an opportunity for those with a vested interest in the defeat of reform to call on the support of the unprivileged commons. Attempts to extract new sources of revenue from British America; to institute a general land tax in the Habsburg Empire and to impose a stamp duty and/or a *subvention territorial* in France all resulted either in ignominious retreat or revolution.[11] While the last two decades of the eighteenth century revealed the (literal) bankruptcy of traditional financial administration they also attested to the limitations of programmatic reform. Impecunious sovereigns who wished to eschew the most draconian authoritarianism were faced with an awkward paradox. Survival demanded reform but since that risked entailing unpredictable political consequences there was no telling that the remedy might not prove more lethal than the disease.

The Dutch Republic was well and truly caught on the horns of this dilemma. Arguably there was no state in Europe in more urgent need of financial overhaul yet none so institutionally ill-equipped to carry it out. The regents and pensionaries of the republic were neither complacent nor oblivious to the problem, but their periodic efforts to set their house in order stopped short of the basic constitutional changes which reform must have entailed. In 1716, guided by Secretary van Slingelandt the Council of State issued an 'extraordinary summons' to the States-General to consider measures for the renovation of the exhausted finances of the Generality. And on becoming Grand Pensionary van Slingelandt made a further effort to reinstate the principle, expressed in article 5 of the Union of Utrecht, that the defence of the state be financed by common and general taxes.[12] The absence of a Stadholder and the gradual recrudescence of the power of the regents vitiated any hopes that the Generaliteits Rekenkamer (limited to the declaration and receipt of the provincial Quotas) might be turned into an effective financial executive. Even in 1748 when the 'restoration' of William IV (Friso) provided a new opportunity for reform it was impossible for the Stadholder to tackle the roots of the problem without incurring the accusation that he wished to destroy the federal union and impose an Orangist despotism. At least the more flagrant excesses of the tax farmers (which had contributed to the revolt against the regents) were abolished in Holland, Zeeland and Friesland, and a 'controller of collectors', Jacob Vosmaer, appointed to supervise the army of officials responsible for collecting indirect taxes. In 1751, following further debate in the States of Holland, a comprehensive regulation was enacted prohibiting fiscal officials from plural appointments and interests. But Vosmaer's minimal establishment, and the limp judicial sanctions, administered by men who had a direct vested interest in the commerce of tax-collection ensured that thorough-going reform failed to survive the early death of the Stadholder in 1752.[13]

The final opportunity to shore up the financial defences of the republic before the inundations of war and revolution hit it came and went in the 1780s. In May 1785, 'in the sorrowful circumstances in which this Republic finds itself since the (Fourth) Anglo Dutch War' the States-General commissioned yet another enquiry on finance. To some degree it was intended to answer the increasingly bitter complaints of the maritime provinces and Utrecht, that they were shouldering a disproportionate burden for the repair of the army and navy following the debacles of the war.[14] The deliberations of the commission were interrupted by the upheavals of the Patriot revolution. But following the restoration of William V in October 1787, courtesy of the diplomacy of Malmesbury and the bayonets of the Duke of Brunswick, van de Spiegel, promoted to Grand Pensionary, was in a position in 1790 to supply the Prince with his 'succinct and accurate account' of the financial damage. The report of 1790 occupies in the history of Dutch fiscal reform a position analogous to Necker's *Compte Rendu au Roi*. Both set out, with some garnishing, the full extent of public indebtedness, and both were equally bereft of adequate means of redress. The grievances against the Quota were partly met by the recommendation of regular twenty-five-year revisions, based on full information on the resources – demographic, territorial and capital – of each province. Future inter-provincial disputes and appeals were to be dealt with by an independent commission appointed by the States General, and pious hopes were expressed that annual budgets would be declared and published. The land tax in the territories administered by the Generality (Flanders, Brabant, Venlo and Maastricht) was to be rationalised along physiocratic lines; and the Stadholder's court was to suffer swingeing retrenchment not the least painful of which was the strict rule that 'the total of postilions and horses maintained must not exceed the limits imposed by the circumstances of the times.'[15]

The lameness of these proposals and the inability of van de Spiegel to live up to his honourable intentions reflected the fact that, like his predecessors, he too was a prisoner of the circumstances which had brought him to power. Unlike his father, William V, as he often pointed out, was 'no friend of novelty'. The trauma of his eviction from the Hague in 1786 and the stripping of his titles by the Patriot States-General had persuaded him that beneath every trimmer there lay a revolutionary waiting to pounce. Nor were the more obdurate Orangists like Ocker Repelaer and Bentinck van Rhoon who had mobilised the repression and plunder of the Patriots in 1787 inclined to countenance anything but the most uncompromising reaction. Those conservative regents and patricians who had thrown in their lot with the prince once the Patriots had begun to adopt menacingly democratic notions were, if anything, even more hostile to fiscal innovation. They had not defended the patrimony of their offices and magistracies against the demagogues to have them taken from them by a Grand Pensionary – let alone a parvenu like van de Spiegel. Only the long-awaited Quota reapportionment would be tolerated. The inevitable result of this drearily familiar obstructionism was the usual catalogue of expedients to which van de Spiegel was forced to resort: bills secured against anticipations of revenue; a forced loan of 4 per cent on property in 1788 (yielding fl.53m) and of 2 per cent in 1793 (yielding only 19.3 of the estimated 25m).[16]

Confronted by the cameralist's nightmare that was Dutch taxation it is understandable that the nerve of men as courageous and intelligent as van de Spiegel should have wilted. The financier who was to have the unenviable task of attempting a root and branch reform, I. J. A. Gogel, later remarked that the necessary remedies 'could not have been undertaken without causing a violent shock to a state already languishing in its own impotence'.[17] That was the nub of the matter. To tackle the major defects of the fiscal system was to challenge the constitution of the Republic. A section, at least, of the Patriots of the 1780s had embarked on their campaign against the Stadholder in order to liberate provincial and municipal sovereignty from executive encroachments.[18] True, the Union of Utrecht, which they claimed to restore to its pristine validity had actually provided for common taxes for the defence of the fatherland established 'on a uniform and single footing'. But the historical development of the republic had been in the opposite direction. Six months after its signature it was decided that each province should furnish its own allotment to the Receiver-General. With the hardening of provincial sovereignties it was assumed both impractical and improper to standardise the plethora of taxes, dues and imposts inherited in many cases from ducal and episcopal, as well as communal, government. Apart from the levy of 'extraordinary pennies' at times of national emergency (such as 1672–3) and the collection by the five admiralties of the 'convooien en licenten' customs, the revenue of the state was furnished by Quota. The first assessment was made in 1582 and thereafter at very irregular intervals, Holland making up between 57 per cent and 65 per cent of the aggregate.[19] It was left to the individual provinces to employ whatever means they judged efficacious to supply their portion.

Naturally those ways and means differed markedly from province to province. The pattern of direct taxation was affected by its importance as a component of the total revenue as well as the economic characteristics of the province. In the land provinces of Groningen and Overijssel where direct taxes accounted for between 40 and 60 per cent of revenue, the land tax was levied (not unlike the French taille) at near 20 per cent of rental value.[20] In Holland where the 'verponding' (land tax) brought in just 20 per cent of the overall income, the 1732 tariff levied at $12\frac{1}{2}$ per cent of land rental value and $16\frac{2}{3}$ per cent of house rent. In Friesland a maritime province with an important rural hinterland, four separate direct taxes (apart from succession duties) were imposed: on houses, land, woodland (where the sale value of timber was taken as base) and the traditional 'floreen renthe' originally levied by the Duke of Saxony in 1511. In Utrecht the provincial treasury left it to the principal municipalities (Utrecht, Amersfoort, Montfoort) to impose any number of a range of direct taxes: hearth, capitation, property and the antiquated 'oud schild geld' on old coinage. Even in Brabant administered directly by the Generality, the standard rate of $16\frac{2}{3}$ per cent varied in the enclaves of Kuik, Breda, Grave en Lande and the Meijerij of 's Hertogenbosch all of which inherited their ancient ducal taxes. The most bizarre situation of all obtained in the Stadholder's own backyard in Gelderland where a province of some 217,000 souls yielding a total revenue of 1½m guilders a year (compared, in the 1780s with Holland's 23m) was *sub-divided* into the three 'kwartieren' of Nijmegen, Zutphen and the Veluwe, each with its own receivers, collectors and exchequers. Thus the Zutphen verponding (1656) differed both in incidence and object from the Nijmegen verponding (1651) both of which differed again from the five categories of property tax levied in the Veluwe.[21]

The array of indirect taxes was no less miscellaneous or exhaustive. In Holland, as Gogel remarked 'everything was taxed except light and air'.[22] Neither the esoteric – elephant tusk and cochenil – nor the common-place – soap, salt, flour, butter, sugar, tea and beer – escaped their duties. Peat, the most common fuel for domestic and some industrial purposes, was taxed twice in Holland, once at the stage of cutting and again at purchase for consumption. There were three different kinds of tax on spirits; three on cattle and no less than eight on flour, related to the type and quality of grain. Comprehensive duties such as the 'waag' (by weight) and 'rondemaat' (by measure on dry goods) added further to the duplication of administration and the costs of collection. And aside from skimming 'additional' pennies from off the top of provincial taxes, many municipalities were entitled to impose their own duties, in particular local tolls and rights of passage. Despite the burden this placed on the ordinary consumer – or possibly because of it – indirect taxation was popular in the land provinces as well as their more commercial neighbours. In Nijmegen kwartier alone there were twenty-four separate duties.[23] A certain body of opinion, including the pensionary of Rotterdam and future champion of the Orange cause in 1813, Gijsbert Karel van Hogendorp, advocated indirect taxation as combining the merit of dependable and relatively inelastic source of revenue with the alleged virtue of being least oppressive (because least concentrated) for the payer. Van Hogendorp went so far as to suggest that it amounted to voluntary contribution, adjustable through varying patterns of consumption.[24] The Patriot economists, and notably Gogel and Metelerkamp insisted to the contrary that such duties were 'voluntary' only to those sacrificing items such as sugar, bread and beer from their diet, and that their indiscriminate incidence made them necessarily socially inequitable. They added the insight that it was these taxes which, by driving up the price of labour, had contributed to the uncompetitiveness of Dutch manufactures.[24] The bitter complaints of manufacturers, made to Johannes Goldberg the 'Agent for the National Economy' on his national tour in 1800, bore out the allegation that high duties, especially those on soap, grain and fuel, had played a part in aggravating the general economic distress.[25]

The advocates of Quota adjustment (in the 1780s) and of national taxes (in the 1790s) argued that the relative contraction of revenue was due, in part, to the shrinkage of inter- and intra-provincial commerce and to a quantitative decline in consumption during the latter half of the century. Modern research, notably that of Drs de Vries and van Dillen, has confirmed van de Spiegel's more optimistic contention that such a decline is difficult to establish and was restricted to specific commodities.[26] Certainly the more reliable *fiscal* indices of internal trade and consumption: 'waag' and 'rondemaat' show no marked downturn until the disasters following 1793 overtook the Republic. And, given the interruption in colonial supply, receipts from the duties on sugar, tea and coffee in Holland show little significant fluctuation.[27] But by the end of the eighteenth century these items had become relative luxuries in the diet of the common people. In the range of 'necessities': flour, fuel, beer, there is a decline in receipts ranging from 30 per cent and 40 per cent in the first two items to 400 per cent in the case of beer, suffering from the double trouble of Schiedam gin and the spreading ruralisation of local brewing.[28] The figures in Table 1, taken from the published five-yearly Holland receipts are not adjusted to take account of price fluctuations, but in almost all cases, and especially that of grain, any inflationary trend would accentuate the per item contraction.[29]

Table 1. *Holland: indirect tax receipts* (fl.)

	1750–6	1781–6	1791–6	1796–1801
Flour	17,361,847	13,665,376	12,848,812	12,241,844
Butter	1,672,229	1,158,248	1,125,302	?
Peat	12,380,954	7,757,455	7,593,169	7,486,710
Beer	4,091,438	2,318,917	1,719,221	1,355,944

Indirect taxation, to be sure, accounted for between 50 and 60 per cent of the average revenue of Holland between 1871 and 1794. But the trend of receipts is sufficiently discernible to lend at least a grain of plausibility to the complaint that the disproportionate liability of the maritime provinces no longer reflected changing economic circumstances. In fact by the time that the revolutionary wars had bitten deeply into the Dutch economy it was apparent that manufactures outside the maritime provinces, even those that had performed relatively successfully in the earlier eighteenth century – Amersfoort bombazines; Henegelo linen; cotton spinning at Eindhoven and Tilburg; tobacco at Groningen, had been levelled virtually flat along with more traditional products made in Holland.[30] This did not prevent Gogel from hammering home the point that it was no easier for an artisan in one of the most afflicted centres – Haarlem or Gouda – to pay his taxes than his counterpart in Arnhem or Delfzijl. Arguably it was the population of Zeeland and southernmost Holland (Maassluis and Middelharnis) who had been hardest hit. First French then British naval patrols had cut off the fishing fleets from their deep-sea catches and the annexation of Flanders by France in 1795 had deprived the artisans of their principal market for made-up goods.[31] The estimated per capita contributions given by the Schiedam regent Keuchenius in 1803 (Table 2) graphically illustrates the differentials.[32]

Table 2. *Ordinary tax receipts 1803* (*Keuchenius*)

	Souls	Ordinary taxes	per capita
Holland	828,532	24,375,000	fl.30
Gelderland	217,828	1,594,223	fl.7
Zeeland	82,212	2,100,000	fl.25
Friesland	161,513	3,455,000	fl.21.10
Utrecht	92,894	1,800,000	fl.19.10
Groningen	114,555	1,478,152	fl.13
Overijssel	135,060	932,773	fl.7

Correspondingly, Holland's quota which in the first twenty-five years of the republic's existence had risen from 52 to 57 per cent, remained at between 60 and 65 per cent for most of the eighteenth century. When, in 1672, Utrecht, Gelderland and Overijssel fell to the French its share rose to 68 per cent to cover the deficit.[33] It was one of the reformers' contentions that when, as in 1672–5 and again in 1781 and 1793–4 the Quota system collapsed under military strain, the burden of rescuing the republic from defenceless-ness was shouldered by extraordinary taxes levied principally from the mari-time provinces.

The most telling factor, however, was not that Dutch revenues had seriously contracted during the century between the two periods of protracted war. If anything they had slightly increased.[34] But the rate of increase had been dramatically overhauled by the steeply rising costs of equipping and maintaining naval and military forces equal to the task of keeping the wolves from the Republic's door. Comparing the figures in Table 3, it should be borne in mind that though for comparable seven-year periods, virtually the whole of the earlier period was one of active hostilities (and includes subsidies to allies and mercenaries) while of the later period (including fl.1,684,453 paid to the Prussian army in 1787) only two were war years.[35] The effects of this strain during the last years of the old republic showed up in the debt charges of Holland. Its capital sum had risen from around 150m in 1678 to over 400m in 1713. But mid-century retrenchment had succeeded in confining interest charges to below 15m. By 1789, however, the accelerating momentum of extraordinary loans, 'dons gratuits', lotteries and levies had begun to take its toll and in 1791 interest reached the record level of fl.18,276,015.[36] By comparison the debts of the other provinces were trifles. Together they amounted to a third of that of Holland. Friesland's debt, for example, stood at around 30m with an annual interest charge of about 1½m guilders. A far more serious liability was the moribund East India Company whose debt on the eve of the Batavian revolution in 1795 stood at fl.118m with charges of around 4m a year. Interest rates in general which throughout the century had remained around 2½ per cent went into reverse at the end of the 1780s when rates of 4 and even 5 per cent became common. At the finish of van de Spiegel's ministry the government was resorting to contracts with financiers at even 10 per cent and more.[37]

Table 3. *Holland: revenues and expenditures* (fl.)

	1671–7	1788–94
Ordinary revenue	147,914,115	169,171,241
Average per annum	21,130,587	24,238,734
Extraordinary revenue	23,222,457	58,628,803
Average extraordinary revenue p.a.	3,317,393	8,375,543
Aggregate revenue	171,136,752	227,800,044
Provincial debt	44,117,154	112,732,916
Military expenditure	100,281,720	103,185,248
Total expenditure	168,014,373	228,300,044

However grim the situation may have appeared in 1794 it was but a fore-taste of what was in store for the long-suffering Dutch in the years ahead. The fraternal embraces exchanged between General Pichegru and the euphoric Batavian Patriots in January 1795 did not extend to granting the Dutch their liberty gratis. Despite the pleas of the Batavian Revolutionary Committee to spare the country the worst evils of conquest, and the French profession to have waged war not on the Dutch people but the 'tyrant of Orange', it was obvious from the scouting mission of Citizens Cochon and Ramel, sent to make an inventory of Dutch wealth, that France was set to exploit its victory to the hilt.[38] The worst fears were duly confirmed in May when, after a concentrated campaign of bullying Sieyes and Reubell arrived in the Hague to oblige Pieter Paulus, the de facto leader of the new republic, to put his signature to a document of pure extortion. The Treaty of the Hague committed the Dutch to pay an indemnification of 100m guilders to their French brothers for delivering them from the Stadholder's yoke. A fleet of forty warships and an army of between 30,000 and 40,000 men was to be contributed to the alliance and a secret clause obliged the Dutch to pay and maintain 25,000 French troops until the conclusion of a general peace.[39] The burden of these penal obligations combined with the afflictions of requisitions and the obligatory reception of the *assignat*[40] combined to ensure that the Treaty of the Hague was, at the same time, the birth certificate and the death warrant of the Batavian Republic. It set off a chain of social and economic fission from which the new state never properly recovered.

Holland, of course, bore the brunt of the crisis. On his departure to England the Stadholder had obligingly issued a decree ordering all Dutch ships in British or allied ports to surrender to their custody. Paulus, who had himself been an officer of the Admiralty of the Maas, estimated that the rebuilding of a fleet in compliance with the Treaty would cost in the region of 10m guilders. 7m to 8m were to be raised in Holland. Ship-building had become an expensive business at the end of the eighteenth century. In 1782 van de Spiegel had ruefully reflected that de Ruyter's fleet of a hundred ships with forty pieces each would scarcely be adequate to the demands of contemporary naval warfare. The largest ships of the line in the 1790s had seventy pieces and fully equipped could cost anything between 700,000 and 800,000 guilders.[41] It says much both for the energy of the revolutionary authorities and for the eagerness of the Rotterdam and West Zaandam yards for work that by March 1796 the fleet was almost at full strength. The French army proved an expensive bodyguard. In the first year it cost the Batavian Republic nearly 13m guilders – though in succeeding years its costs diminished to an average of 10m, along with its numbers.[42] The result of these engagements was a deficit on ordinary revenue in Holland of 32m in 1795 and 41m in 1796.[43] The difference was made up by a cascade of extraordinary impositions which in retrospect made van de Spiegel's exactions seem like a light shower. Few of them yielded their optimised estimates. Thus an elaborately designed levy on incomes, stepped progressively from 3 per cent to 37.5 per cent and bearing interest of 3 per cent was superseded in August by a forced levy of 6 per cent on property bearing $2\frac{1}{2}$ per cent. A lottery launched in February 1796 for 18m raised only 10m.[44] And the voluntary loan announced by the States-General in June 1795 eventually became a 'don gratuit' accompanied by severe sanctions of confiscation or arrest for malefactors.

Although the 'Provisional Representatives of the People of Holland' protested that the inquities of the old regime were being perpetuated in a de facto Quota, the land provinces were certainly not profiting at Holland's expense. Brabant had been the theatre of war in both 1793 and 1794 and Gelderland and Overijssel had experienced the double plague of a chaotic British retreat followed by comprehensive French requisitioning. In the Gelderland kwartieren direct taxes were increased by two and three times and the authorities in Brabant were forced to take anticipations on revenue not only for 1796 but 1797. Utrecht levied special taxes on all corporations and in Groningen and Brabant the daring step was taken of taxing the property of the Reformed Church.[45]

Despite this confused improvisation the revolution of 1795, at least in theory, liberated the republic from the shackles which the federal Union had placed on reform. The abolition of the Stadholderate and the sovereign assemblies of the States; the dissolution of the States-General in November 1795 and its replacement by an elected constituent national assembly the following March gave an unprecedented opportunity for the establishment of a national system of taxation. Such an outcome, however, was far from a foregone conclusion. The more the orators of the Assembly chorused the unity of the republic 'One and Indivisible' (a motto which took on a special resonance in the Netherlands) the more obvious it became that the impact of war and revolution had been, initially, to shatter the country into its constituent cells. Power had passed – for the most part bloodlessly – to a multitude of local notables: lawyers, predikants, journalists, professors, notaries, petty officials or suburban tradesmen whose authority often extended no further than the district club or parish church where their committees were elected by acclamation.[46] The elections to the National Assembly; the abrasive press campaigns and the militant posturing of the radical clubs in the cities all revealed that almost the only feature uniting the legatees of Orangist power was their common hatred of the departed enemy. A fundamental cleavage separated not only democrats from patricians but those who saw the Batavian Republic cast in the matrix of a unitary sovereign state, and those who clung to the federalism of the old Union. The paradoxical (but predictable) situation came about whereby the body elected to offer to the Dutch people their national constitution was itself dominated by a majority of relatively conservative federalists. Pending the ratification of that constitution by popular vote the Assembly was bound by its governing ordinance not to encroach on the sovereign jurisdiction of the provinces.[47]

It was recognised at the outset by both parties to the conflict that the power of the purse would in all likelihood decide the fate of the constitution. The initial skirmishes between groups identified as 'federalist' and 'unitarist' involved the vexed issue of the amalgamation of the provincial debts, an obvious prelude to full fiscal unification. The motion to this effect introduced on 2 May 1796 by Vreede, Blok and Bosch (respectively a textile manufacturer and two zealot predikants) was decisively defeated. The representatives of the land provinces considered the disproportion between their respective deficits and the monstrous growth of Holland's 600m and regarded the invitation to assume their 'patriotic duties' as an offer of ball and chain. Nor were they much appeased by the reasoning of the ex-pensionary of Haarlem, van de Kasteele, that they consider not the outsize capital sum but the piddling 20m of interest.[48] By the spring of 1797 the situation had become more fluid. The die-hard federalists had not budged an iota in their opposition to amalgamation. But riots in Rotterdam and Amsterdam and the tirades of the radical clubs and newspapers had persuaded the less doctrinaire members to go some way to meeting the unitarists' principles. With an eye on producing a constitutional draft with some chance of finding acceptance in the primary assemblies it was agreed to establish a sub-committee to amend it in accordance with the general premise of financial unity and the amalgamation of the debts.[49]

The compromise constitution, however, ended by pleasing nobody. Both ultra-federalists and radical democrats had cause for complaint and their combined vote ensured its rejection by the primary assemblies on August 8 1797. This was grist to the unitarists' mill. In the second National Assembly elected a few days before the plebiscite they were on virtually equal terms with the federalists and held the whip-hand in the vital constitutional sub-committees. The more aggressive among them like Vreede and the ex-predikant journalist Willem Ockerse determined not only that the principle of financial unity be embodied in the constitution but that it provide for the introduction of a national system of taxation within a specified period of time.[50] Even before the work of drafting had been completed, however, an opportunity arose to test their strength in the altered balance of political forces. On 11 October the Texel fleet restored by so much effort and at so great a cost was destroyed by Admiral Duncan in the last of the great Anglo-Dutch naval engagements, the battle of Camperdown. Admiral de Winter had fought doggedly, surrendering only when his flagship was dismasted and wrecked by broadside fire. The city of Amsterdam which fêted his return from British captivity seemed to treat the occasion as one for epic stanzas rather than mourning. But the more sober members of the National Assembly understood only too well the magnitude of the calamity. Somehow more money would have to be found to rebuild the fleet from scratch. It was agreed that a 'general tax on all the citizens of the Republic without exceptions or distinctions' would have to be imposed, but the precise ways and means were left open to debate. Orthodox interest-bearing levies on property were initially proposed but on 14 November van de Kasteele's committee on finance produced a more radical suggestion. Possibly taking their cue from Pitt's administration, an 8 per cent tax on income was proposed, beginning at a floor of 300 guilders.[51] Its [reception was stormy. The federalist rearguard insisted, quite correctly, that any imposition levied on a national basis constituted a violation of the assembly's terms of reference. In reply many of the representatives from Holland declared that in future they would deny assent to *any* tax unless it were raised equally from the whole nation. Van de Kasteele himself presented the measure as one of patriotic emergency which as in 1672 overruled legal niceties and it was in this vein of high moral principle that the tax was advertised from press and pulpit. After the first vote was lost by the hair's breadth of 42–44, journals like Gogel's *De Demo-craten* and Hespe's *Constitutioneele Vlieg* printed petition papers urging support 'For Freedom and Fatherland'. In Amsterdam a consortium of businessmen clubbed together to present an entire ship of the line to the nation, and a wealthy widow in Haarlem engaged to equip a frigate. Such was the lather worked up by the campaign that public opposition to the tax began to smack of treason. At the end of November the Eindhoven unitarist Jan van Hooff declared in the Assembly with Cromwellian finality 'No more discussion. We must have a fleet. Without a fleet the Fatherland cannot be saved.'[52] On the 30th of that month the tax was carried by fifty-eight votes to fifty-four. A whiff of pyrrhic victory lingered over the decision since at the same time it was agreed to seek the consent of the provinces for the measure. But such was the momentum behind the tax that notwithstanding the negative verdict returned by every province bar Holland and Utrecht (with Zeeland undecided) the Assembly endorsed its implementation on 16 January 1798.

Like other disputes between the maritime and the land provinces earlier in Dutch history, the navy tax debates of 1797 marked an important political turning point, but they also eroded the resistance to financial unification. But even though the 8 per cent tax went into effect in April 1798 it was in political circumstances which ensured that the issue would remain in the balance for seven years. On 22 January a section of the radical democrats, led by Wybo Fijnje and Pieter Vreede and egged on by the French minister Charles Delacroix carried out a coup d'etat against the assembly, purging it of two-thirds of its members and arresting the federalist leaders.[53] The long period of executive vacuum was ended with the establishment of a five-man Directory occupying much the same relationship to the legislature as its French counterpart.[54] The new constitution (which would certainly have been enacted without the assistance of armed purges) was ratified on 23 April by a majority almost as large as the veto of the previous August. It was meant as the seal on the liquidation of the old federation of the seven United Provinces. Provincial sovereignty was abolished in favour of the collective and indivisible 'sovereignty of the Batavian people'; local administrations reduced to impotent satraps of the central government and the boundaries of the historic provinces radically re-drawn to create eight new 'departments'.[55] In addition to the Directory ministerial 'Agencies' including (in 1800) that of National Economy, and Finance, were appointed by, and responsible to, the national executive. Commissioners were assigned to each departmental administration to ensure that the will of the government was obediently executed. In short, conditions seemed ideal for the realisation of financial reform. But the radical leaders, with a perverse dedication to political suicide, frittered away their advantage by alienating all but the militant democrats through indiscriminate and clumsy electoral purges and the flouting of their own constitution.[56] The counter-coup; the 'floréal' to January's 'fructidor' which eventually materialised on 12 June was actually instigated by three of the agents, among them the Agent for Finance, Isaac Gogel.[57]

It was, therefore, only in the autumn of 1798 when a constitutionally elected 'Representative Assembly' had convened that Gogel could turn his attention to the interrupted business of fiscal reform. The April constitution had stipulated that a draft scheme be presented to the legislature within the year and that a 'system of general taxation' be in operation in two years at the outside. This timetable was no hardship for Gogel who had been ruminating on his grand design since 1796 when its basic principles had been set out in *De Democraten*.[58] The centralisation of finance and the equalisation of liability was to entail the abolition of not only the autonomy of provincial treasuries but all locally imposed dues and taxes. The costs of departmental adminstration were to be underwritten by national funds and their budgets approved by the government. Where necessary they would be supplemented by the authorisation of 'additional pennies' imposed as a surcharge on national taxes. The weight of the fiscal burden was to be shifted from indirect to direct taxation and the range of excises and imposts reduced to a standard seven or eight. A single national verponding was to replace all the differing provincial land taxes and new sumptuary taxes were to ensure that the burden of contributions fell on those best able to support them. The whole system was to be administered by a hierarchy of salaried officials strictly accountable to government and legislature for all their transactions. Gogel's draft law was set before the legislature on 30 June 1799, but the distraction of the Anglo-Russian invasion that September and the less than mercurial pace at which the Assembly conducted its business meant that the commission assigned with its review could not report until the following July. Its criticisms, directed principally at the emphasis on direct property taxation and the costs of administration were collated into a counter-project by Gogel's rival the young Zeelander J. H. Appelius and were adopted by the First Chamber. It was only due to the peculiarities of the bicameral procedure for legislation that Gogel's original plan finally prevailed on 25 March *1801*.[59]

No sooner had the reform surmounted its last legal hurdle, however, than it was confronted by fresh political obstacles. In September 1801 the reactionary climate of Consular France caught up with the Batavian Republic. Frustrated in their efforts to induce the legislature to amend the unitary constitution out of existence three of the patrician Directors, abetted by General Augureau (who was something of an expert in matters of this sort) killed it off by decree, forcibly liquidating the Assembly at the same time. The ci-devant marquis de Sémonville, the French minister at the Hague, had little difficulty in persuading Bonaparte that the Dutch would prove more efficient, and less grudging clients if governed by their traditional oligarchs and according to the conventions of the federal union. A 'Dutch mediation' was thus imposed based on the reversion to provincial sovereignty and decentralised administration. The Directory was replaced by a twelve man 'State Regency' and the agencies by collegiate councils, very much as under the old republic. The legislature was reduced to the ornamental status of the Consular bodies and lost the right of initiative. In the provinces those patricians and even Orangists who had lost their offices in 1795 were restored and their administrations resumed full responsibility for finance. A national 'Council of Finance' presided over by a 'Treasurer-General' (initially the Overijssel baron de Vos van Steenwijk) was confined to 'those matters not otherwise entrusted to other Persons or Colleges'.[60] The overall effect was counter-revolutionary.

A farcical plebiscite in which mass abstentions were counted as 'tacit affirmatives' in order to reverse the verdict of the votes cast demonstrated that the restoration of federalism was not particularly popular. Nor was it financially salutary. Three years of fumbling equivocation followed by four of administrative chaos despatched what was left of the Republic's finances to its ruin. The costs of defeating the Anglo-Russian expedition had inflated the expenditure for 1799 and 1800 to well over 70m and the deficit over ordinary revenue to nearly 40m. The impermanence of the peace of Amiens had been a bitter disappointment as the revival of trade during the brief respite had given some grounds for optimism.[61] It was quite clear to the leaders of the Batavian Republic that their French ally was bent on bleeding the Netherlands white but so long as neither the Prussians nor the British would hear of neutrality sans Stadholder they were trapped by the compact of 1795. Bonaparte, who had initially seemed receptive to their complaints about the enormities of French privateering against neutral shipping, remained sympathetic only so long as he believed he could soak the Dutch for an easy loan prior to the Italian campaign of 1800. Not a man to forgive rejected overtures the failure to secure those funds from Amsterdam ensured his future indifference to the gradual destruction of all economic life in the Netherlands in the years ahead. Far from responding to requests for a commercial treaty, high tariff walls cut off not only France, but important traditional markets like Brabant, Flanders and the Rhineland from Dutch manufacturers as well as vital raw materials.[62] Any concession had an exorbitant price tag. The *promise* of an eventual reduction of French troops on the conclusion of peace in 1801 cost the Batavian Republic 6m guilders; the return of Nassau property taken by the French 3m more. In 1803, on the resumption of hostilities a new convention required the Dutch to furnish three flotillas for the invasion of England: supplies and transport for 25,000 men and 2,500 horses; five frigates; a hundred armed longboats and 250 small gunboats.[63] That same year it was calculated that citizens of the French Republic were paying, per capita, 15.18 francs in taxes; those of the Batavian Republic the equivalent of 64.25 francs. Between 1795 and 1804 it was estimated that the Dutch had paid over 229m guilders to the French or rather more than the gross annual income of the entire republic.[64] Since 1787, 340m had been paid in forced levies on property; 35m on income;

90m as 'dons gratuits' and 280m in interest-bearing paper had been issued which by 1804 had depreciated to 114m specie value.[65] The unnerving and seemingly endless succession of extraordinary impositions had swollen the already bloated debt to the grotesque capital figure of fl.1,126m, and to the fateful point where annual interest charges were overtaking ordinary revenue (Table 4).[66]

Table 4. *Dutch deficit 1800–1805* (fl.)

	Estimated military expenditure	Estimated total expenditure	Estimated debt interest	Deficit on ordinary revenue
1800	32,203,823	77,993,884	28,792,139	44,193,884
1801	32,308,714	71,353,319	29,662,448	38,874,393
1802	18,137,000	65,992,569	29,935,306	32,192,569
1803	appr. 32.1m	73,497,628	30,903,084	38,497,628
1804	26,030,112	72,944,779	31,990,249	37,944,779
1805	31,732,513	72,236,936	33,882,694	37,232,936

By the autumn of 1804 the Batavian Republic was dead on its feet. The predicament of the national government was mirrored in the steeply rising deficits of the principal cities unable to carry the expanding burden of poor relief without subsidies from the departmental and national treasuries.[67] The foundation of the old federation – the financial autonomy of towns and provinces – was threatened far more seriously by economic crisis than by unitarist ideology. Schimmelpenninck, the ambassador in Paris who in 1796 had written to Gogel that 'the financial state of the nation is parlous but not altogether hopeless', was more fatalistic eight years later. Attempting to make Bonaparte comprehend the plight of his country he described it to him

impoverished by huge losses, surcharged with a terrifying debt; crushed by the weight of intolerable taxes and the forcible extraction of both capital and income; undergoing all the torments of a dreadful agony and having before it only the dismal vision of its imminent disintegration.[68]

Aware that such appeals rarely succeeded in tugging at the heart strings of the First Consul Schimmelpenninck added that his remarks were prompted not by 'a panic-stricken terror' but were 'the fruit of long reflection and a profound knowledge of the true state of affairs'. What really appalled him, however, was that 'in the view of this (French) government our country no longer has any political or civilian existence. This land is one great military camp and ours is but one of its forward posts.'[69] Only two factors prevented Bonaparte from administering the coup de grâce. First he was not at all anxious to saddle France with the Dutch debt. And secondly, for all their pleas of poverty, he continued to believe that vast hoards of treasure lay stockpiled in the vaults of Amsterdam. As long as there was more to wring from the Dutch it would be foolish to abrogate the contract by which they paid their protection money for even a simulacrum of national independence.

On the other hand the pretensions of Dutch sovereignty could under no circumstances be permitted to sabotage the efficiency of the French military machine. The presence in the national and departmental administrations of confessed Orangists; their suspected connivance in the smuggling of British goods and their hankering for neutrality at a time when they should have been devoting themselves to the preparations for the invasion of Britain persuaded Bonaparte, in April 1804 that more dependable men had to be placed in charge of the troublesome satellite. Taking advice from Schimmelpenninck and (via Marmont, the commandant at Zeist) Gogel, a 'Batavian Common-wealth' was concocted with a constitution the exact antithesis of the 1801 model. The titles of 'Grand Pensionary' for its presidential executive and 'Their High Mightinesses' for the members of the rubber-stamp legislature were meant to appeal to historical sentimentality and the Dutch penchant for republican ceremony, while a highly centralised and *dirigiste* bureaucracy, eradicating all anachronisms of local and corporate jurisdictions was to pull together a disjointed administration.[70] The formula was to be: Schimmel-penninck for popularity; Gogel for efficiency. The 'Pensionary' would him-self have much preferred an 'American' hybrid of federal and unitary principles (with himself as the Dutch Washington). But what proved persuasive was Gogel's insistence that the general tax system, as well as an executive power-ful enough to give it effect, were the sine qua non of a new government. After elaborate diplomacy in the autumn of 1804 Gogel and his taxes were foisted on Schimmelpenninck whether he liked them or not.[71] On 1 January 1806 the new system came into effect and when the Pensionary's blindness gave Bonaparte the pretext for placing his brother Louis on the throne of a 'Kingdom of Holland' the minister and his administration were retained along with much of the constitution of 1805. With modifications in 1807 and 1809 it remained the basis of Dutch public finance until 1812 when the re-latively lighter French taxes were introduced into what had become the Dutch departments of the French Empire. In 1814 Gogel declined to accept office from William I. But the advice he gave (in circumstances of somewhat elaborate secrecy) in 1821 served as the basis for a system which was, in part, a resuscitation of the principles of 1805.[72]

The introduction of his fiscal reforms under regimes for which he had little political sympathy may perhaps be taken as evidence of Gogel's addic-tion to bureaucratic formulae. And it may well be that he inflated both the significance and the novelty of the new system. Neither the British govern-ment which introduced the income tax in 1797 nor the Austrian ministry

which imposed the *Klassensteuer* two years later are remembered as inno-
vators of daring radicalism. Both were obliged by military exigency to adopt
unpopular means of raising additional revenue. That the cause at stake for
the Dutch was one of national life or death might be said to be but a matter
of degree. Nor did Gogel take kindly to suggested amendments. When, in
1808 Louis appointed a committee of his Council of State (headed, it is true
by Appelius, the man who had blocked Gogel's way in 1800) the minister
of finance took violent umbrage, seeing the proposal as implied criticism of
his own administration. After a period of prolonged strain between the king
and himself he finally resigned in April 1809.[73]

Gogel's sensitivity to criticism was not, as the king supposed, the reaction
of an offended martinet, unable to tolerate the least tampering with the
bureaucratic machinery he had lovingly assembled, and quite deaf to the
protests of the suffering taxpayer. To the contrary it was the response of a
doctrinaire egalitarian. As a young man he had been a founder member of
the Amsterdam insurrectionary committee and through all the vicissitudes
of the Batavian Republic had preserved his democrat's convictions. Even
under a Bonapartist monarchy he cast himself in the role of the protector
of the little man, the honest burgher who worked 'by the sweat of his brow'
and who was 'infinitely worthier than the wealthy, proprietors of landed
estates and rentiers of funds, men who practise no occupation or trade for
their livelihood'.[74] It was the class of patricians and grandees – social dross
and public parasites – who had sacrified the republic to their own selfish
interests, obstructed reform and had brought it to its present shame and
impotence. Ejected by the revolution, they had wormed their way back to
office and even now infested the court and the legislature. Their claims to
speak up for popular grievances were nothing more than a hypocritical
disguise for a campaign designed to sabotage his efforts to redress the balance of fiscal liability.

As long, Sire, as taxes struck only at the labouring class nothing was heard from
these gentlemen, for no-one was interested in their lot; only the aristocracy was
exempt or evaded liability; it was a true scandal that much of their property was
self-assessed . . . and who now is interested in the poor artisan in this time of
distress when all means of commerce are lacking. . . ?

Certainly there was an aroma of the Patriot pulpit about such utterances.
Like much of the levelling evangelism in the Netherlands, Gogel's social
nostalgia harked back to a commonwealth of free citizens, thrifty and indus-
trious, which during the course of the eighteenth century had somehow
degenerated into a society of perruques and paupers. He subscribed to the
commonplace that an imbalance on the side of speculative finance had dis-
torted the Dutch economy and had placed it on hazardous foundations, and
he looked forward to the renascence of the staple market under more peaceful conditions. A great deal of this was wishful thinking, but in two respects

at least Gogel showed a better grasp of contemporary reality than his opponents. Van Hogendorp, who regarded extremes of wealth and poverty as a healthy feature of the natural economic order, also took the general diffusion of prosperity in a revived mercantile economy for granted. Gogel, on the other hand, addressed himself to a situation in which social differentiations were becoming more rather than less marked.[76] And if his critique at times verged on Jacobin platitudes, van Hogendorp's complacency eulogised a past that was really defunct.[77]

Gogel was equally unsentimental about the decease of the United Provinces. He insisted that 'nothing has done more harm to governments than the repeated resistance of towns based on their pretended powers and privileges'.[78] Van Slingelandt had said as much albeit in less combative style. For better or worse Gogel believed that the old, loose federation had crumbled under a pyramid of debt. Those who stood on the dignity of local autonomy he regarded as scavengers scrabbling to protect their perquisites at the expense of an impoverished community. Briefing Louis in 1806 he emphasised that the extreme decentralisation of government had contributed to the weakness of the republic.

It is easy to perceive that an edifice, so badly secured, was bound to collapse from the moment where the misfortunes of state had reached the point at which it was no longer possible to save it from total destruction without replacing the monstrous system of administration with another more suited to its needs.[79]

And to those who insisted on the impracticability of a single sovereign authority, Gogel reminded them that the whole country was no bigger than what, under the French monarchy had been the Generality of Rennes !

He was under no illusions that an increase of the national revenue could be accomplished without adding to the hardships of the people. But as will be apparent from his social views, Gogel was determined that the 'necessary evil' be more equitably distributed. In his memorandum on taxation written in 1820, he reiterated the fundamental axiom.

When a government finds itself in such calamitous circumstances that it is obliged to tax the people *heavily*, it behoves it, when, and in so far as it may, to see that every contributor pays according to his means, and that some assessment of them may be made in advance; that the middle class are not overburdened in order to spare the rich; that the taxes do not oppress the poor so that they may still have the possibility of bettering their condition; that work may be encouraged and industry not disheartened and the trades remain free and restricted as little as possible.[80]

This highly idiosyncratic melange of social paternalism and domestic *laisser faire* had not yet turned into the cliché of nineteenth-century liberal democracy. Coming from the Dutch financial official it was a distinct novelty. But without doubt it shaped Gogel's approach to the immediate business of staving off disaster. It meant, for example, that he wished to avoid the by now almost monthly excursions to the punch-drunk money market in search of loans at exorbitant rates of interest. And it was the inherently arbitrary nature of forced loans and levies which, he believed, was aggravating the predicament of those of modest means. Nor was he much attracted to the expedient, pressed on him by Bonaparte, of cutting or suspending interest payments on the national debt. 'Bankruptcies are easily declared and even more easily executed' he remarked, but did more harm than good in the long run. Although Dr Zappey suggests that it was only Goldberg's opposition in 1806 which prevented Gogel from toying with the idea, we know that in January 1807 he came out strongly against it. Apart from jeopardising the good faith of Dutch credit without which the whole house of financial cards might come tumbling down, Gogel appreciated that such a measure would bring ruin to thousands of small creditors of the state who at a time of relative commercial stagnation depended on interest payments as the major component of their livelihood.[81]

It was apparent, then, that the necessary increases would have to be made on *ordinary* revenue. Although the impact of the blow would be greater Gogel believed it might be cushioned somewhat if seen to be based on social equity and if known in advance. It was equally important to remove at least some of the most onerous duties on articles of primary consumption. The 1805 system did away with duties on butter, beer, sugar, tea, coffee and a few other lesser commodities and lowered the tariff on some dry goods. But however charitable he may have felt disposed towards the consumer, there were a number of valuable indirect taxes which the treasury could not afford to be without: peat, salt, soap, livestock and the 'weight' tax all remained and to make up for the losses incurred by the abolitions, the duty on spirits (on which Gogel frowned) substantially increased.[82] The immediate result was that while, in the land provinces the proportion of direct to indirect taxes remained very much the same, in Holland it rose from 40 to 60 per cent of total revenue. Gogel also took the view that the reduction in the number of indirect taxes, the abolition of local tariffs and the collection of the remaining duties by a staff of national officials would cut the costs of administration and necessarily reduce smuggling. The receipts for the more straightforward duties like salt and soap bore out his optimism, but the elaborate system of receipts, designed to share costs between producer and consumer, undoubtedly created problems for officials inured to less demanding habits.[83]

The principal innovations, however, were in the field of direct taxation. Their chief virtue, so far as Gogel was concerned, was their sensitivity to changes in personal circumstances and the possibilities offered for equitable assessment. Though influenced in his views by both Adam Smith and Necker, he was not an enthusiast for the physiocratic *impot unique*, nor was he so blinkered as to imagine that a tax on land would be exclusively appropriate for an economy so heavily oriented towards trade and finance. Both in 1798 and in 1804 he considered the possibility of introducing a general income tax, possibly on British lines, but ruled it out as involving unacceptable resorts to search, sequestration and imprisonment.[84] Gogel's guiding principle was that those components of an income which were accessible to accurate and relatively painless verification should serve as indices for a progressive assessment. As individual components (a servant or a second villa) were added or subtracted, the overall fiscal liability would alter correspondingly. The verponding (*not* as some historians have seemed to assume, a land tax, but an imposition on all forms of property) was adopted as the most important direct tax because the rental revenue or rental valuation on which it was based was open to legal certification. In the case of unrented property it would be liable to official assessment. Yielding between 20 and 25 per cent of total revenue (as against 10 per cent under the old Holland verponding) it was intended to tax the proprietor more heavily than the tenant. But generous allowances for the operational overheads of commercial premises; for the maintenance of dykes and polders in the case of agricultural land (and exemption for philanthropic, educational and religious properties) were so designed as to try and ensure that the tax imposed principally on fixed and not working capital.[85] Indeed Gogel was concerned to avoid discouraging capital investment in anything that could be construed as productive or commercial enterprise. Thus the only form of direct taxation on business was a stamp duty (also payable on legal deeds) proportionate to the value of the transaction. Unproductive forms of capital were heavily liable under the categories of sumptuary taxes on servants, pleasure carriages and horses; jewellery, furniture and estate duties. Even here Gogel was alert to the social ramifications. The furniture and movables tax began at a floor of 500 guilders aggregate value and the succession tax was remitted in the case where a household was peremptorily bereaved of its principal earner. The minister's own novelty was the 'personeel' levied according to rent *paid* and therefore in effect a 10 per cent rental surcharge. On the face of it this seems particularly unjust to the tenant who might be faced with a double penalty, from state and landlord, through an inflated rent. But Gogel's assumption was that rent formed a relatively inelastic proportion of overall domestic expenditure and therefore provided, through lease or contract, a simply verifiable guide to *net* means. His more important rider was that the correspondingly higher verponding liability would act as a bracing disincentive to proprietors raising their rents unreasonably. Personeel was meant to (and did) yield only a third of the sum produced by the verponding. The two taxes were opposite faces of the same coin. Either way, they fell neatly into the coffers of the state.[86]

The simplification and standardisation of the Dutch taxation system was accompanied by corresponding economies of administration. Instead of a

profusion of independent staffs of officials competing for the available perquisites the national hierarchy of officials was appointed by the ministry at
the Hague, was to be salaried according to the volume of fiscal turnover,
and subject to monthly certification of accounts. In essence there were to be
three separate sets of officials. The two hundred odd receivers (and a greater
number of sub-collectors) were organised into twenty-one districts, each
with a receiver-general, and were sub-divided into offices for direct and
indirect impositions.[87] A special commission for the regulation and assessment of the verponding was to be responsible directly to the minister (much
to the objection of the Council of State). The forty-eight inspectors comprised the second staff. Their duties were to report on the operation of the
whole fiscal system, check the relation of estimate and yield; monitor social
and economic effects and make recommendations for improvements to the
ministry and the king. Finally there was to be an independent corps of
advocate-fiscals appointed to hear cases of administrative abuse or complaints lodged by taxpayers against any member of the financial personnel.
Conscious of the tendencies of bureaucracies (however high-minded their
executives) to act arbitrarily, Gogel put up a stern resistance to the notion,
canvassed by the Council of State, that the fiscals were an expensive luxury
and could be conveniently absorbed into the duties of the prefectoral land-
drost. There was no doubt that the new system was more economic in
administration than the old. Before 1798 there had been nineteen receivers-
general for Holland alone. In 1806 there were twenty-one for the entire
kingdom. All told there could have been no more than six hundred officials
on the books of the ministry including the separate corps of customs men.[88]
In 1808 Gogel calculated that a revenue of around 50m guilders cost
fl.3,800,000 in administrative expenses and wages, or 8 per cent of the total.
Ten years later, under the Appelian system, it would cost King William 17
per cent of his revenue.[89]

Table 5. *Revenues and expenditures under the reformed tax system* (*fl.m*)

	Revenue	Verponding	Estimated expenditure
1805	35.78	—	72.2
1806	42.68	9.48	77.28
1807	46.59	9.19	75.73
1808	46.7	9.2	78.04
1809	50.5	10.45	70.0
1810	48.0	9.04	74.0

How far did the General Tax System fulfil the ambitious expectations of
its author? In one respect at least, he earned the sobriquet (not, I suspect

awarded by Appelius to flatter) of the 'juggler' (in Dutch, *gogelaar*!) In the first year of its operation the general system produced for the ordinary revenue of the state a net increase of 7m guilders (or 20 per cent) and in subsequent years increased again until the magic figure of 50m was finally achieved in 1809 (with the help of the annexation of East Friesland). This was notwithstanding the loss of 3½m guilders in customs revenue as a result of the application of the Continental System and the enforced closure of all Dutch ports in 1808. As Table 5 suggests, however, the increase was far from sufficient to meet the escalating demands of the war.[90] Louis, who all along was less optimistic than his minister of finance was forced to the gloomy conclusion that

as long as this war continues we cannot flatter ourselves that we shall succeed since it is impossible to reduce our armaments which constitute the principal items of expenditure. How can we think of a definitive amelioration when instead of concentrating on the liquidation of the arrears of the debt, it is necessary to contract new ones in order to provide for the excess expenditure?[91]

It was indeed the most depressing feature of the new system that it was unequal to Gogel's own primary objective of avoiding the evils of extraordinary finance. To cover the deficit and arrears accumulating in 1806, Louis was obliged, in March 1807, to place a loan for 40m in the hands of a consortium of guarantors which included the leading houses of Amsterdam – de Smeth, van Brienen, Hodshon, and Willink – most of whom were councillors of State. Redeemable in eighteen years the loan carried an interest of *seven* per cent and was to be serviced and redeemed by an income of 4m extracted from the revenues collected at Amsterdam. This was as nearly like tax farming as makes no difference and like similar expedients adopted in France represented a pure reversion to the practices of the old regime. Even worse was to follow. For the following April another loan, this time for 30m (reduced later in the year to 20m) was negotiated, to be serviced and redeemed by a special tax of 3m a year (reduced to 2m) imposed by *quota* (!) throughout the country and assessed according to the presumed fiscal income of each district. In terms of the principles on which the general tax system was based this was the purest heresy but even Gogel could see no alternative. As a result the interest payments on the national debt continued their dizzy ascent, reaching 38.8m in 1807 and 40.8m the following year.[92]

Moreover the operation of the new system demonstrated fairly conclusively (not least from the figures supplied by Gogel himself in 1821) that the long-standing grievances over inter-provincial fiscal allotment had been something of a red herring. For the difference between the yield of the new 'department' and the apportionments of the old Quota was not in fact very marked. In 1807, for example, Holland's share of the total revenue was in the region of 55 per cent against 62 per cent in the Quota of 1790. A comparative estimate of respective contributions *excluding* the verponding produces an even closer correspondence between reformed and unreformed shares.[93]

	Geld.	Brab.	Fries.	Overij.	Gron.	Zd.	Utr.	Dte.
1790	6%	5%	9%	3%	5%	3%	4%	1%
1807	5%	5%	9.3%	3%	4.9%	5%	7%	1%

The significant adjustments were in fact confined to the verponding where the shares in 1807 were, for 'Holland' 49%, and for the other departments:

Geld.	Brab.	Fries.	Overij.	Gron.	Zd.	Utr.
5.2%	6.2%	12.5%	2%	7%	7%	6%

Whether, as Gogel hoped, the social incidence of direct taxes was more evenly distributed within each province is very difficult to ascertain with any confidence. Certainly there is a great deal of circumstantial evidence in the shape of protests from landowners and proprietors of urban real estate not only in the land provinces but in Utrecht and Holland on the severity of the verponding and the 'injustice' of the rental valuations.[94] In 1808 Appelius took it on himself to bring these grievances to the attention of the king who, always anxious to please the 'nobility' of the court, took Gogel to task for the failings of his administration. The contention of the Council of State was that assessment would be fairer if based on current market values rather than the rental average over fifteen years. They also urged that verification be carried out by locally appointed men familiar with the circumstances of the area concerned. Gogel replied to the king that since market prices were depressed due to the war recession the treasury would certainly not profit from the amendment and that the proposed changes in valuation were tantamount to the re-introduction of self-assessment. It was vital, he remarked, that assessment be carried out by government-appointed officials with *no* interest in the neighbourhood rather than by men 'who could arrange the valuations according to their tastes and frustrate the purposes of the law.[95]

Doubtless Gogel was being prudent in his concern for impartial evaluation – all the more so since the receipts of the verponding fell below their estimates by 2m in the first two years of operation. But his inflexibility in this matter did little to ease the obviously formidable problems of administration. Appelius was not merely carping when he commented of the general system that 'it was viewed in the departments (accustomed to the old routine) with a very jaundiced eye, so that the officials there did only what they were absolutely required to do and the authorities charged with its supervision have shown the greatest inertia'.[95] Much of this was confirmed by the reports of the departmental inspectors. Van Swinderen in Groningen complained not only of the uncooperative attitude of local authorities, and of their reprehensible failure to regard themselves as 'national' officials, but also of the inexperience, casualness and even drunkenness of many of their own collectors and assessors. He added the observation that wages scaled to estimated receipts were an invitation to upward falsification, and recommended instead an increase in the fixed salary grades.[96]

Part of the problem undoubtedly lay with the quality of the personnel. Gogel would, of course, have liked to have initiated his system with a staff uncorrupted by ancient and time-honoured frauds yet sufficiently professional to carry out its duties efficiently. He was fortunate in that his immediate subordinates in charge of each sub-section of the ministry – Elias Canneman, Pieter Quint Ondaatje, Copes van Cattenburgh – were exceptionally able young men. In addition he was willing to take on capable and trustworthy officials like van Bruegel, the Commissioner for the Verponding, who had served their apprenticeship under the old regime. To some extent, moreover, the economies in the numbers of staff and the stipulation that all collectors and receivers be between twenty and forty-five years of age, numerate and literate, weeded out the more outrageous pluralists, fraudulent and superannuated. But the recruitment for many of the complicated tasks of assessment obviously left much to be desired. Schoolmasters, ex-predikants, and local notaries are prominent among the novices, but they also include the odd lamp-lighter and retired sexton. And despite the stringent prohibitions against pluralism, many continued to take second jobs to supplement what was not, by any criteria, a handsome wage. A bureaucracy equal to the rigorous demands of what, by 1809, had become the government of a single Dutch state, could not be created overnight. Nor was inexperience and confusion assisted by the immense sheaves of regulations and ordinances issuing from the Hague ministries, and which, in the years after 1814, would prove so noxious to King William's southern subjects.

There were, in any case, sound reasons why local authorities should have done their best to avoid the unwelcome attentions of the collectors and assessors. The intensity of the economic depression after 1807 was, for all Gogel's good intentions, obviously compounded by the weight of the general system. The enquiry into the condition of the national economy conducted by the landdrosten in 1808 revealed that many manufacturers attributed at least part of their difficulties to the level of duties imposed on a range of essential raw materials, and in particular, soap, grain and fuels.[97] With much of the Dutch economy (save the agricultural boom) in a derelict condition, and with nearly half the population of Amsterdam and a third of Rotterdam and Leiden on poor relief, it was little wonder that complaints against tax assessment were so ubiquitous and so bitter. In Nijmegen, for example, the local 'maire' complained that a householder who had paid four guilders twelve stuivers under the old kwartier-verponding was now assessed at eleven guilders four stuivers, when his maximum liability should in fact have been six guilders, seven.[98] The protests against the special 1808 tax of three (later two) millions revealed an even more pitiful plight in the smaller villages and towns. At Gansoijen in Brabant twelve souls, gathered in just three households (for like so many others this was a depopulated village), of which one was a hut and another inhabited by a widow and three children, were assessed at fifty-five guilders payable virtually on demand. Bleiswijk in south Holland, with 1,070 souls, nearly a third of them on relief and much of its cultivable acreage under water was billed at fl.1,970. The better-armed of the local magistrates made sure that they were in a position to challenge the estimates of the official assessors. At Soetermeer, near Leiden, the council insisted that, according to acreage and population they fell due for 1/379th part of the departmental quota, a figure computed at fl.2,180 and not the fl.3,025 given on their statement.[99]

Such protests were legion. If Gogel was fond of professing his compassion for the condition of the people, the affection was rarely reciprocated. It may not have been too much for Appelius to have suggested, in 1810 that since the Dutch were, in any case, enjoying only the most spurious counterfeit of national sovereignty, they would be prepared to submit to the humiliation of annexation if in return they were given some relief from the terrible burden of taxation. To put it another way, the price of survival *had* finally become too expensive. The French system did prove to be lighter than the Dutch. The *impôt foncier* was fixed at about 70 per cent of the verponding, and levied at 20 per cent of landed income rather than the mean 25 per cent of the Dutch tax. Dutch officials, not least Gogel himself, who became the 'Intendant-Général des Finances' were prepared to collaborate in the implementation of the imperial system in 1812 in the hope that it might give a much-needed respite to their countrymen. But the relief proved to be a very mixed blessing. Napoleon's decision to order a two-thirds reduction of interest payments on the debt was attended by all the miseries predicted by those who had opposed such a measure under the Kingdom. And if some taxes were lighter, others, just as onerous such as that on doors and windows, were newly introduced. The conduct of the armed French customs officials who set up special posts in the ports and in the centre of the major cities rapidly won them the execration of the population. It was not fortuitous that, at the moment of rebellion in 1813, it was the customs posts in Amsterdam which served as the beacon of revolt.[100]

It was paradoxical, then, that when the Dutch finally abandoned the unequal struggle to defend their national integrity against both ally and enemy, the lot of the mass of the population certainly got no better, and in some respects, notably conscription, hit a nadir under the French Empire. But as both Louis Bonaparte and Gogel conceded in their memoirs, no system of finance, however radical or inventive, could have satisfied the appetite of a war to which their native resources were simply no longer equal. These unhappy years were a watershed in the collective life of the Dutch people. For in spite of the patriotic heroics of the Batavian revolutionaries they were

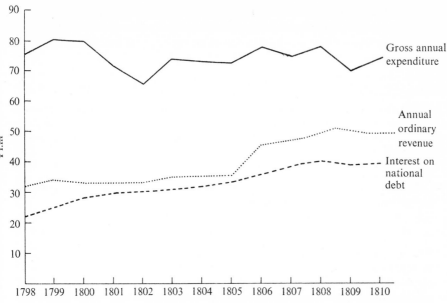

Fig. 1 The Dutch deficit 1798–1810, in fl.m. (Sources: GS, IV, 471–4; 483–6, 486, n. 1, 514–17, 516, n. 2. ARA, Gogel 29, 31, 142, 149; Canneman 30–1; Staatssecretarie 514, 516; Min. van Financian 390. Gogel, *Memorien*, Bijlage FF; Metelerkamp, II, pp. 68f., 81.)

forced to come to terms with a more modest future based on less remarkable but no less sensible institutions than under the old republic. Hence the true beneficiaries of the reforms were the administrators of the nineteenth-century liberal monarchy, and if Groen van Prinsterer consigned the Batavian Republic to a special category of treason and folly, Thorbecke, the constitutionalist of 1848, was at least prepared to give generous credit to his Batavian antecedents.[101] In the longer perspective the work of Gogel and his colleagues may well be seen as a necessary condition for the foundation of the second Dutch state. In 1805 Johannes Goldberg, Gogel's friend and associate had compared the Batavian Republic to a building in which a new superstructure had been placed precariously over foundations not yet properly demolished.[102] The establishment of a single sovereign government after two centuries of loose confederation meant that those who undertook the demolition work did so while they were still unsure of the shape of the new edifice. Had they been granted the luxury of peace their achievements might have been more considerable. But they were never to escape from the cruel predicament that the war which supplied the necessary condition of change also ensured the immediate frustration of reform. If the extraordinary epic of the expansion of republican France was financed by the genial cynicism that 'la guerre nourrira la guerre' the wretched experience of the Dutch,

5

as one of them observed, brought to mind the altogether more sober Colbertian adage that 'l'impôt ruine l'impôt'.[103]

NOTES

1 Crawfurd to Schimmelpenninck, 28 October 1804, Algemeen Rijksarchief, 's Gravenhage (hereafter ARA), Verzameling I. J. A. Gogel, 28.
2 In 1695 Gregory King put the per capita contributions of Englishmen, Frenchmen and Dutchmen at, respectively, £1.4.0, £1.5.0, £3.1.7. See Charles Wilson, 'Taxation and the decline of empires, an unfashionable theme' in *Bijdragen en Mededelingen van het Historisch Genootschap*, LXXVII (1963), p. 16; Adam Smith, *The Wealth of Nations* (Everyman's Library Edition, London, 1910), Book v, ch. II, Art. IV, p. 388. See also R. Metelerkamp, *De Toestand van Nederland in Vergelijking met die van Enige Andere Landen van Europa*, 2 vols. (Amsterdam 1804), II, pp. 106 ff.
3 ARA, Gogel 6; see also the figures given in L. P. van de Spiegel's 'Schets tot een vertoog over de intrinsique en raletieve magt van de Republyk' (1782), (ed. J. de Vries) in *Economisch Historisch Jaarboek*, XXVII (1955–1957), p. 97; P. Geyl, *Geschiedenis van de Nederlandse Stam* (Amsterdam and Antwerp, 1958), II, p. 298.
4 Metelerkamp, *De Toestand van Nederland*, II, p. 73.
5 Wilson, 'Taxation and the Decline of Empires', p. 20.
6 For the conduct of Dutch policy in the mid-century, see Alice Clare Carter, *The Dutch Republic in Europe in the Seven Years' War* (London 1971), passim.
7 For an account of the elaborate diplomatic manoeuvres at the climax of the Patriot revolution see Alfred Cobban, *Ambassadors and Secret Agents* (London 1954), pp. 139–83.
8 Van de Spiegel, 'Schets tot een vertoog', p. 98.
9 It was only in July 1787 that de Castries and Montmorin, the advocates of military support for the Dutch Patriots, were outvoted in Council. Even after this they despatched two hundred artillerymen to the Woerden garrison and for two months bluffed the British and Prussians into believing that a 'camp' had been established at Givet, at the southern extremity of the republic, adjacent to the Bishopric of Liege, ready to parry threatened intervention on the Stadholder's behalf. When the bluff was called the Patriots found to their cost that there was no money – and no troops.
10 For a sympathetic account of the continuity of the efforts to reform financial administration in France, see J. F. Bosher, *French Finances, 1770–1795* (Cambridge 1970); in particular pt 2, chs 7–11.
11 R. R. Palmer, *The Age of Democratic Revolution* (Princeton 1959–1964), vol. 1, chs II–IV, emphasises the role of administrative and financial reform in sparking the revolts of 'constituted bodies' which in due course was to assume a more radical character.
12 Article 5 of the Union stated that at regular intervals taxes 'for the common defence' should be levied 'on one footing' should be levied in all the provinces. This was taken by successive generations of reformers in the eighteenth century as their authority for introducing greater uniformity of taxation. See ARA, Gogel 6; J. A. Sillem, *De Politieke en Staathuishoudkundige Werkzaamheid van Isaac Jan Alexander Gogel* (Amsterdam 1864), p. 167.
13 See J. Smit, *Inventaris van het Archief van de Financien van Holland* (ARA typescript, 1947); for details of the 1751 regulations – and of their liberal

violation – see ARA Gogel 7 (Financien van het Voormalig Gewest van Holland).

14 *Memorie houdende het Generaal Rapport van het Personeele Commissie van het Financie Wezen* (May 1790). See also ARA, Gogel 7 for the petition of the States of Zeeland and the 'request' of Greffier Fagel to the States-General concerning the enquiry.

15 *Ibid.* para. 61.

16 Metelerkamp, *De Toestand van Nederland*, pp. 47–9.

17 'Mémoire relativement à l'organisation et aux opérations du ministère des finances', ARA, Gogel 40.

18 The classic rehearsal of the arguments of the 'constitutional purists' was the *Grondwettige Herstelling van Nederlands Staatswezen*, 2 vols (Leiden 1784–6). for a discussion of its place in the Patriot revolution and its highly prescriptive appeal, see C. H. E. de Wit, *De Strijd tussen Aristocratie en Democratie in Nederland 1780–1848* (Heerlen 1965), pp. 38–41.

19 Metelerkamp, *De Toestand van Nederland*, II, p. 19.

20 One of the most informative accounts of the historical idiosyncrasies of provincial financial administration is to be found in the report prepared for the constitutional debates of the Batavian National Assembly and published in 1797 as *Stukken betrekkelyk den Staat der Financiën ven de respective gewesten der Nederlandsche Republiek*; see also ARA, Gogel 6, 7.

21 *Ibid.*

22 ARA, Gogel 40.

23 ARA, Gogel 6.

24 See, for example, ARA, Collectie Goldberg 59, 'the greater expense of the necessities of life is inextricably connected with the higher taxes of the State, and from these the higher wages of labour have contributed to the damaging of industry and commerce'; Wilson, 'Taxation and the Decline of Empires', pp. 20–6.

25 ARA, Goldberg 27, 'Journaal der Reize van den Agent van de Nationale Oeconomie der Bataafsche Republiek' (1800); L. van Nierop, 'Eene enquete in 1800. Eene bijdrage tot de economische geschiedenis der Bataafsche Republiek', *De Gids*, LXXVII, 3 (1913); W. M. Zappey, *De Economische en Politieke Werkzaamheid van Johannes Goldberg (1763–1828)* (Alphen aan den Rijn-Brussels 1967), pp. 48–52. Soap-boiling was one of the surviving industries of any magnitude in Amsterdam, and the duty affected the bleachers and starch-makers in addition; the distillers at Delft and Schiedam were among those protesting most urgently against grain and fuel taxes.

26 J. de Vries, *De Economische Achteruitgang der Republiek in de Achttiende Eeuw* (Amsterdam 1959), passim; J. G. van Dillen, *van Rijkdom en Regenten* ('s Gravenhage 1970), pp. 616–48.

27 ARA, Gogel 47, 49. Figures from five-yearly returns of 'Collectieve Middelen' for Zuider and Neder-Kwartieren. The tea and coffee duties for the period 1750–56 amounted to fl.1,774,283; for 1796–1800, fl.1,469,430.

28 *Ibid.* Distillers, as well as brewers, were affected by high duties and the expense of grain and juniper during the war, but their difficulties led to a thinning-out rather than the destruction of what, in the eighteenth century, had been something of a boom industry. The Frisian distillers were particularly concerned that their local markets were being captured by cheaper Holland brands. See ARA Goldberg 27. Brewing suffered particularly from the high French tariff on Flemish hops.

29 ARA, Gogel 47–9.
30 For graphic documentation of the experience of Dutch manufactures between 1800 and 1808, see ARA (1795–1813) Binnenlandse zaken 783–6. At Amersfoort, for example, the number of finished bombazine pieces fell from 39,000 in 1804 to 19,877 in 1808; at Tilburg of the five remaining cotton manufactures only one was operative at the later date.
31 ARA Goldberg 27. In 1793 the French had seized twenty-three fishing boats from the Maasluis herring fleet and twenty-four from Vlaardingen; from 1795 to 1800 the British had taken a further twenty-five from Maassluis and forty-one from Vlaardingen. Over *half* the population of Maassluis was supported by poor relief in 1800.
32 W. M. Keuchenius, *De Inkomsten en Uitgaven der Bataafsche Republiek Voorgesteld in Eene Nationale Balans* (Amsterdam 1803), p. 102.
33 The exceptional 1672 quota was divided: Holland, fl.68; Zeeland fl.10; Friesland fl.13; Groningen fl.6; the 1781 Holland share was fl.62 (of 100); Metelerkamp, *De Toestand van Nederland*, II, p. 19.
34 The 'collective ordinary taxes' (excluding customs and verponding) for the seven years 1671–7 amounted to fl.51,287,882; those for the corresponding period 1788–94 to fl.72,504,079. Metelerkamp, *De Toestand van Nederland*, pp. 33, 47, 57.
35 *Ibid.*
36 *Ibid.* p. 81.
37 ARA, Archief Wiselius 10; Geyl, *Geschiedenis van de Nederlanse Stam*, II, pp. 192–4; J. van der Meulen, *Studies over Het Ministerie van van der Spiegel* (Leiden 1905), p. 405 ff., Metelerkamp, *De Toestand van Nederland*, II, p. 25.
38 See H. T. Colenbrander (ed.), *Gedenkstukken der Algemeene Geschiedenis van Nederland 1789–1840* (s' Gravenhage 1905–1911), I, pp. 612–25.
39 The Batavian Republic continued to pay for the 25,000 troops (at a cost of about 10–11m guilders a year) even when, as in 1798 there were no more than *ten* thousand French actually stationed in the country.
40 In 1795 the provisional government of the republic instituted a scheme by which Dutch traders received assignats at a fixed exchange rate, and were then reimbursed in guilders (or bills) at the rate of 1 livre = 9 stuivers. Local and provincial authorities saddled with this onerous responsibility were nearly bankrupted in the process. See, for example, Joh. Theunisz, *Overijsel in 1795* (Amsterdam 1943), pp. 42–50, 68, 73.
41 Van de Spiegel, 'Schets tot een vertoog', p. 98. See also C. N. Fehrmann, *Onze Vloot in de Franse Tijd* ('s Gravenhage 1969).
42 ARA, Gogel 40; F. N. Sickenga, *Geschiedenis der Nederlandse Belastingen, Tijdvak der Omwenteling* (Amsterdam 1865), pp. 12–26.
43 ARA, Gogel 7.
44 *Ibid.* Sickenga, *Geschiedenis des Nederlandse Belastingen*, p. 12.
45 See E. van Voorthuijsen, Hz., *De Directe Belastingen* (Utrecht 1848), ch. VI, pp. 192–9.
46 As in France 'the' revolution and the events in the metropolitan centres concealed an infinite number of local revolutions, each governed by the particular issues of the region: religious cleavages; bitterness between town and country, or against a particular family or group of particians. In some areas the situation simply reverted to the status quo ante Brunswick, 1787; in others new issues emerged. In Brabant, for example, the relationship of what had been the Generality's territory, and thus deprived of provincial rights, to the central

government, was a highly emotive issue both in the clubs and popular assemblies and at the level of provincial administration. See *De Vrijwoording van Noord Brabant* (Voorlezing, G. W. Vreede) ('s Hertogenbosch 1859). For an account of the municipal revolutions in Holland, see C. Rogge, *Tafereel van de Geschiedenis der Jongste Omwenteling in der Vereenigde Nederlanden* (Amsterdam 1796), pp. 260–320.

47 The guarantee against encroachment on provincial prerogatives and, it was assumed, against a forcible consolidation of the debts, were the *conditions* insisted on by the delegates of the land provinces, and Overijssel in particular, for assenting to the dissolution of the States-General and the election of a national representative legislature. See Rogge, *Tafereel van de Geschiedenis*, pp. 591–610.

48 ARA, Gogel 6; Sickenga, *Geschiedenis der Nederlandse Belastingen*, pp. 40ff. The second largest provincial debt was that of Friesland (1796), capital fl. 31,706,933; interest fl.1,232,653.

49 Having failed to win consensus for an impotent formula which, while proclaiming the *principle* of 'unity and indivisibility' would have left the provincial financial autonomy intact, Schimmelpenninck, the 'archi-moderate' bowed to unitarist criticism. For the critique of the first constitutional draft clauses on finance and proposals for unification see C. Rogge, *Geschiedenis der Staatsregeling voor het Bataafsche Volk* (Amsterdam 1799) pp. 190–4; *Dagverhaal der Handelingen van de Nationale Vergadering*, III, pp. 683–93; *Advies van den Burger P. L. van de Kasteele op het Overgegeven Plan Van Eener Constitutie voor 't Volk van Nederland* (1797) (Knuttel Catalogus 22704).

50 ARA, Verzameling Ockerse, i–iv.

51 *Gedenkstukken*, II, p. 331.

52 See the reports in *De Democraten*, ARA Gogel 173; Geyl, *Geschiedenis van der Nederlandse Stam.*, III, p. 575.

53 For an account of the coup of 22 January 1798 see de Wit, *De Strijd tussen Aristocratie en Democratie*, pp. 153–9.

54 There were some very important differences between the French constitution of 1795 and the Dutch of 1798, overlooked by Colenbrander and emphasised by de Wit, *De Strijd tussen Aristocratie en Democratie*, Bijlage II, pp. 397–403. The 1798 constitution gave greater weight to the primary assemblies in the election of the legislature and elected a *unicameral* body which then divided *by lot* into two equal, but separate chambers.

55 For the constitution see J. van der Poll, *Verzameling van Vaderlandsche Wetten en Besluiten* (Amsterdam 1840), pp. 11–93. The new 'departments' were drafted with all the perversity of political cartography, taking, as a basis, not regional or geographical characteristics but numbers of primary assemblies and demographic density. Thus Amsterdam and its hinterland became the 'Department of the Amstel'; Friesland and Groningen (which spoke different languages) the 'Department of the Eems' and most of north Brabant was amalgamated to a chunk of Gelderland to make the 'Department of the Dommel'. See the *Nieuwe Kart der Bataafsche Republike*, 1798, Collectie Hingman 1.

56 For the purges, see ARA, Binnenlandse zaken 186–94. The breaking point came when on May 4, at the urging of Delacroix, it was decided that elections should be held not for the whole legislature but for just one third of the incumbent (post 22 January) body.

57 The co-conspiratorial Agents were Pijman (War) and Spoors (Navy), but the

principal mover, as much to settle a personal score with Fijnje and Delacroix was for political reasons, was General Daendels.

58 ARA, Gogel 173, *De Democraten* (10 and 24 November 1796): *Iets over de Een-en Ondeelbaarheid der Financien in de Bataafsche Republiek.*

59 Sillem, *Gogel*, p. 24; Sickenga, *Geschiedenis der Nederlandse Belastingen*, p. 65. It was the complicated machinery of legislation which gave a further opportunity to the Gogel plan even after it had been rejected by the First Chamber and the Appelian counter-plan adopted in July 1800. The Second Chamber reversed that decision.

60 The records of the Treasurer and the Council (which included Appelius) reveal, to a surprising degree, the frustration of the executive in imposing its will over the provincial administrations to which, after all, it had restored almost full autonomy. The important exception from the status quo ante 1795 was the provision for local authorities to submit their budgets in advance for the approval of the Regency of State before being permitted to allocate expenditure. See ARA, Archief van Financien 386; Gogel 29.

61 The figures given by L. van Nierop, 'Amsterdam's scheepvaart in den Franschen tijd', in *Jaarboek Amstelodamum*, xxi (1924), p. 146, reveal that 1802 was something of a boom year, with 2,967 ships entering at the Texel and Vlie and 1,723 at the Goeree and Maas, a total actually *exceeding* the average shipping for the years 1785–9. Although this total of 4,690 fell to 1,787 in 1803 and 2,863 in 1804 it was not until after the Berlin Decree (1806) that the commercial depression became severe. See also, I. J. Brugmans, *Paardenkracht en Mensenmacht* ('s Gravenhage, 1961), pp. 22–31.

62 Given only the vaguest promises, the Dutch had made repeated attempts, in 1795, 1796 and 1798 to get the French to conclude a commercial treaty which would have opened French, Belgian and German markets and eased problems of raw material supply, In March 1799 the Bordeaux merchant Lubberts was sent to the Netherlands to sound out the possibilities of a treaty in return for a soft loan of around 6m guilders to finance further French campaigns. See ARA, Archief Wiselius 53; *Gedenkstukken*, iii, pp. 44–56.

63 Sickenga, *Geschiedenis der Nederlandse Belastingen*, p. 28. To Dutch complaints Bonaparte assured Schimmelpenninck that the campaign against the British would be mercifully brief. *Gedenkstukken*, iv, p. 598.

64 *Gedenkstukken*, iv, p. 486 n. 1; p. 541, n. 2. Keuchenius, *De Inkomstenen Uitgaven der Bataafsche Republiek*, (through rather doubtful extrapolation from tax receipts) p. 92, gave the gross annual general income of the Netherlands as 221m.

65 ARA, Gogel 29.

66 ARA, Staatssecretarie 514–17; Gogel 24.

67 In the year 1798–9 Rotterdam reported a deficit of fl.84,000; Haarlem nearly fl.60,000, much of it due to increased costs of supporting the poor. In Friesland towns like Harlingen and Franeker received substantial subsidies from the provincial administration whose budget had doubled from its commitments in the 1780s. See ARA, Staatsbewind 230–1; Uitvoerend Bewind 381, 360.

68 ARA, Gogel 17; G. Graaf Schimmelpenninck, *Rutger Jan Schimmelpenninck en Eenige Gebeurtenissen van Zijnen Tijd* ('s Gravenhage and Amsterdam 1845), ii, Bijlage C, p. 314.

69 *Ibid.* p. 83.

70 For the 1805 constitution see van der Poll, *Verzameling van Vaderlandsche*

Wetten, pp. 281–5; for the important Gogel memoranda to Marmont, *Gedenkstukken*, IV, pp. 514–17, 530–5.

71 Napoleon let Schimmelpenninck know that 'he did not want an American President on his doorstep since he would be concerned that that form of government might become contagious in Europe', Graaf Schimmelpenninck, *Rutger Jan Schimmelpenninck*, p. 105. See also de Wit, *De Strijd tussen Aristocratie en Democratie*, p. 255.

72 I. J. A. Gogel, *Memorien en Correspondentien betrekkelijk den Staat van 's Rijks Geldmiddelen in den Jare 1820*, ed. J. M. Gogel (Amsterdam 1844); H. R. C. Wright, *Free Trade and Protection in the Netherlands 1816–1830* (Cambridge, 1955).

73 Much ill-feeling was generated between the Council of State and the ministry of finance by Gogel's refusal to disburse sums without a full account of their allotted expenditure being submitted in advance. He looked on some of the councillors and some of his fellow-ministers as idle aristocrats first and officials a poor second, and as the reign progressed felt that Louis was unduly taking the part of 'the court' rather than the administration. When the king, in 1808, sought the advice of the financial section of the Council rather than the minister Gogel wrote to him that he bitterly resented 'after ten years of hard labour, after being persuaded to undertake and to complete a task which no-one else dared to take on; to be deprived of the sole satisfaction of perfecting it. This decision can only serve to destroy the one ambition remaining to me, and which, if I may be permitted to say so, has already suffered much because in spite of my appeals I have never received from Your Majesty, the necessary support, nor from your financial servants (in the council), nor the least assistance, encouragement or mark of approbation. To this it is also necessary to attribute much weakness and slackness in the executive.' Sillem, *Gogel*, pp. 61–2. In his memoirs Louis called Gogel 'an indefatigable worker ... honest, patriotic and with much integrity. Unfortunately, to these qualities he added faults which cancelled them out to a great extent ... in the distribution of public charges he could see only the interest of the fisc and the success of his system; nothing else existed for him ... he could not suffer the slightest reform in this administration.' Louis Bonaparte, *Documens Historiques et Reflexions Sur Le Gouvernment de la Hollande*, 3 vols (Gand – Bruges – Amsterdam 1820), II, p. 57.

74 Gogel, *Memorien*, p. 38.

75 *Gedenkstukken*, V, p. 415.

76 For a discussion of social changes, see Th. P. M. de Jong, 'Sociale Verandering in de Neergaande Republiek', *Economisch- en Sociaal-Historisch Jaarboek*, XXXV (1972), pp. 1–27.

77 Gijsbert Karel van Hogendorp, *Gedagten over 's Lands Finantien* (Amsterdam 1802), p. 35 cheerfully predicted 'Give the Netherlander, peace, a free sea and colonies once more and trade will flourish again; prosperity will return and the State will stay firm on its old foundations'; for his remarks on the poor and the rich see pp. 78–9.

78 Sillem, *Gogel*, p. 39.

79 ARA, Gogel 40.

80 Gogel, *Memorien*, p. 39.

81 Zappey, *Goldberg*, p. 73; Gogel, *Gedenkstukken*, V, pp. 283–4, pointed out to the king that at a time when 40 per cent of people's means were taken in taxes interest payments from the debt were very often the principal means of income.

Cutting interest rates would 'infallibly plunge (thousands) into misery and their ruin would bring about that of innumerable individuals dependent on them'. On the other hand Gogel was not particularly sympathetic to rentiers as a class, and although he had been an Amsterdam businessman since his adolescence, as a Brabander of obscure German origins he had always remained outside the charmed circle of the great patrician houses such as Hope and Willink.

82 Of the twelve indirect taxes of the 1805 system, the most prolific were, as under the old regime, those on peat, (fuel), livestock, grain/flour; salt and the three duties on wine, imported and domestic spirits which together brought in some 4.5m for 1807. See the published estimates and yields in Gogel, *Memorien*, Bijlage FF, pp. 514–15.

83 Gogel admitted that taxation at source was the simplest form of indirect taxation for administrative purposes but was economically undesirable as falling heavily on the already overburdened producer. On the other hand he certainly did not wish the retailer or consumer to bear the whole cost of the revenue. The system was, therefore something of a clumsy compromise. Wholesalers or retailers wishing to stock a specific quantity of goods paid the tax in advance to the official Receiver for which he obtained a receipt which entitled him to his delivery. He then presented a duplicate to the supplier-producer who had then to pay up his share before finally delivering the order. Needless to say vigilant and very unpopular surveillance was needed to see that the system operated satisfactorily. See Sillem, *Gogel*, pp. 231ff. ARA, Gogel 59.

84 See ARA, Gogel 28. An interesting income tax scheme was sent to him in 1796 by one Cornelis van Vijen of Leiden based on an elaborate sliding scale from $1\frac{1}{2}$ per cent (before allowances) on an income of fl.1,300 for a family of seven, to 56.25 per cent for bachelor incomes of fl.20,000 or over. Another scheme anticipated 'PAYE' administration, recommending responsibility being given to employers to dock tax from workers' wages and pay direct to the state.

85 Owen Connelly, *Napoleon's Satellite Kingdoms* (New York, 1965), p. 150, for example, appears to equate the verponding with a *land* tax and overlooks the fact that property, even landed property, was the hallmark of both fortune and status, even for those whose wealth was based on financial and commercial concerns. A stroll by the banks of the Vegt will confirm the lavish expenditure of the eighteenth-century Amsterdam patricians on summer-house estates between the city and Utrecht and it was this form of 'leisured' fixed capital, not operational funds, which Gogel was most concerned should bear liability. Connally also appears to believe that the 'personeel' was a tax on *income*, when it was a surcharge on expenditure. He provides figures, which are based on Louis Bonaparte's *Memoirs*, are far from reliable, and neglects, in attempting to measure the difference in yield effected by the Gogel tax system, to supply the figures for the last year of the old system (1805). For details of the verponding see ARA, Gogel 59; Sillem, *Gogel*, pp. 211–12.

86 The verponding yielded, on average, 9.9m of the 11m estimated by Gogel; the personeel 4.75m so that proprietorship rather than tenancy bore, as Gogel intended, the heavier liability. See Gogel, *Memorien*, Bijlagen CC, FF.

87 See *Provisioneele Instructie voor de opzieners over de Middelen . . . over alle de Gaarders en Ontvangers en Verdere Bedienden* (20 December 1805); ARA, Gogel 60; 59, no. 52.

88 ARA, Gogel 40, 60.
89 Gogel, *Memorien*, pp. 239–41, 244; Sickenga, *Geschiedenis der Nederlandse Belastingen*, p. 96.
90 ARA, Staatssecretarie, 514, 516, 517; Gogel, 31, 34, 142.
91 ARA, Staatssecretarie 637.
92 *Gedenkstukken*, v, p. xxxviii; p. 192; pp. 207–8; pp. 215–18; Archives Nationales, Paris, AF ɪv 1069 (Trésor); 1820; 1741.
93 Metelerkamp, *De Toestand van Nederland*, ɪɪ, p. 25; Gogel, *Memorien*, Bijlage 00, pp. 520–1; FF, pp. 514–15; CC, pp. 510–11; pp. 134, 136.
94 ARA, Gogel, 78: 17, 18, 23.
95 ARA, Archief Canneman 6.
96 ARA, Archief Canneman 13.
97 ARA, Binnenlandse zaken 784.
98 ARA, Gogel 78.
99 ARA, Ministerie van Financien 847.
100 For the difficulties of financial administration in the years from 1811 to 1813 see ARA, Gogel, 142; Sillem, *Gogel*, pp. 86–119.
101 J. R. Thorbecke, *Historische Schetsen* ('s Gravenhage 1860), p. 99; see also the pioneering essay by L. G. J. Verberne, *Gogel en Uniteit* (Nijmegen-Utrecht 1948) passim.
102 ARA, Goldberg 59.
103 Ermerins-Gogel, 22 March 1807, ARA, Gogel 26.

7 War and the failure of industrial mobilisation: 1899 and 1914[1]

Clive Trebilcock

It is not often that one can attempt a comparative study of industrial mobilisation in war-time. Wars rarely arrange themselves in time and scale so that the tasks involved in the conscription of industrial effort are comparable. In this sense, for example, World War II clearly posed problems for a number of manufacturing disciplines – those providing for mass aerial and armoured campaigns most especially – that were simply not present, or present in a much lower order, during World War I. There are, however, a limited number of exceptions – 'pairs' of wars – where the *matériel* demanded, the technologies involved, the industrial problems confronted, the armament 'best practice' available *are* comparable and offer useful parallels. The first war of the 'pair' in such circumstances is often said to constitute a 'proving ground' for the techniques and products to be used in the second. Quite frequently the Spanish Civil War and World War II are said to 'pair' in this way. Very seldom is it realised, however, that the wars and confrontations around the turn of the nineteenth and twentieth centuries – particularly the Boer War (1899–1902) and the Russo-Japanese War (1904–5) – provide a set of prototypes, of potential 'pairs' for World War I, in industrial as well as military terms. Of these early wars, the Boer War was the most neglected of all, yet possibly the most significant in its lessons for the future.

The purpose of the following argument is to make good the neglect and to make clear the lessons. In turn, this involves the definition of two further objectives: satisfactory proof that the Boer War was, in economic terms, a major war – fitted to be a 'pair' for World War I – and, effective demonstration that this war acted as an entirely unrecognised precedent for the nearly calamitous breakdown in industrial mobilisation in 1914–15. Here we are not dealing with the testing of a respected hypothesis against objective and quantifiable criteria, in the style of the 'new economic historian', but rather in the presentation of a fresh hypothesis concerning the behaviour of the British economy in war-time, employing materials rarely used by the economic historian. Any novelty in the analysis lies not in its mathematical rigour but in its location within the area of interaction between economic, political and military affairs.[2]

[139]

Conventionally, it is with World War I that the problem of industrial mobilisation is first associated. The economic historian and the historian of war have agreed in recognising that the requirements of modern hostilities, such as those of 1914–18, in pressing upon an advanced manufacturing system, create unique problems of supply. The armed forces need engines of destruction which, although individually of high technical complexity, must be produced to extremely demanding levels of standardisation – thus combining the difficulties of technology – intensiveness with those of precise replication. Moreover, these destructive equipments, turned out in peacetime by a handful of specialised armourers, must be produced during wartime in the greatest quantity possible and at the highest possible speed – adding the difficulties of mass production under crisis demand to those of quality and reiteration. Radical solutions are needed to such problems: repeat manufacture of an unprecedented scale must be organised; rarified machines and scarce raw materials must be accumulated; skills that were previously the province of a few industrial specialists must be spread across a wide expanse of manufacturing capacity. Such are the trials and the tasks of industrial mobilisation, as all analysts are agreed. And they are also agreed, with virtual unanimity, that these trials and tasks were *first* meted out to the industrial structure during the Great War of 1914–18. The opinion of Charles Rothwell may be taken as typical: he writes, 'The wars which preceded 1914 only *partially* absorbed the energies of the nations involved, and their economic demands did not exceed the adaptability and productive capacity of free enterprise.'[3] Similarly, it is argued that the experience of 1914–15 revealed, for the first time, the inability of advanced factory industry to provide adequate supplies of weaponry for a modern army in the field: the making machines could not provide enough destroying machines. World War I created, according to one post-war commentator, 'the greatest transaction in the annals of commerce',[4] or, put another way, it generated the largest boom experienced by a single industry up to that time. Yet the armourers proved unable to absorb this demand, and, in failing, created a military problem. On these grounds the study of industrial mobilisation usually begins with the Great War.

Certainly the analysis can, with virtue, be restricted to the period after 1899. The concept of industrial mobilisation – the expansion of the defence sector across a wide segment of civilian industry – requires an economy with highly developed inter-industry and inter-sectoral relationships. And it necessarily implies the existence of a technically complex weaponry product, manufactured by a technologically advanced defence industry – for if a basically simple product, obtainable from a wide variety of producers were at issue, the need for mobilisation would scarcely arise. Consequently, it is not possible to identify industrial mobilisation within a period – the years of the Seven Years, American, and French Wars for example – when the armament technology was of relatively low order, when any ironmaster might choose to produce cannon or any shipbuilder a timber man-of-war. The basic preconditions were indeed established only around the last third of the nineteenth century as the level of armament technology underwent an abrupt upwards adjustment and the armament product began to take on its modern aspect of complexity and specialisation.[5] From this point it was simply the lack of large wars which forestalled the need for full-scale industrial mobilisation.[6] After 1870 Britain – though steadily accumulating more sophisticated weaponry – entered an era of modest colonial wars, a period described by the Esher Committee in 1904 as 'one of immunity from real stress when the provision of relatively small expeditionary forces to operate against unorganised and ill-armed peoples had been the principal occupation of the War Office'.[7] In such a context, a small côterie of professional armourers, working alongside the royal ordnance factories, could supply the nation's needs, and industrial mobilisation remained many battles distant.

However, there is no virtue in extending this interpretation down to 1914; in reality, it ceased to be operationally accurate in 1899, upon the outbreak of the Boer War. Most observers failed to notice. Historians in general have omitted to give the war its due weight, acquiescing in the view of incompetent generals and incautious politicians, that it was merely another colonial episode. Economic historians in particular have ignored the war very thoroughly: almost the sole mention it receives is as a culminating influence upon the great home investment boom of the nineties, and, even then, the reasons for this are not examined. Such attitudes succeed only in imitating the misplaced nonchalance of contemporaries. The Treasury, for instance, calculated that the cost of the war would not exceed £10m and expected to recoup most of this from a swift annexation of the Transvaal gold mines.[8] By the time that the War Office had 300,000 men under arms in South Africa, the Treasury began to notice its mistake. There were some other features which historians might have noticed. In 1901 the average British infantryman was costing the taxpayer 50 per cent more than in the last peace-time year, 1898.[9] He was also requiring one ton of bullets, costing £140, to incapacitate a single Boer farmer.[10] Unsurprisingly, the direct cost upon eventual completion of operations was high – not £10m but £250m or 14.4 per cent of the net national income of 1902, the year in which the bill was presented, if not paid. This was considerably more than the sum paid out by the effective Japanese in their military and naval campaigns against the Russians in 1904–5 – some £182m – and rather more than the £200m disbursed by the Russians for the privilege of being thrashed by the Japanese. Perhaps most significantly of all, the thirty-one months of the Boer War cost Britain very nearly as much as the notably more extensive campaigns conducted in the first eight months of World War I – by which time the bill represented 12.6 per cent of net national income for 1915.[11] Significantly,

Peacock and Wiseman in their survey of British Public Expenditure argue that the 'displacement effect' in government spending which they associate with modern wars is detectable for the first time in the case of the Boer War,[12] and is then repeated in greater amplitude during World War I and World War II.

As is shown by figure 1, the pattern of state spending for the period 1890–1905 clearly reveals the massive influence of the South African War: the

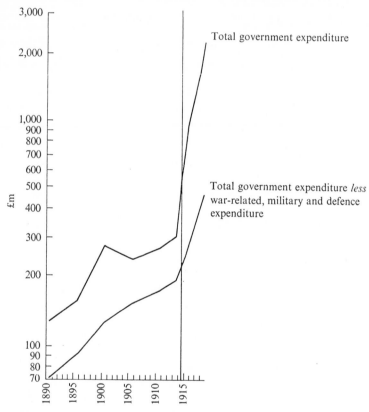

Fig. 1 Total government expenditure and war-related expenditure (current prices).

sudden jagged peak in total government expenditure contrasts obviously with the more gentle 'humped' movement of government expenditure less all war-related, military, and defence costs.[13] Partly this activity in expenditure represents the steadily rising cost of killing, but it also serves to indicate the scale of the war fought in South Africa.

If 'real stress' on account of war had been absent from British economic and industrial affairs before 1899, it became sufficiently obvious thereafter.

The National Debt was increased by £160m, reaching the highest point since 1867; national savings over thirty-six years were wiped out; a downward slide in consols began, and was not terminated before 1914. Even worse were the disruptive effects of war upon the financial system: bank rate rose from 3 per cent in April 1899 to 6 per cent by November, the highest point since the Baring Crisis, and the yearly average for 1900 was the worst since the bleak year of 1890. South African gold supplies were also, naturally, denied to London for the duration of the war. In order to accommodate the unexpected expenditure and to restrain the damaging forces at work within the economy, governments were forced to employ instruments which underlined the unusual nature of the situation: even the Tory government of 1902 felt in necessary to add 7d to the income tax and the Liberal chancellors, Asquith and Lloyd George resorted to budgetary policies of extreme novelty after 1906. Death duties, yet higher income tax, and even the People's Budget of 1909, were in part related to the high costs of defeating the Boer republics. Fittingly, the Royal Commission on the War in South Africa concluded in 1904, reversing all initial impressions, that the Boer War had been 'a great war'.[14]

The industrial counterpart of the problems in expenditure, in finance, and in fiscal resources was, inevitably, a gruelling production test for the armament manufacturers. And this test was set not only by a large war but by the last of the free enterprise wars, a war in which there was no state direction of resources, no supervised industrial expansion – as there was to be painfully in World War I and more efficiently in World War II. The Boer War stands at an important cross-roads; it was the final *laissez-faire* war, but it involved, for Britain, an unparalleled commitment of industrial resources; it devoted an advanced armaments industry to all-out war work, yet lacked the modern methods of controlling it.

The interim situation of this war inevitably made for problems in the supply of weaponry. And these were not eased by the fact that the major portion of war supply depended on the power of output; the *reserve* stocks of defence goods on the outbreak of hostilities were minimal. Artillery reserves were deficient by October 1899 and virtually extinguished by Christmas. In the first days of 1900 the replacement equipment for the entire Royal Artillery amounted to a total of six field guns.[15] The ammunition situation was no better; at the beginning of the war the guns in South Africa had only eight week's supply of shell apiece, and, back in Britain, the exodus of the expeditionary force left behind for home defence a reserve of rifle ammunition counted in hundreds of cartridges rather than the necessary millions.[16] The supply position in 1899 was, in fact, a non-supply situation: there was a universal lack of modern land service artillery, a complete absence of ordnance reserves, and a perilous shortage of all major classes of ammunition. Moved to fury by such deficiencies, the army's chief *matériel*

officer, the Director General of Ordnance, Major-General Sir Henry Brackenbury wrote on 15 December 1899: 'I am charged . . . with supplying the
Army with warlike stores, equipment, and clothing. The stores of warlike
stores, equipment, and clothing at the beginning of the present war were
utterly inadequate to enable me to carry out this duty . . . We are attempting
to maintain the largest Empire the world has ever seen with armament and
reserves that would be insufficient for a third class military power.' The consequences, he concluded, were 'full of peril for the Empire'.[17] And his remedy
was drastic: under threat of his own resignation, he demanded a rapid
armament manufacturing programme costing £15m and providing some one
thousand guns. Everything considered, Brackenbury's revelations and accusations of 1899 unleashed a procurement scandal within the War Office
which offers early parallels for the Shell Scandal of 1915, unleashed by very
similar charges from Field Marshal Sir John French. Not without reason,
Brackenbury's report on the munitions crisis was described by his Comman-
der-in-Chief, Lord Wolseley as 'the most serious public document I have
ever seen'.[18]

The importance of the shortfall in reserves revealed by the 'Empire in
peril' memorandum was crucial. It made explicit a cheese-paring assumption
common to governments of the 1890s: that however desirable in general
terms the manufacture of defence reserves might be, they would always be
struck out as unnecessary luxuries when a particular annual vote was in the
process of composition. 'Every government that I have ever known in
England has shrunk from it', said one senior military official. 'They gave
you a little addition every year but very small, and the result is that we were
found in 1899 without those supplies we required for the mobilisation of the
Army.'[19] Political pressure for economy in peace-time thus produced, neither
for the first nor the last time, an embarrassing military impotence in war-
time. But this was not all; it also produced industrial crisis. For the necessary
sequel to the repeated postponement of manufacture for reserves was the
government's conviction that the armament industry would make up all
deficiencies when the need arose, that is under conditions of actual warfare.
Acidly, Brackenbury reported to a post-war enquiry, 'Everybody at the War
Office was under the impression that there was no reserve kept for the war
upkeep of the Army because it was supposed that the Ordnance Factories
and the trade would supply what we wanted from week to week.'[20] Put
another way, this meant that the War Office had tacitly but definitely committed itself to a policy of industrial mobilisation in war-time, but had
assumed no responsibility for executing or even supervising this task. It
was a most unwise choice; the difficulties of producing modern weaponry in
quantity for a large war could not have been more resoundingly under-
estimated. The outcome was never in doubt: by the end of 1899 Brackenbury
was recording not the ready supply from week to week that the military

authorities had assumed but rather that, 'the output of the country is insufficient to meet current demands ... we have no reserve of output ... we are at the end of our tether now'.[21]

Worse was to come: with heavy artillery orders already placed with the arms trade and causing congestion in the factories, Brackenbury had still to introduce the emergency three-year armament programme devised to remedy the critical shortages of 1899. After eight months of haggling with the Treasury – which, even in war-time, cut some £5m out of Brackenbury's list of requirements – weaponry contracts worth £10m, by far the most valuable land service orders placed before 1914, were at length agreed. The effect was to pack the overworked armouries tighter still and to protract yet further the already chronic delays in deliveries. It was at this time, in 1900, as frantic efforts were made to erase the supply backlog, as the 'Brackenbury orders' rolled out to the trade, that it gradually became obvious that the modern style of warfare had increased the gap between peacetime and war-time demand for munitions to wholly novel and virtually unbridgeable dimensions. Thus the Director of Army Contracts found in 1900 that his department, the main procurement agency for both services, was purchasing in a single month quantities of defence goods which would have sufficed for the consumption needs of the previous twenty *years*.[22] This form of drastic disparity would appear again in 1914, but by that time it already had its prototype.

In 1899, when the disparity *first* occurred in this magnitude, the industrial consequences were more than sufficiently acute. Gunmakers encountered a level of demand between 1899 and 1904 that was some four times greater than the 'normal' level for the nineties, while, in the first twelve months of war, manufacturers of rifle ammunition faced contracts running at five times the peace-time requirements, shell manufacturers at twelve times, and some explosives firms at twenty-five times.[23] A few armament firms, especially rifle and ammunition producers, coped well with this production test. But neither the great private gunmakers nor the Royal Arsenals, concerned mainly with artillery requirements, could produce even remotely satisfactory results.

It was not for lack of promises. The biggest weaponry concerns approached the war with breezy confidence. They had enjoyed booming export orders to South America and the Far East in the years since 1896 and were convinced that they could switch capacity to war production with few problems; they appeared to attach little significance to the fact that their recent pitched activity had left them devoid of any reserve capacity. It was thus in optimistic vein that the most influential trade spokesmen, Captain Andrew Noble of Armstrongs and Sir Trevor Dawson of Vickers assessed their power of output for the government's secret committee of enquiry into armament matters, the Mowatt Committee of 1900. Noble promised that his firm alone could complete the whole of Brackenbury's armament programme in two years,[24] and Dawson, while allowing four years for the guns, promised the entire ammunition allocation of the defence scheme within a single year.[25] Both witnesses were adamant that the ordnance factories should not be expanded and that the private sector was fully equal to the task. They were hopelessly over-sanguine. By May 1901 the two main contractors were between sixteen months and two years in arrears on the field artillery orders placed early in the war. And rather than the completion of the entire Brackenbury pro-gramme within two to four years as they had promised, they could show only long delays on the *share* of the programmes which they had each been awarded.[26] These lamentable results recalled Brackenbury's gibe to the Mowatt Committee that these firms, 'will undertake anything, but they do not keep their promises'[27] – a remark which most uncannily anticipated military complaints in 1915.

Government inspection of the major armament factories in November 1900 revealed the sources of the problem. It found the arsenals in disarray, clogged with work, expanding haphazardly in a desperate attempt to provide manufacturing space. At Armstrongs' Elswick plant, the inspectors dis-covered a classic expression of these difficulties: extensions had been poorly implemented; the layout was cluttered; modern machines were wasted in cramped and outmoded shops. On closer examination, more disturbing disproportions come to light: Armstrongs' foundry capacity was insufficient to keep its gunshops well supplied with ingots; steel production was limited by the inadequate number of presses; the shell shops were not equipped for supply in bulk; crucially, the equipment for rifling heavy guns and for shaping breech mechanisms could not operate sufficiently rapidly to meet a crisis demand. The Vickers works earned rather better opinions from the inspectors, but, once more, insufficient forging power was singled out as a serious bottleneck. The officials concluded that the armourers had entered into promises too lightly, but, on the credit side, had energetically set to work to put matters right with new plant and equipment.[28] Clearly, the private manufacturers simply did not realise what the Mowatt Committee had partially perceived – that 'whatever the *latent* power of output possessed by the trade of the country . . . it is not at present so organised as to enable it at once to increase materially its deliveries, and there is even reason to doubt whether a considerable time may not pass before the power of the trade can be fully developed and the needs of the country . . . adequately met'.[29] The mobilisation of the armament sector of a major free trade economy was gradually, if dimly, revealed to be an extremely complex task.

The greatest private manufacturing concerns in Britain were pushed to the limits of their productive resources by this mobilisation. It was a mis-fortune which could strike with impartiality at an internationally respected armament emporium like Armstrongs', capable of producing nearly a thou-sand guns and a million shells in a year, or at a brisk new armoury like

Vickers with its modern machines and competent management. And it could strike even though Armstrongs' might spend nearly £3m on new capacity between 1896 and 1903 and Vickers some £2m between 1898 and 1903.[30] That firms like these were among the biggest and the best equipped within the economy appeared to offer little effective defence. Thus Vickers had to record that ... 'the Government made most imperative demands on the whole of the establishment of Messrs. Vickers Son and Maxim Ltd ... and Messrs. Vickers own works [were] employed at their fullest extent during this period', and concluded, 'The period referred to was one of great stress and considerable anxiety.'[31] Certainly, Major-General Brackenbury would have agreed with this interpretation. His verdict after the war, was 'I thought you could get anything you wanted out of the trade of this country at short notice. I found it impossible.'[32] In fact, important sections of the private arms trade, including some of Britain's most powerful industrial organisations, very nearly broke under the 'stress' that Vickers found so uncomfortable. It would seem, then, that during the Boer War 'the adaptability and productive capacity of free enterprise' did not exactly live up to Rothwell's expectations.

Nor did matters go much more smoothly in the public sector. Against the high rates of expansion asked of the trade, the ordnance factories could boast only a rapid initial increase in output – by 50 per cent within the first four to six weeks of hostilities – and then a more or less stable level of production. In the long run they could point to nothing similar to the fifty or one hundred fold expansion achieved by some private arms concerns over the war as a whole.[33] Yet it could be argued that it was the *purpose* of the state factories to carry the burden of munitions demand only at the commencement of a war, and until such time as the private sector shifted into higher gear. Such was War Office policy, and, within these terms, the government arsenals seem to have accomplished their task without undue strain. But this impression of moderate activity was in fact an illusion. It was partly created by military officials who, in reporting to post-war enquiries, were loath to admit that their factories – seen as army 'commands' – had shared in the production problems of the private trade, or that their workshops had a naturally lower margin of expansion than the commercial armouries. In fact, however, the Royal Arsenal at Woolwich had to work a seven-day week and a three-shift day at some stages of the war, and it had to add £½m worth of equipment to its capital stock.[34] And still its production would not rise satisfactorily. The restricting factor was the state of the Arsenal's equipment; it was not fully up to standard and its forging capacity was markedly deficient. The fact that the Royal Gun Factory did not have a drastically busy war and made few heavy guns – while orders were heaped on the trade and the army in the field cried out for heavy guns – is explained by such bottlenecks within the state factories. Some military industrialists, of the more forthright kind, certainly argued that their production levels remained stable only because the forging and foundry sections of the Arsenal could not supply sufficient material to justify expansion.[35] Quite possibly, then, orders were transferred to the over-worked private sector because the public sector could not meet them. The trade press certainly seized upon this interpretation, and wrote in a flush of misplaced enthusiasm, 'private establishments are beginning to benefit from the inadequacy of the Government [manufacturing] departments to fit in supply with demand'.[36] In fact, private establishments, which had very similar problems of their own, could only have agreed with the underlying deduction, and seen it confirmed by a new trend in the distribution of orders: if the trade received, on average, only 45 per cent of the sums spent annually on munitions during the nineties, this share rose sharply to 58 per cent in 1899–1900 and to 75 per cent in 1900–2.[37] If the government factories worked on a moderate level of orders throughout the war, therefore, it was not because there were only moderate needs to be fulfilled but because they were inadequately equipped to meet far larger needs.

The Boer War, then, was large enough to severely embarrass both the public and the private sectors of an industry that was, in technology, a leading sector in the economy of its day. Casting around desperately for an explanation, the military came up with a catchphrase which merely underlined the scale of the hostilities. Everything was to be explained by 'unprecedented demand' – a force sufficiently powerful to excuse *all* deficiencies of supply. Superficially, the concept possesses some appeal but in reality has a limited validity – as its use by interested parties in *both* the Boer War and the Great War demonstrates. Thus Sir Ralph Knox, Permanent Under Secretary at the War Office, argued in 1901, 'delays *necessarily* occur before unprecedented demands . . . when the resources of the country are taxed to the uttermost'. Interestingly Sir Ralph was insistent that the resources of the country *were* taxed to the uttermost but in his conclusion – 'I certainly believe they [the delays] were not in the slightest degree due to the faults of the system',[38] he merely testified, as did precisely similar statements in 1914 and 1915, to the current inability to conceive or to implement any better system. In reality, the private armourers made considerable errors during the Boer War, disposing their plant maladroitly, and gauging their capacity inaccurately; and the system, relying on undirected free enterprise, allowed them to do so. Not only that, but precisely similar errors were made in the public sector. Perhaps worst of all, however, was the ineptitude of the state departments – the perpetrators of the system – in organising themselves for the procurement of weaponry in war-time. If the system allowed the armourers to come perilously near to failure in the production test, the government's performance in the procurement test commanded no more confidence.

In this department the army showed a disconcerting inability to phase its contracts smoothly over the first crucial war-time months. Orders – especially for shell – were placed in an apparently random manner, that was, most unfortunately, to be exactly duplicated in 1914. Just before the outbreak of hostilities in 1899, for instance, Armstrongs' asked the War Office whether, in view of the increasing international tension, they should not begin to increase their output of shrapnel shell – and received a negative reply. Yet less than two months later the army, possessing only the shrapnel stacked in its limber boxes, approached the firm with the requirement that production of the shell should be expanded forty-fold.[39] With artillery it was the same: Vickers – who had not made a single field gun for the military before 1899 – received no warning whatsoever of the huge orders which deluged their factories in the first weeks of the war.[40] The armourers' complaint that they could have done better had they been given more notice that unusually large orders were imminent is fair criticism of the confusion among the supply officials. Any mismeasurement of productive power on the part of the trade was thus fully matched by the army's failure to realise, within an acceptable order of magnitude, what its contract needs might be in the autumn of 1899. As in the early stages of the Great War, the services grossly under-estimated their initial requirements, and then, as recognition dawned, simply poured contract upon contract into the groaning armouries.

And once they had succeeded in inducing the manufacturers to accept the contracts, the service administrations proved notably deficient in acquiring the products. The Army Contracts Directorate was more accustomed to maintaining good relations with its specialist suppliers than to harrying them for belated deliveries. As later enquiries found, its officials failed to maintain an alert watch over the progress of manufacture and were insufficiently active in 'accelerating' work that had fallen behind.[41] Although these shortcomings provoked much debate in the early 1900s,[42] the Contracts Directorate was still the army's main link between the fighting service and the industrial supplier in 1914. And it was by no means fully reformed: the visiting contracts inspectors suggested by a government committee of 1901 and intended to solve the problem of 'acceleration', were not in fact appointed for another thirteen years.[43]

Even more dangerous, however, in this context was the persistent strength of the 'special relationship' between the Contracts Directorate and the small group of professional armament firms.[44] From 1899 through to 1915 this bond militated against the extension of the area of munitions supply outside the select côterie of specialist armourers. It mattered little to the Director of Contracts that, as the trade press observed, 'war brings as fresh recruits firms full of hopes and fine promises, quick deliveries, low prices, and lofty ambitions'.[45] On the contrary, the War Office proved singularly resistant to the attractions of such outsiders. And before long, the same trade journal was complaining 'with the exception of two well-known makers, *no* encouragement has been given to other firms. There are at least a dozen capable and willing firms who could manufacture guns.'[46] Clearly, the state did not do enough to create or to employ new armament capacity during the Boer War; it did not procure *sufficient* industrial mobilisation. Yet it was not for lack of need, since in 1900 the War Office was forced to place large artillery orders with *German* armament firms. It was rather that the administration's 'special relationship' system, designed in peace-time to keep a group of picked contractors clustered in attendance around the state purchasing departments, as a safeguard against possible crisis needs, operated in actual large-scale crises to *limit* the official taste for recruiting new suppliers from outside the charmed circle. This was certainly an element in War Office thinking which reappeared in 1914. Together with the unwillingness of the officials to put pressure upon well-known contractors, this element must surely suggest that the War Office procurement system was neither so fault-less, nor 'unprecedented demand' so wholly to blame as Sir Ralph Knox and his colleagues had innocently believed. In fact, the procurement officials were little better at getting the guns than the field commanders were at keeping them.

Economically, industrially, and militarily the Boer War was thus more than a simple colonial episode. It incurred great expenditures, disrupted both private and public sectors of the armaments industry, and revealed within the military procurement system failings which could claim full kin-ship with the more noticeable misdeeds of a Redvers Buller or a Methuen. Above all, it demonstrated the mistakes and the lack of planning that one might expect from *any* free enterprise industrial system confronting the prob-lem of armament supply in a new type of war and lacking assistance from the competent executive authorities. That much perhaps was excusable because it was the first time. But if the war left behind unfortunate memories of stress and strain, it should also have provided important lessons. Some military historians argue that this was so and that the lessons were digested. Thus Colonel John Dunlop writes, 'The South African War was a lesson, and a bitter one, but to the credit of the entire nation, the lesson was learned and was not ignored.'[47] If such arguments were to concentrate entirely upon the Expeditionary Force of 1914, or upon Haldane's reforms of army organisation, they might perhaps convince, but Dunlop calls attention also to the 'satisfactory armament of 1914'.[48] There would appear to be more than a little confusion here. The armament and supply lessons of the Boer War were clear: that, in modern warfare, the possession of heavy artillery firepower was essential; that small calibre automatic weapons were of great value; that immense supplies of shell with serviceable fuses were required; and, above all, that mobilisation of the state and private sectors of the armament industry was an immensely intricate and delicate task. Yet the impact on the military equipment of 1914 and 1915 was scarcely profound. At that time the British army was as inferior to the Germans in heavy artillery as it had once been to the Boers; one historian of the armaments industry has called it 'an Army almost without heavy guns'.[49] It was clearly deficient in machine-guns. It experienced in 1915 a very nearly disastrous shortage of shells and fuses. And, on the home front, the armament firms failed to perform according to their promises and the War Office gave out contracts with a total disregard for order or for the contractors' capacities. Exactly what had been learned is open to debate.

Most of these points were not only emphasised by the Boer War experience but were clearly and publicly presented by military experts to the series of Royal Commissions which sat in *post-mortem* upon the South African fiasco. In this way the Shell Scandal of 1915 was not only anticipated as a fact by the acute ammunition shortages of 1899 but was openly and accurately diagnosed as a risk in any future engagement by 1902. The problem in 1899 in regard to shell had been the manufacture of the fuse, the most intricate part of the projectile. In November, the industrial journal, *Arms & Explosives* reported sadly that 'the trade has failed to provide the War Department with fuses which can pass inspection'. Nor did the government factories fare better: in the early months of the war, the Royal Laboratory at Woolwich, supposedly the country's main repository of expertise in this line, suffered a complete breakdown in fuse output. The eventual solution was to gather together a group of high-quality engineering firms – and to wait fifteen months for some of them to make their first deliveries.[50] Yet in 1914 no special provision whatsoever was made for the supply of fuses, and expansion of output was left entirely in private hands. And, more than any other factor, it was delay in fuse deliveries which reduced British guns on the Western Front virtually to silence in the spring of 1915. The parallel could scarcely be more precise, the problem scarcely more avoidable.

There had been no lack of warnings. Reflecting on his 'lessons' from the Boer War, the Director of Army Contracts considered the problem of shell and fuse manufacture and wrote prophetically in 1902, 'If we should be involved in a campaign involving long and extensive employment of field batteries and guns of position, there would be considerable difficulties in meeting requirements, *particularly at first*, and this difficulty would be seriously enhanced if we should, at the same time, be engaged in a naval conflict.'[51] More graphically, the Superintendent of the Royal Laboratory, the army's chief shell expert, testified to an enquiry, as late as 1906, 'If we ever come to a really big war, ourselves, the trade, and everybody, working as hard as they can go, will never keep pace with what the [services] will want us to supply ... the productive capacity of the country would be stretched *almost to breaking point*.'[52] Exactly this combination of circumstances and dangers did arise when the 'big war' came, and 'particularly at first' in 1914 and 1915.

Other more general lessons in the arts of industrial mobilisation were equally poorly assimilated. In this connection, the most useful legacy of the Boer War was the demonstration that the private armourers tended to produce both extravagant promises and inadequate deliveries early in the war and then to improve their performance as it progressed. It followed, therefore, that the role of the public sector was to expand rapidly in order to plug the initial gap in supply. By 1907 it would seem that this point had made some impact upon opinion close to the government.[53] Yet in 1914, the authorities apparently expected a forced draft, short-order expansion from the private trade, treated their promises seriously, and provided a public sector so reduced in scale as to be incapable of swift expansion. In 1900 the Mowatt Committee had attempted to provide some long-term safeguards and to preserve a capacity for industrial mobilisation: it recommended simply that the private sector should be kept reasonably active in all peace-time years and that a margin of ready capacity should be kept up in the state sector. Unfortunately, when the exigencies of war production slipped away from the forefront of the official mind, it proved all too easy for the trade share of orders to fall below the recommended level – about two-thirds of total contracts – and for the government factories to be cut back in the name of economy until their reserve machinery crumbled away in idleness. Most especially, the armaments industry fell victim to the re-trenching measures of Liberal governments after 1906.

The major villain in this respect was the Government Factories and Workshops Committee (Murray Committee) of 1906–7, briefed to enquire into the problem of armament output and to examine, 'the economy of production in time of peace and the power of expansion in time of war'. Its preoccupation with the first of these objectives – economy – did more to obscure the lessons of the Boer War and to prepare for the munitions crisis of 1914–15 than any other single influence. Historians have not so far seized upon the point, but many of the difficulties of the Kitchener Armies in 1914 and 1915 began with this committee.

The policy of the Murray Committee was, in the name of economy, to reduce the size of the ordnance factories and to throw the whole burden of expansion and contraction in armament supply on to the private armouries. The restricted public sector was to be kept more or less constantly busy while the private manufacturers – again for economy's sake – were to idle in lean years and to leap to their lathes as soon as the first shot was fired. Nothing could have been more alien to the best opinion of 1902 which considered it imperative, 'that the trade proportion does not fall below normal in quiet years'.[54] In bad times in contrast, the Murray Committee accepted, the trade must simply 'look after itself',[55] receiving compensation from the great orders that would come in war-time. The problem of what might occur when a crisis demand followed immediately upon several lean years – as happened in land services munitions between 1908 and 1915 – was not considered. In this way, the perilous gap between peace-time and war-time levels of demand, revealed by the South African incident, was very effectively *widened*. The swings of production were made more gentle where they were already gentle – in the ordnance factories – and more severe where they were already severe – in the private arsenals.

But the public sector did not escape the 'Murray axe'. Despite the entreaties of contract officials, military industrialists, and artillery officers,[56] the labour force of the government factories was savagely pruned – by some 50 per cent between 1899 and 1914 – and a large segment – almost half – of the Arsenal's machinery was laid aside as reserve capacity. Even as the factory management insisted that they needed a force of 15,000 men to maintain their works as a going concern, the Murray Committee cut back their labour provision to 10,600.[57] The results were entirely debilitating – by 1907, 43 per cent of the Arsenal's machinery was idle, 'in reserve', and by 1910 most of it was so decayed as to be useless.[58] In 1913 the labour force was still being reduced and by 1914 had sunk below even the Murray Committee's own 'irreducible minimum'. And this was done despite the fact that, as one interested observer put it, 'those who were responsible for the internal working of the factories warned the Government that to increase suddenly the staff of the Ordnance Factories almost threefold would lend to hopeless breakdown'.[59] At the outbreak of war, the arsenals, denuded of skilled labour and encumbered with obsolete machines, were in no condition to provide the initial spurt of output defined by the Boer War as their proper contribution to the war effort. Still less were they in any position to supervise the expansion of the private trade or to assist in the recruitment of new industrial capacity.

The Murray Committee contrived to choose the worst of the available options and to negate the most obvious lessons of recent experience. No interest, public or private, gained. Having sacrificed ease of expansion in the state sector, the Committee did not concentrate upon the independent armourers, but instead left them only a small residual of the orders available. The policy was to hold the share of the reduced public sector approximately constant, but in years when total orders were small – and army orders in particular were often small from 1908 to 1914 – this intention might involve giving two-thirds of all available work to the state factories and leaving the trade with very lean pickings indeed. At these points, the independent armourers were adamantly required to 'look after themselves'. Any argument which pointed to the special powers of the trade and recommended careful support of its capacity for expansion was simply turned about: if the powers of the trade were so considerable, it was maintained, the armourers could safely be left to their own devices for, whatever the burdens, part of their formidable talents would surely survive. And any argument which suggested the creation of a public sector equipped to provide a concentrated burst of output, or to supervise industrial mobilisation, was immediately suppressed by a view of public expenditure of the most disapproving Gladstonian type. The historians who believe that *laissez-faire* was 'dying'[60] in this period would do well to examine the attitudes of the Murray Committee regarding the resourcefulness of private enterprise (it could do anything if let alone) and the proper role of government expenditure (it should do the least possible) – and this in the defence sector, traditionally a suitable place for infringements of the economic orthodoxy.

The consequences in the production test of 1914–15, unlike those in the parallel case of 1899–1900, are well known. The War Office went into the fray, pinning its faith as before upon a specialist group of weaponry suppliers and expressing a reluctance to spread the supply net any further. As a result no arrangements were available to hand when it became obvious that, in this war, industrial mobilisation would have to spread *outside* the armament sector and to incorporate large sections of the 'civilian' engineering industry. To begin with, it was even assumed, wholly inappropriately, that the responsibility for any such expansion should rest not with the government departments but with the great private contractors – despite the manifest fact that the private industrial interest and the general national interest clashed rather than coincided when any extension of armament manufacture was at issue.[61] Nor could the ordnance factories, debilitated by the strokes of the 'Murray axe', offer any relief from the effects of this misconception. And equally unattainable were the central controls on essential war resources: no provision existed at the commencement of the war, and none was to come until early 1915, for the rational administration of the desperately scarce supplies of raw materials, skilled labour, and machine tools – all vital inputs for the rapid mass output of munitions. In sum, the state in 1914 was once more *committed* to industrial mobilisation in wartime yet had failed to provide any mechanism for *obtaining* industrial mobilisation in wartime. Instead, the government's reaction to the armament crisis, as the number of customers swelled from thirty army divisions in August 1914 to seventy by summer 1915, was simply to increase the volume of its contracts, reproducing the unruly torrent of orders that had crashed down on the private armouries in 1899.[62]

As legend has it, the response of the manufacturers was to promise everything and to supply very little. But in fact they faced immense difficulties. By October 1914 they had managed to recruit only a small band of 'outside' subcontractors – some three thousand firms – and were discovering that shortages of machines, labour, and gauges set severe limits to further progress. And they received little help. Despite suggestions in Cabinet for the nationalisation of the armaments industry in October 1914 and March 1915,[63] and despite proposals for the creation of French-style armament cooperatives, *laissez-faire* principles remained sufficiently strong to preserve the great private armouries as the principal sources of supply. The task of unlocking the doors of the closed shop within which the armourers had worked since the 1880s, was left, impossibly, to the members themselves. Not until spring 1915 did cooperative schemes, enrolling teams of 'civilian' manufacturers in armament production, bring some relief. The vital innovations within the government departments – the War Office Armament Output Committee and the Treasury Munitions of War Committee – arrived only in March and April 1915, and not before then did the rudiments of an efficient procurement machinery come into existence. Central allocation of labour, machine tool, and raw material supplies had similarly to wait upon the creation of special government agencies in April and May 1915. It was only at this juncture that a realistic sense of what private industry could, and could not, do began to form. As the Armament Output Committee realised, 'It was the duty of the Government, not of the main contractors, to inquire into this [problem], for a contractor could have no possible *locus standi* in such an investigation.'[64] With such views gaining ground, it was not surprising that, on 9 June 1915, the machinery of the two existing munitions output committees should have been combined and converted to ministerial status, forming the major supply innovation of the war – the Ministry of Munitions. A primarily free enterprise system of weaponry production was replaced by a primarily statist system. It thus appeared that the only solution to the problem of munition supply in war-time was to demolish the mixed form of weaponry production that had existed since the 1880s and to terminate the classical phase of the capitalistic armaments industry. When Vickers, Armstrongs', BSA, and Nobel's became 'controlled establishments' an era ended. The radical change of direction was explained by a simple fact: it was preceded by the virtual breakdown of armament supply. By early June 1915 the arrears in fulfilment of the weaponry programme ranged across most categories of armament: the shortfall varied from 12 per cent on rifles, 19 per cent on artillery through 55 per cent on machine guns, and rose to a startling 92 per cent on high explosive shell.[65] This last deficiency counted most heavily. Exactly the problems in shell manufacture, and especially in the delicate business of fuse production, which had been revealed during the Boer War, and so painstakingly analysed in the early 1900s, reappeared once more, and with devastatingly increased effect. Their history on this occasion was brief but violent. In February 1915 the shortages were already acute: Field Marshal French, secure in the title of the armament industry's most dissatisfied client, recorded that his ammunition allotment would scarcely allow the expenditure of ten rounds per gun per day.[66] By May the shortages were unbearable: on the 9th, during the battle of Festubert, French found himself answering overwhelming German firepower with a pitiful forty minute barrage. At this point he decided, like Brackenbury before him, that 'the Empire was in jeopardy'.[67] His solution was to release the details of the armament predicament to the press – and thus to unleash the Shell Scandal, to bring down the Asquith Government and, to provide the prime condition for the creation of the Ministry of Munitions.

The chronic munitions deficiency of early 1915 thus brought to fulfilment a danger which had threatened since 1899 – the failure of the private defence industries in war-time. This allowed the first Minister of Munitions, David Lloyd George to conclude, 'When it came to the need of increasing our supply of munitions on an enormous scale, the private firms broke down completely'[68] and his successor Christopher Addison to reflect that, 'I know of no case in our history where a great industry has been so disastrous a failure in time of need.'[69] According to this interpretation the 'greatest transaction in the annals of commerce' simply overwhelmed the manufacturers.

But, in fact, it was not the armaments industry that failed. Nor was it, as the official histories tactfully argued, that the entire supply system had been overcome – once more – by an attack of 'unprecedented demand'.[70] The precise *level* of the demand may have been novel, but the problems relating to its fulfilment had been encountered before and had been accurately analysed more than once in the early 1900s. The true origin of the crisis lay in the system – or, more pertinently, as Brackenbury had observed in 1899, 'the vicious want of system' – under which armament contracts were placed in the early months of war. Once again, the service ministries issued contracts in a wholly disorganised style, building up in the armouries a tottering pyramid of unprocessed demand. The examples are legion, but two must suffice. Ammunition firms capable of turning out 3m rounds per week for the Lee Enfield rifle found themselves by the end of August 1914 confronting an expeditionary force with an immediate need for 176m rounds. And for artillery manufacturers it was the same: in the five weeks after 25 August the War Office issued contracts for almost as many of the standard field guns and howitzers as it had purchased over the previous *ten years*.[71] As in 1899, these phenomenal orders came immediately after a period of very modest activity – the shell requirements for 1913–14 for instance were on the minimum peace-time scale – and came very suddenly – the storm broke only at the end of August, two weeks after the declaration of war.

Infamously, the armourers are supposed to have answered the cascade of orders with a major stroke of capitalistic wickedness: 'the over-inflated promises of 1914'. These undertakings to supply, upon which the government counted so heavily and which were subsequently broken so thoroughly, have provided materials of defamation for many attacks upon the war-time armaments industry. In the inter-war period every variety of critic, from politician to honest pacifist, fastened upon this piece of industrial bombast as proof positive of the private armourer's deep-rooted irresponsibility and deceitfulness. Qualifications are needed even here. There is a good deal of evidence that the 'over-inflated promises' were not lightly given by the armourers but forcibly extracted by the government. The instrument of extraction was a specially appointed Cabinet Committee on Munitions Supply briefed, in effect, to create an armament programme that would at least look convincing on paper. It met in Kitchener's room at the War Office from 12 October onwards into January 1915.[72] Its activities were interesting if uncongenial. The armourers summoned before it to give their assessments of supply potential were not impressed, and their accounts of its dealings, mostly submitted to the Royal Commission on the Private Manufacture and Trading in Arms (Bankes Commission) of 1936, were notably hostile. One of their number, Sir Vincent Caillard of Vickers spoke of its 'inquisitional methods'.[73] Another, Sir Reginald Bacon of Coventry Ordnance Works, 'never ceased to marvel that Lord Kitchener tried to get my firm to supply *more than we could*', and concluded that the munitions crisis was 'very largely owing to the pressure put upon [the armourers] to try and give an *optimistic* estimate'.[74] A third, A. J. Grant of Firth-Brown Ltd, argued that the firms 'were pressed to do a great deal more than they could possibly perform'.[75] And yet another, Saxton Noble of Armstrongs' reported, 'We have accepted the wish of the Cabinet Committee . . . . and we will do our best, but mind you we are not going to be pilloried because we have not done it; because it is outside our actual work.'[76] Of course Noble was wrong: the armourers were pilloried just the same and even observers as dignified as the Official Historian of the Ministry of Munitions joined in, 'It was necessary,' he wrote, 'as bitter experience proved, to discount the promises or sanguine estimates of the manufacturers'.[77] Fortunately, however, the armourers' version of events was not only remarkably consistent, but was confirmed by virtually every non-political eye-witness. Thus the Master General of Ordnance in 1914, Major-General Sir Stanley von Donop, considered the charge relating to the 'over-inflated promises', 'rather a libel on the armament firms',[78] and, even more significantly Colonel Sir Maurice [later Lord] Hankey, the Secretary to the Cabinet during the Great War, observed that, 'there is no doubt that they [the Cabinet Committee] pressed these firms pretty hard . . . I do not think that they [the armourers] ever concealed their misgivings.'[79] Elements of this alternative explanation for the 'overinflated promises' have been available for some time. The historian of Vickers Ltd, J. D. Scott, has hinted at unusual pressures placed upon the firms, at impossible targets set for them by the *Cabinet Committee* which somehow became transposed into the 'sanguine estimates' of the *armourers*. 'If they argued', wrote Scott, 'they were looked at askance; the moral pressure upon them to say that they would attempt the impossible were crushing'.[80] Even the Official History of the Ministry of Munitions speaks briefly of contractors being 'induced' to accept every high production targets.[81] Yet the available evidence has never been satisfactorily correlated nor given the correct emphasis. The explanation appears to be that historians have neglected the central significance of the depositions made to the Bankes Commission in the 1930s by the armourers and the supply officials, and the remarkable parallelism between these two series of accounts. Hankey himself underlined this consensus for the commissioners by a characteristically sardonic remark, 'I do not know whether the Royal Commission have appreciated the significance of their evidence.'[82]

The true objective of the Cabinet Committee is fairly clear. Caught without adequate stocks, a desperate government again pushed the responsibility for the future military situation on to private industrialists who could not carry it – and protested that they could not. The government turned to a fantasy solution, forcing contractors to make paper promises as a substitute for the mobilisation policy they had themselves neglected to develop. There could be no more clear advertisement that the true failure in munitions supply lay not in the workshops or boardrooms of the industry but in the government's system for procuring weaponry. If it needs emphasis, the point was made eloquently and irascibly in 1915 by Max Muspratt of United Alkali – 'as Chairman of the largest chemical company in the country I wish immediately and emphatically to put on record a protest against Lord Kitchener's implications that any delay – in production – is the fault of the manufacturers. Fault if there is any must be put entirely to the account of the War Office . . . If they really knew the requirements of this great contest, they should have known that their system was totally incapable of meeting the new conditions.'[83]

It was not that alternative systems were unavailable. As early as 1900 an unusually intelligent Financial Secretary to the War Office, Francis Powell Williams, had suggested to the Mowatt Committee that the best way of preserving a reserve capacity of output among the trade would be for the state to introduce a subsidy scheme for the major armament contractors. This would provide compensation for the greatest burden involved in the need to maintain industrial readiness – the cost of idle plant. The proposal was constructed around a sensible system of financial relief and inducement similar to that used by the German government to ensure that the Krupp armoury would 'keep itself in a position enormously to increase its output . . . whenever called upon'.[84] Another possibility would have been the creation of a 'laboratory' arsenal in the public sector, entrusted with the design of plans for industrial mobilisation and with the provision of the jigs, gauges, and instruction necessary for the enrolment of 'civilian' firms as armament makers. Almost anything would have been more useful than the decaying workshops produced by the Murray Committee.

The problem did not lie with the lack of alternative proposals. The impediments to efficient industrial mobilisation in the Britain of 1899 or 1914 were of a different order. It could perhaps be argued that they were impediments which would attach to any free enterprise, democratic, style of industrial society as it embarked upon large-scale hostilities in the early twentieth century. After all, in both wars of this 'pair', there was a striking measure of administrative incompetence of a type commonly found in governments of this era. But the really remarkable feature is surely the lack of continuity between the various British military administrations of the period 1899–1914. Useful insights and intelligent analyses like those produced for the Boer War enquiries simply disappeared into the labrynthine files of the War Office as governments and officials changed. So, in *1906* when a member of the Murray Committee advised the Director of Artillery to examine the supply experience of the Boer War, the gallant officer expressed frank ignorance of what that experience might be.[85] In the light of *this* problem it is perhaps unsurprising that the military procurement and supply system could succumb twice to similar problems within two decades.

Commonly, it is alleged that the British War Office suffered, in the early stages of World War I, from an excess of 'Boer War thinking'. There is a violent irony to this charge, for in one field of military and industrial endeavour, the problem was precisely that 'Boer War thinking' had been forgotten. Quixotically, however, the military bureaucracy, if it thoroughly forgot some useful lessons, held tenaciously to others, frequently less useful. In this way, the State, in the interval between the wars, tended to become the victim of its own 'special relationship' philosophy: having depended for munitions supply on a small group of expert firms in peace-time, it chose to rely upon them also for industrial mobilisation in war-time, apparently unaware that this task lay beyond the competence of any private agency. The inability to distinguish between economic tasks that are properly within the sphere of government and those that are properly within the sphere of private interest is the mark of an economic philosophy, which, though still influential, had lost its relevance to actual events. In turn, this form of error was compounded by a failure to support those private firms upon which the State had decided to depend – thus leaving the entire system very precariously balanced. Economising agencies such as the Murray Committee could still direct the full apparatus of *laissez-faire* at proposals such as the Powell-Williams subsidy scheme, and, employing an orthodox economic vocabulary of great power, execrate it thoroughly. Situated squarely between the two wars of the 'pair', retrenching influences like these would strongly reinforce any tendencies making for breakdown in continuity. Such forces might perhaps explain the *double* failure in industrial mobilisation.

If it is to be effective, however, this case should take account of two qualifications frequently applied to military planning after 1902: it is often argued that military preparations were affected, firstly, by the conviction that the next war would be a confrontation of *naval* armament and secondly that, in military terms, it would be a *limited* and rapidly concluded war.

The naval hypothesis might suggest that if land armament was inadequately provided for up to 1915, the sea forces were more than sufficiently equipped. And, since the maritime element was the dominant one in British strategic planning, this would argue that industrial mobilisation did *not* fail in the more important area of supply. In fact, however, the state of naval armament in 1914 did not reflect only 'blue water' priorities in strategy; and it certainly did not reflect high efficiency in manufacturing. It followed rather from the nature of naval armament itself: navies are built up of extremely large weaponry units which require a very considerable production period. There is thus a clear need, not for the sophisticated apparatus of industrial mobilisation in war-time, but for the annual accumulation of a few very capital-intensive units in a *pre-war* situation. The navy, in fact, planned as far as possible to hit maximum output two years before the onset of hostilities. Army readiness, in contrast, requires the capacity to manufacture a myriad of relatively small and complex units in a very great hurry. The industrial problems are of divergent species and, of the two, the naval procurement offers much the less taxing form of demand. But where the navy did require rapid supply in war-time – in ammunition, for example – it is significant that the problems immediately converge. According to one pre-war observer, the navy could 'fire away a horrible amount of metal'[86] – which was exactly what the factories could not provide. And, according to one naval authority, the shell they did provide was so poor in quality that 'it would be necessary to literally pound enemy ships all day before they could be put out of action, before they would do any harm'.[87] In this sense, there was a naval shell scandal, alongside the military one. Generally, mobilisation in naval armament did not fail because it was not needed; where it was needed it did fail.

The 'limited war' hypothesis might suggest that, given the expected scale of hostilities, it was *appropriate* to cut back the public sector and rely entirely upon the few industrial giants within the 'special relationship'. But even a limited war requires an efficient supply organisation and the acceptance of a certain responsibility by the state: by no standards can a policy which decimated the ordnance factories, left the trade to its own devices, and accepted no official responsibility for supply problems be said to constitute adequate preparation for any scale of warfare. One war had already indicated the dangers inherent in some of these attitudes. Moreover, in a limited war, industrial expansion would be needed in the very short term – precisely the style of growth that shrunken government factories and neglected private armouries would be unable to attain. Nor, finally, is the hypothesis itself invulnerable: exactly how justifiable was it to formulate a philosophy of limited land war in Britain after 1902? The question lies properly in the field of the military historian, but given the direction of this analysis a single point might be permitted. If a land war fought against

Boer farmers – also expected to be limited – turned into a 'great' colonial war lasting nearly three years, an indication had surely been given that small wars turned all too easily into large ones. To this extent the creation of a limited war philosophy – even allowing British naval strength – was another product of shattered continuity.

Any expectation that the British service ministries should have equipped themselves with contractors and procurement systems capable of supplying the war needs of Armageddon is clearly nonsensical, the scale of Armageddon being unguessed before 1914. What might legitimately be expected, however, is that the military and naval authorities should have created a defence supply system which drew upon recent experience, corrected the deficiencies revealed by the last round of hostilities, and prepared effectively for the kind of war which was anticipated. The remarkable feature is that none of these objectives was accomplished.

It would not seem, therefore, that either of these two qualifications need deflect the general direction of this argument. The conclusion remains that the traditional interpretation is seriously amiss. It is not sufficient to say that in 1914 and 1915 a production and procurement system organised for the colonial scale was broken by a continental war. The truth is that it was almost broken by an earlier great war, a colonial great war, which advertised its extent by the economic strains it created. Not only that, but many of the weak points in the industrial and military apparatus – over-reliance on the private sector, 'contractors' promises,' poor procurement methods, faulty fuse and shell production – were the *same* points at which weaknesses developed in 1914 and 1915. What is worse, these exact flaws were identified and analysed by the commissions of inquiry of the early 1900s. Highly placed officers and officials knew beyond a shadow of a doubt that, had the Boer War included a naval, as well as a land confrontation, the armament system of the British Empire would have failed. They examined one munitions crisis and predicted a second. The point of this essay is perhaps best made by one such prediction. The Royal Commission on the War in South Africa in its report of 1904 pointed out that, 'insofar as any cause is assigned for the occurrence of so serious a scandal [as that in military supply] no sufficient safeguard [has been] suggested to prevent its recurrence'.[88] And, for this reason, the Boer and Great Wars 'paired' in more than the style of weaponry and the type of production problem – they paired too in the collapse of supply.

NOTES

1 This essay was first presented as a paper to the Annual Conference of the Economic History Society held at the University of Leicester in April 1973.
2 In a recent inaugural lecture, Professor D. C. Coleman drew attention to the remarkable neglect of this 'border-country' by economic historians. See

D. C. Coleman, *What has happened to Economic History?* (Cambridge, 1972), p. 29.

3 C. Rothwell in J. D. Clarkson and T. C. Cochran (eds.) *War as a Social Institution* (New York, 1941), p. 202. My italics.

4 Quoted by A. G. Enock, *The Problems of Armaments* (London, 1923), p. 70.

5 See C. Trebilcock, '"Spin-off" in British Economic History: Armaments and Industry, 1760–1914'. *Economic History Review*, 2nd ser., xxii (1969), pp. 478–9.

6 Demand from the Franco-Prussian War did cause some stir in Birmingham and business was so hectic – and so profitable – that skilled gunmakers could afford to dress, ride, smoke, and drink like gentlemen. But this was not Britain's war and the Birmingham gunmakers did not need to accept more orders than they could fulfil.

7 *War Office (Reconstitution) Committee* (Cd. 1932), 1904, p. 8.

8 F. W. Hirst, *The Political Economy of War* (London, 1915), p. 146.

9 *Ibid.* p. 85.

10 *Arms & Explosives*, August 1902.

11 Absolute figures for war costs from Hirst, *Political Economy*, pp. 298–306.

12 A. T. Peacock and J. Wiseman, *The Growth of Public Expenditure in the U.K.* (London, 1967), Ch. iv and pp. 62–70.

13 Graph extracted from Peacock and Wiseman, *Public Expenditure*, p. 54.

14 *Royal Commission on the War in South Africa* (Elgin Commission, Cd. 1789), 1904, Report, para. 55, p. 29.

15 *Elgin Commission*, Memorandum of 21 May 1900 presented in evidence by Lord Landsdowne, Q21280.

16 *Arms & Explosives*, June 1901.

17 Brackenbury to C-in-C, 15 Dec. 1899. The memorandum is bound with the War Office copy of the *Secret Committee on Reserves* (Mowatt Committee, unpub.), 1900, War Office A-paper 617. Some mention of it is made in Col J. K. Dunlop, *The Development of the British Army 1899–1914* (London, 1938), pp. 84–8, but its more remarkable aspects appear to have gone unnoticed.

18 C-in-C to Secretary of State, 18 Dec. 1899, Annexe to *Secret Committee on Reserves*, WO A617.

19 *Elgin Commission*, Evidence of Col Sir Ralph Knox, Q8945.

20 *Ibid.* Evidence of Maj-Gen Sir H. Brackenbury, Q1732.

21 Brackenbury to C-in-C, 15 Dec. 1899, WO A617, Annexed Memoranda.

22 *Committee on War Office Contracts* (HC 313), 1900, Evidence of Director Army Contracts, Q177.

23 'Secret Report of Director-General Ordnance on the Armaments and Matériel of the War', WO A617, Annexed Memoranda; *Ibid.* Evidence of Asst Director Army Contracts, Q869; *Government Factory and Workshops Committee* (Murray Committee, Cd. 3626), 1907, Evidence of Col Sir H. Barlow, Q1408; and see the table compiled by the author for W. J. Reader, *Imperial Chemical Industries, A History*, vol. 1 (London, 1970), p. 512A.

24 WO A617, Noble, QQ1199–1211.

25 *Ibid.* Dawson, QQ1251–1276.

26 'War Office Report on the Works and Current Contracts of Messrs. Armstrong Whitworth and Vickers Maxim, 1900.' PRO WO/32/300 7101/2474.

27 WO A617, Brackenbury, Q1442.

28 'Report on Works and Contracts of Armstrong Whitworth and Vickers Maxim.'

29 WO A617, Report (unpub.) My italics.

30 *Elgin Commission*, Noble, Q20899; Dawson, Q20945.
31 Vickers Archive, Letter Books, Maj-Gen R. A. Montgomery to Albert Vickers 7 Jan. 1910.
32 *Elgin Commission*, Brackenbury, Q1732.
33 *Murray Committee*, Evidence of Asst Accountant-General, QQ1952–4.
34 *Ibid.* Evidence of Chief Superintendent Ordnance Factories, Q502 and Q2424; also *Conference on Utilization of Arsenal Machinery* (Cd. 3514), 1907.
35 *Ibid.* Evidence of Maj Fisher, QQ1223–5.
36 *Arms & Explosives*, May 1901.
37 Calculated from *Director of Army Contracts Reports* 1899–1902.
38 *Committee on War Office Organization* (Dawkins Committee, Cd. 580), 1901, Evidence of Knox, Q2336. My italics.
39 *Murray Committee*, Noble, Q2187–8.
40 *Elgin Committee*, Dawson, QQ20908–14.
41 WO A617, Brackenbury, Q1451–7.
42 See the evidence presented to the *Dawkins Committee*, particularly that of Major and Brackenbury.
43 PRO WO/32/1046 1/Estab./806.
44 See C. Trebilcock, 'A "Special Relationship" – Government, Rearmament, and the Cordite Firms', *Economic History Review*, 2nd ser., XIX (1966).
45 *Arms & Explosives*, April 1901.
46 *Ibid.* May 1901. My italics.
47 Dunlop, *British Army*, p. 306.
48 *Ibid.* p. 152.
49 J. D. Scott, *Vickers, A History* (London, 1962), p. 99.
50 *Murray Committee*, Evidence of Asst Accountant-General, Q1945, and Col Sir H. Barlow, Q1408.
51 *Director of Army Contracts Report*, 1902. My italics.
52 *Murray Committee*, Col Sir H. Barlow, Q1408–9. My italics.
53 See *Murray Committee*, Report, para. 30, p. 8. The impact was not profound: the Committee paid lip-service to the principle and by its recommendations made the practice impossible.
54 *Director of Army Contracts Report*, 1902.
55 *Murray Committee*, Compare evidence of Director of Artillery, Q827–9 with the general tenor of the Committee's Report.
56 Cf. Sir George Clarke's Memorandum to the *Murray Committee*, 'So with the experience of the Boer War before us, I venture to deprecate most earnestly any reduction of the establishments of the factories below those existing before the pressure of the South African War began.' Cd. 3626, Appendix 19.
57 *Murray Committee*, Evidence of Chief Superintendent Ordnance Factories, Q433–443.
58 PRO WO/33/476.
59 Gilbert Slater, *War and Peace in Europe* (London, 1915), p. 76.
60 See, for example, J. W. Grove, *Government and Industry in Britain* (London, 1962), pp. 27–35.
61 Compare Lloyd George's statement that 'The policy of the War Office relieved it of the dreadful responsibility of the control of work . . . but at the cost of interposing between the crying needs of our front line . . . and the vast manufacturing capacity of Britain, the narrow bottleneck of a handful of over-worked firms.' D. Lloyd George, *War Memoirs* (2 vols, London, 1938), vol. I, p. 83.

62 No adequate comparison of munitions requirements with industrial capacities was in fact carried out until the Treasury Munitions of War Committee executed such a survey in April 1915. *Official History of the Ministry of Munitions*, (12 vols, London, 1922), vol. I, pt III, p. 7–8.

63 *Ibid.*, vol. I, pt I, p. 98; PRO CAB 37/124/40 and PRO CAB 37/125/3.

64 Quoted by *Official History, Ministry of Munitions*, vol. I, pt III, p. 86.

65 *Royal Commission on the Private Manufacture and Trading in Arms*, (Bankes Commission, Cmd. 5292) 1936, Evidence of Dr Christopher Addison, written statement, Exhibit A.

66 PRO CAB 22/1/1.

67 Field Marshall Lord French of Ypres, *1914* (London, 1919), p. 347.

68 *Bankes Commission*, Evidence of Lloyd George, Q3864.

69 *Ibid.* Addison, Appendix to Evidence, para. 65, p. 117.

70 *Official History, Ministry of Munitions*, vol. I, pt I, p. 7; p. 134.

71 *Ibid.* vol. I, pt I, p. 72–4 and p. 84–5.

72 *Ibid.* vol. I, pt I, p. 93.

73 Vickers Archive, Caillard correspondence, microfilm 246.

74 *Bankes Commission*, Evidence of Adm Sir Reginald Bacon (of Coventry Ordnance Works), QQ1509–11. My italics.

75 *Ibid.* Evidence of A. J. Grant, Q3294.

76 *Ibid.* Evidence of Maj-Gen S. von Donop, reporting remark of Saxton Noble, Q1229. It is interesting to compare the description given to these events by Lloyd George, a leading member of the Cabinet Committee. He recorded simply that the contractors 'engaged to increase their output by every possible means'. *War Memoirs*, vol. I, p. 89.

77 *Official History*, vol. I, pt I, p. 43.

78 *Bankes Commission*, von Donop, Q1221–6.

79 *Ibid.* Evidence of Hankey, Q4320ff.

80 Scott, *Vickers*, p. 98.

81 *Official History*, vol. I, pt I, p. 95.

82 *Bankes Commission*, Hankey, Q4320ff.

83 Muspratt to Runciman, 19 May 1915. PRO BT/13/62 E27867.

84 WO A617, Annexed Memoranda, and Evidence of Powell Williams, QQ786ff.

85 Cd. 3626, Q830.

86 *Murray Committee*, Barlow, Q1413.

87 Rear-Adm W. S. Chalmers, *The Life and Letters of David Beatty*, (London, 1951), p. 276.

88 *Elgin Commission*, Report, para. 55, p. 29.

8 War and economic development: government and the optical industry in Britain, 1914–18

Roy MacLeod and Kay MacLeod

INTRODUCTION

Among the changes wrought in British society during the First World War, those affecting science and the science-based industries are among the most notable. In particular, the economic and professional mediations between objectives and innovation deserve careful attention.[1] For it was in the process of mediating between necessity and tradition in the first great 'scientific war' that time-honoured conventions governing free enterprise, state intervention and the neutrality of science were speedily repealed, frequently with far-reaching implications for the conduct of scientific and industrial affairs.[2] This essay explores these mediations in the particular context of government activity in the optical and scientific instrument industries in the period 1914–18.

Historians have long debated the role of wars as complex motive agents, impelling both scientific growth and technological innovation.[3] At present, however, we are concerned to describe the mechanisms by which this stimulus occurred, rather than to enter the lists in the detailed discussion of war as either incentive or distortion in scientific and economic development.[4] Neither are we concerned in this essay with determining ways in which the application of scientific knowledge in any of its aspects affected the conduct or the outcome of the war.[5] These developments, widely discussed by contemporaries,[6] already form a growing literature. Much less notice, however, has been paid to the institutional processes by which science and technology acquired a new prominence in British industry. Given specialised knowledge, techniques and manufacturing methods, and given the necessity of improving, developing and applying these to immediate military purposes, British science-based firms were obliged to expand, collaborate and eventually form part of a great national network. The means by which this transformation occurred illuminate an entire spectrum of issues central to the relationship between industrial education, scientific research and government policy.

In exploring this spectrum, the optical trade is particularly instructive.[7]

First, the effects of the war on optical development were appreciated well before 1914. For example, it was as a result of the British blockade of France during the Napoleonic wars that the manufacture of glass was encouraged in France; similarly, optical glass was developed in the USA as a direct result of the war against Mexico and the consequent demand for field glasses. In Britain, the Boer War provided an important (although temporary) stimulus to the domestic manufacture of optical glass and munitions.[8]

Secondly, the experience of the industry illustrates the difficulty of reaching a monochronic interpretation of the malaise allegedly afflicting British industry between 1870 and 1914. Historians have offered several explanations for the apparent failings of this period,[9] including a 'failure of entrepreneurial nerve' reflected in poor management and resistance to innovation, increasing capital outflows between the 1850s and 1870s which deprived domestic industry of vital resources, and slow output, diminished by sluggish demand and falling profit margins, which in turn discouraged increasing capitalisation, particularly in small firms. In science-based industries, these factors were usually compounded by a neglect of technical education, resistance to cultivate applied research, and a pattern of demand and economic protection which strongly favoured continental competitors.

Given that the issue of British industrial 'failure' is by no means simple, and that its overall dimensions, in particular with regard to the resource limitations of capital and skilled labour, have yet to be agreed, we recognise that any adequate diagnosis of Britain's industrial position in applied science at the outbreak of the war, must rely not on one but on a combination of explanations, some of which remain intractably speculative.

If this is true for the dyestuffs and explosives industries,[10] it is no less true for the optical industry. In these industries, the conditions for success in technological innovation (with varying levels of market demand and technical sophistication, among firms of varying size, complexity, resources and entrepreneurial skill) provide important common ground for economists and historians.[11] We have been unable to look in detail at individual optical technologies (e.g. rangefinders, prism binoculars or dial sights), nor have we explored the business history of individual firms, or the diffusion of innovations and choice of techniques within the industry. Rather, we have concentrated upon the broad questions presented by the changing situation of the optical industry during and after the war and upon the constraints and consequences of state intervention through the Ministry of Munitions and the DSIR. In particular, we have called attention to the role of government in providing 'coupling agents' between technical knowledge and social demands, which, within the favourable climate to specific innovations created by the war, transformed the relationship of industry and the economy.[12]

OPTICAL GLASS AND THE OPTICAL INDUSTRY

Historically, the manufacture of optical glass and the growth of the scientific and optical instrument industries have been interdependent.[13] Since the seventeenth century, the availability of good quality optical glass[14] has been essential to the improvement of experimental techniques in medical and scientific research, in navigation and surveying, and in the development of methods of warfare. However, there were both technical and economic factors inhibiting the growth of a domestic optical industry in Britain. Until the middle of the eighteenth century, the lenses of the most familiar scientific instruments, telescopes and microscopes,[15] were made from thick 'crown' or 'plate' glass. Technical progress in instrument design and production was limited by the difficulty of removing from the single lens the colour of the image caused by refraction. Chester Moor Hall in 1729, and later John Dolland in 1758, found that by combining convex and concave glasses of suitable refractive indexes, a composite glass – the 'achromatic lens' – could be made to give refraction without colour. However, a 'secondary spectrum', a further fringe of colour around the image, persisted as an outstanding problem until the late nineteenth century. In 1824 increasing continental rivalry in the improvement of telescopes and microscopes led to the formation of a committee under the Royal Society to investigate optical glass manufacture. Between 1825 and 1830 Michael Faraday investigated the refractive powers of lenses made with borax oxides using a platinum crucible, but with little success. The outlook for British optical manufacture was not promising.

These technical difficulties were compounded by economic constraints, in particular, the expense involved in manufacturing glass, and the economic restrictions placed on its manufacture by government under the Excise Acts.[16] In 1835, however, a report by the Commissioners of Excise concluded that the tax not only retarded 'the accumulation of national wealth' but also hindered 'the free progress of invention and improvement, first in the manufacture of glass itself, and secondly in the numerous other arts and sciences to which the glass is subsidiary'.[17] The commissioners urged the 'expediency . . . of repeal at the earliest possible period',[18] and the Duty was removed in 1845. One of the glass manufacturers who gave evidence to the Commissioners was Lucas Chance, 'head of one of the greatest crown glass works in the country',[19] at Spon Lane, Birmingham. Chance, aware of the implications of the repeal of the glass duties, negotiated with the French glassmaker Georges Bontemps in 1837 for the patent of a new manufacturing process which, by 1851, gave Chance a dominating position over the British and European markets.[20]

While Chance secured the market in optical glass, British men of science, particularly George (later Sir George) Stokes and the Reverend William Harcourt,[21] pursued the technical problems. In particular, they attempted to eliminate the 'secondary spectrum' through the addition of metallic oxides. In Germany, research also continued on the improvement of optical glass, and at the scientific instrument workshop of Carl Zeiss (1816–88) at Jena, Ernst Abbe (1840–1905),[22] physicist and oculist, applied himself to the improvement of the microscope through the use of achromatic lenses. By 1883 Abbe, in conjunction with Zeiss and the glassmaker Otto Schott, had extended the earlier work of Harcourt and Stokes so successfully that the Prussian government awarded grants of RM60,000 to permit experiment and manufacture of a new range of optical glasses and lenses on a commercial scale. The combination of experimental skill, large-scale manufacturing facilities and government assistance proved irresistible. By 1898, Schott and Genossen had achieved a unique range of optical glasses and an annual profit of £30,000 from the export of optical glass, while the value of optical instruments manufactured annually in Germany reached £250,000. In the meantime, by the 1890s, Chance's optical department had begun to show a loss.[23] By 1900 the excess of imports over exports of scientific instruments into Britain had reached an annual value of over £200,000.[24]

One possible opportunity for Britain to recover the initiative came with the onset of the Boer War and the introduction of new methods of fighting,[25] which not only created demand for quantities of magnifying devices (particularly field glasses and telescopes), but also for new types of optical munitions.[26] In order to meet demand for telescopes, for example, additional plant was set up, but did not survive the end of the war.[27] The opportunities opened to the instrument trade were shortlived since many orders placed by the War Office for instruments were later discontinued, and 'much of the newly installed optical instrument making machinery had to be sold for little more than scrap value to be converted to other uses'.[28]

By 1900 the outlook for the optical industry seemed bleak. There were three alternative diagnoses offered for its malaise: first, that the economic and commercial structure of the industry militated against its success; second, that manufacturers neglected scientific men and scientific research; third, that the trade had few technically trained workmen or optical designers.[29] The third criticism had an immediate popular appeal in the context of the public debate on the relationship of technical education, scientific research and industrial growth, waged in Britain since the 1860s.[30] The argument for technical education, and in particular for educational training for optical designers and computers, was highlighted by the conspicuous contrast between German and British practice. In Germany, technical education was divided between the technical universities such as Charlottenburg, and four specialised technical schools offering theoretical and practical training in technical optics and instrument making.[31] In Britain there was no equivalent provision. By 1910 there were only 139 evening students and 20 part-time day students (mostly employees in instrument and spectacle-making firms) attending the limited courses offered at the Northampton Institute in Clerkenwell, the traditional centre of the London optical trade.[32] Compared with Germany, one commentator complained bitterly, 'the best we have to offer are evening classes, where body and mind are more often than not too tired out by the labours of the day to benefit by the instruction'.[33]

Not only was there limited instruction for workmen and designers, there was a 'shortage, almost an absence of technically qualified men'. It was estimated that in the glass industry, closely related to the optical industry, there was 'only one works in the kingdom' (probably Chance) 'that . . . had a well-qualified scientist'.[34] Moreover, in the optical industry, optical computation 'could be done by perhaps five persons in the country and original optical design by perhaps a dozen',[35] while not more than seven optical instrument firms possessed 'an efficient design department'.[36] Moreover, many of the most skilled workmen in the industry came from Belgium, France, or even Germany.[37]

Between 1903 and 1910, in an effort to overcome these weaknesses, the British Optical Society[38] mobilised a campaign for a central institute of technical optics[39] at the Northampton Institute. Their efforts culminated in 1910 in a review by the Higher Education Sub-Committee of the London County Council. On the basis of responses to a questionnaire circulated to 350 individuals and firms associated with the industry,[40] the sub-committee recommended the creation of a Central Institute of Technical Optics.[41] This recommendation was rejected, however, first by the LCC and then, in turn, by the War Office and the Admiralty, on grounds of economy. For the next four years, the campaign for technical training came to a standstill.

The movement to promote scientific research in the optical industry also met with indifference. As with technical education, German practice was held up to view. In Germany, as Richard Glazebrook told the Optical Society in 1904 'the majority of leading firms retain one or more experienced mathematicians or physicists in their permanent service'.[42] The Zeiss works employed no less than fourteen scientific graduates,[43] but in Britain 'the scientists were regarded as unpractical people with their heads in the clouds'.[44] Even at Chance the research laboratory under the direction of Walter Rosenhain[45] had closed down in 1905 owing to the prohibitive cost of experiments. It reopened on a limited scale in 1909 but on patriotic rather than commercial grounds.[46] Equally disappointing was the record of optical research at the National Physical Laboratory (the NPL),[47] modelled on its German forerunner, the Charlottenburg Reichanstalt, which was well known for its 'numerous and intimate' relations with German industry.[48] However, the combination of Treasury parsimony, and the pressure of other work at the laboratory frustrated an attempt in 1912 to mount a programme of optical research.[49] By the outbreak of the war, therefore, there was no evidence of any large scale industrial or government sponsored research in the composition or manufacture of optical glass other than the work of Chance's optical glass department.

If much popular attention focused on the limited extent of technical training and scientific research, there were, in addition, economic factors to frustrate the optical manufacturers. Some contemporary observers believed that high tariff walls protected Germany from imported goods while British firms suffered from cheaper imports, produced by cheaper labour and longer working hours.[50] However, perhaps the most important was the difference in the volume and structure of demand in Germany and Britain. Traditionally, the German army had placed large orders with German instrument firms.[51] A guaranteed flow of orders with product specialisation and lower costs of mass production, enabled German firms not only to supply their own domestic market but to obtain the bulk of orders for other European armies. The British War Office was a customer for German dial sights and prism binoculars, a policy which had led to the active discouragement of British firms in this area. Moreover, when the War Office placed orders for instruments with British firms they were not for thousands, but for tens.[52] In a misguided effort to stimulate competition, the War Office placed small contracts with several firms which proceeded to manufacture hand made instruments of high quality. The net effect was to force up unit prices and to discourage mass production.

In 1914, therefore, the optical instruments industry remained essentially a fragmentary collection of craft-based family firms, many entirely concerned to retail German goods.[53] Secretiveness and hostility between the various sectors of the trade (the instrument makers, lens makers and spectacle makers) discouraged cooperation. Moreover, the scarcity of capital for investment and research,[54] the absence of a general apprenticeship scheme, no modern methods of 'costing', and 'no policy of commercial or economic expansion'[55] presented a gloomy picture. In June 1914 the British Science Guild (BSG) drew attention to the fact that: 'Great Britain has fallen so far behind in the development of her optical manufacture that not only is she unable to supply her scientific and industrial requirements, but at the present moment she could not, unaided, produce sufficient quantities for the service of the Army and Navy of the optical aids which are so important in modern warfare.'[56]

THE OPTICAL INDUSTRY AND THE WAR

With the outbreak of the war and the cessation of German imports, the full extent of British dependence on German optical glass and instruments was revealed. In August 1914 sixty per cent of optical glass was imported from Jena, while a further thirty per cent was imported from the French firm Parra-Mantois; it was anticipated that French imports could not be expected to continue in the event of increasing domestic demand in France. Chance was supplying only 10 per cent of British needs. In addition, the mobilisation of the British Expeditionary Force brought an unprecedented demand for optical munitions. In November 1914 the British Optical Society were told:

the Army had been increased to . . . something like a million men, six or seven per cent of whom would want field glasses, and one quarter of whom would want telescopes of different sorts, both for sighting guns and for observation . . . Every hundred men would want that very expensive instrument, a rangefinder . . . [and] when they remembered the enormous number of surveying instruments and of heliographs with their mirrors accurately silvered, they could form some conception of the amount of work which the Government required to be done.[57]

The only instrument in assured supply was the rangefinder. In September 1914 Lord Roberts issued an 'almost despairing appeal' that all field glasses in private hands should be donated to the Army. By the third week of September over 2,000 instruments had been forwarded (including four pairs each from the King and Queen). However, this proved totally inadequate and throughout the spring the advertisement columns of the daily papers carried requests for optical instruments from soldiers en route to the Front.[58]

In October 1914 the Institute of Chemistry made the first attempt to provide immediate scientific assistance to the optical and glass industry by appointing an advisory committee on glass under the direction of Professor (later Sir) Herbert Jackson at King's College London.[59] The first task of the committee was to define formulae for the most scarce types of chemical, scientific and optical glass, all unobtainable from Germany; within six months ten formulae for the most urgently needed glasses were available for manufacture.[60] In addition the same advisory committee also asked the BSG to investigate optical glass supply. To the surprise of some, the BSG's report, published in March 1915, accepted the evidence of Chance that 'the supply of optical glass for the manufacture of telescopes, binoculars, rangefinders and other services instruments is sufficient for the purpose'.[61] The BSG was less sanguine, however, about the 'serious inconvenience' which would result if supplies from Germany were cut off for any length of time and recommended 'a considerable development of British glass manufacture in this direction', particularly through a programme of fundamental research on optical glass at the NPL, and the creation of a central institute for technical optics.

In fact, despite Chance's apparent confidence, it was becoming increasingly clear that the demand for all types of optical glass was rapidly outstripping supply, and by April 1915 the firm was forced to announce that they would, in future, be able to supply optical glass only to manufacturers of optical instruments with War Office or Admiralty contracts. Throughout the late spring of 1915, demands for state intervention in optical glass production became audible. In an attack on the government launched in *The Times* on

28 April, Mullineux Walmsley of the Northampton Institute drew attention to the state of the industry, and drew the popular analogy with what had already been achieved in the case of aniline dyes.

The case is one for prompt government action. Government departments are well seized of the facts, and the capital expenditure required would be quite small compared with that in the aniline dye case, and a start could be made at once by taking over the optical glass branch of Messrs Chance Brothers Works ... Last but not least, the urgent necessity for thorough education in optics which I and others have been advocating for many years and which, had we been listened to, would have done something to have lessened the loss of life, especially in the early stages of the war.

Between April and May, Philip Magnus, MP (formerly Secretary of the Department of Technology, City and Guilds of London Institute) kept up a barrage of parliamentary questions on the government's plans to overcome the shortage of optical glass, but official replies betrayed no sense of urgency.[62] On 19 May, in an atmosphere of rumour and anxiety following the revelations of shell-fuse shortages, Magnus adopted more aggressive tactics, and in a detailed speech to the House of Commons, described the country's predicament with regard to optical glass. He urged that the sole solution lay in government intervention, but before he could pursue this argument, the debate was interrupted by Asquith's announcement of the formation of a coalition government.[63] When the debate resumed, Magnus had lost his audience, but Christopher Addison,[64] Parliamentary Secretary to the Board of Education, replied with a promise that the government soon hoped 'to have a comprehensive scheme to deal with this somewhat complicated and technical question'.[65]

The Ministry of Munitions, Chance Brothers and optical glass supply, June 1915 to 1918

Government intervention in the optical industries was accelerated by two developments. The first was the creation of the Advisory Council for Scientific and Industrial Research in July 1915,[66] which took its place with other advisory bodies set up to bring scientific expertise to bear directly on the conduct of the war.[67] The second, more immediately important to the future of the optical industries, was the creation of the Ministry of Munitions,[68] under Lloyd George, and his close colleague, Christopher Addison.

Before the creation of the work of the Ministry of Munitions, the supply of optical munitions had been the responsibility of the gun department of the War Office. When supplies proved inadequate, a branch of the Ministry of Munitions (CM6) was created to promote the supply of optical glass and munitions, by providing financial aid, raw materials and technical assistance to the industry.[69] F. J. Cheshire[70] joined the branch as technical adviser on optical questions and A. S. Esslemont[71] was appointed administrative head. The two formed a remarkable partnership.

Within a few weeks, in view of the demands placed on CM6 by the new gun programme, an Optical Munitions and Glassware Department (OMGD) was organised and divided into functional sections or branches: (1) a *technical section* which had by February 1916 a staff of four, including one optical instrument maker, a draughtsman and two experienced assistants. The branch tested new designs and instruments, revised specifications and provided a constant source of technical and scientific expertise for the trade; (2) a *contracts section* with a staff of six responsible for making and revising all contracts; (3) a *statistics section*, with a staff of six clerks; and (4) a *general section*, with a staff of nine, dealing with the control, supply and distribution of optical glass, the issue of licences, and the control and distribution of optical munitions and the direction of labour.

The OMGD did not underestimate the task before it. Its first objective was to accelerate the supply of optical glass to the optical instruments in industry. Chance was producing only 1,000 lbs a month (or about 10 per cent of pre-war demand), and about twenty types of simple optical glass. The supply from the French firm, Parra-Mantois, continued, however, in exchange for guarantees that rangefinders by Barr and Stroud would continue to be exported for French troops.[72] Finally, there was, in reserve, a small stock of Jena glass.

Between the outbreak of the war and June 1915, discussions on financial assistance to Chance for the extension of buildings, plant and machinery, had gone on between Chance and the War Office in a rather desultory fashion. These were brought to a rapid conclusion in June 1915 by Esslemont who persuaded the firm that with government assistance the output of optical glass could be raised to 120,000 lbs annually, H. J. Stobart, leading the negotiations on behalf of Chance, at first rejected this target as totally unrealistic. He reminded the government that 'for many years we carried on this Department at a loss; kept it alive mainly from patriotic motives'. Not only did the firm not have the capacity for expansion, but production of glass would, he argued, be hampered by the lack of technical staff.[73] However, while the firm was prepared to make every effort to respond to the national emergency, Stobart felt that they had the right to ask for 'a formal undertaking from the Government as to working conditions in the future'.[74] He suggested a fixed guarantee for one third of the cost of any sales falling below that figure. In addition, he asked that the government give Chance a monopoly with sufficient price guarantees.

Despite Chance's initial reluctance to undertake the OMGD's targets, they were persuaded by Esslemont's optimism and his assurances that guarantees could be given to safeguard the future of the firm. The first contract, whereby Chance agreed to enlarge their premises, extend plant and install machinery to provide a monthly output of 8,500 lbs, was ready by January 1916. The agreement provided for a ten year partnership between Chance, the Ministry of Munitions, the War Office and the Admiralty. The firm would be responsible for all plant and machinery, which would remain their property. In return, Chance was required to maintain a specified reserve of glass, adequate staff and, at the conclusion of the war, to keep the plant prepared to increase output to a specified minimum at three months' notice. In addition, the firm agreed to pay the government 5 per cent of all receipts derived from the sale of goods. Finally, it was agreed that government departments would, for the duration of the agreement, place orders exclusively with the firm. The total cost of plant installation was estimated at £40,000.[75]

In fact, with additional plant, labour and machinery, Chance had already increased its output until by November 1915 its estimated output was 70,000 lbs.[76] By the end of 1915, however, it was also clear that earlier estimates of demand for optical glass were still too low, and in April 1916 a further agreement was made with the OMGD to increase monthly output to 14,200 lbs. This target was fulfilled by May 1917. By that date, as Chance's works were within the range of German Zeppelins, a further supply of optical glass had been secured by an agreement between the department and the Derby Crown Glass Company. Chance and Derby supplied all domestic demand for the remainder of the war. Chance's output for the first half of 1918 reached the total of 92,000 lbs, with a capital employment of £150,000 while the value of government contracts with the optical glass firms reached £78,000.[77] By the end of the war Chance was producing 'about twice the world's peacetime consumption'[78] or about four tons of optical glass a month – an achievement all the more remarkable in the light of the worldwide shortage of glass.[79]

As the war continued, and military techniques grew more sophisticated, the technical problems created by the demand for increasingly complex lenses proved more difficult than those of accelerating production. In fact, thanks to the efforts of Chance's scientific manager, Samuel Lamb, some of the major technical problems associated with the manufacture of complex lenses had been partially solved by the outbreak of the war,[80] and the firm was able to supply the most commonly required lenses involved in instrument design. By June 1917 Chance's research laboratory had come into operation under the direction of F. E. Lamplough, and the full complement of staff in the laboratory reached 125 by the end of the war.[81] Chance's research team concentrated on both fundamental and applied research – for example, on colour free lenses, on tinted and coloured glasses, and after 1917 on photographic lenses for cameras used in aerial reconnaisance. The research undertaken by the laboratory resulted in improved methods of testing and producing glasses, and major innovations in the quality and range of glasses. By the end of the war Chance had placed on the market seventy-two types of optical glasses, many of which were previously made only in Germany, using formulae which had been determined from first principles.

The question arises as to how this was possible, given the time available, and the few qualified scientists 'on tap'. Most contemporary commentators believed that Chance had been helped in the production of new glasses by academic scientists, particularly Sir Herbert Jackson, but the firm resisted this view, and was at pains to stress that 'Messrs Chance have neither asked for nor required any assistance from outside sources to produce types of glass required.'[82] Despite the much vaunted superiority of German glass, and the weight of German tradition in optical glass making, it would seem that the concentration of a handful of optical physicists, together with the resources of the manufacturing laboratory with no expense spared, had proved sufficient to overcome major technical problems which had inhibited the domestic optical glass industry in Britain for twenty-five years.

The Ministry of Munitions and the optical industry: economic assistance

In July 1915, while negotiations for an increased supply of optical glass were near completion, the OMGD turned to the shortfall in optical instrument production. While there were an estimated 190 firms concerned in some way with the manufacture of optical munitions, the bulk of the contracts placed by the OMGD with the trade were awarded to about twenty major manufacturing firms which dominated the trade and which were potentially capable of meeting targets.[83]

By November 1915 all unsold instruments in private or commercial hands (a total of 33,019), were commandeered, inspected and purchased by the OMGD.[84] At the same time a further, more bizarre step was taken when, as with chemical dyes, negotiations were actually begun with Germany to exchange British supplies of rubber for German optical instruments, through the neutral office of Switzerland. The German War Office promised 30,000 binoculars by the end of 1915 and 15,000 monthly thereafter. In the event, however, the success of British optical firms made this distasteful agreement unnecessary (although, in the case of chemical dyes, exchanges were arranged). In August 1916 a further requisition of photographic lenses for the camera programme of the Air Board was announced. Despite these efforts, however, certain instruments, particularly binoculars and dial sights, remained in short supply throughout the war despite the valiant efforts of the domestic industry and the import of instruments, where possible, from France, USA and Japan.[85]

There was no systematic attempt to organise optical munitions production however, until the creation of the OMGD in July 1915. 'No real help had been given to the manufacturer except by indiscriminate doles' and Sir William Hart-Dyke (of the Spectacle Makers Company) complained bitterly that 'we can do nothing without capital and machinery . . . If we get the capital, the machinery will come'.[86] The OMGD introduced a system of long-term loans, which eventually took the form of grants-in-aid for the extension and purchase of materials, and the payment of labour. Direct contracts for large quantities of single instruments and elements were placed with major firms, including Barr and Stroud, Heath & Company, Ross, Taylor, Taylor and Hobson, Beck, and Watson & Company.

The contracting policy of the OMGD immediately proved controversial since usually all munitions contracts were handled centrally by the Ministry's contracts department, which argued that in the interests of uniformity of control, contracts awarded to the optical firms should be administered by the contracts branch. The contracts branch was particularly offended that no arrangements had been made to have a 'contracts officer' oversee the important contracts drawn up with Chance.[87] Cheshire resisted these attempts at conformity, emphasising that:

The supplying firms are for the most part small and already overburdened with work, and a very large proportion of the production to be undertaken is more or less experimental in character. Moreover, the question of price and rate of delivery is enormously complicated by the shortage of trained labour and machine tools, difficulties in supply of optical glass and other raw materials, and by frequent revision of specifications to meet these difficulties. Practically every contract is reduced to a matter of individual negotiation requiring detailed and expert knowledge on the part of the supply system.[88]

For his part, Esslemont was particularly anxious that the interference of the contracts branch 'would threaten the delicate relationship between the OMGD and the firms and would create more, and perhaps disastrous delays in production'.[89] After protracted correspondence the contracts branch gave way, and although a few optical firms voluntarily came under direct control,[90] the majority of firms continued to negotiate directly with OMGD.

In addition to assisting the expansion of firms manufacturing optical munitions, national factories were set up in specific areas. The most important of these was the Periscope Prism Company, established in late 1917 to supply optical sights for aeroplane guns, telescopic rifles and gun sighting telescopes. In early 1918, a national factory was built at Enfield for the manufacture of photographic lenses, and in July 1918, an additional photographic lens factory began work at Birmingham.[91]

To ensure that contracts were placed with firms capable of filling them, and to act as liaison between the trade and the OMGD, an inspection section was set up in November 1915 to act as 'the eyes and the ears of the branch'.[92] The majority of the inspectors were scientific graduates – men or women with experience in scientific management or government institutions such as the Patent Office.[93] The functions of the inspection section were: to ensure deliveries on contracts, to 'ascertain and recommend fresh sources of supply of finished instruments, manufactured or semi-manufactured parts of instruments and raw materials',[94] and to oversee the introduction of machinery and diluted labour into the firms.

The introduction of mechanical, standardised machinery into the industry was as important as the provision of capital, and proved more contentious since it immediately threatened the replacement of craft traditions by mass production techniques. Using machine tools, the manufacturing time of a prism for binoculars was reduced from eight or nine hours to half an hour. Prior to the war there were few British engineering firms making machine tools for the optical industry. The result was the local manufacture of a range of idiosyncratic machine tools by the optical firms themselves: each optical worker had a different type of machine tool 'often of his own design and construction'.[95] A specialist from the machine tool branch of the Ministry of Munitions was commissioned to design machine tools for hire, hire purchase or sale from the OMGD. Most firms chose to buy, rather than hire machinery (the bulk of which was built in Switzerland), and by the end of the war an estimated £267,225 worth of machinery had been, bought[96] After the war many firms took up the production of standard types of machine tools themselves.

At the outbreak of war, therefore, 'the ideas of the trade, with a few notable exceptions were ... those of handicraftsmen, not manufacturers',[97] and thus the opposition of the workmen hardened as the introduction of machinery was accompanied by the introduction of 'dilutees' or unskilled women labour into the instrument trade. The return of skilled workmen recalled from the services had proved inadequate, and the absence of any general apprenticeship scheme meant that there was no reserve of 'boy labour'. But although women were already working in parts of the trade, hostility towards them, particularly in the lens-working firms, was very great. 'The industry would not have them at any price and declared almost unanimously that if they were introduced the wastage incurred in training them and the opposition offered by the men would so seriously hamper output that it would be suicidal for the department to insist on their introduction.'[98] *The Optician* tried to temper objections towards the employment of women by pointing out that:

War is an even mightier leveller than poverty. It promises to obliterate sex distinction... Our optical manufacturers are today more productive than they have ever previously been...

It is indeed, a craft that is so varied in its field that employment can be found in it for every grade of ability and intelligence. The entry of women into this arena need not depress the wage market... They could be drafted into what would be to a large extent a new industry so far as this country is concerned.[99]

Eventually, women were mostly employed on grinding and polishing of lenses. Criticisms of lack of skill were overcome when, beginning in March

1916, the women were given basic theoretical and practical training at Northampton Institute. The first ten women students with 'a fairly good education'[100] were admitted in May 1916, and the first intake of twelve students included three women graduates who later became inspectors. Ultimately the school provided sixty places.

On their entry into the firms, it was later recorded that many women faced allegations from the workmen[101] that their clumsy unskilled ways ruined finely turned optical instruments and that their lack of experience slowed down production. Although most complaints were found to be groundless, many manufacturers chose to placate their workmen by either introducing the women at the earliest stage of the manufacturing process, by restricting them to an all-woman factory, or by restricting them to the simplest processes such as engraving, painting or assembling instruments. As the employment of women became a more familiar occurrence, responsibility for recruitment and training was assumed by the firms, but, sadly, many women were under-employed in terms of the training they had received at the Northampton Institute.[102] By the end of the war the total number of employees in the optical and scientific instrument trades had increased by about three times, and the number of women by as much as fifteen times.[103] Eventually, as *The Optician* commented:

Women were brought into the industry in large numbers. Maids of all work, shop girls, educated women of all sorts and kinds were brought in. They had never heard of a sighting telescope, a rangefinder or a clinometer. It did not matter. They were put through a three to six months training course, they were distributed among the various workshops and in a short time they were grinding and fine polishing and edging optical glass for the most complex ... instruments of precision ... As to the lenses, the vast bulk of them were ground and polished by women, work hitherto regarded, not unreasonably, as delicate and highly skilled.[104]

The introduction of women dilutees solved only part of the labour shortage. Equally serious, and vindicating the arguments of the education and research lobby before the war, was the extreme shortage of skilled designers and computers which was widely acknowledged to be a major threat to production schedules. As Esslemont complained: 'In many instances the loss of a simple calculator, designer, or prism worker may hamper the entire output of a firm.'[105] In February 1916 one of the OMGD inspectorate referred to the absence of expert technical and theoretical knowledge and the grave difficulty of producing sufficient achromatic lenses, the manufacture of which depended on skilled computation. In the absence of skilled designers: 'it is not clear that at the present moment this difficulty is not an insuperable one. When glass is delivered in batches varying *inter se* in their optical properties ... to such an extent that modification is required of the grinding tools, then an attendant optical expert becomes a prime necessity.'[106] The inspector suggested that there were three alternatives open to the OMGD to overcome this situation. First, those firms with designers should be encouraged to share them with firms who had none; second, training could be provided by the firm; third, standard publications on optical design and computation could be distributed by the OMGD to the firms. But in each case, as he acknowledged, any solution would inevitably take too long to make a material difference to the immediate shortages.

By the end of the war, however, despite all obstacles, the record of the optical industry was one of considerable achievement. The combination of financial assistance, standardised machinery, diluted skilled labour and the watchful guidance and commercial expertise of the inspection section of the OMGD had resulted in an increase of production to 'something like twenty times' pre-war output.[107] A few illustrations will serve to show the extent of these changes. The weakest area of supply was the manufacture of prism binoculars which were made by only four British firms before the war. By the end of the war fifteen firms were making binocular parts, and total output had increased by 500 per cent. The number of lens and prism manufacturers had increased from thirty to fifty.[108] According to the official historian, the 'annual value' of the industry (we presume at constant prices) had grown from a pre-war figure of £250,000, to £5m in 1918.[109] Moreover, the introduction of mass production had made possible the production in enormous quantities of types of instruments never before manufactured.

The Ministry of Munitions and the optical industry: technical assistance

In addition to the challenge of modernising the industry and coordinating demand and supply, the OMGD faced the fact that the war had thrown up many intractable technical problems which threatened to disrupt and delay production. These problems were of three main types. First, the war had prevented the import of some key raw materials used in the optical industry, such as sand, barium or potash; second, there were fundamental technical problems involved in the use of materials, and processes, and the manufacture of certain products which had to be solved before manufacture could go ahead on any scale; third, there were specific problems relating to the design, development and innovation of optical elements and instruments. The solution of these three types of problem demanded the collaboration of university scientists, technical experts and the manufacturers themselves.

There were three sources of expertise available to the OMGD. First, university scientists, of whom the most active was Sir Herbert Jackson, scientific adviser to the OMGD on glass. Jackson with his research team at King's College, London, undertook fundamental research on a wide range of questions. He was joined, in the course of the war, by other specialist advisers, such as Professor George Boswell (raw materials), and Professor J. W. Cobb (furnaces and refractory materials).[110] In addition to specialist advisers, the

OMGD also had access to the research laboratories of the department of glass technology of the University of Sheffield (after 1916) and the department of technical optics at the Imperial College of Science and Technology (after 1917). Furthermore, eminent scientists were invited to assist the OMGD on an *ad hoc* basis. For example, Sir William Crookes,[111] who for some years had studied the composition of tinted and coloured glasses, continued his research on behalf of the OMGD throughout the war and in 1916 a limited number of coloured glasses were manufactured commercially. The experience of collaboration forced scientists, technical designers and manufacturers into a new realisation of their mutual dependency, for it was evident that:

The inventors and computers who introduce new designs, the men who manufacture, sell and use the apparatus thus evolved, all have their share in the development of productivity . . . For the day of exclusiveness, even in formal academic science, has gone by. The scientist, or at any rate, the optical scientist, must collaborate with technical workers if he is to justify fully his existence at this critical time.[112]

The outstanding needs of the manufacturer dominated the direction of scientific help, and the enthusiasm of university scientists was tempered by the anxiety of the OMGD to apply their talents to the specific problems facing the department and the trade. Many scientific men were 'anxious to help', but 'they wanted to help in their own particular and often quite unpractical way'. The OMGD insisted that the department maintain control of the 'business direction' of the investigation, and make 'itself responsible for seeing that the knowledge derived from their work was usefully assimilated'.[113]

A further source of assistance to the OMGD and the industry was the NPL, where in 1915 a research programme on optical glass was finally begun under Walter Rosenhain. The research followed closely the programme proposed first in 1912, but following representations to the trade to determine the most stubborn scientific and technical problems facing manufacturers, scientists at the NPL concentrated on the definition of refractive and dispersive indexes of optical glass. In the course of time, as new difficulties arose, the laboratory undertook investigations on a wide range of related manufacturing problems including the development of photographic lenses for aerial reconnaissance and the composition of refractory materials for furnaces.[114]

A third source of expert assistance to the trade was that provided by the scientific, technical and engineering branch of the OMGD which formed a bridge between specialist advisers, the trade, and the OMGD. Its main function was to locate and define outstanding technical problems of design or manufacture and to refer such problems to the most appropriate individual or institution for solution. The following examples, although representing only a fraction of the achievements of the technical branch, demonstrate the variety of ways in which it was able to stimulate, organise and promote research. Some technical developments were largely the results of independent work by one manufacturer; other cases represented collaborative work between manufacturers and the OMGD or between scientists and manufacturers. The following examples briefly illustrate three categories of research and development: the creation of substitutes for imported raw materials; developments and improvements related to materials, processes or products used; and the design, development and innovation of weapons.

Raw materials. Among the vital raw materials imported for the manufacture of optical glass were pure sand, barium and potash. Although a supply of sand was maintained, its import was obviously threatened. George Boswell, a lecturer in the department of geology at Imperial College, was commissioned to test certain native British sands with a view to their substitution. As a result of his work, deposits were found in the north of Ireland which proved appropriate, and Boswell, assisted by the OMGD, arranged trial melts of the sands and glass manufacture on a commercial scale.[115] This proved successful – and work on charting British deposits continued under his supervision throughout the war. Equally serious was the shortage of barium – an essential constituent in certain optical glasses. The Derby Crown Glass Company discovered that excellent results could be obtained by the use of selective native carbonate in the form of witherite; this was used as an adequate substitute for barium until the end of the war.[116]

Another important technical development came in the wake of the cessation of potash imports from Germany which had an estimated pre-war value of £915,867. According to estimates in 1916[117] Britain consumed about 30,000 tons annually for fertilisers, soaps, dyes, cocoa and matchmaking, in addition to carbonate for glass making. In April 1915, Kenneth Chance, Managing Director of the Cyanides Company of Oldbury, Worcestershire, began research into the production of potash in the form of waste from blast furnaces, both by increasing the temperature of the furnace and by the addition of common salt to the blast charges. The latter method was cheap and effective and 'a complete success'. As *The Optician* recorded, 'Through chemical action the potash comes off in fumes and solidifies into minute particles. It is then extracted by technical processes from the rest of the fume dust.' The 'great German monopoly' had been 'defeated by a waste product',[118] and *The Optician* looked forward to an annual production of 30,000 tons.

In the event, this was to prove an over-optimistic forecast. In June 1917 the potash production branch was formed under the direction of Esslemont, when the British Potash Company Ltd was set up to develop Chance's process. It was not until March 1918, however, that the potash factory near Oldbury, Manchester was in production. By the end of the war the factory had achieved a total output of 1,700 tons, but the difficulties associated with large-scale potash production made the continuing importation of potash essential throughout the war.

Fundamental research into materials, processes and products. Three examples of this type of investigation reflect various processes in the manufacture of optical glass. First, the composition of glass; second, the development of sophisticated photographic lenses; third, the manufacture and composition of fireclay pots.

In addition to optical glass the OMGD was responsible for the production of laboratory and scientific glassware which were also in short supply at the beginning of the war. The major research effort to overcome this shortage was that of Sir Herbert Jackson and his team. Most of Jackson's work was done in his laboratory at his home where he developed more than seventy successful formulae, from which more than 500 'melts' were made. In May 1916 Jackson's team submitted an impressive report on their work on chemical and scientific glassware since the outbreak of the war.[119] Among their major achievements was the composition of a glass with 'a high resisting power for chemical reagents' which had been a German monopoly. Such a glass was of outstanding value to the pharmaceutical industry, and Jackson reported triumphantly that the problem was 'attacked and successfully solved . . . in two weeks'. The derivation of a formula for 'fluor glass', which had taken German scientists fifteen years, took Jackson ten weeks. In addition, the list of new formulae included that for the manufacture of anti-glare glasses, X-ray bulbs, glasses for artificial eyes, vacuum flasks, thermometers and heat resisting chimneys.[120]

From the composition and manufacture of new types of glass came the introduction of complex lenses. One of the most outstanding developments in this field was the research and manufacture by Chance of camera lenses for aerial photography. The use of the aeroplane for aerial reconnaissance following the formation of the photographic section of the Royal Flying Corps was among the most successful and dramatic developments of the war, and stimulated the improvement of photographic techniques in all fields. The aerial definition of the infamous 'Hindenburg Line' in March 1917 finally established the value of reconnaissance beyond all doubt, and there came an insistent request from the Air Board for photographic lenses of great magnification and accuracy. This was referred to Chance's research laboratory in mid-1917. The task was formidable. As the Board of Trade recalled:

When it is remembered that these aerial photographic lenses are about 5″ in diameter, and consist of four or sometimes five glasses each from one to one and a half inches in thickness and that the glass had to pass the most stringent tests, it will be recognised that a still further strain was put upon an already heavily burdened industry.[121]

The combination of required lenses demanded the production of 'a light barium crown, two light barium flints, two dense barium crowns, and an extra light flint'.

The last three glasses of the most extreme types made by Schott. The experimental work for these was carried out without assistance from analysis, as samples were not at once forthcoming, and the glasses were successfully made, two of them having properties rather more extreme than the corresponding Jena types whilst the third glass (extra light flint) was decidedly more durable than the sample of [Parra] Mantois submitted towards the end of the investigation.[122]

This constituted one of the most impressive technical achievements of the war, to which post-war commentators referred as an outstanding example of British scientific and technical skill.[123]

One further instance of the successful impact of fundamental research on glass manufacture occurred when the acute shortage of firing pots threatened the disruption of optical glass production. Traditionally, it had been that the pots, once manufactured, were not used for twelve months to avoid breakage. The effect was an unacceptable time lag between manufacture and use. In 1916 the lack of pots was so serious that manufacture was brought under the direct control of the department,[124] while at the same time research by Jackson into the composition of the clays and the traditional manufacturing processes (including the practice of treading the clay with the feet) showed that the twelve-month drying time was 'largely due to the lack of scientific treatment in the drying and heating process'.[125] Experimental work on a laboratory and manufacturing scale determined that four months was adequate, a discovery which immediately alleviated the problem by releasing pots into use more quickly. Later in the war a fruitful research programme on refractory materials and furnace structure resulted in further improvement in the materials and processes used in glass manufacture.

Development and innovation in instrument design. Throughout the war the OMGD were called upon to provide a whole range of traditional and new optical munitions. Many of the suggestions for innovations came from serving men. Depending on the nature of the request or suggestion, the OMGD sometimes referred the question directly to the independent scrutiny and manufacture of one firm or a group of firms; on other occasions, a collaborative effort was mounted by manufacturers and scientists; in some cases, the technical branch itself undertook the simplification and modification of design before putting it forward for manufacture.

As an example of an independent innovation undertaken at the suggestion of the OMGD, there was the introduction of a revolutionary process for marking 'graticules' – the delicate etchings giving scale and direction – onto lenses. This had traditionally been done with spider web filaments and later by diamond-engraving the markings onto the lens – a process performed exclusively in Germany which involved every possibility of damaging the lens. Following a suggestion from F. J. Cheshire the firm of Julius Rheinburg undertook to investigate alternative methods. Subsequently, Rheinburg recalled: 'Fifteen months were spent on research work at considerable outlay at my own expense, and led to a satisfactory article being produced by new methods of grainless photography. A plentiful supply of Government orders being immediately forthcoming, a small organisation was started for their production in quantities and for continuous research work on the new photographic methods.' The process developed by Rheinburg was to burn the markings onto the glass by means of a thin file of metal. The designer later recorded that intermolecular action seemed to take place between the metal and the bonding surface of the glass, enabling the disc to be cleaned without damaging the rulings. By the end of the war, 'graticules' had become 'an established industry' in the UK.[126]

Collaboration between the OMGD technical department and manufacturers occurred in the manufacture of periscopes – rarely made in Britain before the war. One modification of the orthodox periscope was the design by the technical branch of a periscope which could be balanced on top of a trench to measure both horizontal and vertical angles. This modification, the inspiration of a serving soldier, later went into production by the firm of Kershaw.[127] Other suggestions coming from the trade brought about the simplification of designs. The gun-sighting telescope, for example, was made by one firm (Watson) which, in response to a request to share its design with other firms, supplied the technical branch with a simplified design, thus enabling the manufacture of the periscope by other, less well equipped, firms.[128]

New instruments and components were also designed by the technical branch in cooperation with the NPL and the trade. These included the production of luminous sights (using radium) for rifles, angle measuring periscopes, compass binoculars, and telescopic sights for rifles. The telescopic sight was of particular importance to trench warfare. At the beginning of the war their use by German sharp-shooters 'made sniping a fine art'. *The Optician* recorded: 'It turns out that one or two men in every German infantry company, the most skilled shots, possess rifles fitted with telescopic sights ... The worst of the British situation ... is that the Germans have developed the telescopic sight and with the exception [of one American firm] make the only practical instruments of this sort for the fighting rifle.'[129] Only one firm – Aldis and Sons – was capable of mounting gun sights. They were commissioned to manufacture telescopic sights in 1916, but had little success. It was not until 1917 that a captured German sight, after investigation by the NPL, gave a clue to the appropriate lens composition. The glass was of Schott origin and could be reproduced. Thus, 'the data obtained from the NPL was ... of much material assistance in computing the new system in so much as the preliminary work on approximations was saved',[130] and in

September 1917 work began on the production of the sights at the Periscope Prism Company.

Another product of collaboration between the technical branch and industry was the manufacture of a 'Giant Land Periscope'. At the end of 1915 the army commissioned a periscope for use in dug outs. The lenses were designed by Alexander Conrady, designer to Watson and Sons, and the periscope was completed by the firm of Kelvin, Bottomley and Baird by March 1916. It was 24 ft long and had tubes of 5 ins diameter, and its optical qualities were described as 'excellent'.[131] Another request for a new type of optical instrument came from the kite balloon section of the Air Board, which wanted a prismatic binocular for the 'observer' riding in a balloon attached to a ship in convoy, whose function it was to detect submarines. The observer was to be equipped with an instrument which would give him both optical magnification and a compass bearing so that on sighting a submarine he could immediately give coordinates. Three separate designs were made by the branch and manufactured by the firm of Piggott and Beck, but the end of the war prevented the distribution of this ingenious instrument.

By the end of 1918 the technical branch had compiled an impressive record of the scientific and technical developments in both fundamental and applied research undertaken in university or government laboratories and in industrial workshops. While some projects had been conspicuously successful (such as the production of new types of glasses, and instruments), others were, if less obvious, equally important in drawing manufacturers closer to the applications of science. The war had demonstrated that the commercial and technical success of the industry depended upon a willing alliance of manufacturers, scientists and technical men. As *The Optician* proclaimed: 'This marvellous thing [has] been brought about [by] . . . Esslemont, Chance, Jackson. The organiser, the pioneer manufacturer, the man of science. They may be styled the Glass Trinity.'[132]

State intervention, technical education and scientific research

The immediate problems of supply and production did not silence the demand for technical training for the optical industry, and indeed the arguments were reinforced by the knowledge that the industry's ability to meet its production targets were constantly threatened by the limited pool of skilled workmen, designers and computers available.

In June 1916, while discussions on alternative educational schemes continued between the LCC and the Board of Education, the governors of Northampton Institute brought the case for an institute of technical optics to public attention, with a pamphlet rehearsing the disappointing history of the proposals of 1903–16.[133] In the same month, Robert (later Sir Robert) Blair, Education Officer of the LCC, put before the County Council a revised plan for a national scheme of training in technical optics. Reviewing the debate, he concluded that with the experience of the war, the trade was now less preoccupied with the need to train workmen, than with the need to secure advanced postgraduate and research work. He therefore recommended a division of training and research. First, places would be made available at evening courses in junior technical schools; second, the existing courses at the Northampton Institute would be strengthened and improved; and third, a new department of technical optics would be created at Imperial College to cater for advanced students, postgraduates, and researchers.[134] The whole scheme would be coordinated by a committee representing the trade, the colleges and universities and the government.

The scheme was accepted by the DSIR, the Board of Education, the LCC and Imperial College. There were critics, however, chief among whom were the supporters of Northampton Institute's continued demand for a central Institute of Technical Optics. Moreover, there was criticism that the emphasis in the Government's proposals had changed from technical training to advanced and postgraduate instruction, and also of the limited provision made for 'the manufacture and use of optical instruments'.[135] The LCC and the Board of Education, however, weathered these complaints, and the scheme went into operation in November 1916. Administrative and educational costs were shared between the LCC and the Board of Education.[136] To encourage coordination, an advisory committee on technical optics was quickly constituted.[137]

In May 1917 F. J. Cheshire, while retaining his position as expert adviser in technical optics to the OMGD, was appointed professor of technical optics at Imperial College; he was later joined by Alexander Conrady, previously chief designer to Watson and Company, as professor of optical design and L. C. Martin as lecturer. In August 1917, in an open letter to the trade, Cheshire described the significance of the decision to create a systematic course in optical design. Not only had the shortages of skilled workmen and designers almost jeopardised the optical munitions programme, the experience of the war had forced manufacturers to a keen realisation that 'trial and error' had been overtaken by 'scientific method'.[138] The programme at Imperial College was an immediate success. During its first year eighty-six students took the advanced courses, and in their *First Report* the Technical Optics Committee commented:

We feel that the work done during the year, although only a beginning, has gone some little way towards meeting the urgent need of a recognised and deplorable dearth in the optical trade of this country of first class designers and computers. We hope that when the Department settles down to its fuller work with a systematic course of instruction extending over at least three years leading up to an associate-ship of the College . . . and with adequate facilities for research, a sufficient supply of men adequately trained for the higher positions in the industry will be assured.[139]

Educational provision was accompanied by strengthened relationships between the optical and glass trades and the scientific community, particularly through the formation of the Society of Glass Technology in November 1916. This organisation, although of more direct interest to glass manufacturers, bore indirectly on the optical industry, and brought together scientists and manufacturers concerned with technical and scientific problems in the composition and manufacture of glass.[140] Following from this, and as a result of the great efforts made by Dr W. E. S. Turner, a department of glass technology was created in the University of Sheffield in 1916, in part supported by the DSIR, offering both advanced work in technical optics and opportunities for research. The Society of Glass Technology flourished throughout the war, and encouraged visits by university scientists to glass-works to study manufacturing techniques at first hand. By 1919 an unqualified success, the society boasted a large library, several major publications, and 516 members.[141] Its very existence was tangible proof of the new commitment to scientific method and research which the experience of the war and the close collaboration of scientists and manufacturers had produced.

Many of the links which sprang up between the universities and industry were welded firmly by the DSIR which had long-term responsibility for encouraging the supply of scientific manpower and promoting the applications of science to industry. As such, the DSIR became involved with the support of the optical industry on several levels: first, directly through its grants to the University of Sheffield department of glass technology and the department of technical optics at Imperial College; second, through the creation of research committees of scientists and manufacturers; third, through the establishment of research associations for the optical industry. The DSIR research committees included the Standing Committee on Glass and Optical Instruments, and the Committee on the Standardisation of Instruments. These expert committees identified outstanding problems, sponsored research and kept a watchful eye on the progress of research throughout the country. In fact: 'The considered opinion of these subcommittees might be regarded as the best all-round advice available which could be obtained on a given technical subject connected with the industry.'[142]

While the research committees were concerned with the immediate problems presented by the war, the research associations, the first venture of the government into the large scale support of industrial research and the first attempt by industry to cooperate on research of mutual importance, were designed to equip industry with a vital scientific base for the era of peace. The first research association created was the Photographic Research Association, which had direct relevance to the optical industry, reflecting as it did the vast improvements in camera techniques developed during the war. The second research association to receive a licence (and now the oldest and one of the most successful research associations to have survived), the Scientific

Instrument Research Association (SIRA), was in part the culmination of the campaign waged to interest manufacturers in research from 1900 onwards. Again, Conrad Beck was the leader of the campaign to establish SIRA,[143] and Sir Herbert Jackson became its first director. By 1919 SIRA had already extended itself to include eleven electrical and X-ray instrument manufacturers, and the same year it claimed to be 'the representative industrial body dealing with the application of science to the manufacture of scientific instruments'.[144] The third, which lasted from 1919 to 1925, was the Glass Research Association.[145]

An observer comparing the optical industry in 1914 and in 1918 would have noticed marked changes in its condition. By the end of the war the industry exhibited many external signs of prosperity – large plant, modern machinery, techniques of mass production and an evident capacity for design and innovation. However, while the achievements of the industry were self-evident, the return of peace ironically brought, as elsewhere in British industry, the threat of bankruptcy and unemployment. The expansion and modernisation of the industry had largely been 'a question of orders of reasonable size, and above all, continuity of orders'.[146] With the liquidation of contracts following the armistice, the trade stood on the brink of a recession.

The precarious economic condition of the optical industry was recognised by both government officials and manufacturers. Throughout the war, successive government reports had emphasised the need for a measure of postwar 'protection' for certain science-based industries. Lord Moulton, for example, warned that although

It is not essential to prop up for ever an industry that does not make itself industrially remunerative ... when you look back upon the consequences of national neglect during a whole series of years and find yourself obliged at the beginning of the war to call on industries to take up new branches, to extend their capital upon them, to develop research and to turn out in a few months that which must rival the result of years of work abroad ... you must not think your duty has come to an end when the crisis is over.[147]

The most enthusiastic champions of postwar 'protection' for the optical industry were the architects of its success – Cheshire and Esslemont – whose intimate knowledge of the forced growth of the trade convinced them that the economic and commercial factors which had frustrated the growth of the trade before the war had not been entirely removed, and that once again exposed to German competition, the industry would founder. In evidence to the Balfour Committee on Essential Industries, set up in 1917,[148] and a committee of the Ministry of Reconstruction concerned with scientific apparatus in 1918,[149] they emphasised that the future of the industry could only be secured if specific steps were taken to discriminate positively in its favour. For example, they endorsed a policy of 'buying British' by government departments: They argued that no foreign glass or instruments should be imported without licence; that working capital should be provided after the war; that skilled labour be employed; and, most important, that the functions of the OMGD – to provide commercial, economic and scientific assistance and to supervise methods of manufacture and costing – should be continued after the war.

Their evidence, and that of the trade itself, keenly anxious for continued State support, was accepted by the Balfour Committee who recommended that the optical industry was a prime candidate for 'key industry' status.

Although comparatively small as regards the amount of capital required to be invested and of labour employed therein, these industries are of vital national importance, both on naval and military ground and for all the purposes of applied science and scientific research ... We are satisfied that the continuance of commercial and scientific assistance and of detailed control on the lines already followed will be necessary for a considerable period ... in view particularly of the great strength and reputation of the German firms ... We think that these measures will be regulated most effectively by means of the prohibition of imports from whatever source, except under licence, of certain kinds of glass and optical instruments.[150]

These conclusions were endorsed by the Ministry of Reconstruction Committee which recommended, in addition, that government departments continue to place contracts with the British firms, that standardisation and specialisation be encouraged and the collection of Excess Profit Duties be postponed.

Despite this overt sympathy, however, the trade had no guarantee of future 'protection'. Esslemont died in 1919 and the industry lost its chief ally. In February 1921 *Nature* recorded that the trade possessed 'the buildings, the plant, the organisation, the technical knowledge and the technicians and the skilled labour needed to maintain these industries at their present high level of efficiency'.[151] But the German home market was still very much larger than the British, and cheaper methods of production continued to be reflected in cheaper goods. The recession was swiftly felt in optical glass. In 1922 Chance's sales of optical glass reached a postwar low of 3,500 lbs, and the staff of the research laboratory had shrunk to three.[152]

In August 1921, despite fears that this would result in the inhibition of scientific research in Britain, the Safeguarding of Industries Act was passed, which provided for an import duty of $33\frac{1}{3}$ per cent on optical glass and instruments. The Act, in the words of Sir Hugh Chance, saved the optical industry from 'complete collapse'.[153] This measure of protection was insufficient, however, and the next five years were very harsh for the twenty major optical instrument firms. The Balfour Committee on the operation of the Safeguarding of Industries Act[154] reported in 1926 that three optical firms had gone into liquidation; in addition, large stocks of optical munitions remained unsold, decreased orders from the fighting Services, devalued foreign currencies, low wages and foreign tariffs against British imports, handicapped the industry severely. Prices of instruments were reduced drastically, and by 1925 unemployment caused by automation had reduced the workforce to only 1,200. (This was about 60 per cent of the numbers employed in 1913 – 78 per cent of those employed in 1921.)[155]

The only encouraging factor, according to the Board of Trade enquiry, was that 'The result of private and coordinated research which has been effected in the postwar years has served to place the products of the British optical industry on a very high plane'.[156] In particular, the Scientific Instrument Research Association had proved a complete success, and 'many problems of considerable importance to the industry have thus been successfully solved'.[157] By 1925 SIRA membership had increased to twenty-nine – including manufacturers of scientific and X-ray instruments, and was no longer 'merely an industrial research association for the exclusive benefit of its industrial members, but something more, partaking of a national or quasi-national character'.[158] In 1926, however, the Balfour Committee concluded that despite all their efforts the optical industry had not been able to take full advantage of the Safeguarding of Industries Act because of external economic forces 'beyond their control', which had prevented them embarking on 'new methods of manufacture and new research to the extent to which is desirable'. The committee recommended in view of the 'very substantial progress' made in both the range and quality of the products, that protection be increased from 33 per cent to 50 per cent.[159]

Although badly hit by the Depression the optical industry, aided by SIRA, had achieved a reputation for excellence which was 'out of all proportion to its financial resources and limited facilities'.[160] In 1935 the government took steps to re-equip the armed forces, announcing that the output of optical instruments would be increased by two and a half times.[161] It seemed that, once again, the industry had been saved by government intervention. A similar decision aided the optical glass industry when, in 1932, after taking over the Derby Crown Glass Company, Chance signed an agreement with the Admiralty on behalf of the three Services for an enlarged programme of research on the manufacture of optical glass. In the five years preceding the war the manufacture of optical glass increased 'five fold', and by 1938 it was possible for Chance to export glass. On the outbreak of the Second World War, a 'shadow' factory was established at St Helens, and by 1942 the volume of optical glass production was twice that of 1939, which made possible the export of optical glass to many of the allied countries.[162]

CONCLUSION

In the historical study of war and economic change, the interaction between science, technology and industrial development acquires special significance. This is particularly visible in the science-based industries which assumed special importance between 1914 and 1918. Forced to meet the demands imposed by total war, science, technology and the optical industry were brought into a new economic juxtaposition, mediated by the intervention of the state. The transformation embodied dramatic changes in resources, procurement, supply, machinery, wage levels and price controls. Rationalisation and product specialisation followed, stimulated by the concentration of scientific and technical assistance made directly available to the manufacturer.[163] Significantly, as in other nations, including France, Italy and the USA, the argument for technical education and scientific research in optics had been overwhelmingly won.

The scale and rapidity of changes brought about by the 'coupling agents' of the Ministry of Munitions and the DSIR suggest that the optical industry – at the extreme end of the science-based industries by virtue of its absolute reliance on scientific knowledge and application – was particularly responsive to swift state action. In the optical case, as in organic chemicals and explosives,[164] it seems that the war, in creating circumstances which mobilised capital and technical assistance, liberated a capacity for technological innovation and diffusion which had remained unexploited before the war. Moreover, the forced collaboration between skilled technician, scientist and manufacturer, sent a quickening impulse along the entire route of innovation from 'pure' research to product and process development, to manufacture and to diffusion.[165]

The achievements of the industry in war-time, however, could not be sustained in peace-time without a similar level of government aid. The demise of the Ministry of Munitions was followed by the decline of the industry, and by 1920 the optical trade was in recession.[166] In part, the trade was a victim of its own wartime success. Overproduction of instruments for military use, over-extended capitalisation, and uncertainty as to future government assistance, undermined the industry's confidence. If the economic intervention of the state had made a temporary difference to the trade, state intervention in providing university departments for optical research and in stimulating collaboration between manufacturers and men of science, had a more permanent effect. Here, the working basis of cooperative research wrought by the war produced one of the most successful research associations in British industry.

The war and the problems of the postwar world demonstrated the dependence of the optical industry and other science-based industries upon the State. This dependence upon government support (and subsidy) has eventually led to the massive development of products which conceivably would not have been undertaken independently by industry. Since the Second World War, this partnership has acquired enormous importance.[167] The circumstances of war which made government intervention desirable, were succeeded by the conditions of peace which made it a continuing necessity. The experience of the First World War showed that an economic and scientific alliance between government and industry was, whether immediately or in the long term, of vital interest to both.

NOTES

We are grateful to Sir Hugh Chance and Mr D. J. Bryden (Whipple Museum of the History of Science, Cambridge) for their helpful suggestions on sources of information on the history of the optical glass industry. We would also like to acknowledge the kindness of Professor Peter Mathias, Professor Christopher Freeman, Mr Andrew Robertson, Dr Jay Winter and Mr Russell Moseley, in commenting on earlier drafts of this essay.

1 General texts rarely supply this dimension: e.g. A. J. P. Taylor, *The First World War* (London, 1953), and *English History, 1914–45* (Oxford, 1965) scarcely consider scientific mobilisation. A. Marwick, however, devotes space to the subject in *The Deluge* (London, 1964) and *Britain in a Century of Total War* (London, 1969).

2 Cf. H. and S. Rose, *Science and Society* (London, 1969), ch. 3, 'The Chemists' War'; N. Vig, *Science and Technology in British Politics* (London, 1968), ch. 2. A most important contribution is Michael Sanderson, *The Universities and British Industry, 1850–1970* (London, 1972), ch. 8, 'The Universities and the War, 1914–18'.

3 Cf. G. N. Clark, *Science and Social Welfare in the Age of Newton* (Oxford, 1937, 1949, 1970), esp. ch. 3, 'Social and Economic Aspects of Science'; H. Levy, *Modern Science* (London, 1939); J. D. Bernal, *The Social Function of Science* (London, 1939), esp. ch. VII, 'Science and War in History'. For a possible synthesis, see D. de Solla Price, *Science Since Babylon* (New Haven, 1961).

4 See the Introduction to this book, pp. 4–7.

5 Many fields of science with known military applications were rapidly stimulated. Thus, the new uses found for knowledge, accelerating research (if not always new discovery) in pharmacology, physiology, bacteriology, agricultural science, not to mention in military psychology, surgery, psychiatry and industrial sociology, in the specific applications of chemistry, in poison gas and high explosives, and in the 'new physics' of aeronautics, aerial bombardment, sound ranging and submarine detection – are all well known. Cf. the *Oxford War Pamphlets*, especially Sir William Osler, 'Bacilli and Bullets' (no. 30, 1914) and J. O. Arnold, 'British and German Steel Metallurgy' (no. 72, 1914–15). Cf. also Daniel Kelves, in 'Testing the Army's Intelligence: Psychologists and the Military in World War I', *J. Amer. Hist.*, LV (December 1968), pp. 565–581; cf. also R. MacLeod and Kay Andrews, 'Scientific Advice in the War at Sea, 1915–1917: The Board of Invention and Research', *Journal of Contemporary History*, VI (1971), pp. 3–40; and the authors' *Scientists at War, 1914–18* (in preparation).

6 Cf. E. B. Poulton, *Science and the Great War* (London, 1915); Sir William Osler, *Science and War* (Oxford, 1915); A. C. Seward (ed.), *Science and the Nation: Essays by Cambridge Graduates* (Cambridge, 1917); J. F. C. Fuller, 'Science and War', *Nineteenth Century*, 103 (1928), pp. 88–96. For the Second World War references abound. Cf. J. G. Crowther and R. Waddington, *Science*

at War (London, 1947); S. Zuckerman, *Scientists and War* (London, 1966), p. 13 *et passim*; R. Clark, *Tizard* (London, 1965); and *The Rise of the Boffins* (London, 1962).

7 Throughout this paper the term 'optical industry' is used as a shorthand for 'optical glass and optical instruments industry'. The optical glass industry was in the period in question confined largely to the activities of one firm – Chance Bros; the term 'optical instruments industry' includes manufacturers of optical elements (i.e. lenses and prisms); 'technical optics' refers to the scientific and technical knowledge of optical design and computation and the design and construction of optical instruments; 'optical munitions' refer to optical instruments used in war (field glasses etc.).

8 *The Optician and Scientific Instrument Maker*, 1 September 1916, p. 7; 19 July 1918, p. 222. On the early manufacture of optical glass in the United States, cf. Sir Hugh Chance, 'Edmond Feil: The first successful manufacturer of optical glass in America', *Transactions of the Society of Glass Technology*, xxvii (1943), pp. 113–32. Interesting comparisons may be drawn with the study of munitions production and procurement in the Boer War; Cf. C. Trebilcock, 'War and the Failure of Industrial Mobilisation: 1899 and 1914', above, pp. 139–64.

9 For a review of the debate, see Donald McCloskey, 'Did Victorian Britain Fail?', *Econ. Hist. Rev.*, xxiii (1970), pp. 446–59; C. W. Wilson, 'Economy and Society in late-Victorian Britain', *Econ. Hist. Rev.*, xviii (1965), pp. 182–98.

10 For important similarities and contrasts, cf. Lutz Haber, *The Chemical Industry, 1900–1939* (London, 1971), and W. J. Reader, *Imperial Chemical Industries: A History* (2 vols, London, 1970, 1972).

11 For discussion of the characteristics of innovation, see K. Pavitt, *The Conditions for Success in Technological Innovation* (OECD, 1971); for discussion of the production factors in the relations of technological development and economic growth, see the classic treatment of Joseph A. Schumpeter, *The Theory of Economic Development* (New York, 1934, 1961), and Jacob Schmookler, *Invention and Economic Growth* (Cambridge, Mass., 1965), and his critics, e.g. R. Nelson, M. Peck, and E. Kalachek, *Technology, Economic Growth and Public Policy* (Washington, 1967).

12 Pavitt, *Conditions for Success*.

13 For an excellent summary of the present 'state of the art' in the study of this interdependence, see G. L., E. Turner, 'The History of Optical Instruments: A Brief Survey of Sources and Modern Studies', *History of Science*, viii (1969), pp. 53–93. See also the major bibliography on glass prepared for the Society of Glass Technology, by G. S. Duncan, *A Bibliography of Glass* (London, 1960).

14 Optical glass differs from ordinary 'crown' or 'plate' glass in several important ways. It must be more transparent, in that it must be able to transmit light without diminution and distortion; it must be free from colour and impurities and from internal strain. It must be sufficiently resistant to withstand the abrasive action of lens grinding and polishing and sufficiently durable to withstand the effects of moisture and carbon dioxide. In addition, it is distinguished from ordinary glass by certain 'optical properties' – the most important of which are its higher refractive and dispersive powers. See W. Rosenhain, 'Optical Glass', *Journal of Royal Society of Arts*, lxiv (4 August 1916), pp. 649–58; (11 August 1916), pp. 663–72; (18 August 1916), pp. 677–87.

15 For the history of lens manufacture, see F. Twyman, *Prism and Lens Making*

(London 2nd edn, 1952); see also, H. C. King, *The History of the Telescope* (London, 1955) and S. Bradbury, *The Evolution of the Microscope* (Oxford, 1967).

16 The Excise taxes on glass were imposed in 1743. By 1828 they amounted to 7d a pound on flint glass (which sold at 1s a pound) and glass manufacturers were agreed that the duty prevented 'any improvement in the article; because to improve, experiments must be made, but a man with a duty of 125 per cent over his head is not very likely to make experiments'. *Reports from Commissioners: Excise Inquiry: Digest of Thirteenth to Sixteenth Reports*, XXXI, 1835, pp. 66, 67.

17 *Ibid.* p. 60.

18 *Ibid.* p. 62.

19 *Ibid. Mins. Evid.*, p. 131. The firm of Chance was founded about 1790 by John Robert Lucas and William Chance at Nailsea, Bristol. In 1832 William's son, Robert Lucas Chance, set up as glass merchant in London and became proprietor of the British Crown Glass Company's business at Spon Lane, Smethwick in 1834. In 1837 the firm became Chance Brothers Company. See J. F. Chance, *A History of the Firm of Chance Brothers* (privately printed, 1919). See also Sir Hugh Chance, 'The Centenary of Optical Glass Manufacture in England', Second Chance Memorial Lecture, *Chemistry and Industry*, XXVII (December 1947), pp. 795–802.

20 This process, acquired by Bontemps from its Swiss inventor, Pierre Guinand, involved stirring the molten glass with a hollow cylinder of burnt clay to eliminate impurities and promote homogeneity. In 1848 Bontemps fled the revolution in France and joined Chance's firm. In 1851 the technical achievements of the firm were publicly noted when Chance received a Council Medal at the Great Exhibition for the largest lens ever manufactured. Cf. Chance, *Chemistry and Industry*, pp. 796–7. For a contemporary description of the manufacture of optical glass, see Apsley Pellatt, *Curiosities of Glassmaking* (London, 1849).

21 George (later Sir George) Stokes (1819–1903), mathematician and physicist; FRS, 1851; secretary, Royal Society, 1854–85; president, 1885–90; Conservative MP for Cambridge, 1887–91. Rev. William Harcourt (1789–1871), general secretary, first meeting of the British Association at York, president, British Association, 1839; FRS, 1824.

22 See Felix Auerbach, *The Zeiss Works* (1903), translated by Siegfried Paul and F. J. Cheshire (London, 1904). Cf. also Chance, *Chemistry and Industry* (note 19), p. 798, for a full account of the developments in optical glass and lenses at Jena.

23 Chance, *History* (note 19), p. 182.

24 *Report of the Education Committee of the LCC* (1 March 1911), p. 7 (hereafter *LCC Report, 1911*). The report, published in March 1911 by the Education Committee of the LCC, remains an invaluable source of information on the comparative condition of the German and British optical industry with particular reference to education.

25 Mullineux Walmsley, Address to the Optical Society, *Transactions of the Optical Society* (22 March 1900), 1–3, p. 35.

26 One of the most important developments in optical munitions during the Boer War was that of the rangefinder to which 'hundreds of inventors' had applied their talents (Mullineux Walmsley, *ibid.*, pp. 36–7). It was an optical measuring instrument consisting of two connected telescopes with a single eye piece

which enabled objects to be measured at any distance. Cf. F. J. Cheshire, *The Modern Range Finder* (London, 1915).

27 *The Optician*, 31 March 1916, p. 35.

28 *The Optician*, 14 July 1916, p. 222.

29 Concern over the future of the industry coincided with the wave of anti-German paranoia particularly manifest in the publication of E. E. Williams' polemic *Made in Germany* (London, 1896), reprinted by Harvester Press, 1973. See also, Geoffrey Searle, *The Quest for National Efficiency* (Oxford, 1971).

30 Cf. A. J. Meadows, *Science and Controversy: A Biography of Sir Norman Lockyer* (London, 1972); Frank Foden, *Philip Magnus, Victorian Educational Pioneer* (London, 1972); D. S. L. Cardwell, *The Organization of Science in England*, 2nd edn (London, 1973).

31 By 1910 the four technical schools specialising in optical instruction had 500–600 pupils. In addition, at Zeiss's works the optical instruction in the local technical school was 'practically under the firm's control'. The experimental work 'is supervised by a staff of no less than 18 mathematicians, physicists and chemists . . . [at a cost of] £6,000 to £10,000 per annum'. H. F. Angus, 'On the Secret of German Progress', *Trans. Opt. Soc.*, 1–3 (23 January 1902), p. 5 and *LCC Report, 1911* (note 24), pp. 4–6.

32 The first systematic courses in optical design were begun at Northampton Institute in 1898 following the introduction of examinations for spectacle making. In 1902, as a result of pressure from the British Optical Society, the Technical Education Board of the LCC agreed to give an annual grant of £200 towards a new department of technical optics at the Northampton Institute. At its demise in 1903, the board specifically recommended the creation of a central institute of technical optics at Northampton to its successor, the Higher Education Subcommittee.

33 H. F. Angus, *Trans. Opt. Soc. 1–3* (note 31), p. 35.

34 F. J. Gooding and Edward Meigh, *Glass and W. E. S. Turner*, Society of Glass Technology (Sheffield, 1961), p. 16. According to Sir Hugh Chance, 'Chance Brothers were one of the earliest firms to be managed by people with scientific education. James Chance (7th Wrangler) and his brother Henry were scholars of Trinity College, and James Chance's sons George and Frederick were both Cambridge graduates. Frederick started the first works laboratory at the glass works in the 1880s.' Personal communication to the authors, 18 January 1974.

35 *Official History of the Ministry of Munitions*, vol. XI, pt III, chs I–V (hereafter, *Official History*), p. 15.

36 *Ibid.*

37 Hansard, *H. C. Deb*, CXLIV, 20 July 1921, col. 2295; *Official History*, p. 95.

38 The British Optical Society, founded in 1899 had a membership of 400 by 1911, including most of the leading optical firms and many leading men of science among whom were Sir Norman Lockyer, editor of *Nature*, Professor Sylvanus Thompson, professor of applied physics at Finsbury Technical College (1885–1916) and Dr (later Sir Richard) Glazebrook, director of the NPL.

39 In 1905 the British Optical Society organised the first of three optical conventions (the others were in 1912 and 1926) to promote discussion on technical commercial and educational problems of the trade. Following the convention, Conrad Beck of the firm of R. and J. Beck and leader of the educational campaign, led a deputation to the Higher Education Subcommittee of the LCC to urge the establishment of a central institute of technical optics. He

emphasised the total absence of theoretical instruction: 'The theories of making corrections in lenses for chromatic or spherical aberation, astigmatism, curvature of field and distortion can be learnt at no institution in this country, while they can be acquired at several German institutions while, without a knowledge of German the literature is not available to the English.' *LCC Report, 1911* (note 24), p. 11.

40 Evidence was received from only fifty-four firms, but these represented 'almost all the firms of any size or standing'. *Ibid.*, p. 12.

41 'The final results of the investigations made . . . point to the necessity for the establishment of the proposed institute for industrial, scientific and national reasons – industrial because the lack of progress in the British optical industry compared with the rapid progress in Germany and the fact that the value of an optical instrument lies almost wholly in the scientific knowledge and skilled labour applied to its making; scientific because of the necessity to the scientific worker of the production on the spot of the best and most suitable instrument for the purposes of pure and applied science; national because of the necessity of the home production of instruments for various branches of the public service.' *LCC Report, 1911* (note 24), p. 1.

42 Presidential Address to the British Optical Society, *Trans. Opt. Soc.*, 2–5 (21 April 1904), pp. 135–6.

43 *LCC Report, 1911* (note 24), p. 10.

44 Gooding and Meigh, *Glass and W. E. S. Turner* (note 34), p. 16. In German industry in 1897 there were an estimated 3,000 chemists while in Britain the equivalent number was between 180 and 200. See Haber, *The Chemical Industry* (note 12), p. 14, and Cardwell, *The Organization of Science* (note 30), p. 208.

45 Walter Rosenhain, 1875–1934; metallurgist; FRS, 1913. Born in Melbourne he went to Cambridge with an 1851 scholarship. In 1900 he became scientific manager for Chance, and in 1906 became superintendent of the metallurgy laboratory at the NPL where he remained until 1931. Author of one of the first standard textbooks in English on glass manufacture, *Glass Manufacture* (London, 1908, reprinted, 1919). See Royal Society, *Obituary Notices of the Royal Society*, vol. I (1932–5), pp. 353–9.

46 Chance, *Chemistry and Industry* (note 19), p. 799.

47 Cf. Russell Moseley, *The Origins and Development of the National Physical Laboratory* (forthcoming D.Phil. dissertation, University of Sussex).

48 Cf. *LCC Report, 1911* (note 24), p. 10; Cf. also, Frank Pfetsch, 'Scientific Organisation of Science Policy in Imperial Germany, 1871–1914: The Foundation of the Imperial Institute of Physics and Technology', *Minerva*, VIII (October 1970), pp. 557–80.

49 Cf. Moseley, *The NPL* (note 47).

50 H. F. Angus, *Trans. Opt. Soc.* (note 31), pp. 33–4.

51 *Board of Trade Journal*, 26 February 1920, p. 202.

52 Letter to *Nature*, reprinted in *The Optician*, 13 April 1917, pp. 85–6.

53 *LCC Report, 1911* (note 24), p. 12; *Official History*, (note 36), p. 9.

54 *LCC Report, 1911* (note 24), p. 8. It was estimated that in 1909 'the capital invested in the British optical industry might lie between £1,300,000 and £2,500,000'.

55 *Official History* (note 35), p. 13.

56 The British Science Guild was set up by Sir Norman Lockyer in 1903 to promote scientific research and education. It won the active support of many

leading educationalists, politicians and men of science. Cf. BSG, *Report of the Technical Optics Committee respecting the Proposed Establishment of an Institute of Technical Optics*, June 1914, Appendix C to the *Ninth Annual Report of the BSG* (July 1915), pp. 29–31.

57 Major C. A. Williams, Inspection Department, Woolwich, to the British Optical Society, *Trans. Opt. Soc.*, 7 (12 November 1914), p. 14.

58 *The Optician*, 13 November 1915, p. 126, for example reprinted a letter to the *Daily Telegraph* which announced that 'Major Carey, RE . . . would be very glad indeed to receive . . . a suitable rangefinder.'

59 Herbert Jackson (1863–1936), chemist; FRS, 1917. assistant professor of chemistry at King's College, London, 1902; professor of organic chemistry, 1905; professor of chemistry, 1914–18; emeritus professor, 1918–; president of the Institute of Chemistry, 1918–21; and first director of the Scientific Instrument Research Association.

60 The formulae were published in *Nature*, xcv (15 April 1915), pp. 192–3.

61 *The Optician* disagreed: 'We do not know what are the steps that have been taken to collect information on that subject, but if the Guild had applied to us we could have put them in communication with manufacturing firms whose experience since the outbreak of the war leads to a very different conclusion', *The Optician*, 2 April 1915, p. 2.

62 *Nature*, xcv (6 May 1915), p. 67. *Nature* caustically remarked that 'so optimistic is the government that it has declined the patriotic offer of Lt Col J. W. Gifford to hand over to the nation free of cost practically the whole of a collection of optical glass, considerably over a ton in weight'.

63 By May 1915, the failure of the 'Spring Offensive' in France and the campaign in the Dardenelles, compounded by the revelations of the extreme shortages in fuse and shell production, precipitated the resignation of Asquith's Liberal government, and the creation of a coalition government with Lloyd George as Minister of Munitions.

64 Christopher (later Sir Christopher) Addison (1869–1951); physician, taught at the Charing Cross Hospital, 1901–7; Liberal MP for Shoreditch, Hoxton Division. Helped Lloyd George draft the National Insurance Bill, 1911; parliamentary secretary to the Board of Education, August 1914–May 1915; parliamentary secretary to the Ministry of Munitions, May 1915–July 1917 when he became Minister of Munitions.

65 Hansard, *H. C. Deb*, LXXI, 19 May 1915, col. 2423.

66 See R. MacLeod and Kay Andrews, 'The Origins of the DSIR: Reflections on Ideas and Men, 1914–16', *Public Administration*, XLVIII (1970), 23–48.

67 These advisory bodies were the munitions invention department of the Ministry of Munitions, headed by Sir Ernest Moir, and the board of invention and research, chaired by Lord Fisher, First Sea Lord of the Admiralty until his resignation in May 1915. See R. MacLeod and Kay Andrews, 'Scientific Advice in the War at Sea: The Board of Invention and Research', *Journal of Contemporary History*, VI (1971), pp. 3–40.

68 See the twelve volumes of the unpublished *Official History of the Ministry of Munitions*; for an account of his work at the Ministry, see David Lloyd George, *War Memoirs*, 6 vols (London, 1933).

69 CM6 was also responsible for the production of scientific and chemical glassware, and in 1917 assumed responsibility for potash production, when its title was changed to the Optical and Glassware Munitions and Potash Division.

70 F. J. Cheshire, author of *The Range Finder* (London, 1915), was an examiner

of patents before the war. He had 'an extensive knowledge of the trade and of ... its lack of organisation and technical equipment.' *Official History* (note 35), p. 1.

71 Alfred Sherwood Esslemont's personal contribution to the success of the optical industry during the war was widely acknowledged by his manufacturers. At his early death in the autumn of 1918, the Optical Society recorded that 'Mr Esslemont was preeminently the man for the hour. Under his inspiration and guidance the British optical industry rose magnificently to the tasks imposed upon it ... He sacrificed his life for his country as surely as if he had fallen in the trenches'. *Trans. Opt. Soc.*, 20 (October 1918–June 1919), p. 3. The glass trade gave a substantial sum to his widow. *Official History* (note 35), p. 5.

72 Before the war Barr and Stroud had been 'practically supported' by orders from the French government who had been supplied with 2,000 rangefinders while the British War Office had ordered only twenty. PRO, BT66/1 (MMW 4), 27 July 1915. In exchange for a continuing supply of rangefinders a small quantity of optical glass from the firm of Parra-Mantois continued to be available for import. PRO, BT 66/2 (MMW 11) *Optical Glass from France*, July–February 1916.

73 PRO, BT 66/1 (MMW 5), Stobart to Secretary, War Office, June 1915. H. J. Stobart, George Chance's brother-in-law, and a qualified engineer, became responsible for Chance's optical department in 1895 (Chance, *Chemistry and Industry* (note 19), p. 799). Stobart pointed out to the War Office representatives in June 1915 that the firm had only one foreman and one manager in the optical glass department and would therefore require an immediate increase in technical assistance.

74 PRO, BT 66/1 (MMW 5), Stobart to Secretary, War Office, June 1915.

75 Chance, *History* (note 19), p. 185.

76 PRO, BT 66/1 (MMW 7), *Optical Munitions – Memorandum as to Development of Output* (November 1915).

77 Chance, *Chemistry and Industry* (note 19), p. 800 n.; Hansard, *H. C. Deb*, CXLIII, 27 June 1921, col. 1806.

78 *Board of Trade Journal*, 19 February 1920, p. 252.

79 Chance was approached by many of the allies to supply optical glass and in many cases had reluctantly to refuse. In the winter of 1915 two Russian scientists sought Chance's assistance in setting up an optical glass factory in Russia where 'the Russian Army is in dire stress for optical munitions'. Stobart refused to spare his scarce technical assistance for the project, pointing out that it would take at least two years for an optical glass works to be established, but an eventual compromise was agreed whereby Russian technicians and workmen came to Chance for instruction, and 'On this small foundation the Soviet Government later set up its own optical glass industry.' Cf. PRO, BT 66/3 (MMW 20), *Suggestions for Chance and Co. to assist the Russians to set up an optical glass factory* (November 1915). Cf. also *Chemistry and Industry* (note 19), p. 800.

80 Chance, *Chemistry and Industry* (note 19), p. 799.

81 Chance, *Chemistry and Industry* (note 19), p. 800.

82 *The Optician*, 30 August 1918, p. 4.

83 Leading firms included Heath and Company (nautical instruments), E. R. Watts (clinometers, directors), Adam Hilger (optical elements), Taylor, Taylor and Hobson (optical elements), Ross (photographic objectives), Aldis (photo-

graphic objectives), Watson (photographic and microscope objectives); Dallmeyer (photographic objectives); Ottway and Cooke (theodolites); Grubb (astronomical telescopes); Kershaw (binoculars); Barr and Stroud (range-finders). Most of these firms (with the exception of Hilger, Taylor, Taylor and Hobson and Aldis who produced only optical elements) made elements and assembled the instruments.

84 *Official History* (note 35), pp. 42–3.

85 *Ibid.*

86 *The Optician*, 23 July 1915, p. 222. The OMGD recorded that only 'in a few cases could firms obtain financial help from their backers . . . in the majority of cases, special arrangements were made'. PRO, Mun 5/30, *Memorandum on the Function and Organization of OMGD.*

87 PRO, Mun 7/96, Draft Memorandum from Contracts Department to DGMS (nd but probably February 1916).

88 PRO, Mun 7/96, Col Wedgwood to DGMS, 23 March 1916.

89 As Esslemont pointed out: 'Makers of optical munitions stand in a class by themselves. They are few in number and are practically all cases fully engaged in Government work. As a result of our attendance at a meeting of the optical trade we have secured, we think, that the maximum of effort will be made . . . the speed of delivery depends very much upon goodwill and individual effort.' PRO, Mun 4/55, Esslemont to DDGO, 22 July 1915.

90 These were Ross, Barr and Stroud, and Kershaw.

91 PRO, Mun 5/365, *History of National Factories for Optical Munitions.*

92 PRO, BT 66/4 (MMW 31), Report of the Chief Inspector, 16 February 1917.

93 The Chief Inspector, given responsibility for supervising Chance's contract, was a science graduate previously employed at the Patent Office. The deputy chief inspector responsible for the supply of prisms and binoculars was a science graduate; the three other inspectors included one recent science graduate, and two ex-employees of the Patent Office. Finally, there were three women sub-inspectors, graduates in science with additional training from the Northampton Institute. Cf. PRO, Mun 4/943, *The Organization of OMGD* (nd).

94 *Official History* (note 36), p. 4.

95 *The Optician*, 16 June 1916, p. 174.

96 *Official History* (note 36), p. 18.

97 *Official History* (note 36), pp. 17–18. The use of precision tools inevitably meant that 'a great deal of the responsibility was removed from the operator'. S. Bradbury, *The Evolution of the Microscope* (note 15), p. 272.

98 *Official History* (note 36), p. 18; pp. 96–8. Most skilled workmen in the industry belonged to the Society of Instrument Makers. For a contemporary account of the introduction of dilutees into the engineering and metal trades, see A. M. Anderson on 'Women in Industry in Wartime', in S. J. Chapman, *Labour and Capital after the War* (London, 1918), and on the extent of the hostility to women dilutees in British industry see ch. VIII, 'Women', in S. J. Hurwitz, *State Intervention in Great Britain* (London, 1968).

99 *The Optician*, 24 March 1916, pp. 28–9.

100 PRO, BT 66/2 (MMW 13), Walmsley to Esslemont, 4 March 1916. The first women dilutees, in addition to possessing a 'fairly good education', were also 'of good character', and were recruited personally by the 'lady members of the Governing Board of the Institute'. The OMGD was 'one of the first Branches of the Ministry to realise the need for preaching dilution' and the optical munitions training programme was begun before a training section was

established at the Ministry. PRO, BT 66/1 (MMW 8), *Review of Labour Conditions, 1914–18: Labour Supply*, p. 1.

101 *Official History* (note 35), p. 97.

102 This was implicitly recognised by A. M. Anderson in a footnote to her discussion on 'Women in Industry in Wartime', emphasising that scientific and optical glass manufacture was an industry 'where the field for intelligent women is possibly greater than is yet realised'. (S. Chapman, *Labour and Capital after the War* (note 98), p. 84.)

103 PRO, BT 66/7, Ministry of Reconstruction, Engineering Trades (New Industries), *Report of the Committee on Scientific Apparatus* (3 December 1918).

104 *The Optician*, 18 April 1919, p. 117.

105 PRO, Mun 4/55, Esslemont to DDGO, 22 July 1915.

106 PRO, Mun 4/55, Monroe to OMGD, 26 February 1916.

107 PRO, BT 66/7 (MMW 63), *A Record of the Work of the Scientific, Technical and, Research Branch of the Optical Munitions and Glassware Supply Department of the Ministry of Munitions* (hereafter: *Record of the Technical Branch*).

108 *Board of Trade Journal*, 20 February 1920, p. 293.

109 *Official History* (note 35), p. 9.

110 Percy George Boswell. FRS, 1913; demonstrator in geology, Royal College of Science, 1914–17; professor, 1917–30; professor of geology, University College, London, 1930–8. J. W. Cobb D.Sc., FRIC; Livesey professor of gas and fuel industries, University of Leeds, 1912–38.

111 Sir William Crookes (1832–1919); chemist, OM, 1910; PRS, foreign secretary, Royal Society, 1908–12; proprietor and editor of *Chemical News*. See 'The coloured glass situation from an opthalmic lens point of view', *The Optician*, 1 September 1916, pp. 12–13: 'the discovery and commercial manufacture of this glass assuredly represented the greatest peaceful victory in the optical world over the forces of nature'. See also, PRO, BT 66/1 (MMW 6), *On the Production of Tinted or Coloured Glasses*, September–October 1916.

112 *The Optician*, 16 February 1917, p. 308.

113 *Official History* (note 35), p. 16.

114 Cf. *The Optician*, 23 August 1918, pp. 271–3, and for the work of the Laboratory on Optical Glass see the Annual Reports of the NPL.

115 PRO, BT 66/7 (MMW 63), *Record of the Technical Branch*, p. 56.

116 *Ibid.*

117 *Official History* (note 36), p. 73. For an account of work on potash production, see the *Official History*, pp. 71–89.

118 *The Optician*, 18 April 1919, p. 117.

119 PRO, BT 66/2 (MMW 14), *Memorandum of an interview held between Jackson, Merton, Esslemont and Cheshire on research work on chemical and optical glassware*, 26 May 1916. Royal Society *Obituary Notices*, ii (1936–8), p. 313.

120 *Ibid.* Of his war work it was later said: 'It is impossible to speak too highly of the value and importance of his work in the production of glass during the war period. In recognition of it . . . he was created Knight Commander of the British Empire in 1917 and elected to the Royal Society', Royal Society, *Obituary Notices*, ii (1936–8), p. 313.

121 *Board of Trade Journal*, 19 February 1920, p. 252.

122 *Ibid.* See also 'Recent Progress in Aerial Photography during the War', *The Optician*, 5 December 1919, pp. 191–5.

123 *The Daily Mail* recorded that 'It was in this connection that the optical industry

felt the greatest pinch of the war [and] it is now admitted . . . that the lenses
used by British aerial photographers are better than any of those captured
from the enemy or used by any of our allies.' Quoted in *The Optician*, 14
February 1919, p. 310.

124 PRO, BT 66/3 (MMW 18), *Supply of Pots for Glass Making*, May 1916.
125 *Ibid.* p. 2.
126 *Trans. Opt. Soc.*, *20* (May 1919), p. 277; see also Julius Rheinberg, 'Pressing Need
of the Moment with Regard to Scientific and Industrial Research' (12 April
1919) (MS copies donated to the University of Sussex, by the firm of Rheinberg).
127 PRO, BT 66/71 (MMW 63), *Record of the Technical Branch*, pp. 23–4.
128 *Ibid.*
129 *The Optician*, 27 August 1915, p. 279.
130 PRO, BT 66/7 (MMW 63), *Record of the Technical Branch*, p. 29.
131 *Ibid.* pp. 30–1.
132 *The Optician*, 18 April 1919, p. 117.
133 PRO, DSIR 17/54, *An Imperial School of Technical Optics*, May 1916. The
pamphlet carried a *Foreword* by Lloyd George in support of the proposal.
134 PRO, DSIR 17/54, Report by the Education Officer to the Higher Education
Subcommittee of the LCC (1 June 1916), p. 2.
135 PRO, DSIR 17/54, Board of Scientific and Technical Societies, *Report of a
Committee appointed to consider and Report on National Instruction in Technical
Optics* (1916), p. 2.
136 The contribution of the Board of Education towards the department of technical optics at Imperial College amounted to £1,500 for equipment and an
annual grant of £2,000; while the LCC contributed £1,000 equipment grant
plus £1,000 annual maintenance for the technical training. Cf. PRO, DSIR
17/54: L. A. Selby Bigge, Board of Education to Secretary, Treasury, 2 November 1916. Imperial College later made an additional grant of £2,000 for the
department.
137 The technical optics committee included A. H. D. Acland (then chairman of
the executive committee, Imperial College), Sir Alfred Keogh, Rector, Imperial
College; Otto Beit, Governor, Imperial College; L. B. Sebastian, chairman of
the governing body, Northampton Institute; F. Twyman, Conrad Beck,
Watson Baker, and H. J. Stobart, representing the optical trades; Dr A.
Schuster, FRS, representing the Royal Society; Dr R. T. Glazebrook, representing the NPL; A. D. Esslemont, representing the Ministry of Munitions,
Captain F. Creagh Osborn, RN, representing the Admiralty, and Lt Col A. C.
Williams, representing the Army Council. Two representatives of the glass
and metal workers were later added. Cf. PRO, BT 66/5 (MMW 40): *Proposals
for the Organization of Instruction in Technical Optics.*
138 *The Optician*, 3 August 1917, p. 267. The article outlined the advanced courses
available at Imperial College and Cheshire emphasised that manufacturers
were finally coming to appreciate that 'The performance of a system can be
determined by a skilled optician by calculation alone . . . to an order of
accuracy which cannot be attained by the testing of a workshop sample.'
139 PRO, DSIR 17/54, *First Report of the Technical Optics Committee*, July 1918,
p. 2. For a discussion of the research work of the technical optics department,
see Michael Sanderson, *The Universities and British Industry* (note 3), pp.
224–6.
140 On the work of the Society of Glass Technology and particularly the record of

the glass industry in the inter-war years, see Meigh and Gooding, *Glass and W. E. S. Turner* (note 34), pp. 13–23 and the *Journal of the Society of Glass Technology*, edited primarily by W. E. S. Turner, between 1919 and 1939.

141 W. E. S. Turner, 'A Professor looks at the Glass Industry', Twenty-first anniversary of the Society of Glass Technology, *Journal of the Society of Glass Technology*, VII (1937), p. 7.

142 *Official History* (note 35), p. 17. For an account of the work of the Standing Committee on Glass and Optical Instruments, see PRO, DSIR 3/314–18, and for the Committee on the Standardisation of Instruments, see PRO, DSIR 3/307–8.

143 The Report of the DSIR for 1918 (Cd. 9144) reviewed the establishment of SIRA. Since many firms anxious to join SIRA were not in a position to guarantee contributions, it was agreed that the DSIR would guarantee £40,000 while the trade would contribute £4,000. The normal arrangement for the financing of a research association was £1 from the government for every £1 from the industry.

144 *Fifty Years of Instrument Research: SIRA, 1918–68* (London, 1968), p. 2.

145 The Glass Research Association came to an end in 1925, reflecting the success of the research department at the University of Sheffield, and public criticism occasioned by the appointment, as director of the Research Association, of a non-scientist. Cf. Michael Sanderson, *The Universities and British Industry*, (note 3), p. 225 and *The Scientific Worker*, I (1920–22), p. 2.

146 Letter to *Nature*, reprinted in *The Optician*, 13 April 1917, p. 85.

147 Quoted by Sir J. Grieg in the Committee Stage of the Safeguarding of Industries Bill; Hansard, *H. C. Deb*, CXLIV, 20 July 1921, col. 2312.

148 *Interim Report on Essential Industries*, 1918, xiii, (Cd. 9032), paras 17–22.

149 PRO, B/T 66/7, Ministry of Reconstruction, Engineering Trades (New Industries), *Report of the Committee on Scientific Apparatus* (3 December 1918).

150 *Interim Report on Essential Industries* (note 148), para. 19.

151 *Nature*, CVI (10 February 1921), p. 749.

152 Chance, *Chemistry and Industry* (note 19), p. 800.

153 *Ibid.*

154 Board of Trade, *Safeguarding of Industries Act*, 1921, pt I (Cmd. 2631), 1926, XV, pp. 9–10.

155 *Ibid.*

156 *Ibid.* p. 12.

157 *Ibid.*

158 SIRA. *Fifty Years of Instrument Research* (note 144), p. 4.

159 Board of Trade, *Safeguarding of Industries Act* (note 154), p. 14.

160 SIRA, *Fifty Years of Instrument Research* (note 144), p. 4.

161 Gooding and Meigh, *Glass and W. E. S. Turner* (note 34), p. 118.

162 *Ibid.* pp. 40, 118.

163 For recent discussions of the relationships between economic, scientific and educational stimuli to innovation, see B. R. Williams, *Technology, Investment and Growth* (London, 1967), Edwin Mansfield, *Industrial Research and Technological Innovation* (New York, 1968), and James Langrish, *Wealth from Knowledge* (London, 1972).

164 Cf. W. J. Reader, *Imperial Chemical Industries* (note 10), vol. I. R. C. Trebilcock, 'A "Special Relationship": Government Rearmament and the Cordite Firms', *Econ. Hist. Rev.*, 2nd ser. XIX (1966), pp. 364–79; R. C. Trebilcock, '"Spin-off"

in British Economic History: Armaments and Industry, 1760–1914', *Econ. Hist. Rev.*, 2nd ser. xxii (1969), pp. 474–90.

165 Cf. M. Fores, 'Technology and Innovation: Some comments on the Literature', *Technology and Society* (Oct. 1973), pp. 94–8. One hopes that future discussion of economic 'decline' will refer more seriously to 'latent capacity' for innovation. In turn, this will probably require, as McCloskey argues, international comparisons of specific industries, not merely statements 'on the aggregate measures about which the controversy on British economic performance has hitherto revolved'. McCloskey (note 9), p. 459.

166 For the plight of British postwar industry, in which the optical industry shared, see R. Tawney, 'The Abolition of Economic Controls, 1918–21', *Econ. Hist. Rev.* xiii (1943), pp. 1–30; and A. C. Pigou, *Aspects of Economic History, 1918–1925* (London, 1947).

167 Cf. e. g. George Eads and Richard Nelson, 'Governmental support of advanced civilian technology: Power reactors and Supersonic Transport', *Public Policy*, xix, 3 (1971), pp. 415–27.

9 War demand and industrial supply: the 'Dope Scandal', 1915-19

D. C. Coleman

According to one's viewpoint or disposition the episode here examined may be variously regarded: as the war-time consequence of the shortage of a component in the aircraft industry; as an incident in the widespread manufacturing processes built upon discoveries in the chemistry of cellulose; as an example of what is fashionably known as 'spin-off'; or as an instance of the typical war-time relationships between governments and business, compounded of patriotism and profits, of opportunism and muddle.

I

It is with the requirements of early aircraft production that the story must begin. Until the use of aluminium the normal material for the outer skin of aircraft was a heavy linen fabric treated with a substance commonly called 'dope' in order to make it taut, wind-resistant and weather-proof. It was also used for airships and balloons. So dope and its ingredients soon acquired industrial and military consequence. Precisely when and how the need presented itself as capable of being met by one of the many products of the newly emerging cellulose chemistry is not clear. Around 1900 nitro-cellulose came into use as a base for making varnishes and lacquers as well as cinematograph film and that unattractive commodity called celluloid. So experiments were made, successfully, with nitro-cellulose as a base for aeroplane dopes in place of the sundry pastes, glues, oil-based varnishes, and rubber compositions which were never of much use. It was discovered that by adding certain chemicals the extreme inflammability of nitro-cellulose dope could be reduced. Nevertheless, its dangers provided a strong stimulus, here as in other fields, to find an alternative base. It was found in the shape of cellulose acetate as a result of experiments proceeding between, approximately, 1900 and 1909 – the year in which Louis Blériot made his famous flight across the English Channel. Even so, the then state of powered flight was unlikely to have induced visions of soaring demand from an aircraft industry. Within the next decade, however, thousands of tons of dope, mainly cellulose-acetate based, were used in hundreds of thousands of aircraft, as the warring powers discovered alike their destructive value and their destructibility.[1]

Since its initial discovery in 1865, cellulose acetate – obtained by treating cellulose with acetic acid and acetic anhydride – had been the subject of various patents and the repository of many hopes. This was especially true after the important patent of the English chemists C. F. Cross and E. J. Bevan of 1894; and thereafter much work was done, with a view to various industrial uses, in England, Germany, France, and the USA. The primacy for the development of a soluble form of cellulose acetate is usually given to the German chemist Arthur Eichengrün, working with the Bayer Company. It was made at that company's Elberfeld works, and in about 1905 was being marketed under the trade name of 'Cellit'. In 1909 he patented another process of dissolving cellulose acetate; and the resulting substance, primarily intended for use in the manufacture of non-inflammable cinematograph film, was marketed under the name of 'Cellon'. The other possibilities of 'Cellit' and 'Cellon' – for both of which names Eichengrün was the registered trade mark holder in Britain and elsewhere – were soon evident, notably as a base for lacquers and varnishes. Sundry companies were set up, including the British Cellon Company, which was registered as a private company in 1913. Its origins lay partly in the enterprise of an Englishman, A. J. W. Barr, in 1911, and partly in the acquisition of Eichengrün's patent rights in 'Cellon'. It planned to make sundry commodities including aeroplane dope, importing its cellulose acetate from Bayer. A company prospectus of June 1912 printed a testimonial from the pioneer aviator S. F. Cody; its wording nicely illustrates this particular aspect of the early days of flying: 'Now that I have tested my machine by flying to Hendon yesterday, reaching an altitude of 4,850 feet, encountering 3 rain-showers or traversing 3 heavy rain-clouds, after landing I examined the fabric to find that it was in perfect condition . . . I have decided to varnish my next new machine with "Cellon".'[2]

By the outbreak of war in 1914 no soluble cellulose acetate had been made in Britain on a commercial scale, as distinct from laboratory work. Makers of paints and lacquers who were interested in its use, such as the paint firm, Pinchin Johnson & Company, had to import it; so did a number of firms that had gone in for the manufacture of aeroplane dope; and so too, did the Royal Aircraft Factory at Farnborough which made its own dope. But enemy Germany was not the sole source. In France, the chemical enterprise, Usines du Rhône, had succeeded in developing a form of soluble cellulose acetate and in 1913 had a factory capable of turning it out at the rate of one ton per day. There was one other source open to the British: the enterprise developed by the brothers Henri and Camille Dreyfus at Basle in Switzerland. They had established a factory to make cellulose acetate in 1912. The new demand for aeroplane dope, which military aviation created, now offered to these men a range of remarkable opportunities and produced some equally remarkable consequences.

II

Henri Dreyfus, born in 1882, was a Swiss of French–Alsatian origins. A chemist, he took out numerous patents and, in 1912, in conjunction with his elder brother, Camille, and another Swiss, Alexander Clavel, a silk dyer, set up a company for the manufacture of cellulose acetate and other chemicals. It was called the 'Société de Cellonit Dreyfus et Cie'. To use the word 'Cellonit' in a company's title when 'Cellit' and 'Cellon' were already someone else's registered trade marks for forms of soluble cellulose acetate was perhaps asking for trouble. The validity and originality of the Dreyfus patents and process have been called into question, both then and later, by various chemists.[3] Nevertheless, whatever his claims to originality as an inventor, his firm had apparently made a process work and, in 1914, was the only one to have done so outside France and Germany.

At the beginning of the war the Basle company was developing its business in Britain, as elsewhere, and in September 1914 offered supplies to the War Office.[4] During a commercial visit, in about March 1915, and specifically in relation to the requirements of the Royal Aircraft Factory, Camille Dreyfus met the head of the contracts branch of the aeronautical department of the War Office. According to evidence later given by this official, it was in pursuit of a policy of independence of foreign sources for important war stores, that he then asked Dreyfus whether he would consider manufacturing cellulose acetate in Britain.[5] Dreyfus agreed, provided that there should be a contract for not less than 100 tons. The War Office, after negotiations with firms of dope makers, in July 1915 invited tenders from three firms for 100 tons of cellulose acetate, to be manufactured in Britain. The Dreyfus company alone tendered, but in its tender reserved the right to deliver 50 per cent of the total from its works in Switzerland. The tender was accepted. It should be emphasised that at this date 100 tons undoubtedly seemed an immense amount; in the summer of 1915 it was thought that twenty tons would meet the whole requirements of the army and navy for twelve months;[6] the official estimate for the war department's needs was later increased though only to forty-three tons for the year ending September 1916.[7] There still seemed plenty to spare in the contract, even though a shortage of dope was beginning to be apparent.

The Basle company first tried to take over a small factory in London run by a firm called the Safety Celluloid Company, who were customers of the Dreyfus'. On the strength of these expectations, Camille is alleged to have told the War Office (though subsequently denying making any such statement) that manufacture could begin in a fortnight. That was in November 1915. In fact that particular venture fell through; and the company continued until 1917 to meet the contract from its Basle factory, a factory which was only three miles from the German frontier. Meanwhile, however, the establishment of a company to start operations in Britain had been brought about by a curious amalgam of capitalism and militarism. The catalyst appeared, improbably enough, in the person of a Canadian businessman, Lieutenant Colonel W. Grant Morden, who was also an officer in a Canadian cavalry regiment and a member of the Canadian Expeditionary force. In August 1915, at the age of thirty-five, he was appointed to the post of 'Personal Staff Officer to the Minister of Militia and Defence for Canada, Overseas', the minister in question being Sir Samuel Hughes.

Grant Morden was a financier and a director of various Canadian companies, in shipping and other activities. On his own evidence he had not, before August 1915, ever heard of cellulose acetate, had no official connection with aeroplanes or the air service, and no prior acquaintance with the Dreyfus brothers. But he evidently had a big net of business contacts, into which all sorts of interesting fish swam from time to time. In exactly the same month as his appointment took effect he was visited in London by a M. Magnier, a Frenchman who had been given his name by one of Morden's acquaintances who happened to be head of the British Chamber of Commerce in Paris. Morden had obviously been represented as a company promoter, likely to be interested in speculative ventures. For Magnier promptly set about trying to interest this Canadian officer and shipping director in a new way of making cellulose acetate for aeroplane dope. This was the proposition, helped along with the contention that the British War Office was dependent on supplies from a firm in Switzerland, close to the German frontier and indeed represented as being German.

Morden took it up with gusto. Within a short time he had met the War Office official mentioned above, who told him all about the cellulose acetate position and the desirability of manufacturing in Britain;[8] and had set the ball rolling at the feet of two other businessmen with rather closer interests in the commodity in question. One, already known to Morden but apparently brought in at the suggestion of his chief, Sir Samuel Hughes, was Sir Trevor Dawson, a director of Vickers Ltd; the other was Edward Robson, chairman of Pinchin Johnson Ltd. Neither had any direct chemical knowledge of cellulose acetate or dope but both saw possibilities, for different reasons, in stimulating its manufacture in this country: Robson, because Pinchin Johnson already used it in making paints and varnishes; Dawson, not only because Vickers made aeroplanes and airships – of which department Dawson was in charge – but because, as armaments manufacturers, they were interested in acetone which was used both as a solvent for cellulose acetate and in the making of explosives. In September 1915 they jointly formed a private company called The Actose Manufacturing Company, purchased a factory near London, and tried to make the Frenchman's scheme work.

It was a complete failure: Magnier made no worthwhile quantity of cellulose acetate and by January 1916 the venture was abandoned. But this setback did not deter Morden. He went to Paris; through intermediaries he learnt more about, and got in touch with, the Dreyfus firm; in February 1916 he and Robson went to Basle, and entered into an agreement with the Swiss manufacturers to set up a British company to make cellulose acetate *and other chemicals* (my italics). The agreement named two groups: Morden, Dawson and Robson (called the English Group) and the Dreyfus brothers and Clavel (called the Swiss Group). It provided for the setting up of an English company with a share capital of £300,000–£400,000, to cover an estimated £85,000 thought adequate to erect a factory; the English Group were to raise £115,000 in cash by an issue of 6 per cent bonds; the Swiss Group were to have half the share capital to cover the value which the Dreyfus brothers put on the patents and 'secret processes'; and, out of the £115,000 they were to have £30,000 in bonds as well as a cash payment of £10,000. The agreement also effectively liquidated the Actose venture by providing that the English Group (who *were* the Actose Company) should take over that company's plant at cost; and, finally, it envisaged the creation of separate American, Russian and Canadian companies. Perhaps more than any other clause it was the last which gave the clearest indication of one at least of Morden's real hopes. In his evidence to the British Cellulose Enquiry Committee of 1919 he stressed on more than one occasion that his motives were wholly patriotic and that he 'did not want to make any money out of the war'. When questioned on the contemplated creation of overseas companies, however, and of 'a very big enterprise to work these patents', he answered simply: 'We did that very deliberately. We wanted to get the control of this for all the various countries.'[9]

III

As a direct consequence of this agreement the British Cellulose and Chemical Manufacturing Company Ltd was registered as a private company in March 1916. One important change, however, was made in the arrangements. The Swiss Group were reluctantly persuaded by the English Group to agree to a much smaller initial capitalisation. So the company was floated with a nominal share capital of £4,000; and at the same time it was agreed that it should be reconstructed within two years with a capital of £400,000 or more. The debenture capital was increased to £120,000. The £4,000 was divided into 160,000 6d shares. The choice of this unusually low denomination of share was subsequently explained by spokesmen for the company as having been made for the purpose of 'defining interests'. But from Morden's examination by the Cellulose Enquiry Committee, it is evident that, apart from hopes of capital gains, his reasons for adopting this procedure were two-fold. First, to attract as little public attention as possible: as all the capital was placed privately, without any prospectus, no application was made to the Capital

Issues Committee of the Treasury. Second, to have a supply of nominal, low-denomination shares either to sell or give away as bonuses to brokers, clients or friends who could be persuaded to purchase the highly speculative debentures. Asked by the Cellulose Enquiry Committee what were the terms on which his friends came in, Morden said simply that they were given 400 shares for each £1,000 of debentures subscribed for.[10] The possible results of the whole operation were neatly summarised during his examination by that committee:[11]

Q. So if . . . (the Company) . . . was highly successful the investment of 6d would be an enormously profitable investment?
A. Yes, undoubtedly.

Q. In point of fact, this was a means of securing all the profits of the concern, over the 6 per cent, to the group to whom your 160,000 shares would be issued.
A. Yes.

Q. Without their risking a great deal in taking up the shares?
A. Exactly.

The immediate outcome of this exercise in war-time share-pushing is shown in the following distribution of major shareholders and debenture subscribers (Table I).[12] The Prudential Trust Company of Canada of which, not surprisingly, Grant Morden was a director, was introduced partly to get round the statutory limitation to fifty of the numbers of share-holders in a private company, and partly to assist in keeping voting control together for the English Group. It also acted as trustee for the debenture holders.

One other financial arrangement – which was later to arouse particular suspicion – was negotiated at this time. During the first, abortive scheme for taking over a works in England, consequent upon the War Office's proposal to Camille Dreyfus in 1915, one of the directors of the Safety Celluloid Company suggested that an application should be made to the government for some sort of tax relief.[13] Camille Dreyfus had some discussion with the financial authorities about an exemption such as, it was claimed, 'was very common in Latin America and other countries in order to encourage the establishment of new industries'.[14] The British authorities remained unim-pressed; the request was refused. However, when the 1916 agreement was made the English Group undertook to try to secure relief from taxation for a period of five years. Much heavier guns were then brought to bear upon the financial powers. Dawson wrote to Reginald McKenna, the then Chancellor of the Exchequer; Morden wrote to Walter Long, then president of the Local Government Board and later Colonial Secretary (whose son worked in the London office of one of Morden's companies and subscribed for £1,000 of debentures in the company); Long, senior, in turn wrote to McKenna. After some negotiations it was finally agreed, in November 1916, that the War

Office would refund to the company a sum equal to the excess profits duty actually charged, during a period of five years from the formation of the company, subject to certain conditions.[15]

With all the financial arrangements, public and private, completed or in train; with a board consisting of Morden as chairman and Dawson as his deputy, Henri and Camille Dreyfus, Clavel, and three others; with the Dreyfus brothers installed in England as managing directors: with all this

Table 1

Name	Number of shares allotted	Debentures subscribed (£)
Vickers Ltd	19,800	25,000
Albert Vickers	1	10,000
Douglas Vickers	—	3,000
Edward Robson	1,620	—
Sir A. Trevor Dawson	2,104	1,000
Lt Col Grant Morden	1,705	—
Sir Samuel Hughes	1,000	—
George Holt Thomas	1,600	4,000
Berthold Kitzinger	4,300	10,250
Henry Michael Isaacs	2,000	5,000
Camille & Henri Dreyfus and Alexander Clavel	79,998	30,000
The Prudential Trust Co. of Canada	40,470	—
Main beneficial owners of these shares:		
E. Robson 10,500		—
T. Dawson 12,250		—
G. Morden 12,900		—
35,650		
	154,597	88,250
Others	5,403	31,750
Total	160,000	120,000

done, a start was made in finding sites for a factory. Eventually in June 1916 land was bought from the Derby Corporation at Spondon and sundry orders for plant were placed. There then started a long tale of delays and unfulfilled promises. Difficulties with labour; unfamiliar machinery and consequent late delivery by manufacturers; too low a war-time priority for securing supplies: problems such as these soon combined to make nonsense of an optimistic statement by Camille Dreyfus when he told the War Office that he hoped to begin manufacturing by the end of August. The Basle factory continued to supply cellulose acetate under the 100-ton contract of 1915, and negotiations for a formal contract with the British company were started. It was not, however, until January 1917 that the company got its first contract: for forty tons, the balance still due under the 1915 contract.[16] And it was not until the relevant authorities called for a special report on the situation at Spondon, and the services of yet another Canadian Army officer had been secured specifically to expedite supplies, that finally deliveries started on a very small scale in April 1917, in gradually increasing quantities thereafter (see below p. 216).

Meanwhile, an ominous rumble of troubles to come could be heard. It is difficult precisely to pinpoint their origins. They were unlikely at this stage to have had much to do with the circumstances attending the company's financial birth for this was little known. Some arose from criticisms of the quality of the product supplied from Basle under the 1915 contract. Certain of the officials in the aeronautical inspection department of the War Office, in the Royal Aircraft Factory, and of the Admiralty, said that it was inferior to that of the Usines du Rhône which was also being imported by such dope makers as the British Cellon Company. Others said it was better. It seems, at least, to have been variable.[17] Some troubles may have arisen from the familiar xenophobia of the times. The government had, after all, given its support to foreign entrepreneurs whose optimistic claims were not matched by punctual performance – for whatever reasons. And some may have been helped into being after rival tenders were turned down. United Alkali, the large but technically old-fashioned and economically decaying amalgamation of alkali producers,[18] had made a tentative offer to the Admiralty in about May 1916. Their suggestion was that they should start manufacture using the process favoured by Usines du Rhône; it was referred to the War Office and declined. So too was a further proposition made in October 1916.[19]

These troubles would probably not have mattered very much had it not been for the rapid expansion of the aircraft programme in 1917. (1914, 200; 1915, 2,342; 1916, 6,633; 1917, 14,832; 1918, 30,782; total, 54,799 – of which 52,027 were built at home.) Although, as the above figures show, the rate of increase was faster before then, the absolute numbers of aeroplanes being built became such as to put much heavier pressure on component supplies.[20] The general extension of the air war meant that Allied demands rose accordingly, yet at the same time the intensification of the German submarine campaign was threatening supplies of acetic acid, mainly obtained from America. Moreover, the demand for it was increasing not only from the expanding aircraft programme but because the trench warfare department wanted it for the manufacture of tear gas; acetone, too, was in short supply as demands for it likewise increased. By July 1917 the cellulose acetate position was getting very serious.[21] The output of the Spondon factory, though rising, was still well below expectations:[22] April, 900 lb; May, 1,900 lb; June,

5,500 lb; July, 12,700 lb; August, 17,300 lb; September, 27,200 lb. Moreover, this was now the sole British source for cellulose acetate dope as the French had commandeered the whole output of the Usines du Rhône. So temporary recourse was again had to nitro-cellulose dope. It was used on training machines and others for service at home which were thus spared the dangers of being only too readily set on fire by incendiary bullets. Experiments were made with aluminium wings but there was not enough aluminium. In September 1917 the shortage of acetic acid became so acute that it came under government control. To economise on raw materials, a 'standard' dope with agreed specifications was determined.[23]

As indicated earlier (above p. 209) the Dreyfus brothers, from the beginning of their involvement in Britain, had had it in mind to manufacture chemicals other than cellulose acetate.[24] The shortages of 1916–17, however, created favourable circumstances for moving in this direction. Already in 1916 they were discussing with Vickers Ltd the possibility of making not only acetone but also methyl acetate, an alternative solvent in dope manufacture; synthetic acetic acid; non-inflammable celluloid; and, *inter alia*, artificial silk. Such ambitions would be costly; and the existing capital would be quite inadequate. In November 1916 a scheme was devised by which further capital up to £300,000 was to be provided by a syndicate ('The Explosives Syndicate') consisting of Vickers, Nobels Explosives Company Ltd, and the Chilworth Gunpowder Company. This was to cover the extension of the factory primarily to manufacture synthetic acetic acid. Experimental work was started with the help of an immediate loan of £10,000 from the syndicate.

The main cellulose acetate factory had, however, still to be completed and money was fast running out. In January 1917 a loan of £60,000 was arranged by Morden from the Union Bank of Canada. When the production at last began in April, Camille Dreyfus celebrated the achievement by suggesting to the Ministry of Munitions – which, since February 1917, had taken over responsibility for aircraft supplies – that the company be given a contract for the alternative solvent, methyl acetate; and also by proposing the installation of a plant to make acetic acid, acetone, carbide and ethyl alcohol. In the cause of national self-sufficiency, it was agreed. In June, along with a new contract for twenty-five tons of cellulose acetate per month, came an order for 2,500 tons of methyl acetate or acetone. Work on the new acetic acid and carbide plant was put in hand on a further 190 acres at Spondon acquired with Ministry help, and with the aid of the £300,000 from the Explosives Syndicate; the latter also provided a further £15,000 on account of the scheme for artificial silk and other such items – though little or nothing seems in fact to have been carried out in this direction at that time. Sir Henry McGowan of Nobels Explosives had become a director of the company in April 1917.

IV

Income and expenditure were rising substantially. A further contract, for 700 tons of cellulose acetate, was placed in August 1917. At the agreed price of 9s per lb this was worth over £705,000. But to effect the requisite increases in capacity and to erect the acetic acid and carbide factory (involving an electric power plant) more money than that initially provided by the Explosives Syndicate proved necessary. A further £200,000 was borrowed from the Union Bank of Canada; and the government itself provided money, in the form of a loan of £200,000 from the Ministry of Munitions. But rising prices and the growing scale of the undertaking not only made even these sums inadequate but also served to emphasise the bizarre financial structure of the company. The reconstruction, promised in 1916, became imperative. In September 1917 Morden started negotiations with the Beecham Trust with a view to forming a public company. The scheme was thus dependent on the company obtaining permission from the Treasury Issues Committee, but this was refused. Morden pressed the committee further, even, in the course of correspondence, to the extent of making the incautious claim of the monopolist: 'We are the sole source of supply for the Government and no aeroplane can fly without our product.'[25] Despite the committee conceding, in December, that it might re-consider its refusal, this scheme was abandoned. Instead, a complex series of negotiations was put in train, resulting in the registration, in March 1918, of another private company. This time it had a nominal capital of £3,500,000 and bore the curious title of The British Cellulose and Chemical Manufacturing (Parent) Company Ltd – thus providing the rare spectacle of a parent, albeit a financial one, coming to life two years later than its effective offspring.

In the course of 1917 as the company's operations grew bigger and better known, and as at least some people got to know of the involvement of the Explosives Syndicate, those 6d shares began to change hands privately at larger and larger sums. Around March and April 1917 a few began to change hands between £1 and £2.10.0; then they began to rise so that by the summer £3.10.0 was normal; after October the rise continued to £10. The total number of shares changing hands at £1 and upwards was small, less than 5,000 out of 160,000 and the circle of buyers and sellers very narrow. But a few speculators did very well indeed. Berthold Kitzinger sold 3,290 shares between 13 April 1917 and 1 February 1918 at prices ranging from £2.5.0 to £8.2.6, thereby making a gross profit of over £12,500. Charles W. Small sold 500 shares in March 1918 at £10 per share – a gross return of £4,987.10.0 on an initial outlay of £12.10.0.[26] The implications were obvious. The Cellulose Enquiry Committee, having in 1919 extracted from Morden the information about the sales (though not the calculations about the profits) made its views clear enough:[27]

Q. . . . I can appreciate you were not a seller. It was far too good a thing to sell at
   that time was it not?
A. I did not go into it as a share speculation.
Q. I know, so you told us, but having got into it for other reasons did you not
   appreciate you had got into a gold mine?
A. No, I believed after the War there was a good future for this business. It was
   going to be a key industry.

It was on the future and some 'bullish' buying that hopes rested. The
negotiations with the Beecham Trust had assumed a share value of £10. When
the 'parent' company was formed, the valuation of those 6d shares was
£14.10.0 and the allotted capital of £3,100,000 in £1 shares divided as follows:

	£
To existing shareholders at the rate of £14.10.0 per 6d share	2,320,000
To the Explosives Syndicate in respect of £355,000 cash and	
of £100,000 additional cash from Nobels	780,000
	3,100,000

The 'Parent' company then became entitled to the shares of the 'operating'
company, and indeed began to finance it. As a part of this deal further
finance was provided by the Central Mining and Investment Corporation
Ltd to the extent of a loan of £190,000. The capitalisation of the new money
from the Explosives Syndicate and Nobels posed a problem of the proportion
of the equity to be maintained in the hands of the Swiss Group. As Morden
put it in evidence, 'the Dreyfus people refused to reduce their holding under
$33\frac{1}{3}$ per cent'.[28] They then held 45 per cent; so on the basis of what the
Explosives Syndicate wanted, $33\frac{1}{3}$ per cent meant £14.10.0 per 6d share. It
may have been a convenient calculation but it was soon to have lively
repercussions.

   The distant rumble of troubles ahead became much louder in the course of
1917–18 as the company's monopolistic position and government support,
even before the financial reconstruction, attracted increasingly adverse
comment. Another attempt to breach the monopoly – this time by the
rapidly expanding and extremely successful artificial silk firm of Courtaulds
Ltd – illustrates clearly how it all seemed to the outsider.[29] In October 1917
a meeting took place at the instigation of an official of the technical department
of the Air Board who thought little of the Spondon product. It was attended
by a representative of Courtaulds; and it discussed the supply of aircraft dope
in Britain which was said to be 'seriously inadequate both as to quality and
output'. The upshot was an invitation to Courtaulds to consider the possibility
of going in for cellulose acetate manufacture on a large scale. Courtaulds,
like all other firms apart from the Dreyfus enterprise, had not extended their
laboratory experience of it to the stage of commercial production, even on a
pilot scale. Nevertheless, they signified their interest, saying that they would

be willing to put up all the capital involved. Once the idea was conveyed to the supply department of the Ministry of Munitions, however, it was firmly suppressed. Courtaulds were informed that it was not considered advisable to start any new plant to make cellulose acetate, and that the present and prospective output was adequate. Certain MPs were consulted and requested to investigate the evident discrepancies between the views of the two departments. To no avail. Of course, Courtaulds were no more wholly disinterested patriots than were the businessmen who had promoted the British Cellulose and Chemical Manufacturing Company. They had already investigated the possibilities of cellulose acetate in the manufacture of artificial silk; and they strongly suspected, and rightly, that the Dreyfus brothers were getting, with government assistance, a well-equipped chemical works ready for use in artificial silk manufacture after the war was over. Meanwhile, it was all ammunition for a much bigger attack soon to be launched.

Trouble for the company also arose from a different source. The rate of twenty-five tons per month, specified in the June 1917 contract, was not reached until after January 1918. Thereafter the Spondon factory's output rose satisfactorily as the following figures show:[30]

	(lb.)		(lb.)
1917			
October	46,000		
November	30,700		
December	47,200		
1918			
January	51,900	April	120,000
February	95,700	May	172,200
March	127,200	June	144,900
		July	182,900

But whilst output rose so did prices of raw materials and labour – and by March there were over 5,500 men working at Spondon, of whom 2,334 were employed by the company and 3,206 by the contractors building the massive extensions required by the acetic acid and carbide plants.[31] The company sought a revision in the terms of their contracts. After protracted negotiations with the Ministry of Munitions, entirely new arrangements were made. The most important features of these were: the cancellation of the tax concessions; the drawing up of new contracts worth nearly £3m and, most significantly, more money from the government. These new advances had reached £485,000 by August, had risen to £900,000 in October 1918 and reached £1,450,000 in June 1919. The new arrangements had been embodied in an agreement dated 27 June 1918. By that time deliveries of methyl acetate under the contract of June 1917 had only just started; and no deliveries of acetic acid ever had been made by the time the war ended in November 1918.[32] But within a month of the June 1918 agreement the balloon had gone up in the shape of the Fifth Report of the Select Committee on National Expenditure.[33]

V

The Select Committee on National Expenditure had earlier appointed a sub-committee to enquire into the doings of the Ministry of Munitions; and in October 1917 this body had started to investigate the curious case of cellulose acetate supply. Its pryings soon began to reveal all manner of interesting information supplemented by evidence cheerfully offered by disgruntled potential competitors such as Courtaulds,[34] by officials who disapproved of the Dreyfus product, and by others who felt themselves excluded from the delights of 6d shares which in two years became £14.10s.0 shares. The result was a vigorously critical, partly inaccurate, and far from impartial report. It disliked what it saw as lack of adequate consultation between the supply, contracts and finance branches of the Ministry; berated the supply department for its refusal to sanction alternative sources and its support of a monopoly; commented adversely on the delays in output and variability of quality of the Spondon product; revealed, in general terms, the nature of the company's financial history; and was very critical of the lack of supervision over the substantial programme of capital expenditure consequent upon the extensions sanctioned in the summer of 1917. Its recommendations were threefold and far-reaching: that the works of the British Cellulose Company should be taken over by the government; that a technical committee should be appointed to advise on the completion and management of the factory; and that the Ministry should, without delay, consider the advisability of securing an alternative source of supply.

Signed on 23 July, the report came out on the 26th on which day the chairman of the sub-committee, Godfrey Collins,[35] took the unusual step of promptly sending a copy to the press, underlining in blue pencil various passages relating to the company.[36] It was an obvious invitation to the press to make a meal of it, and in due time they did. Immediate reactions, however, were comparatively subdued. The criticisms in the report were repeated, in some detail, and the *Morning Post* had a leader which accused the Ministry of Munitions of having created 'at vast and still incalculable expense, a monopoly which has hitherto failed to supply the needs of the country'.[37] But an incentive to do better than this was soon provided in the House of Commons on 1 August. Sir Frederick Banbury,[38] launched himself on a speech which opened with the claim that the report laid bare, 'financial methods which had been practised in the old days by a well-known man in the City called Baron Grant, and afterwards by Whittaker Wright and Ernest Terah Hooley.' And it ended by saying roundly that 'a more discreditable transaction has never been brought to the knowledge of this House'.[39] Aside from attacks on the remission of excess profits duty and on delays and monopoly, it was the financial methods which were his chief target. This Tory spokesman of the City was followed by a Liberal, R. D.

Holt,[40] who contended in sweeping terms that he had 'seldom read an account of a more gross scandal than this question of the Cellulose Acetate Company'. Dawson and Morden were presented as sinister company promoters; and Morden's appointment on the staff of the Canadian Minister of Militia evoked the observation that that minister, Sir Samuel Hughes, was 'a person of the worst reputation in Canada and who happens to be one of the shareholders in the £14.10s for 6d transactions'. He claimed to have seen a list of those shareholders: 'When the House sees that list it will be horrified'.[41] The press took up the theme, led by the *Daily Chronicle* which on 5 August published a list of the shareholders and, soon followed by other papers, started to relish what it called the 'Dope Scandal' and the *Evening News*, not to be outdone, called the 'Great Dope Scandal'.

On the same day as the *Daily Chronicle* began its attack the House of Commons took up the debate again. Sir William Bull[42] defending the company, criticised the Select Committee's report as full of misrepresentations, and asked for an independent tribunal to look into the case. F. Kellaway, parliamentary secretary to the Ministry of Munitions, made some very defensive statements and announced that a departmental committee would be set up to enquire into the matter. But Holt persisted, not only making much of the 6d to £14.10.0 share rise but also, following the *Daily Chronicle*'s lead, commenting on the fact that Morden's fellow London director of the Prudential Trust Company of Canada turned out to be connected with another government department.[43] Several other members, including Herbert Samuel (later Viscount Samuel)[44] and J. B. Dillon,[45] pressed for something more than a departmental committee. Finally, the Chancellor of the Exchequer, now Bonar Law, noting allegations of improper influence in high places, intervened to state his belief that something more than a departmental enquiry was needed and to say that he would later announce the form that a tribunal would take.[46]

Whilst waiting for this body to be constituted the press kept up the hue and cry, especially the *Daily Chronicle* which made the running. It continued its revelations about the company by publishing more details of the financial reconstruction and a full list of the shareholders in the 'Parent' company complete with the holdings, addresses, and in some cases, occupations, other business interests, and government connections.[47] Just as frustrated would-be participants in the dope business had helped to feed the Select Committee, it was soon obvious that a disgruntled employee (almost certainly the former secretary[48]) with access to the company's office files, was feeding the *Daily Chronicle*. For the next instalment contained facsimile copies of 1915 trade advertisements by the Société de Cellonit Dreyfus et Cie, one in an English journal and the other in the German *Chemiker Zeitung*. Heavy with xenophobic innuendo, the article also provided the names and holdings of the shareholders in the Basle company; gave details of the agreement between the 'Parent' Company and the Prudential Trust Company of Canada; and claimed comprehensively that 'the more we probe the matter the uglier the sordid story becomes'.[49] The *Westminster Gazette,* which was currently conducting a campaign against the businessmen chosen by Lord Beaverbrook to run the new Ministry of Information, weighed in with the contention that 'on the story as told by the Committee we are in face of the greatest financial scandal of the war'.[50] The suggestion of improper influence was enabling hostile sections of the press to blow up a fairly small scandal into a potentially very large scandal. The *Manchester Guardian* spoke gravely of the need for the enquiry to be 'as deep and as wide as possible unless the scandal is to shake public confidence in the capacity and even in the integrity of the nation's administration';[51] and the *Spectator* observed of 'what is popularly called "The Dope Scandal" . . . (that) no worse instance has yet been revealed of the laxity of financial control'.[52]

Sooner or later the name of Dreyfus was bound to evoke a response in the layers of national anti-Semitism. A very literary one came in the unmistakable prose of G. K. Chesterton in the *New Witness* which he then edited. Supporting the *Daily Chronicle* for, as he said, 'turning the Great Dope Scandal into a formidable feature of the daily press', he picked up a sentence which had occurred in that paper – 'The Dreyfuses . . . were a thoroughly patriotic Swiss firm' – and proceeded to make unpleasant fun of it. Two brief excerpts may serve to catch the flavour:

Camille Dreyfus and Henri Dreyfus are not Switzers violating their own neutrality, they are not Englishmen betraying their own country or serving their own country, they are not Germans betraying Germany or serving Germany. They are ordinary Jews who need have no sort of patriotism for any of these countries. . . .

International Israel is not always positively 'Pro-German' but it is for our purposes always negatively Pro-German.

and

When a Jew has done certain disputed things, or formed certain doubtful connections, it may or may not be just to call that Jew a traitor or to call that Jew a swindler. But if, at the very beginning, we have not even the courage to call that Jew a Jew, we shall certainly do nothing and get nowhere.[53]

On 8 August, Bonar Law announced the composition of the tribunal. It comprised three peers: a judge, Lord Sumner, a Lord of Appeal; and two senior and suitably respectable businessmen, Lord Inchcape, shipowner, and Lord Colwyn (formerly Sir Frederick Smith), cotton manufacturer and colliery owner. Their terms of reference were brief and general.[54] The company promptly engaged leading counsel, including Sir Edward Carson and Douglas Hogg (later Lord Hailsham) to represent them, and at the same time issued writs for libel against the *Daily Chronicle* and the *Saturday Review.*[55] The press continued for some time to keep the pot boiling, displaying much critical interest especially in Morden's activities, not least because he had become Unionist candidate for Brentford and Chiswick. *John Bull* and the *Daily Express* found cause to champion his doings: the latter, already owned by Morden's friend and fellow-Canadian, Lord Beaverbrook, referred to him in glowing terms as one of Canada's 'leading businessmen'. But much of the comment was hostile, especially from the *Daily Chronicle* and even the *Times* viewed his selection as a candidate while the tribunal was sitting as 'most unsatisfactory'.[56] The months passed and the newspaper campaign abated, an abatement aided by the silencing of the *Daily Chronicle*. It had become critical of other and bigger aspects of Lloyd George's administration, so in October 1918 it was bought by one of the prime minister's henchmen, and the offending editor departed rapidly.[57] In November the war was over; in December Morden became MP for Brentford and Chiswick. The 'Dope Scandal' was still far from dead, however, for questions continued to be asked in Press and Parliament alike, about the non-appearance of the tribunal's report.[58] In the summer of 1919, when its publication was known to be imminent, the subject was revived, to herald the report itself which finally appeared in August 1919.

Within the limits of its powers and in the time available, the tribunal had done its job fairly thoroughly, receiving, as the report said 'a very voluminous mass of documents' from the relevant departments; examining thirty-two witnesses, some at considerable length; and having commissioned from a leading firm of accountants a full analysis of the company's finances. The report provided a careful and much more detailed history of the whole episode than did that of the Select Committee. In language and in findings its tone was sober and wholly unsensational. To the vociferous critics it was a whitewash; to the company's supporters, a vindication; to those in the middle, an anti-climax. The tone was bland and the chosen path offered information rather than condemnation. Having, for example, given the details of the tax concession the report went on to use such soporifics as: 'we apprehend that it does not fall within our province to interpret the true meaning of this concession, the terms of which seem to have been variously construed, nor are we called upon to discuss whether it was politic or impolitic'.[59] They were, however, on firm ground in pointing out that in any event it never operated because no profits had been made.

This indeed was crucial. From the unpublished minutes of evidence it is obvious that the committee found neither the conduct of the financial arrangements nor the running of the organisation at all to their liking; though they sensed chaos rather than crime, they patently mistrusted Morden; they had great difficulty in making Henri Dreyfus stick to the point and in detecting his meaning through a fog of words and technicalities; and Camille Dreyfus, who in February 1918 had left to run the associated company set up in America, incurred their explicit displeasure by failing to turn up to give evidence, despite many promises, until July 1919. But whatever pickings were made by a few people in share deals or whatever may or may not have stuck to the fingers of various persons in the company, there was no evidence here of massive profits directly made by the exploitation of wartime scarcity. The report did at least go so far as to observe that the contrast between the nominal capital of the original company and that of the 'Parent' company was 'so glaring that, for much of the criticism to which they have been exposed, we think that the promoters and others connected with the company's financial arrangements have only themselves to blame.'[60] On the question of improper influence, the committee concluded that there had been neither 'favouritism nor corruption'. In examining the position of monopoly which government support had given the company they were, again, on strong grounds in stressing the big difference between 'a general, and even a practical, knowledge of the manufacture of such a chemical product' and the special knowledge and skills needed to provide, regularly, large and reasonably uniform quantities of it.[61] No British manufacturers had such knowledge; and, the report decided, there were good reasons for the government to continue in its support of the company, rather than sanction an alternative factory especially as shortages of men and materials increased in 1917. Finally, this gentle rebuke was given to the company's critics: 'if all the facts, which we have sifted with so negative a result, had been available last year to the critics of the Company and its proceedings we think that their conclusions would, to say the least, have undergone large modifications.'[62] The 'Dope Scandal' was dead.

VI

Its longer-term consequences, however, were only just becoming apparent. In 1920 the British Cellulose and Chemical Manufacturing Company became a public company with the stated intention of making artificial silk. It marketed the latter under the brand name of 'Celanese', and in 1923 became British Celanese Ltd. Across the Atlantic, from similar war-time roots, there sprouted the Celanese Corporation of America and Canadian Celanese. The Spondon plant, equipped as a war-time measure and with the aid of government money, grew into a substantial chemical-textile works. Indeed, largely under Henri Dreyfus' direction, it became in time a remarkable pioneer example of a vertically integrated plant, its activities ranging from the production of basic chemicals, through the spinning of cellulose acetate yarn, to include the weaving of fabrics and the making of garments, mainly women's underwear. A vigorous selling and advertising campaign ensured that by the 1930s, Celanese had become a household name.[63] This was the real pay-off for the Dreyfus' from aircraft dope. The experiments with making artificial silk from cellulose acetate which had been carried out before the First World War in various countries had not resulted in commercial production partly because of technical difficulties and partly because of the striking success of the rival viscose method pioneered by Courtaulds. No doubt if war demand for dope had not been answered in the particular way that it was, someone else would still have developed this branch of artificial fibre manufacture. But the historical path actually followed was a product of those war needs.

Spin-off or pay-off: the coin had another side too. The circumstances of the company's birth and the legacy of its promoters, together with the personalities of the Dreyfus brothers, particularly Henri, helped to give British Celanese a stormy, not to say disastrous, financial history. The investment of government money, transmuted into the form of a holding of £1,450,000 preference shares issued when the company went public in 1920, helped to keep it in the public eye; and questions about it were asked in the House of Commons at intervals throughout 1920–2.[64] By 1927 there was no longer any government money in the company but nor had there been any profits. Instead, there had been, as there were to be in the 1930s, warring groups of shareholders battling with directors over the control and capitalisation of the company. Year after year there were the all too familiar accusations about over-optimistic forecasts. In 1929 the *Economist* observed that the 'disturbing fact about this company has always been, and continues to be, its inability to turn into cash receipts the enormous potential values of which so much has been repeatedly heard'; and in 1936 it was still commenting, wryly, on 'the bumper earnings which remain so persistently round the next corner'.[65] By 1938 the preference dividends were eight years in arrears. And it was not until 1944, the year in which Henri Dreyfus died, during the Second World War and twenty-eight years after its original parent company had been born during the First World War, that British Celanese Ltd ever paid a dividend on its ordinary shares. Meanwhile, during the 1920s and 1930s, not only had the company been the object of sundry rumours, speculations and conflicts, but it engaged in expensive litigation. Once again there were accusations about the dubious validity of Dreyfus patents. Between 1931 and 1937, at Henri Dreyfus' instigation, a series of extremely expensive lawsuits were waged in defence of his artificial silk patents: they were all lost, at every stage right up to the House of Lords.[66] By 1960, British Celanese Ltd, Cellon Ltd, and Pinchin Johnson Ltd had all been absorbed by Courtaulds.

Finally, the Dope Scandal can be seen as providing an example, in microcosm, of the moral dilemma of the capitalist economy in war. For behind the rhetoric of political combat and popular journalism there clearly lay unresolved doubts about that uneasy mixture of patriotism and profits which had already spawned the very word of 'profiteer' and the very act of profiteering. It may be that Morden was, as he claimed both in public speeches and in evidence to the Cellulose Enquiry Committee, out of pocket to the extent of some £20–25,000 and that he had arranged it all in the name of patriotism.[67]

But it was also obvious, whatever the evidence, or lack of it, that all sorts of people found it hard to reconcile such claims with the distribution of 6d shares to well-placed persons and to businessmen of sometimes dubious reputation. The logic of capitalism demanded the inducement of profit. But was this the right way to go about it?

From the evidence given to the Cellulose Enquiry Committee it is clear that Morden was the prime mover in using the tricks of the questionable financier. If the subsequent career of Henri Dreyfus may perhaps have confirmed the view of those who had earlier expressed scepticism about him, that of Grant Morden seems to have amply justified the 1918 critics of this ambitious and too plausible Canadian. Apparently seeking to emulate his friend Beaverbrook, he added newspapers to business and politics. In 1920 he bought *The People* and, shortly afterwards, on playing a major part in arranging the finance for Odhams Press Ltd, when it absorbed *John Bull*, became chairman of Odhams.[68] Never a man to let a chance go by, he celebrated his position by writing to Lloyd George in March 1922 in order to offer the Prime Minister, should he decide to relinquish office, the job of editor of *John Bull* at a salary of £35,000 per annum.[69] But Morden's massive extravagance, in setting himself up as a country gentleman and host to politicians, combined with an over-developed urge for speculation, led to so large a pile of debts that in 1925 he was forced to dispose of *The People*, by then declining in circulation. He relinquished the chairmanship of Odhams; but he still had fingers in all sorts of business pies, including a syndicate interested in cellulose acetate for films and artificial silk.[70] The slump, however, was soon to leave its mark. His assets tumbled in value; despite generosity from Beaverbrook, to whose Empire Preference campaign he gave active support, his liabilities grew; and in 1930 he was bankrupt. Bankruptcy proceedings dragged on over the whole of 1931. In the early months of 1932, nearly penniless and with failing eyesight, his wife and four children were being maintained by the generosity of a few friends who raised a fund to help the family – but ensured that the money was not paid directly to Morden himself, for, as one of them wrote, 'I cannot imagine Grant with a few hundred pounds without "trying a spec".' In June 1932, after a collapse, both mental and physical, he died.

So maybe it was at least one benefit for the British Cellulose and Chemical Manufacturing Company that, after its founders had to relinquish some of their shares on the 1920 reconstruction,[71] Morden transferred his interests and his gambling instincts elsewhere.

Nevertheless, the company had been saddled with a legacy which helped to blight its subsequent financial history and might have been avoided if less brash financial methods had been used in the original flotation and subsequent development. But to the problem of how to finance and organise the supply of aircraft dope, the British government of 1916 had no prepared answer.

For its officials and executives were faced with a product about which they knew virtually nothing, save that it was not made in Britain, and with urgent needs for an utterly new arm of war. In the assorted names of patriotism and profits, of self-sufficiency and private enterprise, they yielded to the sales-talk of the company promoter and thereby generated, albeit on a small scale, one of those characteristic bits of economic policy, the results of which turn out in the end to be so different from what anyone expected.

NOTES

1 *History of the Ministry of Munitions* (12 vols 1922), vol. 12, pt 1, pp. 136–43; L. F. Haber, *The Chemical Industry, 1900–1930* (Oxford, 1971) pp. 213–4, and 214 n. 1, quoting French estimates that on average 120 kg of dope were used per plane. From figures given in H. A. Jones (and Sir W. Raleigh), *The War in the Air* (Oxford, 1922–37), Appendices volume, pp. 154–5, it would seem that Britain, France, USA, Italy and Germany together built well over 200,000 airframes during the war, thus using around 24,000 tons of dope on new aeroplanes alone.

2 A facsimile prospectus of Cellon Ltd is one of a collection of records relating to the 'Dope Scandal' in Courtaulds archives [hereafter: CA] consulted by kind permission of Courtaulds Ltd. Much of the above paragraph is derived from various papers in these files; see also Haber, *The Chemical Industry*, passim; and my *Courtaulds. An Economic and Social History* (Oxford, 1969), vol. II, pp. 178–84.

3 None of the pre-war Dreyfus patents for cellulose acetate was accepted in Germany. Several documents in the files of Courtaulds' own adviser on international patent matters during and after the First World War, Dr E. Lunge, are highly critical of many of the Dreyfus' claims. As Lunge was of German-Swiss origin and had worked with German companies before the war, this is not perhaps surprising. But certainly Lunge's, and other people's, scepticism about Dreyfus' later British patents for making artificial silk by the cellulose acetate process proved well-founded (see above, p. 222).

4 This was the first move in the whole episode described here. My account of it is largely derived from the following sources: the *Report of the British Cellulose Enquiry Committee* (Parliamentary Papers 1919, XI) [hereafter: *Report*] and, in CA, transcripts of its verbatim evidence (which was never published), together with statements of facts, and drafts thereof, briefs to Counsel, copies of correspondence with government departments, contractors and others, as well as sundry supporting documents and a book of press cuttings for 1918–19; the *Fifth Report from the Select Committee on National Expenditure* (Parliamentary Papers 1918, (IV) [hereafter: *Select Committee*] and, also in CA, a typescript of part of the verbatim evidence before that committee (also never published); and the *History of the Ministry of Munitions* loc. cit.

5 CA transcripts: evidence of A. E. Turner, p. 6 and of Camille Dreyfus, pp. 5–6; both stressed that the initiative came from the British end not the Swiss.

6 CA transcripts: evidence of A. E. Turner, p. 10.

7 *History of the Ministry of Munitions*, vol. 12, pt I, p. 138 n. 1.

8 He also disabused Morden about the Dreyfus' alleged German origin.

9 CA transcripts: evidence of Grant Morden, first day, p. 14.

10 *Ibid*. p. 30.
11 *Ibid*. pp. 18 and 19.
12 The full list is published in *Report*, Appendix A.
13 CA transcripts: evidence of Camille Dreyfus, eighteenth day, p. 6.
14 CA draft 'preliminary statement', dated 16 September 1918; in the final version, submitted to the committee, the reference to Latin America was discreetly removed.
15 CA transcripts: evidence of Morden, first day, p. 27; evidence of Sir Trevor Dawson, sixth day, pp. 1–2; correspondence as to remission of Excess Profits Duty. *Report*, p. 10.
16 There was some dispute about whether this was a contract for a further forty tons, but the evidence of A. E. Turner (pp. 15–16) shows that it was intended to be simply the balance of the original 100 tons.
17 Much conflicting evidence was given on this subject. See *Report*, p. 11.
18 On the position of United Alkali, see W. J. Reader, *Imperial Chemical Industries. A History*, vol. I (Oxford, 1970), passim, and especially pp. 229 and 289.
19 This approach had been supported by an Admiralty suggestion that there should be an alternative source of supply – *Select Committee*, p. 8. Nothing came of a direct approach to Dreyfus made in 1916 by Max Muspratt, chairman of United Alkali, suggesting that the latter should take a small interest in the company.
20 *The War in the Air*, vol. III, Appendix VII.
21 *History of the Ministry of Munitions*, vol. 12, pt 1, pp. 139–40.
22 Figures from CA preliminary statement, p. 20.
23 *History of the Ministry of Munitions*, vol. 12, pt 1, pp. 139–43. On the experiments with aluminium see CA transcripts: evidence of A. E. Turner, p. 19.
24 There was indeed a temporary and small-scale manufacture of the chemically related drug, aspirin, at Spondon.
25 CA correspondence with Treasury (Capital Issues Committee), 6 November 1917.
26 Assuming that Kitzinger paid 6d for each of 3,290 shares (his original holding was 4,300) they cost him £82.5.0; the proceeds of his sales were £12,616.3.4. Both Kitzinger and Small had subscribed to debentures. CA transcripts: evidence of Morden, first day, pp. 103–7; preliminary statement, pp. 30–2.
27 CA transcripts: evidence of Morden, first day, pp. 107–8.
28 *Ibid.* evidence of Morden, second day, pp. 5–6.
29 The account of the episode which follows is derived from CA letters E. L(unge) to Air Board 29 October, E. L. to J. D. Kiley, M.P., 13 November, Air Board to Kiley, 29 November, E. L. to Air Board 11 December 1917; E. L. reports to chairman and deputy chairman of Courtaulds, 13 and 24 November 1917; also correspondence between E. L. and Munitions Inventions Department, May–August 1918. Although Lunge's attitude to Dreyfus and his associates was decidedly hostile (it was reciprocated) the outline of the episode in *Report*, p. 13 substantiates this account.
30 CA preliminary statement, p. 20.
31 *Ibid*. p. 16.
32 *History of the Ministry of Munitions*, vol. 12, pt 1, p. 140; also vol. VII, pt IV, ch. 4, p. 70. The great shortage of acetic acid and of dope solvents, which had appeared to jeopardise the whole Allied air programme in 1917, was relieved partly as a result of changes in the poison gas requirements and partly from new sources of supply (*ibid.*, vol. 12, p. 140).

33 Parliamentary Papers 1918, iv.
34 CA Secretary of Select Committee to Secretary of Courtaulds, 5 April 1918, and E. L. to ditto. 11 April 1918.
35 Liberal, Greenock.
36 *Hansard*, vol. 109, 5 August 1918, pp. 1035, 1039–41.
37 *Morning Post*, 29 July 1918.
38 Unionist, City of London.
39 *Hansard*, vol. 109, 1 August 1918, pp. 746–51.
40 Liberal, Hexham.
41 *Hansard, ibid.* pp. 751–3.
42 Unionist, Hammersmith. Bull was an interested party. A lawyer and a friend of Morden and Dawson, he had been consulted over the financial reconstruction of the company. He was also parliamentary private secretary to the Colonial Secretary, now Walter Long whose son, as noted above (p. 210) was a debenture holder.
43 *Hansard*, vol. 109, pp. 1041–6. The director in question was C. G. Bryan, appointed to deal with propaganda in America in the then recently created Ministry of Information.
44 Liberal, Cleveland; chairman of the Select Committee.
45 Irish Independent, East Mayo.
46 *Hansard*, vol. 109, p. 1054.
47 *Daily Chronicle*, 6 August 1918. Amongst the shareholders in the reconstructed company was Professor Sir John Cadman who held various technical advisory posts to the Ministry of Munitions.
48 One Boris Berliand, a Russian, who was sacked by the company in July 1918. CA preliminary statement p. 39; transcripts, sixth day, evidence of M. Greenhill, pp. 47–50; photographic copy of letter Berliand to Camille Dreyfus, 12 May 1918.
49 *Daily Chronicle*, 7 August 1918.
50 *Westminster Gazette*, 6 August 1918.
51 *Manchester Guardian*, 9 August 1918.
52 *Spectator*, 10 August 1918.
53 *New Witness*, xii, 302 (16 August 1918).
54 They were to enquire into and report upon 'the formation and financial arrangements of the British Cellulose and Chemical Manufacturing Co. Ltd and associated companies, and upon their relations with Departments of the Government'. Despite expressed views that the tribunal should have the power to take evidence on oath this power was not granted.
55 The *Saturday Review* had published, on 3 August 1918, an attack on similar lines to that of the *Daily Chronicle*, under the title of 'Dopers and Doped'.
56 *Daily Express*, 11 December; *Daily Chronicle*, 10 August, 21 September, 4 October; *Times*, 6 December 1918.
57 The much bigger aspect was the affair of General Maurice, although the editor, Robert Donald, had also exhibited others signs of hostility to Government policies. On the whole matter, see H. A. Taylor, *Robert Donald* (1934), pp. 165–93; A. J. P. Taylor, *English History, 1914–45* (Oxford, 1965), pp. 117–18 and his *Beaverbrook* (1972), pp. 154–8.
58 E.g. 17 and 22 October, 12 November 1918 (*Hansard*, vol. 110, pp. 305, 593–4, 2497–8); 7 April, 3 and 17 July, 13 August 1919 (*Hansard*, vols 114, pp. 1054–5; 117, pp. 1194–5; 119, pp. 594–5, 1309). *Daily Telegraph*, 23 October 1918; *Times*, 14 March 1918; *New Statesman*, 26 April and 9 August 1919; *Truth*, 19 March 1919.

59 *Report*, p. 10.
60 *Ibid.* p. 14.
61 *Ibid.* p. 12.
62 *Ibid.* p. 14.
63 For some details of these developments, see my *Courtaulds*, vol. II, pp. 183–4, 270–2.
64 See, e.g. *Hansard*, vols. 126, 127, 143, 153.
65 *Economist*, 27 July 1929, 14 November 1936.
66 *Courtaulds*, vol. II, pp. 351–7.
67 CA transcripts: evidence of Morden, third day, p. 17.
68 R. J. Minney, *Viscount Southwood* (1954), pp. 163–4, 178–85.
69 Beaverbrook Library, Lloyd George Papers, Grant Morden to Lloyd George, 21 March 1922.
70 Minney, *Viscount Southwood* p. 185; Beaverbrook Library: Hannon Papers, Box 16. The brief account which follows of Morden's end is largely derived from these papers. I am grateful to Mr A. J. P. Taylor for drawing my attention to them. For reports on Morden's bankruptcy and death see the *Times*, 2 and 6 April, 23 May, 18 July, 1 August, 31 October, 5 December 1931, 30 January, 11 February, 27 and 29 June 1932.
71 CA transcripts: evidence of Morden, third day, pp. 17–20; evidence of Dawson, sixth day, pp. 3–6.

10 Administrators and agriculture: aspects of German agricultural policy in the First World War

Joe Lee

It is a commonplace that pre-1914 military authorities expected a short war. It has been customary to argue that the mistakes of the economic policy makers during the war derived mainly from the difference between the anticipated and the actual course of the war. This, no doubt, was frequently the case. But in agriculture, at any rate, German blunders did not generally result from a failure to anticipate the length of the war. They arose mainly from a failure to understand the basic interrelationships operating in the economy, whether in peace or war, virtually irrespective of the time span involved. The Ministry of the Interior's critique of Georg Froehlich's reflections on German food supplies provides a useful case-study of the functioning of the official mind in this respect. Gustav Schmoller, Froehlich's mentor, thought sufficiently well of his student's work not only to publish it in his *Jahrbuch* in 1912, but also to forward a copy of the manuscript to Bethmann-Hollweg, who asked the Ministry of the Interior for comment.[1]

Froehlich assummed that France and England would be the enemy in any coming war, that England would not be deterred by quibbles about international law from imposing an effective blockade, that Russian food exports would cease, and that the United States would not oppose English interests.[2] Germany must therefore rely almost exclusively on domestic food supplies, which Froehlich considered dangerously inadequate. He calculated that Germany relied on imports for 15–25 per cent of her wheat consumption and 40 per cent of her fodder. Official statistics, he believed, exaggerated domestic yields and thus understated German dependence on imports.[3] A change in the method used to estimate yields after 1898 led to a sudden, unjustified upward revision of yields by nearly 20 per cent. Before 1898 estimates had been based on the returns of local officials and estate overseers. After 1898 the returns, referring to larger areas, were made by local volunteers who were usually outstanding farmers inclined to generalise too generously from their own yields.[4] Even if large numbers of livestock were slaughtered on the outbreak of war, domestic fodder supplies would still prove inadequate to maintain the irreducible minimum of protein supply.[5] As domestic grain stocks were subject to sharp seasonal fluctuations, a war breaking out in

[229]

spring or summer might find Germany dangerously short even of foods, like rye, of which she produced an overall annual surplus.[6] A bad harvest, like that of 1911, would seriously exacerbate this problem.[7] Froehlich suggested two main solutions to these difficulties. Waste lands should be improved in order to substantially expand the domestic peace-time agricultural area.[8] Above all, however, as Germany could never become wholly self-sufficient, he urged a policy of systematic accumulation of wheat stocks to guard against the threat of total blockade.[9]

Many of Froehlich's points were made by other pre-war observers. Schmoller's intervention, however, served to expose official thinking by eliciting a detailed commentary on the article by the Ministry of the Interior.[10]

The Ministry completely rejected Froehlich's diagnosis and prescriptions. It accused him of exaggerating German dependence on wheat imports. Rye and potatoes could easily be substituted for wheat.[11] Froehlich exaggerated the minimum physiological demand for food. Germans could survive on less food than they normally consumed in peacetime, which far exceeded the subsistence levels of earlier generations.[12] Recent Danish experiments had shown that human protein requirements were generally grossly exaggerated.[13] Germany, contrary to Froehlich, could become agriculturally self-sufficient. There was no reason why wheat should not emulate the rapid increase in rye yields since 1880 which 'must be attributed exclusively to the progress of domestic agricultural techniques, especially the cultivation of more prolific strains'.[14] The yield statistics must be reliable because they were based on a series stretching back to 1880.[15] Total meat production could be increased 25 per cent in war-time through reclamation of waste lands.[16] Fodder shortages were unlikely to occur for livestock numbers would be reduced on the outbreak of war.[17] The experience of the bad harvest of 1911 should inspire confidence rather than concern, in view of the ease with which German agriculture had recovered from it.[18] Above all, whatever other shortages might occur, potatoes would prove an inexhaustible source of domestic food supply.[19] Their already huge output could be easily increased through more intensive application of fertiliser and improved techniques.[20]

The memorandum complacently concluded by accusing Froehlich of superficiality and asserting that his contribution had received more attention than it warranted through appearing in the widely respected *Schmollers Jahrbuch*, implicitly criticising Schmoller for an error of editorial judgement and for wasting valuable bureaucratic time.[21] What the memorandum most glaringly revealed, in fact, was the intellectual poverty of the Ministry itself. Four aspects of the reply deserve particular attention: (1) the confusion concerning the time scale involved; (2) the internal contradictions; (3) the failure to perceive basic relationships within agriculture; (4) the failure to perceive basic linkages between agriculture and the economy as a whole.

The Ministry did not appear to anticipate any insuperable problems in the event of a long war. Some of the replies, indeed, seemed to envisage a longer war than Froehlich himself. Where Froehlich demanded a sustained peace-time reclamation policy, the officials predicted a 25 per cent increase in meat production as the result of the initiation of such a policy in war-time. Reclamation on this scale might be feasible in a thirty years war. It was inconceivable in a four year, never mind a 'short', war. Likewise, the suggestion that wheat and potato yields could be easily increased seemed to envisage a limitless time span. Yields were rising on trend, but they certainly could not be increased sharply through policy measures from one year to the next.

The Ministry seemed unaware of the contradiction involved in simultaneously envisaging a sharp reduction in livestock numbers on the outbreak of war and a marked increase in livestock production in the course of the war. It refrained from revealing the precise mechanism by which this rather spectacular reversal was to be accomplished, unless it was silently assumed that a massive instant reclamation programme would solve the problem. The Ministry appeared equally unconcerned about the contradiction between the arguments that abundant rye and potato crops precluded shortages and that shortages didn't really matter anyway because Germans could easily survive on less food.

The claim that the rapid recovery from the bad harvest of 1911 reflected the resilience of German agriculture evaded the central issue. Imports could be increased in peace-time to compensate for domestic shortages. A bad harvest under blockade conditions raised far more ominous implications. The Ministry's reluctance to contemplate the consequences of a bad harvest in war-time appears still more surprising in view of its reliance on the potato, a crop of notoriously variable yield, as the solution to virtually all food problems. In the event the terrible 'turnip' winter of 1916–17, after potato yields plunged 40 per cent in the harvest of 1916, amply justified Froehlich's warning.

The claim that the statistics of harvest yields must be reliable because they covered a long period was, of course, a non sequitur. It ignored the kernel of Froehlich's argument, the spurious sudden increase following the introduction of new collection procedures. It is, in fact, debatable how valid Froehlich's criticisms were in this respect. There appears to be no a priori reason, apart from the fact that they referred to somewhat larger areas, why the later returns should have been less accurate than the earlier. Yields were undoubtedly rising between 1898 and 1914, regardless of the accuracy of the 1898 base itself, and earlier returns may have made inadequate allowance for rising yields in the previous decade. If the yields after 1898 were generally estimated by the best farmers in each district, these were presumably not unaware of their own exalted standards, and it may be thought contrary to human nature had they not made adequate – perhaps even excessive – allowance for their own presumed superiority in estimating average yields in their locality. The whole issue certainly deserves close consideration. The scepticism of the pre-war critics may prove to have been justified. Many later commentators accepted the pessimistic case.[22] That it was in their own interest to do so – for several wrote as apologists for their own war-time performance and were naturally inclined to magnify the problems that had confronted them – does not necessarily mean that their retrospective opinions did not happen to coincide with the truth. The reply to Froehlich, however, raised none of the pertinent issues. It sought edifying but unconvincing refuge in salvation by faith alone.

An intriguing aspect of the Ministry's memorandum was the fleeting reference to the possibility of improving potato yields in war through increased application of fertiliser. Froehlich's failure to consider the impact of a blockade on fertiliser imports, and the resulting implications for yields, was a serious omission in his generally sensible survey. If Froehlich overlooked this possibility, the Ministry adopted an absurd attitude. It actually anticipated rising yields in war-time. It failed to grasp that increasing pre-war yields were due primarily to a rapid growth in fertiliser inputs.[23] It further failed to relate its anticipation of increasing fertiliser application to the probable supply situation. Germany possessed abundant potash, some phosphates, little nitrates. In addition, the fall in livestock numbers, as a result of the slaughter expected on the outbreak of war, would reduce manure input. Table 1 records the actual course of fertiliser inputs during the war.

Table 1. *Fertiliser input (kg per hectare of agricultural land)*

	Nitrates	Phosphates	Potash
1913–14	6.3	18.9	16.7
1914–15	3.3	17.7	14.6
1915–16	2.5	14.5	20.8
1916–17	2.7	12.5	24.8
1917–18	3.1	11.4	26.5
1918–19	3.9	7.9	22.8

SOURCE: H. H. Herlemann, *Die Versorgung der westdeutschen Landwirtschaft mit Mineralduenger* (Kiel, 1950), p. 8.

The increased use of potash partly compensated for the decline in the use of other fertilisers and of manure. However, as potash was an imperfect substitute for the other products, the qualitative decline in fertiliser input was even more severe than the quantitative. The brilliant achievement of the Haber–Bosch process in solving the munitions crisis in the early days of the war has distracted attention from the fact that it did not solve the nitrates problem equally satisfactorily for agriculture. It managed, at best, to supply little more than half the amount used in the last pre-war years, and this was qualitatively inferior to the imported product.[24] Table 2 records movements in yields during the war.

Table 2. *Yields per hectare (kg)*

	Wheat	Rye	Barley	Oats	Potatoes	Sugarbeet
1913	2,350	1,910	2,220	2,190	15,860	
1914	1,990	1,650	1,980	2,060	13,460	29,750
1915	1,930	1,430	1,530	1,300	15,110	27,400
1916	1,830	1,490	1,830	1,940	8,960	24,600
1917	1,520	1,260	1,280	1,040	13,700	24,810
1918	1,720	1,390	1,510	1,430	10,800	24,600

SOURCE: W. G. Hoffmann, *Das Wachstum der Deutschen Wirtschaft seit der mitte des 19. Jahrhunderts* (Berlin, 1965), pp. 280–1.

These figures, sober enough in their own right, convey a misleadingly favourable impression. Far from waste land being brought into cultivation during the war, as officials fondly predicted, the area under crops fell 15 per cent between 1913 and 1918,[25] as lack of fertiliser precluded economic cultivation of the worst soils. Yields for the later war years are therefore inflated because they refer to relatively better soils than the immediate pre-war returns.

Other factors besides falling fertiliser inputs affected these yields. It has, in particular, been frequently argued that labour shortage proved the most important obstacle to maintaining yields, but the experience of non-belligerants during the war, and immediate post-war experience in Germany itself, suggests that fertiliser shortage was the most significant single factor. Denmark and Holland had, like Germany, rapidly intensified their fertiliser inputs in the pre-war decade. Their agricultural labour forces were not seriously affected by the war, but fertiliser imports fell sharply. So did yields.[26] In Germany itself labour streamed back into agriculture in 1919. Yields, however, did not generally recover immediate pre-war levels until 1924–5. This seems to have been mainly due to fertiliser shortages. Potash inputs did continue to fluctuate around their 1918 levels but nitrates input did not recover the 1914 level until 1922 and phosphates input recovered the level of 1918, itself one-third less than that of 1914, only in 1925.[27]

Pre-war prognosticators generally conceded the possibility of reduced food imports in war-time, but assumed that domestic yields would be maintained. In view of the inevitable decline in yields that would follow a fall in fertiliser imports, however, self-sufficiency in peace-time would not have sufficed to ensure self-sufficiency in war, as seemed to be generally assumed even among critics of official complacency. Germany needed 125 per cent self-sufficiency to be confident of maintaining peace-time consumption levels. In the event the shortfall in domestic grain output in the final two years of the war exceeded double the annual grain imports on the eve of the war. It was less the decline in food imports *per se* than the decline in domestic output that crippled food supplies.

The claim that Germans could survive on less food, though physiologically correct up to a point, overlooked the impact of reduced consumption on industrial productivity. The influence of improved nutrition on labour productivity had been a self-evident truth to nineteenth-century commentators. During the war productivity did in fact suffer severely from inadequate food supplies.[28] The Ministry failed to see the connection. Indeed the officials might be interpreted as implying that soldiers no less than industrial workers could thrive on less food, for they simply ignored Froehlich's warning – duly borne out in the event – that as army rations exceeded average adult civilian consumption, the transfer of several million males from below average to above average consumption levels would impose further strain on civilian food supply.[29]

The reply to Froehlich provides a useful opportunity of appraising the quality of bureaucratic thinking in the immediate pre-war years. Several other examples might be cited to reinforce the impression of intellectual inadequacy it conveys. On the immediate eve of the war, for instance, the Ministry not only ignored the little matter of fodder imports in predicting the impact of a blockade on livestock numbers, but also managed to overlook the possibility that the diversion of fodder potatoes and barley to human consumption might reduce the amount of fodder available.[30] The quality of pre-war official thinking did not, therefore, augur well for policy formulation during the war. The official reaction to war-time developments casts further light on the functioning of the official mind.

Pig producers in the hinterlands of Hamburg and Bremen fed their swine mainly on good quality, conveniently imported Russian barley. The cutting off of Russian imports induced these farmers to bring their pigs to market on the immediate outbreak of war, saturating the meat market. Slaughter restrictions were therefore imposed in October 1914. However, as it began to impinge that more pigs would have to be fed on potatoes as a substitute for the missing barley, academics like Max Sering, and representatives of the agricultural organisations, impressed on Moltke in early 1915 the potential gravity of the situation if food stocks could not last until the new harvest.[31] As no government agency had initiated systematic checks on potato returns before the war, there was no tested technique for appraising the widely varying estimates of existing stocks and probable demand. The information was acquired in rather primitive manner in the course of January. Towns were asked to predict their demand until the new harvest, farmers to return their existing stocks. The officials panicked on receiving the returns, which seemed to portend a food crisis by June unless immediate restrictions on the use of potatoes for fodder were imposed. The compulsory pig slaughter of the next three months caused a net fall of 9m, nearly 40 per cent of the total, in pig stocks.[32] By May 1915 it became clear that the January returns had exaggerated the potential human demand, and that farmers had under-estimated their stocks.[33] The pig slaughter was called off. But forces had by then been set in motion which the government failed to contain for at least another year. The severe meat shortage following the temporary glut of the pig slaughter forced meat prices up so sharply in the summer and autumn of 1915 that it became profitable to use not merely potatoes but grain, whose price had been controlled from early in the war, as fodder. A maximum was duly imposed on pork prices in November 1915 but as the price was set unrealistically low the immediate result was to sharply reduce pork supplies as farmers held back pigs for their own consumption.[34] The decline in the supply of pork compelled demand to shift to beef – whose price remained uncontrolled. Beef prices naturally spiralled upwards. Berlin retail beef prices, which had remained roughly stable from July to November 1915, doubled in the next five months.[35] Maximum prices for cattle were finally imposed in March 1916. As the beef maxima were set comparatively high compared with milk prices, however, it became profitable in some cases to kill cows for meat. Cow numbers fell from 9.5m to 8.1m between December 1916 and December 1918.

It took policy makers two years to appreciate the nature of the agricultural price system, and to grasp that no individual price could be regulated without disturbing the whole supply structure.[36] Consequently the measures taken, as with the pork and milk price maxima, achieved results contrary to those intended. Livestock numbers tell an even sorrier tale than crop output. Pig numbers fell from 25m to 6m between 1914 and 1918, cattle numbers from 22m to 17m. Pig weights fell about 50 per cent, cattle nearly as much, milk output per cow almost 30 per cent.[37] In view of the inadequate preparations it may be that German food supplies were beyond human redemption in a long war. But the problems that piled up for administrators in the spring and summer of 1916, before the disastrous 1916 harvest, were largely of their own making.

Distribution difficulties no doubt aggravated the problem of food supply from the consumer viewpoint. But the real crisis occurred in production. Distribution problems – perhaps one-third of the food entering into exchange took the black market route in the later stages of the war – were a symptom of the production crisis. The considerable ingenuity devoted to solving them after the creation of the *Kriegsernaehrungsamt* in June 1916 belongs very much to the bolting the stable door variety. The production crisis, in turn, resulted from the failure to realise the crucial role played by fertilisers in sustaining yields, and the consequent neglect to take any measures to ensure adequate stocks; the casualness concerning the acquisition of systematic information about the structure of agricultural output; the reluctance to concede that agriculture functioned as a system, and not as a series of discrete, parallel production lines – that, in short, every output was someone else's input; the failure to realise that a price system existed, and that individual prices could not be regulated *in vacuo* without disturbing the whole finely meshed price mechanism. It is peculiarly ironic that officials who generally protested the impropriety of interfering with market forces[38] should have displayed so little understanding of the functioning of those revered forces.

Recent research has emphasised that cumbersome bureaucratic structures hampered effective decision making in Imperial Germany. Lack of coordination within and between ministries, between Imperial and state agencies, between civilian and military organisations has been convincingly demonstrated.[39] The case has been so effectively made that it may inadvertently divert attention from the actual quality of thinking of officials in their own departmental recesses, before their proposals began to run the gauntlet of the governmental structure. The allocation of administrative responsibilities was as illogical in agriculture as in many other spheres. But there is little evidence that this was the main problem hampering the formulation of effective policies. The fundamental weakness was more intellectual than organisational. It would be unwise to generalise too freely from the experience of agriculture, whose administration may have raised as peculiar problems for urban administrators as its history raises for urban historians. It is nonetheless difficult to resist the suspicion, despite contemporary boasts that Germany's resilience in the face of the blockade reflected the superiority of German organisation and German intellect,[40] that in this sphere at least the men simply did not measure up to the job.

We have argued that the errors of war-time agricultural policy did not derive basically from a surge of unforeseeable problems. Farmers and consumers both behaved rationally in war-time. It was the failure of pre-war administrators to understand peace-time realities that precluded their early understanding of war-time realities. Why these comprehension gaps existed in a society that prided itself on expertise raises questions that go beyond the limited purpose of this paper – questions concerning the educational system, recruitment and training procedures in the public service, the background and qualifications of the specific officials charged with the administration of agriculture. August Skalweit, himself a leading war-time agricultural adviser, more modest than some of his colleagues, pleaded in extenuation that 'To understand all is to forgive all.'[41] That may be sound theology. Historians, however, are still some distance from understanding all. I hope that this paper, by drawing attention to some neglected techniques of administrative thinking, may promote understanding of the relation between policy and performance in German agriculture.

NOTES

1 Georg Froehlich, 'Deutsche Volksernaehrung im Kriege', *Jahrbuch fuer Gesetz-gebung, Verwaltung und Volkswirtschaft* (Schmollers Jahrbuch) 36 (1912), pp. 575–94; Reicharchiv (ed.), *Kriegsruestung und Kriegswirtschaft, Anlagen zum ersten Band* (Berlin, 1930). Der Staatssekrataer des Innern Dr Delbrueck an den Reichskanzler Dr v. Bethmann Hollweg, 30 March 1912, p. 239.

2 Froehlich, Deutsche Volksernaehrung im Kriege, pp. 575–94, pp. 576–9.

3 *Ibid.* p. 580.

4 *Ibid.*

5 *Ibid.* p. 589.

6 *Ibid.* p. 581.

7 *Ibid.* p. 587.

8 *Ibid.* pp. 593–4.

9 *Ibid.* p. 591.

10 Froehlich's article and the Ministry of the Interior's reply are discussed in Lothar Burchardt, *Friedenswirtschaft und Kriegsvorsorge: Deutschlands wirt-schaftliche Ruestungsbestrebungen vor 1914* (Boppard am Rhein, 1968), pp. 196–7. This book contains a valuable summary of pre-war opinion, but takes a rather different approach from that adopted in this paper. Fritz Fischer refers to the matter from yet a different perspective, in *Krieg der Illusionen* (Duessel-dorf, 1969), p. 285.

11 Reicharchiv (ed.), *Kriegsruestung*, p. 239.

12 *Ibid.*

13 *Ibid.* p. 244.

14 *Ibid.* p. 241.

15 *Ibid.* pp. 242–3.

16 *Ibid.* p. 242.

17 *Ibid.* p. 246.

18 *Ibid.* p. 244.

19 *Ibid.* p. 245.

20 *Ibid.*

21 *Ibid.* p. 247.

22 A. Skalweit, *Die Deutsche Ernaehrungswirtschaft* (Stuttgart, 1927), pp. 6ff; K. Thiess, 'Die Ernaehrungslage in Deutschland zu Beginn des fuenften Kriegs-jahres', *Schmollers Jahrbuch*, 43 (1919), p. 186. L. Burchardt, *Friedenswirtschaft und Kriegsvorsorge*, pp. 98ff., esp. 106, accepts that pre-war returns exaggerated output, but his arguments are not quite conclusive.

23 The best discussion of the influence of fertiliser on pre-1914 agricultural output is in A. V. Desai, *Real Wages in Germany 1871–1913* (Oxford, 1968), ch. 6.

24 Dr Roth, 'Die deutsche und die auslaendische Kaligewinnung', *Schmollers Jahrbuch*, 42 (1918), p. 672; O. Goebel, *Deutsche Rohstoffwirtschaft im Weltkrieg* (Stuttgart, 1930), p. 30.

25 W. G. Hoffmann, *Das Wachstum der Deutschen Wirtschaft seit der mitte des 19. Jahrhunderts* (Berlin, 1965), pp. 273–5.

26 Einar Cohn, 'Denmark', in *Sweden, Norway, Denmark and Iceland in the World War* (New Haven, 1930), p. 491; I. J. Brugmans, *Paardenkracht en Mensenmacht, 1795–1940* (The Hague, 1961), pp. 447–8. F. E. Posthuma, 'Food Supply and Agriculture' in *The Netherlands and the World War* (New Haven, 1928) begins his year by year analysis of government measures with 'Provision for artificial fertilisers' and doesn't include a section on labour at all. For shortfalls in fertiliser supply, see esp. p. 268.

27 H. H. Herlemann, *Die Versorgung der westdeutschen Landwirtschaft mit Mineral-duenger* (Kiel, 1950), p. 8.
28 W. Hahn, *Der Ernaehrungskrieg* (Berlin, 1939), pp. 51–2.
29 Froehlich 'Deutsche Volksernaehrung im Kriege', p. 590; Skalweit, *Die Deutsche Ernaehrungswirtschaft*, p. 83.
30 Burchardt, *Friedenswirtschaft und Kriegsvorsorge*, pp. 170, 181.
31 Skalweit, *Die Deutsche Ernaehrungswirtschaft*, n. 1, p. 27, pp. 84ff.
32 *Ibid.* p. 97. A net decline of about 2.5m might have been expected in numbers over this phase of the normal pig cycle (Hahn, *Der Ernaehrungskrieg*, p. 30). The net wastage attributable to the slaughter, therefore, was about 6.5m pigs – over 25 per cent of the total stock, or about 15 per cent of normal German meat supplies, and this in a country vulnerable to fats shortages!
33 Skalweit, *Die Deutsche Ernaehrungswirtschaft*, p. 97; Mary Stocks, 'German Potato Policy', *Economic Journal*, xxvi (1916), pp. 57ff.
34 Skalweit, *Die Deutsche Ernaehrungswirtschaft*, pp. 101–2, 110–12; Edgar Meyer, 'Die Entwicklung der Vieh- und Fleischpreise und die Regelung der Fleischversorgung in Deutschland waehrend der ersten beiden Kriegsjahre (unter besonderer Beruecksichtigung der Berliner Verhaeltnisse)', *Jahrbuch fuer Nationaloekonomie und Statistik*, IIIF, 54 (1917), p. 595.
35 Meyer, 'Die Entwicklung der Vieh- und Fleischpreise', p. 595.
36 Dr Herbst, 'Die reichsgesetzlichen Massnahmen zur Sicherung der deutschen Volksernaehrung im Kriege', *Jb. f. NÖ. u. Stat.*, IIIF., 53, 54 (1917), contains a detailed survey of regulations concerning food supply during the first two years of the war.
37 Skalweit, *Die Deutsche Ernaehrungswirtschaft*, n. 19, pp. 112, 113.
38 Burchardt, *Friedenswirtschaft und Kriegsvorsorge*, pp. 140, 218–19.
39 For a particularly effective exposition of this view cf. J. Steinberg, 'Germany and the Russo-Japanese War', *American Historical Review*, LXXV (1970), and 'The Tirpitz Plan', *Historical Journal*, xvi, 1 (1973), pp. 201ff.
40 Herbst, 'Die reichsgesetzlichen Massnahmen', p. 82.
41 Skalweit, *Die Deutsche Ernaehrungswirtschaft*, p. 89.

11 Social planning in war-time: some aspects of the Beveridge Report[1]

José Harris

In analysing the impact of modern warfare, many historians have detected a complex interaction between the prosecution of war and developments in social policy.[2] The precise nature of this relationship remains, however, a matter for conjecture. War and war expenditure have sometimes been seen as rivals to expenditure on social welfare; in other cases they have been seen as positively setting the pace for social welfare expenditure and government-sponsored social change.[3] Pressure for social reform in war-time has been ascribed both to an increase in social solidarity brought about by war[4] and to a war-induced heightening of social and political conflict.[5] Whichever of these views is correct – and it seems likely that each of them has validity at different times and in different circumstances – it is certain that warfare in modern times has tended to promote a good deal of public introspection into the nature of social justice and into prevailing social and economic arrangements. An outstanding example of this kind of enquiry was the Beveridge Report of 1942 – a report which has often been seen as the agenda for the British welfare state. This essay will examine certain aspects of the making of the Beveridge Report, its relation to the wider context of war, and its subsequent influence on social policy.

The Beveridge Committee on Social Insurance and Allied Services was established by the war-time Committee on Reconstruction Problems in the summer of 1941. The terms of reference were extremely limited – they were merely to enquire into the possibility of integrating the various compartments of British social security which had grown up piecemeal alongside the Poor Law since 1897. Nevertheless, both historians and contemporaries have seen the work of this committee as far more than a mere 'machinery of government' enquiry of the kind so familiar in Britain in the last few decades. From the start, its deliberations were seen by contemporaries as evidence of a conscious attempt on the part of the war-time government to abolish poverty, as 'one of the essentials for pursuing the National War Effort' and as 'a blueprint for freedom from want'.[6] Retrospectively, the report of the Beveridge Committee was seen as the basis of the social reforms of the post-war Labour government, and Beveridge himself was seen as the originator

[239]

of the comprehensive national insurance system, the family allowance system and the greatly enlarged and extended system of national health.

When examined in the light of historical evidence, however, this account of the Beveridge Committee proves to be in many respects inaccurate; and in this paper I shall attempt to show, firstly, that the Beveridge plan was in no sense an expression of the aims and ideals of the war-time coalition government; secondly, that Beveridge himself contributed little that was intrinsically original to the discussion of war-time plans for social reconstruction; and, thirdly, that the significance of his report lay much less in its substantive proposals than in its synthesis of secondary opinions and its transmission to a popular audience of ideas which – among journalists, academics, trade unionists and public administrators – had long been in vogue.

Let us first consider the position and reputation of Beveridge himself. He has often been portrayed as a collectivist liberal with a continuous commitment to social reform dating back to his days as sub-warden of Toynbee Hall in the early 1900s;[7] but in fact his ideas on politics and society were a good deal more ambivalent than this view would suggest. Ideologically he veered between an almost total commitment to the free market, and a belief that the free market was corrupt and inefficient and should be replaced by a strong, impartial administrative state. As a young man he had helped to frame the first national insurance bill, and had been personally responsible for some of the more restrictive clauses of the original unemployment insurance scheme – notably the clauses which imposed behavioural constraints on beneficiaries and limited the ratio of benefits to contributions to one in five.[8] Even at that stage he had toyed with schemes for more comprehensive social insurance,[9] and in 1924 he had produced a Liberal pamphlet on *Insurance for All and Everything*, which outlined a scheme for covering the whole of the population against a wide spectrum of social risks. Since 1934 he had been part-time chairman of the Unemployment Insurance Statutory Committee, which advised the Ministry of Labour on variations in rates of benefit and relations with the public. On this committee he had made some interesting policy innovations, not merely in technical aspects of social insurance, but in using insurance funds as a means of anticipating cyclical depressions of trade.[10]

Nevertheless, by 1940 Beveridge had very little connection with, and only a limited interest in, the wider issues of social security: and quite the last kind of job that he was hoping to be given by the War Cabinet was the job of enquiring into problems of post-war reconstruction. Beveridge at the outbreak of war was a man of sixty with a long, distinguished, though rather erratic career behind him. He was the master of an Oxford college, an ex-director and virtually the creator of the London School of Economics. As a civil servant in the First World War, he had been one of the youngest men ever to reach the rank of Permanent Secretary. He had an inflated opinion of himself as an economist, and a deservedly high reputation as an expert on manpower and labour organisation; and it was in these two fields – in economic planning and in problems of manpower – that he hoped to serve the government as a war-time advisor, if not actually as a member of the government itself. After a lifetime of speaking his mind however, Beveridge had few friends in high places. He had curiously little understanding of the limited scope in establishment politics for the non-party 'expert' and the political outsider; and his name was 'mentioned in the Cabinet as one who criticised the Government too much'.[11] Consequently, at the beginning of the war, Beveridge far from finding himself – as he had hoped – at the head of an economic general staff, found himself virtually unemployed. His friend and rival, Maynard Keynes, found himself in a similar position; and for the first nine months of the war Keynes, Beveridge and other disgruntled liberal economists used to meet together in Keynes' house in Bloomsbury, where they denounced the Chamberlain government's lack of policy, and wistfully and rather unhistorically recalled their own share in the successful running of the previous war.[12]

When Churchill replaced Chamberlain and Labour joined the Coalition, Keynes was taken into the Treasury, but Beveridge still remained for some time without an official position – possibly because he offended Attlee and Dalton, the new Deputy Prime Minister and the new Minister for Economic Warfare, by treating them as though they were still junior lecturers and he still the director at the LSE. Eventually he was given the task of conducting a special enquiry into war-time manpower requirements; but in this capacity he was used merely as an 'investigating satellite'[13] without executive or policy-making authority. At the end of 1940 he became a temporary assistant secretary in Ernest Bevin's Ministry of Labour, and there he hoped that Bevin might place him in charge of the coordination of labour supplies and civilian mobilisation. As a veteran trade unionist, however, Ernest Bevin regarded Beveridge's interest in labour with suspicion and hostility – almost certainly because he associated Beveridge with the curtailment of trade union liberties in the First World War and, more recently, with the advocacy of policies of industrial conscription.[14] Beveridge was literally one of the last men in England with whom Bevin would have entrusted any kind of real control over the organisation of labour. But Beveridge was too eminent and too persistent to be summarily dismissed from government service, and he had to be employed in some way or another. Hence, Bevin grudgingly approved the appointment of Beveridge to the chairmanship of the Committee on Social Insurance and Allied Services in June 1941. Beveridge himself was under no illusions about what was happening to him. It is recorded that tears stood in his eyes when the appointment was offered to him; and twenty years later he recalled that Ernest Bevin 'pushed me as Chairman of the Social Insurance Committee by way of parting from me . . . My removal in 1941 from the Ministry of Labour to Social Insurance was a "kicking upstairs".[15]

Beveridge was right in believing that his new appointment was not initially seen by the government as an important one, and certainly not as a prelude to a massive programme of social reconstruction. In fact, the decision to appoint a social insurance committee was taken almost by accident and came about in the following way. Since 1938 the workmen's compensation branch of the social security system had been under investigation by a Royal Commission, a commission called into being by the demand of trade unionists that greatly increased benefits should be paid in cases of industrial disease and accident, and that the whole of this benefit should continue to be paid for solely by the employers. This commission had virtually folded up early in 1941 through lack of cooperation from the employers, who argued, firstly, that they could not present evidence on such a subject in war-time and, secondly, that industrial disease should be dealt with, not as a special problem but, like other forms of sickness, through the contributory national health insurance scheme set up by Lloyd George in 1911. Rates of benefit under national health insurance were, however, considerably lower than those which prevailed under workmen's compensation; and there was therefore no possibility that the trade unions would accept the transfer of industrial injuries to the national insurance system – not, at any rate, without a substantial *quid pro quo*. Nevertheless, the employers' proposal raised in an acute form a problem which social insurance authorities had been avoiding for many years – the fact that there was such a wide variation in the extent, duration and coverage of benefits offered by different types of social security. Thus, a man entitled to workmen's compensation received a benefit proportionate to his previous earnings. A man whose earnings were interrupted by unemployment received a benefit at least theoretically related to his subsistence needs, plus an additional allowance for dependents. A man out of work through sickness, on the other hand, received no statutory allowance for dependents, and his rate of benefit was deliberately fixed below subsistence level in order to encourage additional private health insurance. This kind of anomaly was increasingly hard to justify, particularly when the pressures of war were also revealing the enormous geographical and institutional variations which prevailed on the treatment side of the health system. Moreover, the Ministry of Health was under pressure to start planning for a comprehensive state medical service; and its officials argued that this should not be done in isolation from the reform of social security, since 'there is no problem of public health which does not have a common frontier with the treatment or rehabilitation side of social insurance'.[16]

In the spring of 1941, therefore, both the Home Office and the Ministry of Health were keen to establish a social insurance committee, not so much with a view to making long-term plans as with a view to exposing and clarifying some of the anomalies of the existing system.[17] Ernest Bevin initially opposed the scheme, on the ground that 'a Committee consisting partly of civil servants and partly of outsiders would be no good';[18] but he apparently capitulated when he saw that it was a chance of getting rid of Beveridge. Nevertheless, he insisted that the enquiry should not be a 'policy enquiry' but should concern itself merely with technical questions of social administration[19] – a condition which senior officials privately admitted to be quite unrealistic, in view of the controversial nature of many of the financial issues and the 'questions of major policy' to be raised.[20] The Treasury indeed was anxious that the social insurance committee should be a secret committee, fearing that its enquiries would be interpreted as an indicator of future government policy.[21] The committee's terms of reference were in fact never officially disclosed to parliament, although MPs soon extracted from Arthur Greenwood, the minister in charge of reconstruction problems, the information that a special inquiry into the social services had been set in hand.[22] It was Greenwood who recruited the civil service members of the committee, and who announced Beveridge's new appointment to the House of Commons on 10 June 1941.

As I have shown, his appointment to the social insurance committee was a crushing blow to Beveridge – the end of his hopes of being placed in charge of economic planning or civilian mobilisation. During the next few months however, he apparently got over his disappointment and convinced himself that his new job was one of the most important jobs of the war – a prerequisite of military victory as well as the beginning of planning for peace.[23] It was this conviction (rather than any original contribution that Beveridge made at this time to the theory and practice of social security) that transformed his committee from a 'machinery of government' to a 'high policy' committee, and helped to make 'reconstruction' the preoccupation no longer merely of a few reformers and intellectuals but of the whole political nation.

At no time, however, can the discussions of the Beveridge committee be seen as evidence of the policy intentions of the government of the day. Churchill himself believed that the problems referred to the committee were exclusively post-war problems, and that no commitment could be made to social reform until after the restoration of peace.[24] It soon became clear, however, that the government was being trapped in an increasingly paradoxical situation. On the one hand, ministers used the existence of the Beveridge committee to stave off all kinds of demand for social reform; and on the other hand the very fact that issues like family allowances, increased rates of benefit and extended medical care were continually postponed 'until the Beveridge committee shall have reported' created the false impression that ministers were already secretly committed to all these innovations.[25] In fact, with the exception of family allowances, the reverse was the case; and consequently both Cabinet and Treasury were highly alarmed when in the summer of 1942 Beveridge produced virtually single-handed a draft report on social insurance which was obviously nearly ready for publication.[26] This draft differed in very few particulars from the final version of the report. It was based on the assumption that any reconstruction of social security must take place within a context of full employment, universal medical care and the payment of family allowances at subsistence level. Within this context Beveridge proposed that uniform benefits, also calculated at subsistence rates, should be given for all interruptions of earnings to all insured persons, who in future would include not only the working-class but the whole employed and self-employed population. Full rates of benefit would be reached only gradually, and for old age pensioners Beveridge predicted that it would be twenty years before the full rates of benefit could be given. At the end of that period he looked forward to the final withering away of the Poor Law and an end to supplementation.

Beveridge's proposals are often criticised at the present time on the ground that the rates of benefit proposed were much too low and took no account of the need for proofing against inflation. In 1942, however, it is not too much to say that they were seen by the Treasury and Cabinet as needlessly and even shockingly extravagant. As a result of the first intimation of Beveridge's comprehensive plans the civil servant members of his committee had been downgraded from being full members of the committee to being merely 'advisers and assessors'.[27] This was done lest the Beveridge proposals should be thought to represent the official views of their respective government departments. Beveridge was forced to acquiesce in this decision; but he accepted it only with extreme reluctance, presumably realising that it would seriously diminish the political – as opposed to merely popular – impact of his report. In the first draft of the report he implied that it was the production of the whole of his committee, but this was amended at the request of the official members. 'Beveridge cannot properly expect to have "the best of both worlds"', commented the Ministry of Health representative, 'viz. a free hand as to the contents of his Report, coupled with the implication ... that his advisors and assessors agree with his conclusions'.[28] The Treasury meanwhile became increasingly alarmed at the prospective cost of Beveridge's proposals; but at the same time Treasury officials were diffident about making criticisms or suggestions, lest they should appear to 'have committed the Government on matters of policy'. This situation was smoothed over by Lord Keynes, who claimed that Beveridge 'if approached, would be ready and willing to be cooperative'; and he urged the Treasury to give Beveridge's committee every possible assistance.[29] Keynes was in fact in favour of many aspects of Beveridge's plan, believing that it was 'the cheapest alternative open to us';[30] and he and Beveridge eventually agreed together that the Exchequer's share of the cost of the plan should not exceed the fairly generous limit of £100m a year for the first five years, with no limitation thereafter.[31] It was probably largely due to the mediation of Keynes, backed up by the pressure of reforming back benchers, that the enquiry was not at this stage abandoned and the Beveridge Report ignominiously suppressed.

After this hostile official reception of the draft report, it was not perhaps surprising that the War Cabinet virtually refused to acknowledge the final version of the report which was ready for publication early in the autumn of 1942. In October Stafford Cripps told Beatrice Webb that publication of the Report was being postponed 'as some of the Cabinet object to it as too revolutionary'.[32] The Report was, however, published in November 1942, and was instantly seized upon for propaganda purposes by the Ministry of Information.[33] Almost immediately a committee of civil servants was formed to comment on the Beveridge proposals, and this committee, under the chairmanship of Sir Thomas Phillips, rejected the idea of subsistence benefits, severely reduced the proposed level of family allowances, and was sceptical of the possibility of maintaining full employment after the war. Moreover, the Phillips committee advised the Government either to accept or reject the Beveridge plan as a package-deal – thus excluding the possibility, suggested by Beveridge himself, that certain items of reform could be introduced piecemeal when funds became available or as circumstances demanded.[34] At the same time Beveridge himself was given to understand that he would not be personally involved in the implementation of his proposals; and he was expressly prohibited from conducting a further official enquiry into the implications of full employment – an enquiry which had originally been seen as a logical continuation of the enquiry into social insurance. Beveridge himself subsequently carried out a private enquiry into the nature of full employment, but he was denied both official advice and access to official statistics;[35] and neither he nor anyone else during this period seems to have fully understood the potential equation between full employment, inflation and the failure of social security benefits to meet subsistence needs.

I have shown that the Beveridge plan was in no sense part of a government plan for promoting a revolution in British social security. What of my second proposition, that Beveridge himself at this stage of his career contributed little that was original to such a revolution? I do not want in any way to minimise the significance of Beveridge's work; and the papers of his committee which have recently been opened to historians tend to strengthen rather than weaken the common impression that Beveridge himself was mainly responsible for its report. All the members of the committee whom it has been possible to interview were unanimous in believing that Beveridge's influence was crucial in transforming the work of the committee from a mere tidying-up operation into a blueprint for future policy formation. None of the civil service members had instructions from their ministers to deal with wider issues; and most of them were mainly concerned with the problems of 'marginal' cases and with presenting and defending a departmental point of view. They felt, moreover, that in spite of frequent meetings Beveridge gave them little opportunity to discuss questions of principle, and that the preparation of the Report was far too rapid to allow all sides of every question to be thoroughly considered.[36] They were all heavily engaged in other aspects of wartime administration; and few of them had the time, if they had the inclination, to contribute substantially to Beveridge's panoramic vision of future social policy. It was Beveridge himself who insisted on seeing social security as part of a much wider spectrum of economic and social reform. It was he who decided that social insurance should henceforth be imposed on the whole working community, that benefits should be standardised for all kinds of 'interruption of earnings', and that the use of means tests should be reduced to a minimum; and it was he who insisted that the scheme proposed should reconcile the potentially conflicting principles of a state-guaranteed basic subsistence minimum with a wide margin of scope for 'private saving' and 'voluntary effort'.[37] It was Beveridge also who insisted that an attempt should be made to sound out the views and desires of the potential *consumers* of the services under review; and it was at his instigation that a nation-wide enquiry into working-class attitudes to the Poor Law, Assistance Board and National Health Insurance was carried out under the direction of G. D. H. Cole.[38] Cole's survey was technically rather crude even by contemporary standards, and its blanket condemnation of panel practice and of all forms of discretionary welfare was manifestly partisan; but, nevertheless, it was the first systematic attempt made in Britain to inform an official inquiry about popular reactions to the social services, and to find out about the client's own perception of his needs.[39] It was Beveridge also who focused the committee's attention on what he called the 'sinister concentration of poverty upon children in large families';[40] and it was he who won the confidence of employers, and persuaded them to abandon the policy of total non-cooperation which they had adopted towards the Royal Commission on Workmen's Compensation two years before.[41]

Nevertheless, as we have seen, at the outbreak of war Beveridge was preoccupied with subjects very remote from social security, and it was only with reluctance that he eventually turned his mind to integrating and extending the various aspects of social insurance. This does not mean, however, that such problems were being neglected by other social reformers – in fact, the first three years of the war saw a tremendous upsurge of interest in questions of social policy among journalists, civil servants, academics and persons drafted into Whitehall for the duration of the war. The reasons for this movement are difficult for the historian to catalogue precisely. Undoubtedly an important factor was that stressed by Professor Richard Titmuss in *Problems of Social Policy* – that the tremendous disturbance of civilian population underlined the defects of the existing social services, and areas of neglect which had lain concealed in peacetime stuck out like sore fingers in time of war. A second factor was almost certainly the desire to win and keep the support of organised labour, as a prerequisite of maintaining the war effort and ultimately of winning the war. A third factor was the need to foster morale in the armed forces, and the belief that soldiers, particularly soldiers in conscript armies, fight better 'if they believe that the stakes are high, that freedom, justice, civilisation itself are threatened'.[42] Fourthly, the Second World War, like the First World War, induced a tremendous expansion in the spheres of state control and economic management; and reformers, including Beveridge himself, were not slow to seize upon these experiments as creating precedents for peace-time social administration.[43] This argument was strengthened by recollections of the withdrawal of government from social and economic life after the First World War – a withdrawal that had been accompanied by, if not necessarily responsible for, prolonged depression and unemployment. The analogy between the two situations was forcibly expressed in a classic article by R. H. Tawney, in which Tawney's penchant for drawing morals from history was less than usually veiled. 'Looking back from the vantage ground of 1943', he wrote, 'we can see that the sharp antithesis between the economic conditions of war and those of peace was an illusion . . . The view prevalent in 1919 and 1920 . . . that there is a strong presumption in favour of prompt and general de-control is certainly erroneous. If that view still exists, it ought to be discarded altogether and at once.'[44] A fifth and more nebulous factor was the effect of the economic climate produced by the war in redefining the nature of social distress. As surplus workmen were absorbed into the services or into war production and as wages spiralled upwards in key industries, the concern of social administrators and Public Assistance officials shifted away from the problem of unemployment and focused instead upon the problems of low wage-earners, of those on fixed rates of benefit and those with large families. For the first time for thirty years the relief of poverty rather than the reduction of unemployment became the major problem and first priority of social reform.

This change of priorities was rapidly reflected in the public discussion of social policy. From the start of the war backbenchers of all parties were pressing for family allowances, increased old age pensions, higher social insurance benefits and a freeze on profits and prices; and it should be emphasised that there was already in 1940–1 considerable parliamentary pressure for the kind of reform that Beveridge was to propose at the end of 1942.[45] Whilst the Beveridge committee was in session, moreover, a group of economists and political scientists began to meet together at a series of informal conferences in Oxford and drew up plans for post-war full employment and the reform of the public health services that were in many respects strikingly similar to the 'basic assumptions' of Beveridge's Report.[46] Perhaps, however, the most convincing evidence of the widespread dissemination of such ideas well before the publication of the Beveridge Report, was the written and oral evidence submitted by expert witnesses to the social insurance committee during the course of 1942.

Quite how far this evidence influenced Beveridge and helped him to formulate proposals is not at all clear. In July 1942 Beveridge was covertly criticised by Treasury officials for making up his mind on major items of policy whilst many witnesses were still awaiting cross-examination.[47] But this, if true, is a tribute to Beveridge's capacity to interpret the spirit of the times, because again and again witnesses pressed spontaneously and independently for measures which afterwards became the six main policy proposals of the Beveridge Report – namely, family allowances, the maintenance of full employment, a universal free national health service, a uniform system of contributory insurance, subsistence level benefits and the final abolition of poor relief. Insofar as witnesses disagreed with these policies they were mainly differences of detail rather than differences of general principle. Many friendly societies, for example, endorsed the need for greatly increased medical care and for more comprehensive statutory benefits – with the reservation that sickness insurance should continue to be managed through voluntary organisations.[48] Even the industrial assurance companies claimed to favour a great expansion of existing statutory services, provided that they could continue to share in the administration of national insurance and retain the commercially valuable right of door-to-door collection of contributions.[49] In certain cases witnesses in their anxiety for reform were highly critical of their own role in the prevailing welfare system. Public assistance officials, for example, unanimously called for a dismantling of the Poor Law, denounced the 'meanness of the means tests', and condemned existing public assistance provision as 'inadequate, overlapping, ungenerous and inefficient'.[50] Politically perhaps the most significant evidence came from representatives of the Trades Union Congress who, in spite of initially declaring their refusal to compromise,[51] ultimately agreed with Beveridge on every major issue – with the sole exception of whether workmen's compensation should henceforth be integrated with the rest of social insurance.[52] The TUC delegation to the Beveridge committee was in fact in many ways a remarkable embodiment of the traditional sterling virtues of the labour aristocracy. The delegates were strongly in favour of contributory insurance; they were contemptuous of 'dodgers', of the 'very poor' and of 'the type of person who will not join a Friendly Society'; and to the surprise of Beveridge and his committee the leaders of the delegation favoured the withdrawal of public assistance from the wives and children of workers who went on strike.[53] Amongst other witnesses the only serious disparagement of Beveridge's proposals came from the British Employers' Confederation, who advised him to postpone all consideration of social reconstruction until after the end of the war.[54] Very few of those who gave evidence to the committee were critical of the regressive aspects of flat-rate contributions; only P.E.P and the economist J. E. Meade questioned the basic rationale of the social insurance principle – the latter suggesting that contributions were a harmful 'tax on industry', which should be replaced by payments from direct taxation.[55]

The Beveridge Report therefore expressed views that were almost universally popular, and probably never before or since has there been more of a national consensus on issues of social reform. This being so – and if I am right in saying that Beveridge made no original contribution to the debate, merely expressing what people were inclined to think anyway – what can be seen as the historical significance of the Beveridge Report? Did it in any way change the future content of social policy? Certainly, if one examines the report item by item, its direct influence on specific areas of policy seems to have been slight.

Let us take first the case of family allowances, one of the three assumptions on which the more detailed reforms of social insurance were based. Beveridge had supported Eleanor Rathbone's campaign for family allowances since the early 1920s, and as a member of the Coal Commission of 1926 he had tried to persuade the miners to accept family allowances as a bonus for working longer hours without increased pay. By the early 1940s, however, Beveridge had come to see family allowances in a rather different light; and he proposed them as one of the basic assumptions of his report, partly because he hoped they would promote population growth, but mainly to widen what he saw as the dangerously narrow gap between subsistence level insurance benefits and the income of low paid workers when in work.[56] Both of these arguments were influential in winning *popular* support for family allowances, but neither of them appears to have influenced the coalition government, which in any case rejected the principle of benefits at subsistence level. The promise of family allowances was in fact adopted as official government policy in the summer of 1942, several months before Beveridge had actually reported;[57] and the main motive behind this promise seems to have been, not protection of the insurance scheme nor encouragement to population growth, but the palliation of the government's policies of statutory wage restraint and compulsory wartime savings.[58] Family allowances were eventually introduced, at a considerably lower rate than Beveridge had recommended, in 1945.[59]

Secondly, let us consider another of Beveridge's basic assumptions, the maintenance of full employment. Writing retrospectively about his work for the social insurance committee, Beveridge looked upon his proposals as a direct practical outcome of Keynesian economics; and he claimed that his own studies of unemployment and those of Keynes were 'not contradictory but complementary'.[60] But according to Mr Harold Wilson, this was far from being the case. In a lecture to the Institute of Statisticians in 1966, Wilson recalled that it was only with great intellectual difficulty that Beveridge came round to accepting the Keynesian system, and that this conversion did not happen until some time after the publication of the Beveridge Report.[61]

This account perhaps exaggerates Beveridge's lack of sympathy with the Keynesian view; but, nevertheless, it is true that during the inter-war depression Beveridge's view of unemployment had been for a time that of an orthodox classical economist of the most rigid school.[62] In the late 1930s he had somewhat modified this view, but he had strongly criticised Keynes for exaggerating the homogeneity of 'aggregate demand' and for underestimating the problem of promoting regional and occupational labour mobility.[63] Quite what persuaded him to base his social security proposals on the assumption of full employment is not entirely clear. Possibly his experience of managing the unemployment fund on the Unemployment Insurance Statutory Committee had convinced him of the wider possibilities of economic management. Certainly he believed in a purely pragmatic fashion that governments which managed to abolish unemployment in wartime could equally well do so in time of peace. Several economists who gave evidence before his committee suggested that the insurance funds could themselves be used in the post-war economy to regulate the level of effective demand.[64] Possibly also Beveridge was at this time directly influenced by Keynes with whom he was in constant contact over the budgetary aspects of post-war social security.[65] It seems reasonable to suppose that it was this combination of factors which persuaded Beveridge to adopt full employment as one of his so-called basic assumptions; but in so doing he merely reflected, and in no way determined the most advanced Treasury thinking of his time. His own caution about the possibility of full employment was revealed in the *financial* side of his social insurance proposals, which were calculated, not on a basis of full employment, but on an average rate of unemployment of $8\frac{1}{2}$ per cent.[66]

Thirdly, I want to consider in more detail Beveridge's ideas on national insurance, since it is on these that his reputation as an innovator chiefly rests. These ideas, as we have seen, were based on three main principles: that insured persons should receive the same benefit for all different kinds of interruption of earnings; that flat-rate contributions should be paid for flat-rate benefits, irrespective of earnings; and that benefits should be fixed at subsistence level or above. The first of these principles merely rationalised the highly anomalous state of affairs that had arisen because of the previous piecemeal development of social security legislation. It was a necessary and desirable but in no way strikingly original contribution to social policy. The second principle, that flat-rate contributions and benefits, is the one which has been most radically called in question by subsequent reformers; but whatever its faults and merits, the possible alternative of a graduated system was never seriously considered by the Beveridge committee. Beveridge himself was willing at least to explore the possibilities of an earnings-related system;[67] and at one stage he was considering the possibility of transitional pensions graduated according to an individual's contribution record, but this alternative was ruled out by the Treasury in the summer of 1942 as administratively and financially impossible.[68] The third principle, that of subsistence-level benefits, was perhaps the area in which the Beveridge Report can be seen as most constructively original, since it was a striking departure from the Lloyd Georgian view of national insurance as merely a foundation for voluntary private saving. The idea of a subsistence minimum had of course been put forward by the Webbs over forty years before;[69] and Sir John Walley has recently revealed that subsistence old age pensions had been recommended by a secret committee of the Conservative party as early as 1924.[70] Nevertheless, the Beveridge committee was the first official enquiry to support such a policy for all aspects of social security; and almost certainly it was Beveridge himself who imposed the idea on the rest of his committee and made it a central feature of his report. Moreover, contrary to what is often believed, it is clear from the papers of his committee that Beveridge did not view 'subsistence' as a scientifically immutable concept but as a concept that could and should be adjusted in relation to the changing communal standard of living.[71] But, as well as being original, it was also strikingly unsuccessful, since the principle of subsistence benefits was subsequently rejected by the Treasury and by the social policy departments. The responsibility for this rejection, however, lay at least partly with Beveridge himself, because whilst insisting on the subsistence principle he ultimately refused to accept its administrative and financial implications. He went to immense lengths to work out to the last halfpenny how much benefit would be required to provide a subsistence diet, using the detailed evidence on household budgets published by R. F. George, Seebohm Rowntree and Dr Magee; and having made these calculations, he then added a notional ten shillings to cover the cost of rent.[72] But as Rowntree pointed out in a sub-committee of the main Beveridge committee, this addition for rent rendered meaningless all his previous calculations, because rent varied so enormously from region to region and family to family.[73] The average rent paid in many provincial areas was considerably less than ten shillings, whilst the average rent paid by London households was more than fifteen shillings a week.[74] A flat-rate benefit which included a sum of ten shillings for rent would thus be excessively generous in some areas and entirely inadequate in others. A solution proposed by the Fabian Society's research department was that, instead of a flat-rate benefit for all items, insured persons should receive a flat-rate benefit for food, light, heat and clothing *plus* their *actual* rent.[75] Another alternative suggested by the secretary of the Beveridge committee, D. N. Chester, was that a basic rent allowance of eight shillings should be paid, plus any additional rent charge up to a maximum of fifteen shillings a week. Such a compromise, Chester argued, would prevent unnecessary overpayment to low-rented households, and would at the same time secure the vast majority of high-rented households from the need to supplement insurance benefits by recourse to public assistance.[76] These proposals were, however, vetoed by several official members of the Social Insurance Committee, who raised a variety of objections: that low-paid areas like Scotland ought not to subsidise highly-paid areas like London, that it would 'introduce a discordant note into a scheme that is to be free from any suggestion of "Means Test"', and that it might encourage workmen to move to needlessly expensive lodgings.[77] Beveridge therefore allowed himself to be stuck with the paradoxical proposition that benefits should be based on subsistence needs and yet should be uniform in all parts of the country. This paradox was acknowledged in the Beveridge Report; but it was nevertheless seized upon by the Philips committee and used as a reason both for paying less than subsistence-level benefits and for retaining a means-tested system of benefit-supplementation.[78]

In so far as they were original, therefore, Beveridge's ideas on social security did not gain political acceptance. And in conclusion, I think it is arguable that the significance of the Beveridge Report lies, not in any of its substantive proposals – many of which, as I have shown, were not entirely consistent and were subsequently rejected by those in power. Rather its significance lies in its lucid exposition of a series of general principles; in its clear articulation of a wide spectrum of ill-defined views and opinions which many people held already; and in the tremendous publicity which surrounded the report and the popular interest which it aroused. This popular interest was partly due to the pressure of backbench politicians who, as soon as the Beveridge committee was appointed, continually embarrassed ministers by demanding to know *when* it was going to report, *what* its proposals would be and *when* they were going to be turned into public policy.[79] But it was also largely due to Beveridge himself who, whatever his faults as a politique and as a social theorist, was a highly-skilled manipulator of the mass media. 'You have a remarkable gift for dealing with rather humdrum questions of this kind with the maximum of clarity and simplicity', commented a colleague in the Civil Service a few years before, when Beveridge had given a series of popular wireless talks on problems of unemployment insurance.[80] Throughout 1942 he constantly leaked items from his Report to the press, he employed Frank Pakenham as a sort of unofficial public relations officer, and he frequently broadcast on 'social problems' on the BBC, misleading many people into believing that he was the spokesman of the inner counsels of the Coalition government. As soon as his report was published he horrified many civil servants by going on a nationwide publicity campaign to promote discussion of social insurance; and he then repeated the same campaign in America, where again many people appear to have mistaken him for the private ambassador of the British government. It was as a response to this kind of pressure that the Coalition government began to consider the implementation of Beveridge and was eventually forced to commit itself to a national health service, to a systematic overhaul of national insurance, and to serious rather than merely token planning of post-war reconstruction.[81]

NOTES

1 In preparing this paper I have been greatly helped by discussion with Sir D. N. Chester, Dame Marjorie Cox, Professor Arthur Goodhart, Sir Edward Hale, the Earl of Longford, Miss Muriel Ritson, Baroness Stocks and the late Professor Richard Titmuss. I am most grateful for their comments and recollections of the events herein discussed. For the interpretation of those events I am of course alone responsible.

2 E.g. Olive Anderson, *A Liberal State at War. English Politics and Economics during The Crimean War* (1967), ch. VI. B. B. Gilbert, *The Evolution of National Insurance. The Origins of the Welfare State* (1966). Arthur Marwick, *The Deluge. British Society & the First World War* (1965). Philip Abrams, 'The Failure of Social Reform: 1918–21', *Past & Present*, 24 (1963). Richard Titmuss, *Problems of Social Policy* (1950).

3 Alan T. Peacock and Jack Wiseman. *The Growth of Public Expenditure in the United Kingdom* (1961), pp. 25–34, 65–8.

4 Richard Titmuss, 'War and Social Policy', *Essays on the Welfare State* (1960).

5 Olive Anderson, *A Liberal State of War*, p. 181.

6 378 HC Deb., 5s., col. 509; 385 HC Deb., 5s., col. 593.

7 Janet Beveridge, *Beveridge and his Plan* (1954), pp. 53–7. Maurice Bruce, *The Coming of the Welfare State* (1961), pp. 13, 165.

8 José Harris, *Unemployment and Politics. A Study in English Social Policy 1886–1914* (Oxford, 1972), p. 315.

9 *Braithwaite Papers*, II item 8, Memorandum on Sickness and Invalidity Insurance, by W. H. Beveridge, Jan. 1911.

10 *Unemployment Insurance Statutory Committee, Annual Report*, 1937–8.

11 *Dalton Papers*, Hugh Dalton's diary, 8 April, 1942.

12 W. H. Beveridge, *Power and Influence* (1953), pp. 268–9. Roy Harrod, *Life of John Maynard Keynes* (1951), pp. 577–8. Lord Salter, *Slave of the Lamp. A Public Servant's Notebook* (1967), p. 88.

13 M. M. Postan, *British War Production* (1952), p. 141.

14 *Power and Influence*, p. 131. Alan Bullock, *The Life and Times of Ernest Bevin* (1967), II, p. 9.

15 *Beveridge Papers*, IIb 60, Draft of a letter from W. H. Beveridge to Lord Longford, 9 Aug. 1961.

16 PRO PIN 8/85, 'Survey of Social Insurance and Workmen's Compensation', by R. Hamilton Farrell, April 1941.

17 PRO PIN 8/85, Report of Preliminary Conference on Workmen's Compensation and Social Insurances, 29 May 1941.

18 PRO PIN 8/85, 'Workmen's Compensation and Social Insurances', meeting held in the War Cabinet Offices, 16 May 1941.

19 *Beveridge Papers*, IIb 60, Comments by W. H. Beveridge on *Freiheit und Soziale Sickerheit*, by Gabrielle Brenne, July 1961.

20 PRO PIN 8/85, Note by E. G. B. and A. N. Rucker, 19 April 1941. *Ibid.* 'Survey of Social Insurance etc.' Note of conclusions reached at a conference held in the Secretary's room, 24 April 1941.

21 PRO PIN 8/85, Sir George Chrystal to Sir John Maude, 2 July 1941.

22 371 HC Deb., S. 5, col. 1575; 372 HC Deb., S. 5 col. 45. The Hansard index

(375 HC Deb., 5s, p. 412) refers to the announcement of the committee's terms of reference; but this was a mistake for the Nuffield College Reconstruction Survey.

23   *Social Insurance and Allied Services.* Report by Sir William Beveridge, Nov. 1942. (Cmd. 6404) para. 459.

24   PRO CAB 66/34, Note by the Prime Minister on the Beveridge Report, 15 Feb. 1943.

25   378 HC Deb 5s, col. 2128. 380 HC Deb. 5s, col. 1941. 381 HC Deb. 5s, col. 1339.

26   PRO PIN 8/87, Interdepartmental Committee on Social Insurance and Allied Services. First draft of a report by Sir William Beveridge, July–Sept. 1942.

27   PRO CAB 87/79, Arthur Greenwood to Sir William Beveridge, 27 Jan. 1942.

28   PRO PIN 8/87, R. Hamilton Farvell to E. Hale, 3 Sept. 1942.

29   PRO PIN 8/87, 'Beveridge Report. Meeting at the Treasury', 22 July 1942.

30   *Passfield Papers*, II, 4, n. 11. J. M. Keynes to Beatrice Webb, 3 Mar. 1943.

31   *Power and Influence*, p. 309.

32   *Passfield Papers*, Beatrice Webb's diary, 26 Oct. 1942.

33   *Power and Influence*, pp. 316–17.

34   PRO PIN 8/85, Report of the Official Committee on the Beveridge Report. para. 34, 58, 114–16, 128.

35   W. H. Beveridge, *Full Employment in a Free Society* (1944), pp. 12–13.

36   PRO PIN 8/87, E. Hale to W. H. Beveridge, 2 Oct. 1942.

37   PRO CAB 87/77, Interdepartmental Committee on Social Insurance and Allied Services, Minutes of Evidence, Q3076. CAB 87/76, 'Basic Problems of Social Security with Heads of a Scheme', by Sir William Beveridge, 11 Dec. 1941.

38   PRO CAB 87/76, 'Nuffield College Reconstruction Survey', by W. H. Beveridge. 11 Dec. 1941.

39   PRO CAB 87/80, Nuffield College Reconstruction Survey, Statutory Social Services Investigation. Memoranda on 'National Health Insurance', 'Contributory Old Age Pensions', 'The Assistance Board', 'Public Assistance', 'Workmen's Compensation'. For criticisms of the Nuffield Survey by Beveridge's advisors, see CAB 87/80, Note by Sir George Reid, 10 June 1942; and CAB 87/81, Muriel Ritson to D. N. Chester, 17 July 1942.

40   PRO CAB 87/79, 'The Scale of Social Insurance and the Problem of Poverty', by W. H. Beveridge, 16 Jan. 1942.

41   PRO CAB 87/79, W. H. Beveridge to the British Employers Confederation, 28 Jan. 1942.

42   Michael Walzer, 'World War II: Why Was This War Different?' *Philosophy and Public Affairs*, I, 1 (1971), pp. 3–4.

43   *Beveridge Papers*, VIII 27, 'Reconstruction Problems: Five Giants on the Road', by W. H. Beveridge, 3 June 1942.

44   R. H. Tawney, 'The Abolition of Economic Controls, 1918–21', *Econ. Hist. Rev.*, XIII, 1 (1943), pp. 18, 30.

45   369 HC Deb. 5s, col. 527; 370 HC Deb, 5s, cols. 269–70, 575, 702; 317 HC Deb. 5s, 1574–8.

46   G. Worswick, 'Cole and Oxford, 1938–1958', in *Essays in Labour History*, ed. Asa Briggs and John Saville, (1967), p. 31. Sir Arthur MacNalty, *The Reform of the Public Health Services* (1942); *Post-War Employment. Being a précis of Employment Policy and Organisation of Industry after the War* (publ. by Nuffield College, 1943).

47   PRO PIN 8/87, Beveridge Report. Meeting at the Treasury, 22 July 1942.

48   *Social Insurance and Allied Services. Memoranda from Organisations* (Cmd.

6405, 1942) Paper 13. Memorandum of evidence from the National Conference of Friendly Societies, 29 Jan. 1942.

49 PRO CAB 87/77, Interdepartmental Committee on Social Insurance and Allied Services, Minutes of Evidence, QQ1693, 1871, 1877.

50 PRO CAB 87/81, Memorandum from the Local Government Clerks' Association, 20 July 1942. Memorandum from the Assistance Board Departmental Whitley Council (Staff Side), 1 Aug. 1942. Memorandum from the National Association of Relieving Officers, 1 Aug. 1942.

51 PRO CAB 87/88, Interdepartmental Committee on Social Insurance and Allied Services, Minutes of Evidence, Q316.

52 *Ibid.* QQ505–9.

53 *Ibid.* QQ325, 350, 438, 2362, 2374–5.

54 *Ibid.* QQ2844, 2849, 2854.

55 Cmd. 6405, p. 35. *Beveridge Papers*, viii 27, J. E. Meade to D. N. Chester, 28 Aug. 1941.

56 PRO CAB 87/76. 'Basic Problems of Social Security with the Heads of a Scheme', by W. H. Beveridge, 11 Dec. 1941.

57 *Family Allowances: Memorandum by the Chancellor of the Exchequer* (Cmd. 6354, 1942).

58 PRO PIN 8/163. Family Allowances. Summary of Mr Amery's address at the preliminary meeting 15 Feb. 1941. 'Draft note on Family Allowances', by Mary Agnes Hamilton, 23 April 1941.

59 At 5s a week for second and further children. Beveridge had proposed 8s a week, plus additional services in kind.

60 *Full Employment in a Free Society*, pp. 106, 159–60.

61 Harold Wilson, *Beveridge Memorial Lecture* (1966), p. 3.

62 W. H. Beveridge. *Unemployment: A Problem of Industry* (1930 ed.), pp. 368–72.

63 *Beveridge Papers* iib 36, W. H. Beveridge to E. Witte, 30 April 1937. *Passfield Papers*, B. Webb's diary, 17 March 1936.

64 *Beveridge Papers*, viii 29, 'Internal Measures for the Prevention of General Unemployment', memorandum by The Economic Section of the War Cabinet Secretariat, n.d. PRO CAB 87/78, Interdepartmental Committee on Social Insurance & Allied Services, Minutes of a meeting on 24 June 1942.

65 Above, p. 244.

66 *Social Insurance & Allied Services*, para. 441.

67 PRO CAB 87/76. Interdepartmental committee on Social Insurance & Allied Services, Minutes of a meeting on 24 Sept. 1941.

68 PRO PIN 8/87. E. Hale to Muriel Ritson, 31 Aug. 1942.

69 S. & B. Webb, *Industrial Democracy* (1897) ii, pp. 766–84.

70 Sir John Walley, *Social Security: Another British Failure?* (1972), p. 58.

71 PRO CAB 87/79. 'The Scale of Social Insurance Benefits and the Problem of Poverty', by W. H. Beveridge, 16 Jan. 1942.

72 *Beveridge Papers*, viii 28, 'Benefit Rates & Subsistence Needs', by Sir William Beveridge, July 1942.

73 *Beveridge Papers*, viii 28, 'Reply to Queries raised by Sir William Beveridge in the Memorandum SIC (42) 55, dated 29 March 1942' by B. S. Rowntree, July 1942.

74 *Beveridge Papers*, viii 28, E. Ramsbottom, Ministry of Labour Statistician, to Sir William Beveridge, 19 Jan. 1942.

75 *Beveridge Papers*, viii 28, 'Possible Variations of Benefit Rates for Rent' by Sir William Beveridge, 20 July 1942.

76 *Beveridge Papers*, VIII 28, D. N. Chester to W. H. Beveridge, 13 Aug. 1942.

77 PRO PIN 8/87, Note by Muriel Ritson on 'Objections which may be urged against the payment of differential benefits based on rent variations under a scheme of social insurance which compels the payment of a flat rate contribution', Aug. 1942. *Beveridge Papers*, VIII 28, Sir George Reid to D. N. Chester, 27 July 1942; E. Hale to D. N. Chester, 24 July 1942.

78 PRO PIN 8/115, Report of the Official Committee on the Beveridge Report, paras 23–4.

79 377 HC Deb. 5s, col. 1277; 383 HC Deb. 5s, cols 805, 1229, 1633, 1762.

80 *Beveridge Papers*, IIb 36, H. L. French to W. H. Beveridge, 30 June 1937.

81 A Committee of civil servants appointed to consider the practical implementation of the Beveridge proposals began to meet in April 1943 (PRO PIN 8/1, Reports of Central Staff weekly conferences). It was this committee which produced the white paper on social insurance of 1944.

Select bibliography of works on war and economic development

J. M. Winter

CONTENTS

A. ECONOMY, SOCIAL STRUCTURE, AND WAR
General
Economic causes of war
Direct and indirect costs and consequences of war
Population movements, casualties, and the demographic consequences of war

B. WAGING OF WAR
Agriculture
Industry
Labour
The Military
Armies, armaments, and arsenals
Navies and naval dockyards
Prices and incomes
Science, medicine, and the health of civilians and combatants
Trade and investment
War administration
General
Finance and economic policy
Food supply
War supplies and preparations for war
Miscellaneous

This bibliography contains only a fraction of all publications related to the theme of war and economic development. It provides at best a survey of the literature which relates to Western European warfare. All works are published in London unless otherwise noted. I am grateful to Naomi Eilan, Avner Ofer, and Sara Heller Mendelsohn for their help in preparing this bibliography.

A. ECONOMY, SOCIAL STRUCTURE AND WAR

General

Andreski, S., *Military Organization and Society* (1954).
Bayley, C. C., *War and Society in Renaissance Florence: the De Militia of Leonardo Bruni* (Toronto, 1961).
Beeler, John, *Warfare in England, 1066–1189* (Ithaca, New York, 1966).

Blake, J. W., *Northern Ireland in the Second World War* (Belfast, 1956).

Bloch, Camille, *Bibliographie méthodique de l'histoire économique et sociale de la France pendant la guerre* (Paris, 1925).

Bodart, G., *Militär-historisches Kreigslexikon (1618–1905)* (Vienna, 1908).

Bouthoul, G., Guerres et civilisations, *Études polémologiques*, 6 (Oct. 1972).

Boutrouche, R., *La Crise d'une société: seigneurs et paysans de Bordelais pendant la guerre de cent ans* (Paris, 1947).

Boxer, C. R., *The Dutch Seaborne Empire 1600–1800* (1965).

The Portuguese Seaborne Empire 1415–1825 (1969).

Bradon, R. H., The Business Man and the Army, *Journal of the Royal United Service Institution*, LXII (May 1917).

Braudel, F., The Forms of War, in *The Mediterranean and the Mediterranean World in the Age of Philip II*, trans. S. Reynolds, (2 vols, 1972–3), vol. 2.

Bulkley, M. E., *Bibliographical Survey of Contemporary Sources for the Economic and Social History of the War* (Oxford, 1922).

Cipolla, C. M., *Guns and Sails in the Early Phase of European Expansion 1400–1700* (1965).

Clark, G. N., The Character of the Nine Years War, 1688–99, *Cambridge Historical Journal*, XI, 2 (1954).

Clark, J. M., and Hamilton, W. N., and Moulton, G. E., *Readings in the Economics of War* (Chicago, 1918).

Cochin, D., *Les Organisations du blocus en France pendant le guerre 1914–1918* (Paris, 1926).

Contamine, P., Batailles, bannières, compagnies: aspects de l'organisation militaire française pendant la première partie de la guerre de Cent ans, *Actes du collogue international de Cocherel. Les cahiers vernonnais*, 4 (1964).

Guerre, état et societé à la fin du moyen âge (Paris, 1972).

Cornelius, C., *Les Dessous économiques de la guerre* (Paris, 1915).

Court, W. H. B., The Years 1914–1918 in British Economic and Social History, in *Scarcity and Choice in History* (1970).

Crammond, E., Economic Aspects of the War, *Quarterly Review*, CCXXI (Oct. 1914).

Crouzet, F., L'économie de guerre britannique, *Revue d'histoire de la deuxième guerre mondiale*, II (1952).

L'Économie britannique et le blocus continental, 1806–13 (2 vols, Paris, 1958).

Wars, Blockade and Economic Change in Europe 1792–1815, *Journal of Economic History*, XXIV (1964).

Bilan de l'économie britannique pendant les guerres de la Révolution et de l'Empire, *Revue historique*, CCXXIV (1965).

Davis, S. C., *The French War Machine* (1937).

Dearle, N. B., *An Economic Chronicle of the Great War for Great Britain and Ireland, 1914–1919. Supplement: 1920, 1921, 1922* (Oxford, 1929).

Dening, B. C., Disarmament and Economics, *Jnl. Roy. Utd. Ser. Inst.*, LXXV (Nov. 1930).

Dewar, K. G. B., What is the Influence of Overseas Commerce on the Operation of War? *Jnl. Roy. Utd. Ser. Inst.*, LVII (April 1913).

Eichholtz, D., *Geschichte der deutschen Kriegswirtschaft 1939–1945* (Berlin, 1969).

Fauvel, L., *Problèmes économiques de la guerre totale* (Paris, 1940).

Fayle, C. E., The Deflection of Strategy by Commerce in the Eighteenth Century, *Jnl. Roy. Utd. Ser. Inst.*, LXVIII (May 1923).

Economic Pressure in the War of 1739–48, *Jnl. Roy. Utd. Ser. Inst.*, LXVIII (Aug. 1923).

Fowler, K. (ed.), *The Hundred Years War* (1971).

Franz, G., *Der Dreissegjährige Krieg und das Deutsche Volk* (Stuttgart, 1961).

Fuller, J. F. C., *War and Western Civilisation 1832–1932* (1940).

Garcia, Clive, *A Key to Victory* (1940).

Giffen, R., Some Economic Aspects of the South African War, *Economic Inquiries and Studies* (2 vols, 1904), vol. 2.

Grand-Jean, P., *Guerre, fluctuations et croissance* (Paris, 1967).

Greenwood, A., Social and Economic Aspects of the War, in Seton-Watson, R. W., et al., *The War and Democracy* (1914).

Guillebaud, C. W., Hitler's New Economic Order for Europe, *Economic Journal*, n.s., I (1940).

Halperin, J., L'économie sovietique pendant la guerre, *Revue d'histoire de la deuxième guerre mondiale*, II (1952).

Hart, B. H. Liddell, Economic Pressures or Continental Victories, *Jnl. Roy. Utd. Ser. Inst.*, LXXVI (Aug. 1931).

Heckscher, E. F., *The Continental System. An Economic Interpretation* (Oxford, 1922).

Hogg, O. F. C., England's War Effort against the Spanish Armada, *Journal of the Society for Army Historical Research*, XLIV (March 1966).

Hueckel, G., War and the British Economy, 1793–1815. A General Equilibrium Analysis, *Explorations in Economic History*, XI (1973).

Imbert, J., Économie et guerre: les 'militaires aux armées' en 1806, in *Mélanges offert à G. Jacquemyns* (Brussels, 1968).

Jack, D. T., *Studies in Economic Warfare* (1940).

Jaeger, H., *Der Dreissigjaehrige Krieg und die deutsche Kulturlandschaft* (Stuttgart, 1966).

Jones, G. D. B., Civil War and Society in Southern Etruria, in Foot, M. R. D. (ed.), *War and Society* (1973).

Jones, J. H., *The Economics of War and Conquest* (1915).

Kulischer, A. and E., *Kriegs und Wanderzüge. Weltgeschichte als Volkerbewegung* (Berlin, 1932).

Lane, F. C., *Venice and History: The Collected Papers of Frederic C. Lane* (Baltimore, 1966).

Livet, G., *La Guerre de trente ans* (Paris, 1963).

Lourie, E., A Society Organized for War: Medieval Spain, *Past & Present*, 35 (Dec. 1966).

Leutge, F., Die wirtschaftliche Lage Deutschlands vor Ausbruch des Dreissigjaehrigen Krieges, in *Studien zur Sozial- und Wirtschaftsgeschichte* (Stuttgart, 1963).

McFarlane, K. B., War, the Economy and Social Change: England and the Hundred Years War, *Past & Present*, 22 (1962).

A Business Partnership in War and Administration 1421–1445, *English Historical Review*, LXXVIII (1963).

The Wars of the Roses, *Proceedings of the British Academy*, L (1964).

An Indenture of Agreement between Two English Knights for Mutual Aid and Council in Peace and War, *Bulletin of the Institute for Historical Research*, XXXVIII (1965).

The Nobility in War, in *The Nobility of Later Medieval England* (Oxford, 1973).

Mallock, W. H., *Capital, War and Wages* (1918).

Marriott, J. A. R., Economics and War, *Fortnightly Review*, XCIV (Jan. 1916).

Masters, R. D., Développement économique et guerre totale, *Études polémologiques*. 4 (April 1972).

Miller, E., *War in the North: the Anglo-Scottish Wars of the Middle Ages* (Hull, 1960).
Nef, J. U., War and the Early Industrial Revolution, in Wright, C. W. (ed.), *Economic Problems of War and its Aftermath* (Chicago, 1942).
War and Economic Progress, 1540–1640, *Economic History Review*, XII (1942).
La guerre, *Proceedings of the Ninth International Congress of Historical Sciences* (Paris, 1950).
War and Human Progress (Cambridge, Mass., 1950).
Nere, R., Sur la guerre économique, *Revue d'histoire de la deuxième guerre mondiale*, X (1960).
Nolde, B., *Russia in the Economic War* (New Haven, Conn., 1928).
Olson, M., *The Economies of the War-time Shortage* (Durham, N.C. 1963).
Osterheld, T. W., *Economic Phases of the War* (New York, 1918).
Pieri, P., Sur les dimensions de l'histoire militaire, *Annales: économies-sociétés-civilisations*, XVIII (1963).
Pirenne, H., *La Belgique et la guerre mondiale* (Paris, 1928).
Polišenský, J. V., The Thirty Years' War and the Crises and Revolutions of Seventeenth Century Europe, *Past & Present*, 39 (April 1968).
Postan, M. M., *British War Production* (1952).
Prest, A. R., *War Economics of Primary Producing Countries* (Cambridge, 1948).
Ringel, K. R., *Frankreichs Wirtschaft in Umbruck* (Leipzig, 1942).
Robinson, E. V. D., War and Economics in History and Theory, *Political Science Quarterly*, XV (Dec. 1900).
Rosenbaum, E., War Economics. A Bibliographical Approach, *Economica*, n.s., IX (1942).
Rostow, W. W., War and Economic Change: the British Experience, in *The Process of Economic Growth* (New York, 1952).
Sauvy, A., *Histoire économique de la France entre les deux guerres* (2 vols, Paris, 1965–7).
Secerov, S., *Economic Phenomena before and after War: a Statistical Theory of Modern Wars* (1919).
Skalweit, A., Die Eingliederung des friderzianischen Heeres in die Volks- und Wirtschaftskoerper, *Jahrbücher für Nationalökonomie und Statistik*, CLX (1944).
Sombart, W., *Studien zur Entwicklungsgeschiente des Modernen Kapitalismus. II. Krieg und Kapitalismus* (Munich, 1913).
Sorokin, P. A., Fluctuations of War in Intergroup Relationships, in *Social and Cultural Dynamics* (4 vols, New York, 1937), vol. 3.
Man and Society in Calamity (New York, 1942).
Spann, O., *Bibliographie der Wirtschafts und Sozialgeschichte des Weltkrieges* (Vienna, 1924).
Taylor, F. L., *The Art of War in Italy 1494–1529* (Cambridge, 1921).
Thayer, G., *War Business* (Hamburg, 1970).
Thielmans, M.-R., *Bourgogne et Angleterre: relations politiques et economiques entre les Pays-Bas Bourgignons et l'Angleterre, 1435–1467* (Brussels, 1966).
Vickers, C. G., Economic Warfare, *Jnl. Roy. Utd. Ser. Inst.*, LXXXVIII (Feb. 1943).
Wiedenfeld, K., *Die Organisation des Kriegsrohstoffbewirtschaftung im Weltkriege* (Hamburg, 1936).
Wiles, P., War and Economic Systems, in *Mélanges en l'honneur de Raymond Aron: Science et conscience de la société* (2 vols, Paris, 1971), vol. 2.
Wilson, C., *Profit and Power: A Study of England and the Dutch Wars* (1960).
Wright, Q., *A Study of War* (2nd edn, Chicago, 1965).

Economics and War, *Round Table*, xxv, (June 1935).
War Economics, *Round Table*, xxx (Dec. 1939).

Economic causes of war

Abel, D., Economic Causes of the Second World War, *International Conciliation* (1941).
Angell, N., *The Great Illusion* (1910).
Aron, R., *War and Industrial Society* (1958).
Bakeless, J., *The Economic Causes of Modern War* (New York, 1921).
Brailsford, H. N., *The War of Steel and Gold* (1917).
Brandt, G., Socio-economic Aspects of German Rearmament, *Archives européennes de sociologie*, 6 (1965).
Brodie, B., Theories on the Causes of War, in *Mélanges en l'honneur de Raymond Aron: Science et conscience de la société* (2 vols, Paris, 1971), vol. 2.
Cazelles, R., Quelques réflexions à propos des mutations de la monnaie royale française (1295–1360), *Le Moyen Âge*, LXXII (1966).
Cuttino, G. P., Historical Revision: the Causes of the Hundred Years War, *Speculum*, XXXI (1956).
Elzinga, S., La prélude de la guerre de 1672, *Revue d'histoire moderne et contemporaine*, II (1927).
Gill, C., *National Power and Prosperity: A Study of the Economic Causes of Modern Warfare* (1916).
Handman, M., War, Economic Motives, and Economic Symbols, *American Journal of Sociology*, XLIV (March 1939).
Higonnet, P. I. R., The Origins of the Seven Years' War, *Journal of Modern History*, XL (1968).
Hilferding, R. *Das Finanzkapital* (Frankfurt, 1968).
Hobson, J., *Imperialism* (1902).
Johnson, A. S., Commerce and War, *Pol. Sci. Q.*, XXIX (1914).
Lenin, V. I., *Imperialism* (Eng. edn, 1920).
Luxemburg, R., *The Accumulation of Capital*, trans. A. Schwanzchild (1951).
Mason, T., Some Origins of the Second World War, *Past & Present*, 29 (1964).
Noel-Baker, P., *The Private Manufacture of Armaments* (Oxford, 1937).
Robbins, L., *The Economic Causes of War* (1939).
Salter, A., The Economic Causes of War, in Porrett, A. (ed.), *The Causes of War* (1932).
Stalley, E., *War and the Private Investor* (New York, 1935).
Viner, J., Power Versus Plenty as Objectives of Foreign Policy in the Seventeenth and Eighteenth Centuries, *World Politics*, I (Oct. 1948).
Wolff, P., Une problème d'origines: la guerre de Cent ans, in *Eventail de l'histoire vivante: Hommage à Lucien Febvre* (2 vols, Paris, 1953), vol. 2.

Direct and indirect costs and consequences of war

Abrams, P. A., The Failure of Social Reform: 1918–1920, *Past & Present*, 24 (April 1963).
Allen, J. E., Some Changes in the Distribution of National Income during the War, *Journal of the Royal Statistical Society*, LXXXIII (1920).
Allman, C. T., War and Profit in the Later Middle Ages, *History Today*, XV (Nov. 1965).
Anderson, J. L., Aspects of the Effects on the British Economy of the Wars against France, 1793–1815, *Australian Economic History Review*, XII (March, 1972).

Anderson, O., Economic Warfare in the Crimean War, *Econ. Hist. Rev.*, 2nd ser., XIV, 1 (1961–62).

Angell, N., Effect of War on the World System of Economics and Finance, in Inter-Parliamentary Union, *What Would Be the Character of a New War?* (1933).

Antipa, G., *L'Occupation ennemie de la Roumanie et ses conséquences économiques et sociales* (Paris, 1929).

Arribas Arranz, F., Repercusiones economicas de las comunidades de Castilla, *Hispania*, XVIII (1958).

Atkinson, C. T., The Cost of Queen Anne's War, *Jnl. Soc. Army Hist. Res.*, XXXIII (1956).

Aubé, P., Une méthode, un bilan, *Cahiers d'histoire de la querre*, 4 (May, 1950).

Balogh, T., The Economic Problems of France, *Bulletin of the Oxford Institute of Statistics*, VII (7 Apr. 1945).

Baudin, L., *Esquisse de l'économie française sous l'occupation allemande* (Paris, 1945).

An Outline of Economic Conditions in France under the German Occupation, *Econ. Jnl.*, LV (Dec. 1945).

Beauregard, P., *La Vie économique en France pendant la guerre actuelle* (Paris, 1915).

Bergeron, L., Problèmes économiques de la France Napoléonienne, *Annales historiques de la Révolution française*, XLII (1970).

Bernard, A., *L'Afrique du Nord pendant la guerre* (Paris, 1927).

Beutin, L., Die Wirkungen des Siebenjaehriges Krieges auf die Volkswirtschaft in Preussen, *Vierteljahrschrift fur sozial- und Wirtschaftsgeschichte*, XXII (1929).

Bilimovitch, A. D., *The Land Settlement in Russia and the War* (1930).

Boag, H., Human Capital and the Cost of War, *Jnl. Roy. Stat. Soc.*, LXXXIX (Jan. 1916).

Bogart, E. L., Money Costs of War, *Historical Outlook*, 10 (June 1919).

Direct and Indirect Costs of War (1920).

Boom, Ch. de, L'occupation des Pays du Bas-Rhin pendant la guerre de Sept ans, *Rev. d'h. mod. contemp.*, V (1930).

Boudet, F., Aspects économiques de l'occupation allemende en France, *Revue d'histoire de la deuxième guerre mondiale*, XIV (1964).

Bowley, A. L., *Some Economic Consequences of the Great War* (1930).

Brand, R. H., War and the Wealth of Britain, *Round Table*, XXXV (Sept. 1945).

Brosse, T., L'enfance victime de la guerre. Problèmes d'éducation, *UNESCO*, I, 8 (1949).

Butel, P., Crise et mutation de l'activité économique à Bordeaux sous le Consulat et L'Empire, *Annales hist. Rév. fr.*, XLII (1970).

Cahen-Salvadore, G., *Les Prisonniers de guerre, 1914–1919* (Paris, 1929).

Carus-Wilson, E. M., The Effect of the Acquisition and Loss of Gascony on the English Wine Trade, *Bull. Inst. Hist. Res.* XXI (1947).

Chapman, C. H., War and Criminality, *Sociological Review*, IX (Autumn 1916).

Chardonnet, J., *Les Conséquences économiques de la guerre 1939–1946* (Paris, 1947).

Chester, D. N., (ed.), *Lessons of the British War Economy* (Cambridge, 1951).

Clapham, J. H., Europe after the Great Wars, 1816 and 1920, *Econ. Jnl.*, XXXI (Dec. 1920).

Clark, G. N. *War and Society in the Seventeenth Century* (Cambridge, 1958).

Clark, J. B., The Economic Costs of War, *American Economic Review*, VI (March 1918), supplt.

Clark, J. M., *The Costs of the World War to the American People* (New Haven, 1931).

Clarke, R. W. B., *The Economic Effort of War* (1940).

Cohen, D. B., Le pillage de l'économie bulgare par les Allemands, *Revue d'histoire de la deuxième guerre mondiale*, XVIII (1968).

Conant, O. A. *Effect of the War on the Supply of Investment Capital* (New York, 1914).

Courteault, P., *La Vie économique à Bordeaux pendant la guerre* (Paris, 1925).

Crammond, E., The Cost of the War, *Jnl. Roy. Stat. Soc.*, LXXVIII (1915).

The Effect of the War on the Economic Condition of the United Kingdom, *Journal of the Royal Society of Arts*, LXVI (26 July 1918).

Reconstruction and the Real Cost of the War, *Jnl. Roy. Soc. Arts*, LXVI (16 Aug. 1918).

The Economic Condition of the U.K. after Three and a Half Years of War, *Jnl. Roy. Soc. Arts*, LXVI (29 Aug. 1918).

Real Cost of the War and Problems of Reconstruction (1918).

Dejonghe, E., La reprise économique dans le Nord et le Pas-de-Calais, *Revue d'histoire de la deuxième guerre mondiale*, XX (1970).

Devleeshouwer, R., Le Consulat et L'Empire: période de 'take-off' pour l'économie belge? *Annales hist. Rév. fr.*, XLII (1970).

Director, A., Does Inflation Change the Economic Effects of War?, *Amer. Econ. Rev.*, XXX, 1 (March 1940), supplt.

Duncan, G. A., The First Year of War: its Economic Effects on Twenty-Six Counties of Ireland, *Econ. Jnl.*, LI (1941).

Dupré, F., *La Réparation des dommages matériels causés par la guerre de 1939* (Paris, 1943).

Enderes, B., *Verkehrswesen im Kriege. Die österreichischen Eisenbahnen* (Vienna, 1931).

Ergang, R., *The Myth of the All-destructive Fury of the Thirty Years' War* (Philadelphia, 1956).

Exner, F., *Krieg und Kriminalität in Österreich* (Vienna, 1927).

Fayle, C. E., Economic Pressure in the Wars of 1789–1848, *Jnl. Roy. Utd. Ser. Inst.* (1923).

Gide, C. (ed.), *Effects of the War upon French Economic Life* (Oxford, 1923).

Giffen, R., The Costs of the Franco-Prussian War, in *Economic Inquiries and Studies* (2 vols, 1904), vol. 1.

Gignoux, C. J., *Bourges pendant la guerre* (Paris, 1926).

Gore-Browne, F., *Effect of the War on Commercial Engagements* (1914).

Gowing, M., La mobilization économique, *Revue d'histoire de la deuxième guerre mondiale*, 90 (April 1973).

Gratz, G., and Schueller, R., *Die äussere Wirtschaftspolitik Osterreich-Ungarns: Mitteleuropaische Plane* (Vienna, 1927).

Guillehaud, C. W., The Cost of the War to Germany, *Econ. Jnl.*, XXVII (June 1917).

Haensel, P., Financial Consequences of War and of Preparations for War, in Inter-Parliamentary Union, *What Would Be the Character of a New War?* (1933).

Hancock, W. K., and Gowing, M. M., *British War Economy* (1949).

Hay, D., The Division of the Spoils of War in Fourteenth-Century England, *Transactions of the Royal Historical Society*, 5th ser., IV (1954).

Heckscher, E. F., War and Economic Life, *Index*, V (Stockholm, 1930).

Heers, M. J., Difficultés économiques et troubles sociaux en France et en Angleterre pendant la guerre de Cent ans: le Problème des Origines, *Actes du colloque international de Cocherel. Les cahiers vernonnais*, 4 (1964).

Henderson, W. O., Economic consequences of the war, in *Studies in the Economic Policy of Frederick the Great* (1963).
Henning, H., Der Aufbauder deutschen Kriegswirtschaft im ersten Weltkrieg, *Wehrwissenschaftliche Rundschau*, VI (1956).
Henry, A., *Études sur l'occupation allemande en Belgique* (Brussels, 1920).
Herrior, E., *Lyon pendant la guerre* (Paris, 1925).
Himly, F. J., Les conséquences de la guerre de Trente ans dans les compagnes alsaciennes, in *Deux siècles d'Alsace française* (Strasbourg, 1948).
Hobson, J. A., Shall We be Poorer after the War?, *Contemporary Review*, CXII (Jan. 1917).
How Can England Pay the Bill?, *New Republic*, 10 July 1917.
et al., Costs of the War, *Nineteenth Century*, LXXXVIII (Sept. 1915).
Jaquart, J., La Fronde des Princes dans la région parisienne et ses conséquences matérielles, *Rev. d'h. mod. contemp.*, n.s. IX (1962).
John, A. H., War and the English Economy, 1700–1763, *Econ. Hist. Rev.*, 2nd ser., VII, 3 (1954–5).
Jones, J. M., The War and Economic Progress, *Proceedings of the Royal Philosophical Society of Glasgow*, XLVII (1915–16).
Kaldor, N., German Economy, *Review of Economic Studies*, XIII (1945–6).
Kamen, H., The Economic and Social Consequences of the Thirty Years' War, *Past & Present*, 39 (1968).
Kingsford, C. L., Social Life and the War of Roses, in *Prejudice and Promise in XVth century England* (Oxford, 1925).
Kirkaldy, A. W., Some Thoughts on Reconstruction after the War, *Report of the 86th Meeting of the British Association for the Advancement of Science (Transactions of Section F)* (1917).
Knight, B., Postwar Costs of a New War, *Amer. Econ. Rev.*, XXX, 1 (March 1948), supplt.
Kohn, S., and Meyendorff, A., *The Cost of the War to Russia* (New Haven, Conn., 1932).
Lane, F. C., Public Debt and Private Wealth: particularly in Sixteenth Century Venice, in *Mélanges en l'honneur de Fernand Braudel* (2 vols, Paris, 1973), vol. 2.
Laufenburger, H., La vie économique au seuil de l'année 1943, *Revue de l'économie contemporaine* (1944).
Lauterbach, A. T., Economic Demobilization in Great Britain after the First World War, *Pol. Sci. Q.*, LVII (1942).
L'éritier, M., *Tours et la guerre: Etude économique et sociale* (Paris, 1926).
Liepmann, M., *Krieg und Kriminalität in Deutschland* (Stuttgart, 1930).
Lorwin, L. L., *Economic Consequences of the Second World War* (New York, 1941).
Low, A. M., *Benefits of War* (1943).
McFarlane, K. B., The Investment of Sir John Fastolf's Profits of War, *Trans. Roy. Hist. Soc.*, 5th Ser., VII (1957).
Mannheim, H., *War and Crime* (1943).
Marwick, F., *The Deluge* (1964).
Britain in the Century of Total War (1968).
The Impact of the First World War on British Society, *Journal of Contemporary History*, III (1968).
L'impact de la deuxième guerre mondiale sur les britanniques, *Revue d'histoire de la deuxième guerre mondiale*, 90 (Avril, 1973).
Medlicott, W. N., *The Economic Blockade* (2 vols, 1952–59).

Mendelssohn-Bartholdy, A., *The War and German Society: the Testament of a Liberal* (New Haven, Conn., 1937).

Mendershausen, H., *Four Lectures on the Economics of War* (Colorado Springs, 1940).

Milward, A., The End of the Blitzkrieg, *Econ. Hist. Rev.*, 2nd ser., xvii (April 1964).

German Economy at War (1965).

The Economic Effects of the Two World Wars on Britain (1970).

The New Order and the French Economy (Oxford, 1970).

The Fascist Economy in Norway (Oxford, 1972).

Moss, H. St., The Economic Consequences of the Barbarian Invasions, *Econ. Hist. Rev.*, vii (1936).

Murphy, M. E., *The British War Economy 1939–1943* (New York, 1943).

Nathan, O., *The Nazi Economic System* (Durham, NC, 1944).

Nicolai, G. F., *The Biology of War*, trans. by C. A. Grande and J. Grande (New York, 1918).

Oberlé, R., Mulhouse et la crise économique du début de la guerre de Trente Ans (1618–1622), *Revue d'Alsace*, xc (1950–1).

Oliphant, T. L. K., Was the British aristocracy Destroyed by the Wars of the Roses?, *Trans. Roy. Hist. Soc.*, 1st ser., i (1872).

Pankhurst, R., The Effect of War in Ethiopian History: an Essay on the Economic, Social and Demographic History of the Nineteenth and Early Twentieth Centuries, *Ethiopia Observer*, vii (1963).

Pardevin, P., Aspects économiques des negotiations Français-Allemands, *Rev. d'h. mod. contemp.*, xix (1972).

Pigou, A. C., The Economics of the War Loan, *Econ. Jnl.*, xxvii (March 1917).

Polišenský, J. V., The Thirty Years' War, *Past & Present*, 6 (1954).

Postan, M. M., Some Social Consequences of the Hundred Years' War, *Econ. Hist. Rev.*, xii (1942).

The Costs of the Hundred Years' War, *Past & Present*, 27 (1964).

Prato, G., *Il Piemonte e gli effeti della guerra sulla sua vita economica e sociale* (Bari, 1925).

Prestwich, M., *War, Politics and Finance under Edward I* (1972).

Rabb, T. K., The Effects of the Thirty Years' War on the German Economy, *Jnl. Mod. Hist.*, xxiv (March 1962).

Rogers, J. H., *The Process of Inflation in France 1914–1927* (New York, 1930).

Schaeffer, E., *L'Alsace et la Lorraine, 1940–1945* (Paris, 1953).

Scott, N. R., *Economic Problems of Peace after War* (2 vols, Cambridge, 1917–18).

(ed.), *Rural Scotland During the War* (1926).

Sellier, H., *et al.*, *Paris pendant la guerre* (Paris, 1926).

Sering, M., *Germany under the Dawes Plan. Origin, Legal Foundations and Economic Effects of the Reparation Payments* (1929).

Shenfield, A. A., Impact of Reductions of Defence Requirements on British Industry, *Jnl. Roy. Utd. Ser. Inst.*, civ (Feb. 1959).

Skalweit, S., *Die Berliner Wirtschaftskrise von 1763 und ihre Hintergruende* (Stuttgart, 1937).

Smart, J. M., The Economic Dislocation of the War, *Proc. Roy. Phil. Soc. Glasgow*, xlvi (1914–15).

Snapper, F., *Oorlogsinvloeden op de overzeese handel van Holland, 1551–1719* (Amsterdam, 1959).

Sottile, A., Le bilan de la deuxième guerre mondiale, *Revue de droit international de sciences diplomatiques et politiques*, 3 (1945).

Speare, G. F., Cost of a Year of War, *Review of Reviews*, 52 (Aug. 1915).

Speier, H., Militarism in the 18th Century, *Social Research*, III, 3 (Aug. 1936).

Steinberg, S. H., The Thirty Years' War, a New Interpretation, *History*, XXXII (Sept. 1947).

The Thirty Years' War and the Conflict for European Hegemony (1600–1660) (1967).

Stone, L., War, the Economy and Social Change: 16th century England, *Past & Present*, 22 (1962).

Sweezy, M., *The Structure of the Nazi Economy* (Cambridge, 1951).

Tarké, E., *Le Blocus continental et le royaume d'Italie* (Paris, 1928).

Tawney, R. H., The Abolition of Economic Controls, 1918–1921, *Econ. Hist. Rev.*, XIII (1943).

Thuillier, E., Pour une histoire de l'économie rhénane de 1800 à 1830: Les houillères de la Ruhr, *Annales e.s.c.*, XV (1960).

Usher, R. G., The Cost of the War, *Atlantic Monthly*, CXV (June 1915).

Zechlin, E., Deutschland zwischen Kabinettskrieg und Wirtschaftskrieg, *Historische Zeitschrift*, CXCIX (1964).

On the Effects of the War on Credit, Currency, and Finance, *Rpt. 85th Mtg. Br. Assoc. Advan. Sci. (Trans. Sect. F)* (1916).

Population movements, casualties, and the demographic consequences of war

Amourous, H., *La Vie des Français sous l'occupation* (Paris, 1961).

Andrews, I. O., *Economic Effects of the War upon Women and Children in Great Britain* (Washington, 1918).

Arab-Ogly, E., Conséquences démographiques de la guerre, *La nouvelle revue internationale* (1962).

Arnould, M.-A., Les répercussions démographiques de la sac de Binche en 1544, in *Mélange Georges Smets* (Brussels, 1952).

Bauermann, H., Demographic Changes in Post-war Germany, *Annals of the American Academy of Political and Social Sciences*, CCLX (Nov. 1948).

Baumgarten, O., *Der Krieg und die Bergpredigt* (Berlin, 1915).

Der sittliche Zustand der deutschen Volkes unter dem Einfluss des Krieges (Stuttgart, 1927).

Bergues, H., Répercussions des calamités de guerre sur la première enfance, *Population*, III (July–Sept. 1948).

Beskrovny, L. G., Kabouzan, J. M. and Iatsounski, V. K., Bilan démographique de la Russie en 1789–1815, *Annales de démographie historique* (1965).

Biraben, J. N., Pertes allemandes au cours de la deuxième guerre mondiale, *Population*, XVI (1961).

Blayo, C., La population des pays socialistes européens, *Population* XXI, (1966).

Bourgeois, J., La situation démographique, *Population*, I (Jan.–March 1946).

Bouthoul, G., *La Population dans le monde* (Paris, 1935).

Cent milles de morts (Paris, 1946).

Guerres et population, *Revue de défense nationale*, n.s., II (Oct. 1946).

Le Phénomène-guerre, méthodes de la polémologie, morphologie des guerres, leur infrastructures (technique, démographique, économique) (Paris, 1962).

Bowley, A. L., Births and Population in Great Britain, *Econ. Jnl.*, XXXIV (1924).

Burchandt, F. A., Wartime Changes in the Distribution of the Population of Great Britain, *Bull. Oxf. Inst. Stat.*, VI, 15 (4 Nov. 1944).

Chambers, T. G., Eugenics and the War, *Eugenics Review*, VI (1914).

Chaplin, A., The Rate of Mortality of the British Army 100 Years Ago, *Proceedings of the Royal Society of Medicine (History of Medicine Section)*, IX (1916).

Chasteland, J. C., La population des democraties populaires d'Europe, *Population*, XIII (1958).

Evolution générale de la mortalité en Europe accidentale de 1900 à 1950, *Population*, XV (1960).

Corvisier, A., Service militaire et mobilité géographique au XVIIIe siècle, *Annales dém. hist.* (1970).

Darwin, L., The Disabled Soldier and the Future of Our Race, *Eugenics Review*, IX (April 1917).

Devaldès, M., *Croître et multiplier, c'est la guerre* (Paris, 1933).

Doublet, J., Mouvements migratoires d'après guerre, *Population*, II (July–Sept. 1947).

Ducasse, A., Meyer, J., and Perreux, G., *Vie et mort des Français, 1914–1918* (Paris, 1960).

Dumas, S., and Vedel-Peterson, K. O., *Losses of Life Caused by War* (1923).

Duncan, C. L., The Comparative Mortality of Disease and Battle Casualties in the Historical Wars of the World, *Journal of the Military Service Institution*, LIV (March–April 1914).

Dupaquier, J., Problèmes démographiques de la France napoléonienne, *Annales hist. Rév. fr.*, XLII (1970).

Festy, P., Evolution de la fécondité en Europe occidentale depuis la guerre, *Population*, XXV (1970).

Firth, C. H., The Sick and Wounded of the Great Civil War, *Cornhill Magazine*, n.s, X (March 1901).

Fourastié, J., Une population active française pendant la seconde guerre mondiale, *Revue d'histoire de la deuxième guerre mondiale*, XV (1965).

Fowler, G. H., The Devastation of Bedfordshire and the Neighbouring Counties in 1065 and 1066, *Archeologia*, LXXII (1922).

Frumkin, G., Pologne: six années d'histoire démographique, *Population*, IV (1949).

Gedda, L., Serio A., et Mercuri A., *Il metticeiato di guerra e altri casi* (Rome, 1960).

Ginesy, R., La seconde guerre mondiale et les déplacements de population – les organismes de protection, *Population*, IV (1949).

Girardot, R., La société militaire dans la France contemporaine (1815–1939), *Population*, VIII (1953).

Greenwood, Major, British loss of life in the wars of 1794–1815 and 1914–1918, *Jnl. Roy. Stat. Soc.*, CV, pt 1 (1942).

Heer, D. M., *After Nuclear Attack: a Demographic Inquiry* (New York, 1965).

Henry, L., Evolution démographique de l'Europe 1938–1947 après un article de E. Frumkin, *Population*, IV (1949).

Au sujet des pertes de guerre, *Population*, VIII (1953).

Table de mortalité de l'Allemagne occidentale, 1949–1951, *Population*, VIII (1953).

Perturbations de la nuptialité resultant de la guerre 1914–1918, *Population*, XXI (1966).

Hersch, L., *La Mortalité chez les neutres en temps de guerre* (Paris, 1915).

La mortalité causée par la guerre mondiale, *Metron*, VII, 1 and 2 (1927).

Des principaux effets démographiques des guerres modernes (Roma, 1932).

Demographic Effects of Modern Warfare, in Inter-Parliamentary Union, *What Would Be the Character of a Future War?* (1933).

Hodge, W. B., On the Mortality Arising from Naval Operations, *Quarterly Journal of the Statistical Society*, XVIII, pt III (Sept. 1855).

On the Mortality Arising from Military Operations, *The Assurance Magazine and Journal of the Institute of Actuaries*, VII, pts II–V (July 1857–April 1858).

Houdaille, L., Le problème des pertes des guerre, *Annales hist. Rév. fr.*, XLII (1970).

Huber, M., *La Population de la France pendant la guerre avec un appendice sur les revenus avant et après la guerre* (Paris, 1931).

Ibarrola, J., *Les Incidences des deux conflicts mondiaux sur l'évolution démographique française* (Grenoble, 1964).

Jacquemyns, G., *La Societé belge sous l'occupation allemande 1940–1944* (Brussels, 1950).

Jastrzebski, S. de, War and the Balance of the Sexes, *Eugenics Review*, X (July 1918).

Jouary, J.-P., Quelques aspects de la démographie française au XIX siècle, *Guerres et paix*, II (1967).

Kerr, H., The Influence of War Conditions upon the Death Rate from Consumption, *Medical Officer*, XVIII (27 Oct. 1917).

Koehl, R. L., *R.K.F.D.V.: German Resettlement and Population Policy 1939–1945* (Cambridge, Mass., 1957).

Koulicher, A. M., Les guerres et les migrations, *Resumés des communications presentés au VIᵉ Congrès International des Sciences Historiques* (Oslo, 1928).

Lannes, X., Les conséquences démographiques de la seconde guerre mondiale en Europe, *Revue d'histoire de la deuxième guerre mondiale*, V (1955).

Latouche, R., Aspect démographique de la crise des grandes invasions, *Population*, II (Oct.–Dec. 1947).

Ledermann, S., Les pertes militaires allemandes, *Population*, I (April–June, 1947).
Situation démographique de l'Allemagne en 1946, *Population*, 11 (Oct.–Dec. 1947).
L'évolution de la population de l'Allemagne de l'Ouest après la deuxième guerre mondiale, *Population*, V (1950).
and Cercelle, O., Berlin de 1939–1946, *Population*, II (April–June 1947).

Létinier, G., Progrès technique, destructions de guerre et optimum de population, *Population*, 1 (Jan.–March 1946).

Lindsay, J. A., The Eugenic and Social Influence of the War, *Eugenics Review*, X (Oct. 1918).

Lukaszewski, J., La population de la Pologne, pendant et après la seconde guerre mondiale, *Revue de géographie de Lyon* (1963).

Mallet, B., Vital statistics as affected by the war, *Jnl. Roy. Stat. Soc.*, LXXXI (Jan. 1918).

March, L., Some Attempts towards Race Hygiene in France during the War, *Eugenics Review*, X (Jan. 1919).

Markowitz, S., Retardation in Growth of Children in Europe and Asia during World War II, *Human Biology*, XXIV, 4 (Dec. 1955).

Myers, R. J., War and Post-War Experience in Regard to the Sex Ratio in Various Countries, *Human Biology*, XXI (Dec. 1949).

Nixon, S. W., War and National Vital Statistics in Special Reference to the Franco-Prussian War, *Jnl. Roy. Stat. Soc.*, LXXIX (July 1916).

Reinhard, M., Étude de la population pendant le Révolution et l'Empire, *Bulletin d'histoire économique et sociale de la Révolution française* (1959).

Robinson, G., Wounded Soldiers and Sailors in London during the First Dutch War (1652–54), *History Today*, XVI, 1 (1966).

Sauvy, A., Le faux problème de la population mondiale, *Population*, IV (1949).
Besoins et possibilités de l'immigration française, *Population*, V, 2, 3 (1950).
La population de l'Union Soviétique, *Population*, XI (1956).
Malthus el les deux Marx. Le problème de la faim et de la querre dans le monde (Paris, 1963).

Heurs et malheurs de la statistique pendant la guerre (1939–45), *Revue d'histoire de la deuxième guerre mondiale*, xv (1965).
and Ledermann, S., La guerre biologique (1933–45): population de l'Allemagne et des pays voisins, *Population*, ii (1947).
Schechtman, J. B., *Postwar Population Transfers in Europe 1945–1955* (1952).
Tandler, S., *Krieg und Bevölkerung* (Vienna and Leipzig, 1916).
Titmuss, R. M., War and the Birth Rate, *Eugenics Review*, xxxiii (July 1941).
The Effects of the War on the Birth Rate, *Eugenics Review*, xxxiv (April 1942).
Thomson, J. A., Eugenics and War, *Eugenics Review*, vii (April 1915).
Urlanis, B., *Bilanz der Kriege: die Menschenverlaste Europas von 17 Jahrhundert bis zur Gegenwart* (Berlin, 1965).
War and population (Moscow, 1971).
Verdugo, J. S., Influencia de la guerra en algunos fenemenos demografecos, *Revista de Sanidad e Higiena Publica*, xxii (1948).
Vincent, P., Conséquences de six années de guerre sur la population française, *Population*, i (July–Sept. 1946).
Guerre et population, *Population*, ii (Jan.–March 1947).
Vogts, A., Battle and other Combatant Casualties in the Second World War, *Journal of Politics*, vii, 3–4 (1945).
Willcox, W. F., Population and the World War, *Journal of the American Statistical Association*, xviii (1942).
Effects of War on Population, *Br. Med. Jnl.*, 20 May 1916.
Foreign Birth-rates and the European War, *Boston Medical and Surgical Journal*, clxxi (20 Aug. 1914).
The War and the Birth Rate, *British Medical Journal*, 27 May 1916.
War and the Birth-Rate, *Lancet*, 7 July 1945.
War and the Sex Ratio of Births, *Statistical Bulletin of the Metropolitan Life Insurance Company*, xxx, 6 (June 1949).
War Brings More Marriages, *Stat. Bull. Met. Life Ins. Co.*, xxi, 12 (Dec. 1950).
War Wastage and the Birth Rate, *Br. Med. Jnl.*, 15 April 1916.

B. WAGING OF WAR

Agriculture

Antsuiferov, A. N., Bilimovitch, A., Batscheff, M. O., and Ivantsov, D. N., *Russia's Rural Economy during the War* (1930).
Augé-Laribé, M., *L'Agriculture pendant la Guerre* (Paris, 1925).
Boutruche, R., La dévastastion des campagnes pendant la guerre de Cent ans, et la reconstruction agricole de la France, in *Mélanges* (Paris, 1945).
Cépède, M., *Agriculture et alimentation en France durant la IIᵉ Guerre mondiale* (Paris, 1961).
Ciriacy-Wantrup, S. V., The Relation of War Economics to Agriculture with Particular Reference to the Effects of Income and Price Inflation and Deflation, *Amer. Econ. Rev.*, xxx, 1 (March 1940), supplt.
Fussell, G. E., and Compton, M., Agricultural Adjustments after the Napoleonic wars, *Economic History*, iv, 14 (1939).
Habakkuk, H. J., Landowners and the Civil War, *Econ. Hist. Rev.*, 2nd ser., xxviii (1965).
Hibbard, B. H., *Effects of the Great War upon Agriculture in the United States and Great Britain* (New York, 1919).

Hirschfeld, A., Le mouvement coopératif agricole sous l'occupation, *Revue d'histoire de la deuxième guerre mondiale*, xv (1965).

John, A. H., Farming in Wartime, 1793–1815, in Jones, E. L. and Mingay, G. E. (eds.), *Land, Labour and Population in the Industrial Revolution* (1967).

Kirk, J. H., The Output of British Agriculture during the War, *Proceedings of the Agricultural Economics Society*, vii (June 1946).

Maxton, J. P., Rural Scotland during the War, *Econ. Jnl.*, xxxvii (1927).

Minchinton, W. E., Agricultural Returns and the Government during the Napoleonic Wars, *Agricultural History Review*, i (1953).

Mitrany, D., *The Land and the Peasant in Rumania. The War and Agrarian Reform, 1917–21* (1930).

Murray, K. A. H., *Agriculture* (1955).

Ricci, U., *La politica annonaria dell' Italia durante la Grande Guerra* (Bari, 1939).

Serpieri, A., *La guerra e la classi rurali Italiane* (Bari, 1930).

Industry

Aftalion, A., *L'Industrie textile en France pendant la guerre* (Paris, 1924).

Andrews, C. F., *Vickers Aircraft since 1908* (1969).

Armytage, W. H. G., Sheffield and the Crimean War: Politics and Industry 1852–1857, *History Today*, v, 7 (1955).

Belikov, A. M., Transfert de l'industrie soviétique vers l'est (Juin 1941–1942), *Revue d'histoire de la deuxième guerre mondiale*, xi (1961).

Birch, A., The British Iron Industry during the Napoleonic Wars, in *The Economic History of the British Iron and Steel Industry 1784–1879* (1967).

Boudot, F., L'industrie de l'essence synthetique dans le IIIᵉ Reich, *Revue d'histoire de la deuxième guerre mondiale*, xv (1965).

Bowen, I., The Building Industry in Wartime, *Econ. Jnl.*, xlix (1939).

Carpenter, H. C. H., Munition Metals, *Nature*, 15 (July 1915).

Carr, J. C., and Taplen, W., War and Depression 1914–1932, in *The Economic History of the British Iron and Steel Industry 1784–1879* (1967).

Cocks, E. J., and Walters, B., *A History of the Zinc Smelting Industry in Britain* (1968).

Cohen, T., Wartime Profits of Russian Industry 1914–1916, *Pol. Sci. Q.*, lviii (1943).

Coleman, D. C., Reorganization and War, in *Courtaulds: An Economic and Social History. II. Rayon* (Oxford, 1969).

Court, W. H. B., *Coal* (1951).

Dixon, P. H., and Parmelee, J. H., *War Administration of the Railways in the United States and Great Britain* (New York, 1918).

Farrar, M. M., Preclusive Purchase: Politics and Economic Warfare in France during the First World War, *Econ. Hist. Rev.*, 2nd ser., xxvi, 1 (Feb. 1973).

Fayle, C. H., *The War and the Shipping Industry* (1927).

Fetzer, F., *Ölpolitik der Grossmächte unter kriegswirtschaftlichen Gesichtspunkten: Das japanische Beispiel* (Hamburg, 1935).

Fontaine, A., *L'Industrie française pendant la guerre* (Paris 1925).

Foxwell, H. S., The Nature of the Industrial Struggle, *Econ. Jnl.*, xxvii (Sept. 1917).

Gordon, W. R., Coal in War, *Jnl. Roy. Utd. Ser. Inst.*, xci (Nov. 1946).

Haicht, J., Les négociations relatives aux achats d'avions Americains par la France pendant la période qui précéda immédiatement la guerre, *Revue d'histoire de la deuxième guerre mondiale*, xv (1965).

Hall, H. D., *North American Supply* (1955).

Hargreaves, E. L., and Gowing, M. M., *Civil Industry and Trade* (1952).

Hatch, F. H., *The Iron and the Steel Industry of the United Kingdom under War Conditions* (1919).
Homann-Herimberg, E., *Die Kohlenversorgung in Österreich wahrend des Krieges* Vienna, 1925).
Hornby, W., *Factories and Plant* (1958).
Jager, S. J., Sweden's Iron Exports to Germany, 1933–1944, *Scandinavian Economic History Review*, xv, 1 and 2 (1967).
Jensen, W. G., The Importance of Energy in the First and Second World Wars, *Historical Journal*, viii, 3 (1968).
King, H. K., *Armament of British Aircraft* (1971).
Kirkaldy, A. W., *Credit, Industry and the War* (1915).
Kisch, H., Growth Deterrents of a Medieval Heritage: the Aachen-area Woolen Trades before 1790, *Jnl. Econ. Hist.*, xxiv (1964).
Kohan, C. M., *Works and Buildings* (1952).
Layton, W. T., The Effect of War on Industry, *Quarterly Review*, ccxxiii (Jan. 1915).
Lebrun, P., *L'Industrie de la laine à Verviers pendant le XVIIIe siècle* (Liege, 1948).
Le Polemarque, La mobilisation des industries, *Europe Nouvelle*, 22 (Apr. 7, 1939).
Lloyd, A. H., British Machine Tools during the War, *Proceedings of the Institution of Mechanical Engineers*, cliv (1946).
McClaren, C. N., The Organization of Industry in War, *Jnl. Roy. Utd. Ser. Inst.*, xcii (May 1947).
Macht, T., *Die deutsche Fettwirtschaft in und nach dem Kriege* (Hamburg, 1936).
Mikhel'son, A. M. and Apostol, P., *La Lutte pour la pétrole et la Russie* (1922).
Money, Chiozza, The War and British Industry, *Fortnightly Review*, xcvii (March 1915).
Penrose, H., *British Aviation. The Great War and Armistice 1915–1919* (1969).
Peschaud, M., *Politique et fonctionnement des transports par chemin de fer pendant la guerre* (Paris, 1926).
Postan, M. M., Hay, D., and Scott, J. D., *Design and Development of Weapons: Studies in Government and Industrial Organisation* (1964).
Pratt, E. A., *British Railways and the Great War* (2 vols, 1921).
Reader, W. J., The Great War, in *I.C.I.: A History. I. The Forerunners 1870–1926* (1970).
Redlich, R., Plans for the Establishment of a War Industry in the Imperial Dominions during the Thirty Years' War, *Business History Review*, xxxviii (1964).
Redmayne, R., *The British Coal-mining Industry during the War* (Oxford, 1923).
Renwick, W. H., The Coal Industry under War Conditions, *Nineteenth Century*, lxxviii (Aug. 1915).
Roepke, H. G., *Movements of the British Iron and Steel Industry: 1720 to 1951* (Urbana, Ill., 1956).
Rovani, J.-G., *L'Industrie textile française à l'épreuve de la guerre* (Paris, 1948).
Savage, C. I., *Inland Transport* (1957).
Scott, J. D., *Vickers. A History* (1962).
Scott, W. R., and Cunnison, J., *The Industries of the Clyde Valley during the War* (Oxford, 1924).
Shadwell, A., The Mobilization of Industry for War, *Edinburgh Review*, ccxxiii (Jan. 1916).
Shenfield, A., and Sargent, F. P., Labour and the War Industries: the Experience of Coventry, *Rev. Econ. Stud.*, xi (1944–45).
  The Economics and Diseconomics of Industrial Concentration: the War Experience of Coventry, *Rev. Econ. Stud.*, xii (1944–45).

Silverman, H. A., *Studies in Industrial Organisation* (1946).
Speer, A., *Erinnerungen* (Munich, 1969).
Tardy, M., La nationalisation et le controle des industries de guerre, *Revue de France*, 18 (1 Sept., 1938).
Trebilcock, C., A 'Special Relationship'. Government Rearmament and the Cordite Firms, *Econ. Hist. Rev.*, 2nd ser., xix (1966).
'Spin-off' in British Economic History: Armaments and Industry 1760–1914, *Econ. Hist. Rev.*, 2nd ser., xxii (1969).
British Armaments and European Industrialization, 1890–1910, *Econ. Hist. Rev.*, 2nd ser., xxvi (1973).
Truelle, J., La production aéronautique militaire française jusqu'à juin 1940, *Revue d'histoire de la deuxième guerre mondiale*, xix (1969).
Tyerman, D., The Battle of Production, *Listener*, 30 May 1940.
Ward, D. M., *The Other Battle: A History of B.S.A. Company Ltd.* (1946).
Williams, T. I., The Chemical Industry and the First World War, in *The Chemical Industry Past and Present* (1953).
Wilson, C., Between Belligerents, 1914–1918, in *The History of Unilever: A Study in Economic Growth and Social Change*, ii (1954).
Worswick, C. D. N., Aircraft Production, *Bull. Oxf. Inst. Stat.*, v (18 Sept. 1943).
Zaalberg, C. J. P., *The Manufacturing Industry* (1928).
Zagorsky, S., *State Control of Industry in Russia during the War* (New Haven, 1928).
Some Developments in British Industry during the War, *Nature*, 27 Feb. 1919.
The War and the British Chemical Industry, *Nature*, 1 April 1915.
The War and Industrial Organization, *Round Table*, v (June 1915).

Labour

Anderson, B., Early Experience of Manpower Problems of an Industrial Society at War, *Pol. Sci. Q.*, lxxxii, 4 (Dec. 1967).
Armeson, R. B., *Total Warfare and Compulsory Labour* (Hague, 1964).
Billig, J., Le role des prisonniers de guerre dans l'économie du IIIᵉ Reich, *Revue d'histoire de la deuxième guerre mondiale*, x (1960).
Boudet, M., Fonds d'archives relatifs à l'emploi pendant la seconde guerre mondiale, *Revue d'histoire de la deuxième guerre mondiale*, xv (1965).
Boulin, P., *L'Organisation du travail dans la région envahie de la France pendant l'occupation* (Paris, 1927).
Bright, R. H., The Industrial Population of Great Britain and the War, *Jnl. Roy. Utd. Ser. Inst.*, lxxxvi (Nov. 1941).
Women in Industry, *Jnl. Roy. Utd. Ser. Inst.*, lxxxvii (Nov. 1942).
Bullock, A., *The Life and Times of Ernest Bevin. II. Minister of Labour 1940–1945* (1967).
Cole, G. D. H., *Labour in War-time* (1915).
Labour in the Coal-mining Industry, 1914–1921 (Oxford, 1925).
Trade Unionism and Munitions (Oxford, 1923).
Workshop Organisation (Oxford, 1923).
Forchheimer, K., War-time Changes in Industrial Employment, *Bull. Oxf. Inst. Stat.*, vii (24 Nov. 1945).
Gowing, M., The Organisation of Manpower in Britain during the Second World War, *Journal of Contemporary History*, vii, 1 and 2 (Jan.–April 1972).
Halperin, D. B., The Trade Union Movement since the Outbreak of War, *Bull. Oxf. Inst. Stat.*, v (1943).

Hanusch, F., and Adler, E., *Die Regelung der Arbeitsverhaltnisse im Kriege* (Vienna, 1927).

Henderson, H. D., The Influence of War on Employment, *Econ. Jnl.*, XXIV (Dec. 1914).

Hobson, J. A., The War and its Effect on Work and Wages, *Fortnightly Review*, XCVII (1915).

Labour and the Costs of War (1916).

Honze, E. L., *Foreign Labour in Nazi Germany* (Princeton, 1967).

Inman, P., *Labour in the Munitions Industries* (1957).

Jacquemyns, G., Quelques attitudes et réactions des travailleurs belges sous l'occupation Allemande, *Revue d'histoire de la deuxième guerre mondiale*, VIII (1958).

Kalecki, M., Sources of Manpower in the British War Sector, *Bull. Oxf. Inst. Stat.*, V (12 Feb. 1943).

Lorenz, C., *Die gewerbliche Frauenarbeit wahrend des Krieges* (Stuttgart, 1928).

Lueders, M. E., *Das unbekannte Heer. Frouen Kaempfen fuer Deutschland, 1914–18* (Berlin, 1936).

McKowen, H. and Robinson, H. W., Labour Potential in War Time, *Econ. Jnl.*, XLIX (1939).

Nicholson, J. L., Substitution of Women for Men in Industry, *Bull. Oxf. Inst. Stat.*, V (3 April 1943).

Parker, H. M. D., *Manpower: a Study of War-time Policy and Administration* (1957).

Passelecq, F., *Deportation et travail forcé des ouvriers et de la population civile de la Belgique occupée* (New Haven, 1929).

Rawson, S. W., War and Wages in the Iron, Coal and Steel Industries, *Econ. Jnl.*, XXVI (June 1916).

Rowe, J. W. F., Wages in the Cotton Industry, 1914–1920, *Econ. Jnl.*, XXXIV (1929).

Umbreit, P., *Der Krieg und die Arbeitsuerhaltnisse. Die deutsche Gerwerkschaften im Kriege* (Stuttgart, 1928).

Ward, J., Labour and its Relation to the Army, *Jnl. Roy. Utd. Ser. Inst.*, LXVI (Feb. 1921).

Wolfe, H., *Labour Supply and Regulation* (Oxford, 1923).

Wormser, O., Le role du travail concentrationnaire dans l'économie de guerre allemande, *Revue d'histoire de la deuxième guerre mondiale*, IV (1954).

Interim Report of the Conference to Investigate into Outlets for Labour after the War, *Rpt. 85th Mtg. Br. Assoc. Advan. Sci. (Trans. Sect. F)* (1916).

Man Power and Woman Power, *Round Table*, XXXII (March 1942).

Medical Research Council, *A Report on the Causes of Wastage of Labour in Munitions Factories Employing Women*, Special Report Series, no. 16 (1918).

The Problem of Women in Industry, *Round Table*, VI (March 1916).

The Military

Armies and Armaments

Ashlund, Lt. Col., L'armée suedoise de 'soldats-cultivateurs à la fin du XVIIe siècle et au début du XVIIIe siècle, *Revue internationale d'histoire militaire*, XXX (1971).

Barnett, C., *Britain and Her Army 1509–1970* (1970).

Begue, S., Le problème de l'alimentation de l'armée sous Charles X. Une expérience: le ravitaillement des troupes de la division d'expedition en Morée, *Actes du 93e congrès national des sociétés savantes (section d'histoire moderne et contemporaine)*, I (Paris, 1970).

Beller, E. A., The Military Expedition of Sir Charles Morgan to Germany 1627–9, *Eng. Hist. Rev.*, XLIII (1926).

Bertaud, J.-P., Contribution à l'étude des transports militaires dans les Pyrénées (1794–1795), *Actes du 94ᵉ congrès national des sociétés savantes (sect. d'h. mod. contemp.)*, I (Paris, 1971).

Le recruitement et l'avancement des officiers de la Révolution, *Annales hist. rév. fr.*, XLIV (1972).

Blanchard, A., Les ci-devant ingénieurs du roi, *Rev. int. d'h. milit.*, XXX (1970).

Blanco, R. H., Henry Marshall (1775–1851) and the Health of the British Army, *Medical History*, XIV (July 1970).

Bosset, M. A., Essais sur l'histoire des fabrications d'armement en France jusqu'au milieu du XVIIIᵉ siècle, *Mémorial de l'artillerie française*, XIV (1935).

Bouloiseau, M., L'approvisionnement de l'armée de l'Ouest en l'an II, d'après les registres du commissaire ordonnateur Lenoble, *Actes du 93ᵉ congrès national des sociétés savantes (Sect. d'h. mod. contemp.)*, I (Paris, 1970).

Boussard, J., Services féodaux, milices et mercenaires dans les armées en France aux Xᵉ et XIᵉ siècles, *Settimane di studie sull'Alto Medievo*, XV (Spoleto, 1968).

Boyer, F., Armes et munitions vendues en 1860 par Napoléon III à Victor-Emmanuel II, *Rev. d'h. mod. contemp.*, n.s. IX (1962).

Brusten, C., *L'Armée bourguignonne de 1465 à 1468* (Brussels, 1955).

L'armée bourguignonne de 1465 à 1477, *Rev. int. d'h. milit.*, XX (1959).

Le ravitaillement en vivres dans l'armée bourguignonne 1450–1477, *Publications du centre européen d'études burgundo-médianes*, III (1961).

Busch, O., *Militärsystem und Sozialleben im Alten Preussen 1713–1807* (Berlin, 1962).

Carr, A. D., Welshman and the Hundred Years War, *Welsh History Review*, IV (1968).

Casarini, A., *La medicina militare nella leggenda e nella storia* (Rome, 1929).

Chadwick, G. F., The Army Works Corps in the Crimea, *Journal of Transport History*, VI (1964).

Chalmin, P. 'La guerre révolutionnaire sous la Legislative et la Convention', *Revue Histoire de l'Armée*, IV (1958).

Compton, T. E., Supply and Transport in the French Army in 1812 and 1914, *United Service Magazine* (August 1918).

Conturie, P. M. J., *Histoire de la fonderie national de Ruello (1750–1940)* (Paris, 1951).

Corvisier, A., *L'Armée française de la fin du XVIIᵉ siècle au ministère de Choiseul* (2 vols, Paris, 1964).

Les Controles de troupes de l'Ancien Régime (Paris, 1968).

Hiérarchie militaire et hiérarchie sociale à la veille de la Révolution, *Rev. int. d'h. milit.*, XXX (1970).

Vocation militaire, misère et niveau d'instruction au XVIIIᵉ siècle. Les limites de la methode quantitative, *Actes du 94ᵉ congrès national des sociétés savantes (sect. d'h. mod. contemp.)*, II (Paris, 1970).

Quelques aspects de la captivité militaire au XVIIᵉ siècle: le sort des prisonniers de guerre espanols en France de 1635 à 1648. *Actes du 94ᵉ congrès national des sociétés savantes (sect. d'h. mod. contemp.)*, I (Paris, 1971).

Cruickshank, C. G., *Elizabeth's Army* (1946).

Army Royal. Henry VIII's invasion of France, 1513 (Oxford, 1969).

Davies, C. S. L., Les rations alimentaires de l'armée et de la marine anglaise au XVIᵉ siècle, *Annales e.s.c.*, XVIII (1963).

Provisions for Armies, 1509–60, *Econ. Hist. Rev.*, 2nd ser., xvii (1964).
Davies, G., The Parliamentary Army under the Earl of Essex 1642–5, *Eng. Hist. Rev.*, xlix (Jan. 1934).
Recruiting in the Reign of Queen Anne, *Jnl. Soc. Army Hist. Res.*, xxviii (1956).
Defrasne, J., Vie et mentalité des militaires britanniques pendant les guerres de la Révolution et de l'Empire, *Rev. int. d'h. milit.*, xxx (1970).
Drew, R., Medicine's Debt to the Army: a Review of the Army's Contribution to Medical Science, *Journal of the Royal Army Medical Corps*, cx (1964).
Drummond, A., Medicine and the Army, *St. Bartholomew's Hospital Journal*, lxii (1958).
Ffoulkes, C. J., *Gunfounders of England* (Cambridge, 1937).
Arms and Armament (1945).
Firth, C., *Cromwell's Army* (1902).
Fowler, K. A., Les finances et la discipline dans les armées anglaises en France au xive siècle, *Actes de colloque internationale de Cocheril. Les cahiers vernonnais*, 4 (1964).
Gaier, C., Analysis of Military Forces in the Principality of Liège and the County of Looz from the Twelfth to the Fifteenth Century, in Wm. Bowsky (ed.), *Studies in Medieval and Renaissance History*, ii (1965).
L'approvisiennement et la régime alimentaire des troupes dans le duché de Limbourg et les terres d'autre-Meuse vers 1400, *Le Moyen Âge*, lxxiv (1968).
La cavalerie lourde en Europe occidentale du xiie au xvie siècle, *Rev. int. d'h. milit.*, xxxi (1971).
Gaier, M. H., Mentalité collective de l'infanterie communale liégeoise au Moyen Âge, *Rev. int. d'h. milit.*, xxx (1970).
Gerard, P., L'armée révolutionnaire de la Haute Garonne, *Annales hist. rév. fr.*, xxxi (1959).
Godechot, J., *Les Commissaires aux armées sous le Directoire* (2 vols, Paris, 1937).
Golovin, N. H., *The Russian Army in the World War* (New Haven, Conn., 1931).
Gray, A. C., Organization and Pay: Their Influence on the Army's Manpower, *Jnl. Roy. Utd. Ser. Inst.*, xcv (Feb. 1950).
Habakkuk, H. J., The Parliamentary Army and the Crown Lands, *Welsh Hist. Rev.*, iii (1967).
Hanham, H. J., Religion and Nationality in the Mid-Victorian Army, in Foot, M. R. D. (ed.), *War and Society* (1973).
Hay, I., *R.O.F.: The Story of the Royal Ordnance Factories 1939–48* (1949).
Headlam, J., *The History of the Royal Artillery* (2 vols, 1937).
Hoeniger, R., *Die Armeen des Dreissigjahrigen Krieges* (Berlin, 1914).
Hogg, O. F. G., *English Artillery 1326–1716* (1963).
The Royal Arsenal (1963).
Hollister, C. W., The Annual Term of Military Service in Medieval England, *Medievalia et Humanistica*, xiii (1960).
The Military Organization of Norman England (Oxford, 1965).
Jennings, B., *Wild Geese in Spanish Flanders, 1582–1700* (Dublin, 1964).
Jones, K. R., Richard Cox, Army Agent and Banker, *Jnl. Soc. Army Hist. Res.*, xxxiv (Dec. 1956).
Kiernan, V. G., Conscription and Society in Europe before the War of 1914–18, in Foot, M. R. D. (ed.), *War and Society* (1973).
Laws, M. E. S., Army Doctors in the Eighteenth Century, *Jnl. Roy. Utd. Ser. Inst.*, xciii (Aug. 1948).
Leverrie, J., *La naissance de l'armée nationale, 1789–94* (Paris, 1939).

Lewis, N. B., The Recruitment and Organisation of a Contract Army, May to November 1337, *Bull. Inst. Hist. Res.*, xxxvi (May 1964).

Lindsay, A. D., The Organisation of Labour in the Army in France during the War, and Its Lessons, *Econ. Jnl.*, xxxiv (1924).

Lot, F., *L'Art militaire et les armées aux Moyen Âge en Europe et dans le Proche-Orient* (2 vols, Paris, 1946).

Recherches sur les effectifs des armées françaises des guerres d'Italie aux guerres de Religion (1494–1562) (Paris, 1962).

Lovegrove, P., *Not Least in the Crusade: a Short History of the Royal Army Medical Corps* (Aldershot, 1951).

Margerand, J., *Armament et equipement de l'infanterie française du XVIe au XXe siècle* (Paris, 1945).

Mather, F. C., Army Pensioners and the Maintenance of Civil Order in Early Nineteenth Century England, *Jnl. Soc. Army Hist. Res.*, xxxvi (Sept. 1958).

McLaughlin, R., *The Royal Army Medical Corps* (1972).

Mearbreck, L. van, Le service sanitaire de l'armée espagnole des Pays-Bas à la fin du XVIe et au XVIIe siècle, *Rev. int. d'h. milit.*, xx (1959).

Meyer, J., L'armement nantais au XVIIIe siècle d'après les registres des classes: la période 1735–1748; comparaison avec la deuxième moitié du siècle, *Actes du 91e congrès national des sociétés savantes (sect. d'h. mod. contemp.)*, i (Paris, 1969).

Muller, J., Les ingénieurs militaires dans les Pays-Bas espagnols (1500–1715), *Rev. int. d'h. milit.*, xx (1959).

Nutton, V., Medicine and the Roman Army: A Further Reconsideration, *Medical History*, xiii (July 1969).

Parker, G., *The Army of Flanders and the Spanish Road, 1567–1659* (Cambridge, 1972).

Percival, A., The Faversham Gunpowder Industry, *Industrial Archeology*, i, 1 and 2 (1968).

Perjès, M. G., Historie militaire et psychologies, *Rev. int. d'h. milit.*, xxx (1970).

Pieri, P., *La crisi militare italiana nel rinascimento nella sue relazione con la crisi politica ed economica* (Napoli, 1934).

Polišenský, J. V., Gallants to Bohemia, *Slavonic Review*, xxv (1947).

Prestwich, M., Victualling Estimates for English Garrisons in Scotland during the Early Seventeenth Century, *Eng. Hist. Rev.*, lxxxii (1967).

Prince, A. E., The Payment of Army Wages in Edward III's Reign, *Speculum*, xix (1914).

The Strength of English Armies in the Middle Ages, *Eng. Hist. Rev.*, xxix (1914).

Quimby, R., *The Background of Napoleonic Warfare*, (New York, 1957).

Rebouillat, M., Les réquisitions pour la subsistance des armées et des villes à Sercy (district de Châlon-sur-Sâone) pendant la Révolution, *Actes du 93e congrès national des sociétés savantes (sect. d'h. mod. contemp.)*, i (Paris, 1970).

Reinhard, M., Recherches et perspectives sur l'armée dans la Révolution française, *Annales hist. Rév. fr.*, xliv (1972).

Salmon, T. W., *The Care and Treatment of Mental Diseases and War Neuroses in the British Army* (New York, 1917).

Scarborough, J., Roman Medicine and the Legions: A Reconsideration, *Medical History*, xii (July 1968).

Scott, S. F., The Regeneration of the Line Army during the French Revolution, *Jnl. Mod. Hist.*, xlii (1970).

Les soldats de l'armée de ligne en 1793, *Annales hist. rév. fr.*, xliv (1972).

Scouller, R. E., *The Armies of Queen Anne* (Oxford, 1966).

Sherbourne, J. W., Indentured Retinues and English Expeditions to France, 1369–1380, *Eng. Hist. Rev.*, LXXIX (1964).

Stone, N., Army and Society in the Hapsburg Monarchy, 1900–1914, *Past & Present*, 33 (1966).

Tresse, R., Le problème de la nouture des grains de l'armée d'Italie à Nice, (1792–1800), *Actes du 93ᵉ congrès national des sociétés savantes (sect. d'h. mod. contemp.)*, I (Paris, 1970).

Vallée, G., *La Conscription dans le département de la Charente* (Paris, 1936).

Von Loewe, K., Military Service in Early Sixteenth-Century Lithuania: A New Interpretation and Its Implications, *Slavic Review*, XXX, 2 (1971).

Waley, D. P., Papal Armies in the Thirteenth Century, *Eng. Hist. Rev.*, LXXII (1957).

Navies and naval dockyards

Albion, R. G., The Timber Problem of the Royal Navy 1652–1852, *Mariner's Mirror*, XXXXVIII (Feb. 1952).

Aldridge, R. D., The Victualling of the British Naval Expeditions to the Baltic Sea between 1715 and 1727, *Scandinavian Economic History Review*, XXI (1964).

Anderson, M. S., Great Britain and the Growth of the Russian Navy in the Eighteenth Century, *Mariner's Mirror*, XLII (May 1966).

Ayre, A., Merchant Shipbuilding during the War, *Proceedings of the Institution of Naval Architects*, LXXXVII (1945).

Bach, J., The Maintenance of Royal Vessels in the Pacific Ocean 1825–1875, *Mariner's Mirror*, LVI (Aug. 1970).

Barrett, M. K., The Navy and the Clyde in the American War 1777–1783, *Mariner's Mirror*, LV (Feb. 1969).

Bassett, G. A., The Repair and Upkeep of H. M. Ships and Vessels in War, *Transactions of the Institution of Naval Architects*, LXXXXVIII (1946).

Bath, A. G., The Victualling of the Navy, *Jnl. Roy. Utd. Ser. Inst.*, (Nov. 1939).

Bromley, J. S., In the Shadow of Impressment: Friends of a Naval Militia, 1844–74, in Foot, M. R. D., (ed.), *War and Society* (1973).

Brooks, F. W., The Cinque Ports, *Mariner's Mirror*, XV (April 1929).

Naval Administration and the Raising of Fleets under John and Henry III, *Mariner's Mirror*, XV (April 1929).

Buisseret, D. J., The French Mediterranean Fleet under Henry IV, *Mariner's Mirror*, L (Nov. 1964).

Cary, L. H. St. C., Harwich Dockyards, *Mariner's Mirror*, XIII (April 1927).

Coleman, D. C., Naval Dockyards under the Later Stuarts, *Econ. Hist. Rev.*, 2nd Ser., VI (Dec. 1953).

Creswell, J., English Shipping at the End of the Eighteenth Century, *Mariner's Mirror*, XXV (April 1939).

Crowhurst, R. P., The Admiralty and the Convoy System in the Seven Years War, *Mariner's Mirror*, LVII (May 1971).

Dawe, C. H., Diet and Disease in the Navy, *Proc. Roy. Soc. Med. (War Section)*, XX (1927).

Dewar, A. C., The Naval Administration of the Interregnum, *Mariner's Mirror*, XII (Oct. 1926).

Ehrman, J. P. W., Pepys' Organization and the Naval Mobilization of 1688, *Mariner's Mirror*, XXXV (July 1949).

The Official Papers Transferred by Pepys to the Admiralty by 12 July 1689, *Mariner's Mirror*, XXXIV (Oct. 1949).

The Navy in the War of William III, 1689–1697 (Cambridge, 1953).

Fardet, M., La revitaillement des marins de la flotille de Boulogne (septembre 1803–septembre 1805), *Actes du 93ᵉ congrès national des sociétés savantes (sect. d'h. mod. contemp.*), ɪ (Paris, 1970).

Firth, C. H., Sailors of the Civil War, the Commonwealth and the Protectorate, *Mariner's Mirror*, xɪɪ (July 1926).

Glasgow, T., The Navy in Philip and Mary's War, *Mariner's Mirror*, ʟɪɪɪ (Nov. 1967).

The Navy in the First Elizabethan Undeclared War 1559–1560, *Mariner's Mirror*, ʟɪv (Feb. 1968).

The Maturing of Naval Administration 1556–1564, *Mariner's Mirror*, ʟvɪ (Jan. 1970).

Goldingham, R. M. H. T., The Personnel of the Tudor Navy and the Internal Economy of the Ships, *United Service Magazine* (March 1918).

Hampson, N., *La Marine de l'an II: mobilisation de la flotte de l'océan 1793–1794* (Paris, 1959).

Les ouvriers des Arsenaux de la Marine au cours de la Révolution Française (1789–1794), *Revue d'histoire économique et sociale*, xxxɪx (1961).

Jones, A. G. E., Shipbuilding in Ipswich 1700–1750, *Mariner's Mirror*, xʟɪɪɪ (1957).

Kitson, H., The Early History of Portsmouth Dockyard 1496–1800, *Mariner's Mirror*, xxxɪɪɪ (Oct. 1947) and xxxɪv (1948).

Knight, R. J. B., The Administration of the Royal Dockyards in England 1770–1790, *Bull. Inst. Hist. Res.*, xʟv (1972).

Lane, F. C., *Venetian Ships and Shipbuilders of the Renaissance* (Baltimore, 1934).

Lewis, M., *A Social History of the Navy 1793–1815* (1960).

Lloyd, C., *The British Seaman 1200–1860* (1968).

Lombard, M., Arsenaux et bois de marine dans la Mediterranée muselmane (VIIᵉ–XIᵉ siècles) *Deuxième colloque internationale d'histoire maritime* (Paris, 1957).

McCord, N., The Impress Service in North-East England during the Napoleonic War, *Mariner's Mirror*, ʟɪv (May 1968).

MacGregor, D. R., Tendering and Contract Procedure in Merchant Shipyards in the Middle of the Nineteenth Century, *Mariner's Mirror*, xʟvɪɪɪ (Nov. 1962).

MacLeod, N., The Shipyards of the Royal Dockyards, *Mariner's Mirror* xɪ (July, Oct. 1925).

Mauro, F., Types de navires et constructions navale dans l'Atlantique portugais aux xvɪᵉ et xvɪɪɪᵉ siècles, *Rev. d'h. mod. contemp.*, n.s. vɪ (1959).

Merrien, J., *La Vie quotidienne des marins au Moyen Age: des Vikings aux Galères* (Paris, 1969).

Parkinson, C. N., *The Rise of the Port of Liverpool* (Liverpool, 1952).

Patteson, G., Nineteenth-Century Dock Labour in the Port of London, *Mariner's Mirror*, ʟɪɪ (Aug. 1966).

Pool, B., Some Notes on Warship-building by Contrast in the Eighteenth Century, *Mariner's Mirror*, xʟɪx (May 1963).

Navy Contracts in the Last Years of the Navy Board (1780–1832), *Mariner's Mirror*, ʟ (Aug. 1964).

Navy Contracts after 1832, *Mariner's Mirror*, ʟɪv (Aug. 1968).

Powell, J. R., *The Navy in the English Civil War* (1962).

Powell, W. R., The Administration of the Navy and the Stannaries, 1189–1216, *Eng. Hist. Rev.*, xʟvɪ (1931).

Ranft, B. McL., Labour Relations in the Royal Dockyards in 1739, *Mariner's Mirror*, xʟvɪɪ (1961).

Richardson, H. E. (and Macleod, N.), Wages of Shipwrights in H.M. Dockyards, 1496–1788, *Mariner's Mirror*, xxxiii (Oct. 1947).

Richmond, C. F., The Keeping of the Seas during the Hundred Years' War, *History*, xlix (1964).

Scammell, V. G., Manning the English Merchant Service in the Sixteenth Century, *Mariner's Mirror*, lvi (May 1970).

Sherborne, J. W., The Hundred Years War: the English Navy, Shipping and Manpower 1369–1389, *Past & Present*, 37 (July 1967).

Shore, H. N., Shipbuilding during the War with France 1793–1815, *United Services Magazine* (Aug. 1916).

Tanner, J. R., *Samuel Pepys and the Royal Navy* (Cambridge, 1920).

Taylor, R., Manning the Royal Navy: the Reform of the Recruiting System, 1852–1862, *Mariner's Mirror*, xliv (Nov. 1958) and xlv (1969).

Tedder, A. W., *The Navy of the Restoration* (1916).

Turner, W. J. C., The Building of the *Gracedieu*, *Valentine* and *Falconer* at Southampton 1416–1420, *Mariner's Mirror*, xl (1954).

Southampton as a Naval Centre, 1414–1458, in Morgan, J. B. and Pebendy, P. (eds), *Collected Essays on Southampton* (Southampton, 1958).

Webb, J. G., William Sabyn of Ipswich: an Early Tudor Sea-Officer and Merchant, *Mariner's Mirror*, xli (1955).

Prices and incomes

Benham, F., Wartime Control of Prices, *Economica*, ix (1942).

Bowley, A. L., *Prices and Earnings in Time of War* (1915).

Prices and Wages in the United Kingdom, 1914–1929 (Oxford, 1921).

Contract and Retail Food Prices, *Bull. Oxf. Inst. Stat.*, vi (14 Oct. 1944).

Debru-Bridel, J., *Histoire du marché noir, 1939–1947* (Paris, 1947).

Hamilton, E J., *War and Prices in Spain, 1651–1800* (Cambridge, Mass., 1947).

Kalecki, M., Profits, Salaries and Wages, *Bull. Oxf. Inst. Stat.*, v (5 June 1943).

Rationing and Price Control, *Bull. Oxf. Inst. Stat.*, vi (5 Feb. 1944).

Layton, W. T., State Control of Prices and Production in Time of War, *Political Quarterly*, i (May 1915).

Madge, C., *The War-time Pattern of Saving and Spending* (Cambridge, 1943).

March, L., *Mouvement des prix et des salaires pendant la guerre* (Paris, 1925).

Methorst, H. W., *The Cost of Living, Prices, and Wages* (1928).

Nicholson, J. L., Earnings of Workpeople in 1938 and 1942, *Bull. Oxf. Inst. Stat.*, v (12 Feb. 1943).

Earnings and Hours of Labour, *Bull. Oxf. Inst. Stat.*, vi (20 May 1944).

Changes in Consumption, *Bull. Oxf. Inst. Stat.*, vi (23 Sept. 1944).

Wages during the War, *Bull. Oxf. Inst. Stat.*, vi (14 Oct. 1944).

Employment and National Income during the War, *Bull. Oxf. Inst. Stat.*, vii (13 Oct. 1945).

Pigou, A. E., The Control of Prices during the War, *Contemporary Review*, cxiii (Aug. 1918).

Roberts, B. C., *National Wages Policy in War and Peace* (1958).

Rutherford, R. S. G., Guaranteed Prices and the Farmers, *Bull. Oxf. Inst. Stat.*, vi (15 Feb. 1944).

Schultz, T., 'Human Needs' Cost of Living for a Single Person, *Bull. Oxf. Inst. Stat.*, v (26 June 1943).

Working-class Budgets in Wartime, *Bull. Oxf. Inst. Stat.*, vi (5 Feb. 1944), supplt.

Income and Household Expenditure of Working-class Families with Children, *Bull. Oxf. Inst. Stat.*, VIII (Feb. 1946).

Working, H., War and Commodity Prices, *Journal of the American Statistical Association*, XXXV (June 1940).

Worswick, G. D. N., Prices and Retail Consumption in 1942, *Bull. Oxf. Inst. Stat.*, V (13 March 1943).

Wages and Prices, *Round Table*, XXXIII (Dec. 1942).

Science, medicine and the health of civilians and combatants

Addison, E. B., The Radio War, *Jnl. Roy. Utd. Ser. Inst.*, XCII (1947).

Andrewes, F. W., The Work of British Pathology in Relation to the War, *Br. Med. Jnl.*, 23 June 1917).

Appleton, E., The Scientist in War Time, *Proceedings of the Institution of Mechanical Engineers*, CLIV (1946).

Barnsley, R. W., King Charles II's Medical Services, *Army Medical Services Magazine*, XII (Aug. 1963).

Mars and Aesculapius: an address given in the Royal Army Medical College (1963).

Beggam, A., War-time Advances in Medicine which Might be Translated into Civil Practice, *Edinburgh Medical Journal*, LIII (Aug. 1946).

Bernal, J. D., Science and War in History, in *The Social Function of Science* (1939).

Bernard, L., *La Défense de la santé publique pendant la guerre* (Paris, 1929).

Blackett, P. M. S., *Studies of War* (Edinburgh, 1962).

Bolduan, C., Medical Science in the Service of War, *Scientific American*, 7 (Nov. 1914).

Bowlby, A., Wounds in War, *Jnl. Roy. Army Med. Corps*, XXVI (Feb. 1916).

and Wallace, C., The Development of British Surgery at the Front, *Br. Med. Jnl.*, 2 June 1917.

Brockington, C. F., Effects of War-time Nutrition on Children, *Public Health*, LX (July 1942).

Brownlow, C. A. L., Invention: Machinery and War, *Army Quarterly*, LXVII (Oct. 1953).

Buckatzsch, E. J., Reform of the Health Services, *Bull. Oxf. Inst. Stat.*, VI (8 April 1944).

Carslaw, J. S., Military Medicine from the Aesculapius to the Air and Atomic Age, *Jnl. Roy. Utd. Ser. Inst.*, C (Aug. 1955).

Chambers, J., Hospital Ships in Peace and War, *Proc. Roy. Soc. Med. (War Section)*, XVIII (1925).

Clark, G. N., *Science and Social Welfare in the Age of Newton* (Oxford, 1937).

Clark, R., *The Rise of the Boffins* (1962).

Tizard (1965).

Cockburn, R., Science in War, *Jnl. Roy. Utd. Ser. Inst.*, CI (Feb. 1956).

Collar, A. R., Tizard and the Aeronautical Research Committee, *Journal of the Royal Aeronautical Society*, LXXI (Aug. 1967).

Cope, Z., *Medicine and Pathology* (1962).

Surgery (1953).

Coulter, J. H. S., *The Royal Naval Medical Service* (2 vols, 1954–6).

Crew, F. A. E., The War and Ourselves, *Royal Army Medical Corps Journal*, LXXV (Dec. 1940).

The Army Medical Services (6 vols, 1953–62).

Crowther, J. G., and Whiddington, R., *Science at War* (1947).

Curran, D. and Mallinson, W. P., Depressive States in War, *Br. Med. Jnl.*, 1 March 1941.

Cutler, E. C., A Surgeon Looks at Two World Wars, *Lancet*, 30 Sept. 1944.

Military Surgery, *Surgery, Gynaecology and Obstetrics*, LXXXII (1946).

Dakin, H. D., Biochemistry and War Problems, *Br. Med. Jnl.*, 23 June 1917.

Dale, H., Science in War and Peace, *Nature*, 30 Aug. 1947.

Daley, W. A., and Benjamin, B., Tuberculosis in London in Wartime, *Br. Med. Jnl.*, 10 Oct. 1943.

Dawson of Penn, Viscount, Medicine and the Public Welfare, *Br. Med. Jnl.*, 9 May 1942.

Desch, C. H., Metallurgy and the War, *Proceedings of the Royal Philosophical Society of Edinburgh*, XLIV (1917–18).

Dunn, C. L. (ed.), *The Emergency Medical Services* (3 vols, 1952–53).

Eder, M. D., The Psycho-pathology of the War Neurosis, *Lancet*, 12 Aug. 1916.

Ellis, F. P., and Rowlands, A., Health of the Navy in Two World Wars, *Journal of the Royal Navy Medical Service* (1968).

Emslie, I., The War and Psychiatry, *Edinburgh Medical Journal*, n.s., XIV (May 1915).

Ferguson, S., *Studies in the Social Services* (1954).

Fleming, J. A., Science in the War and after the War, *Nature*, 14 Oct. 1915.

Frith, F. A., The Chemistry of War, *Jnl. Roy. Utd. Ser. Inst.*, LXXV (Nov. 1930).

Fuller, J. F. C., Science and War, *Nineteenth Century*, CIII (1928).

Fulton, J. F., Neurology and War, *Transactions and Studies of the College of Physicians of Philadelphia*, VIII (1940).

Medicine, Warfare and History, *Smithsonian Institution Annual Report* (1954).

Gamble, J. H. *et al.*, Symposium on Wartime Advances in Medicine, *Proceedings of the American Philosophical Society*, LXXXVIII (1944).

Gask, G. E., The Medical Services of Henry the Fifth's Campaign of the Somme in 1415, *Proc. Roy. Soc. Med. (Hist. Med. Sect.)*, XVI (1923).

Giao, M., Notes sur le service de santé pendant la guerre de la restauration 1640–1668, Chirurgiens étrangers dans l'armée portugaise, *Rev. int. d'h. milit.*, I (1939).

Gillespie, R. D., War Neuroses after Psychological Trauma, *Br. Med. Jnl.*, 12 May 1945.

Gowing, M., *Britain and Atomic Energy* (1964).

Green, F. H. K., and Covell, Sir G. (eds.), Medical Research (1953).

Hadfield, J. A., War Neurosis, *Br. Med. Jnl.*, 28 Feb., 7 March 1942.

Hartcup, G., *Challenge of War: Britain's Scientific and Engineering Contributions to World War II* (1970).

Howell, H. A. L., The British Medical Arrangements during the Waterloo Campaign, *Proc. Roy. Soc. Med. (Hist. Med. Sect.)*, XVII (1924).

Hume, W. E., The Physician in War in Harvey's Time and After, *Lancet*, 30 Oct. 1943.

Hurst, A. F., The Etiology and Treatment of War Neuroses, *Br. Med. Jnl.*, 29 Sept. 1917.

Irvine, E. D., Civilian Health Risks in War, *Public Health*, LIV (Nov. 1940).

Jameson, W., War and the Advancement of Social Medicine, *Lancet*, 24 Oct. 1942.

Jeffrey, J. S., and Thomson, S., Penicillin in Battle Casualties, *Br. Med. Jnl.*, 1 July 1944.

Jessel, G., Tuberculosis and the War, *Public Health*, XXXI (Aug. 1918).

Jones, E., War and Sublimation, *Rpt. 85th Mtg. Br. Assoc. Advanc. Sci. (Trans. Sect. I)* (1916).

Jones, M. and Lewis, A., Effort Syndrome, *Lancet*, 28 June 1941.

Jones, R. V., Scientists at War: Lindemann v. Tizard, I–III, *The Times*, 6–8 April 1961.

Keevil, J. J., Lloyd, L., and Coulter, J. H. S., *Medicine and the Navy (1200–1900)* (3 vols, Edinburgh, 1957–63).

Lewis, A., Mental Health in War-time, *Public Health*, LVII (Dec. 1943).

Lockwood, A. L., Some Experiences in the Last War, *Br. Med. Jnl.*, 2 March 1940.

MacGregor, A., The Public Health Services in the War, *Public Health*, LV (Jan. 1942).

Macintosh, J. M., *The War and Mental Health in England* (New York, 1944).

MacLeod, R. M. and Andrews, E. K., The Origins of the DSIR: Reflections on Ideas and Men, 1915–1916, *Public Administration*, XLVIII (1970).

Scientific Advice in the War at Sea 1915–1917: the Board of Invention and Research, *Journal of Contemporary History*, VI (1971).

MacNalty, A. S., Advances in Preventive Medicine during the War of 1939–45, *Nature*, 8 Nov. 1947.

Civilian Health and Medical Services (2 vols, 1953–5).

and Mellor, W. F., *Medical Services in War* (1969).

MacPherson, W. G., *Medical Services: Diseases of the War* (1922).

and Beveridge, W. W. O. (eds.), *Medical Services: Hygiene of the War* (1923).

Makins, G. H., The Development of British Surgery in the Hospitals on the Lines of Communications in France, *Br. Med. Jnl.*, 16 June 1917.

Max-Page, C., Some Reflections on the Development of War Surgery, *Royal Army Medical Corps Journal*, LXXIV (April 1940).

Mitchell, T. J., Man-power and the Medical Service in Relation to Some of the Principles of War, *Proc. Roy. Soc. Med. (War Sect.)*, XX (1927).

and Smith, G. M., *Medical Services: Casualties and Medical Statistics of the Great War* (1931).

Mitchiner, P. H., Thoughts on Four Years of War Surgery – 1939 to 1943, *Br. Med. Jnl.*, 8 July 1944.

Mortara, G., *La salute publica in Italia durante e dopo la guerra* (Bari, 1925).

Mott, F. W., Mental Hygiene and Shell Shock during and after the War, *Br. Med. Jnl.*, 14 July 1917.

et al., Special Discussion on Shell Shock without Visible Signs of Injury, *Proc. Roy. Soc. Med. (Psychiatry Sect.)*, IX (1916).

Myers, R. S., *Shell Shock on France 1914–1918* (Cambridge, 1940).

Ogilvie, W. H., Surgical Advances during the War, *Jnl. Roy. Army Med. Corps*, LXXV (Dec. 1945).

Osler, W., *Bacilli and Bullets*, Oxford War Pamphlets no. 30 (1914).

War, Wounds, and Disease, *Quarterly Review*, CCXXIV (July 1915).

Science and War, *Lancet*, 9 Oct. 1915.

Science and War (Oxford 1915).

Patavel, J. E., Engineering and Science during the War, *Rpt. 87th Mtg. Br. Assoc. Advan. Sci. (Trans. Sect. G)* (1920).

Pear, T. H., The War and Psychology, *Nature*, 3 Oct. 1918.

Pirquet, C., *Volksgesundheit im Krieg* (Vienna, 1926).

Poulton, E. B., *Science and the Great War* (1915).

Prinzing, F., *Epidemics Resulting from Wars* (Oxford, 1916).

Read, C. S., War Psychiatry, *Proc. Roy. Soc. Med. (Psych. Sect.)*, XII (1919).

Redenour, L. N. (ed.), *Radar System Engineering* (1947).

Rees, J. R., *The Shaping of Psychiatry by War* (1945).

Rexford-Welch, S. C., *The Royal Air Force Medical Services* (4 vols, 1954–8).
Rivers, W. H. R., The Repression of War Experience, *Lancet*, 2 Feb. 1918.
Ross, T. A., *Lectures on War Neuroses* (1941).
Rousser, J., Médecine et histoire. Essai de pathologie urbaine. Les causes de morbidité et de mortalité à Lyon aux XVIIᵉ et XVIIIᵉ siècles, *Cahiers d'histoire publiés par les universités de Clermont, Lyon, Grenoble*, VIII (1963).
Ryle, J. A., Public Health in Great Britain during the War, *Nature*, 2 Nov. 1946.
Sargent, M. and Slater, E., De l'influence de la guerre 1939–1945 sur la psychiatrice britannique, *Journal Brasiliana Psyquiatria*, I (1952).
Sayer, A. P., *Army Radar* (1950).
Shaw, J. J. S., The Hospital Ship, 1608–1740, *Mariner's Mirror*, XXII (Oct. 1936).
Shekerjian, H., The Chemist's Role in National Defence, *Jnl. Roy. Utd. Ser. Inst.*, LXXXIII (Nov. 1938).
Smith, R. P., Mental Disorders in Civilians arising in Connection with the War, *Proc. Roy. Soc. Med. (Psych. Sect.)*, X (1917).
Stephens, H. E. R., The Influence of War on the Craft of Surgery, *Proc. Roy. Soc. Med. (United Services Sect.)*, XVII (1934).
Symonds, C. P., Anxiety Neurosis in Combatants, *Lancet*, 25 Dec. 1943.
Thorpe, T. E., Sulphuric Acid and the War, *Nature*, 11 April 1918.
Titmuss, R. M., *Problems of Social Policy* (1950).
    War and Social Policy, in *Essays on 'the Welfare State'* (1960).
Tizard, H. T., Science and the Services, *Jnl. Roy. Utd. Ser. Inst.*, XCI (Aug. 1946).
Torrie, A., Psychoanalytic Casualties in the Middle East, *Lancet*, 29 Jan. 1944.
Turner, E. H., Naval Medical Services 1793–1815. *Mariner's Mirror*, XLVI (1960).
Turner, W. A., Neuroses and Psychoses of War, *Jnl. Roy. Army Med. Corps*, XXXI (Nov. 1918).
Valabras, V. C., Observations sur la taille moyenne du conscrit grec, *Académie d'Athènes*, XVI (1941).
    Le taille et le poids moyen des écoliers grecs pendant la guerre, *Académie d'Athènes*, XIX (1944).
Watson, W. N. B., Two British Naval Surgeons of the French Wars, *Medical History*, XIII (July 1969).
Whitby, L., Transfusion in Peace and War, *Lancet*, 6 Jan. 1945.
Willey, F. E., War and the Medical Education of Women, *Lancet*, 9 Oct. 1915.
Wittkower, E., and Spillane, J. P., Neuroses in War, *Br. Med. Jnl.*, 10, 17, 24 Feb. 1940.
Woker, G., Chemical and Bacteriological Warfare, in Inter-Parliamentary Union, *What Would Be the Character of a New War?* (1933).
Wolf, K. M., Evacuation of Children in Wartime: a Survey of the Literature, in *The Psychoanalytic Study of the Child*, I (1945).
Zuckerman, Sir S., *Scientists and War* (1966).
Chemotherapy of War Wounds, *Br. Med. Jnl.*, 9 Nov. 1940.
Committee of Privy Council for Medical Research, *Medical Research in War: Report of the Medical Research Council for the Years 1939–45*, Cmd 7335 (1946).
Effects of the War on Scientific Undertakings, *Nature*, 10 Dec. 1914.
Med. Res. Coun., *An Inquiry into the Prevalence and Aetiology of Tuberculosis among Industrial Workers with Special Reference to Female Munitions Workers*, Spec. Rpt. Ser. no. 22 (1918).
    Report of the Committee on Tuberculosis in Wartime, Spec. Rpt. Ser. no. 12 (1917).
The Organization of the Medical Profession in Wartime, *Br. Med. Jnl.*, 7 July 1945.

Penicillin in Warfare: Special Issue of the British Journal of Surgery (1941).
Progress in the Psychiatry of War, *Br. Med. Jnl.*, 30 June 1945.
The War and the Health of the Country, *Lancet*, 12 Sept. 1914.
The War and the Standard of Medical Education, *Lancet*, 28 Nov. 1914.
War-Time Developments in Metals and Alloys, *Nature*, 30 Aug. 1947.
War-Time Progress in X-Ray Analysis, *Nature*, 24 Aug. 1946.

Trade and investment

Behrens, C. B. A., *Merchant Shipping and the Demands of War* (1955).
Bowley, A. L., *The Effect of the War on the External Trade of the United Kingdom* (Cambridge, 1915).
Butch, P., Guerre et commerce: L'activité du port de Bordeaux sous le Régime des licences, 1808–15, *Rev. d'h. mod. contemp.* xix (1972).
Butel, P., Les difficultés du commerce maritime bordelais sous le Directoire: exemple de l'adaptation à la conjoncture de guerre maritime, *Actes du 94e congrès national des sociétés savantes (sect. d'h. mod. contemp.)*, ii (Paris, 1971).
Cangardel, H., *La Marine marchande française et la guerre* (Paris, 1927).
Chaloner, W. H., Hazards of Trade with France in Time of War, 1776–1783, *Business History*, vi (June 1964).
Clark, G. N., *The Dutch Alliance and the War against Dutch Trade 1688–1697* (1923).
War Trade and Trade War, 1701–1713, *Econ. Hist. Rev.*, i (1927–28).
Davis, R., *The Trade and Shipping of Hull, 1500–1700* (York, 1964).
Devine, T. M., Transport Problems of Glasgow West India Merchants during the American War of Independence 1775–83, *Transport History*, iv (Nov. 1971).
Farnell, J. E., The Navigation Act of 1651, the First Dutch War and the London Merchant Community, *Econ. Hist. Rev.*, 2nd ser., xvi (1964).
Fitton, R. S., Overseas Trade during the Napoleonic Wars as Illustrated by the Records of W. G. and J. Strutt, *Economica*, n.s., xx (1953).
Fohlen, C., La Guerre de Secession et le commerce franco-américain, *Rev. d'h. mod. contemp.*, n.s., viii (1961).
Hillman, H. O., Analysis of Germany's Foreign Trade and the War, *Economica*, vii (1940).
Iatsounski, W. R., De l'influence du blocus continental sur l'industrie cotonnière russe, *Annales hist. Rév. fr.*, xxxvi (1964).
Johnston, J. A., Parliament and the Protection of Trade 1689–1694, *Mariner's Mirror*, lvii (Nov. 1971).
Kendall, M., Losses of U.K. Merchant Ships in World War II, *Economica*, xv (1947–48).
Kent, H. S. K., *War and Trade in the Northern Seas* (Cambridge, 1973).
Kerr, G. F., *Business in Great Waters: the War History of the P & O* (1953).
Kerviler, G. de, *La Navigation intérieure en France pendant la guerre* (Paris, 1926).
Monchy, E. P., de, *Commerce and Navigation* (1928).
Muron, P., *L'Organisation des achats sur les marchés étrangers en France durant la guerre* (Paris, 1945).
Paish, F. W., Economic Incentive in Wartime, *Economica*, viii (1941).
Salter, J. A., *Allied Shipping Control* (Oxford, 1921).
Schweitzer, A., The Role of Foreign Trade in the Nazi War Economy, *Journal of Political Economy*, li (1943).
Syrett, P., *Shipping and the American War, 1775–83: A Study of British Transport* (1970).
Zeller, G., Le commerce internationale en temps de guerre sous l'ancien régime,

Rev. d'h. mod. contemp., n.s., IV (1957).

La mise à la disposition de l'Allemagne de la flotte de commerce française, *Cahiers d'histoire de la guerre*, 4 (May 1950).

War administration

General

Anderson, A. V., Administration of Occupied and Liberated Territories during the 1939–45 War, *Jnl. Roy. Utd. Ser. Inst.*, XCII (Feb. 1947).

Anderson, O., *A Liberal State at War. English Politics and Economics during the Crimean War* (1967).

Asterov, N., The Municipal Government and the All Russian Union of Towns, in Gronsky, P., *The War and the Russian Government* (New Haven, 1929).

Baugh, D., *British Naval Administration in the Age of Walpole* (Princeton, N. J., 1965).

Baumont, M., Abel Ferry et les étapes du controle aux armées, 1914–1918, *Revue d'histoire moderne et contemporaine*, XV (1968).

Cailland, F. C., The Economics of War, *Army Quarterly*, XXIV (1932).

Chappell, E., *Samuel Pepys as a Naval Administrator* (Cambridge 1933).

Crimmin, P. K., Admiralty Relations with the Treasury 1783–1806: The Preparation of Naval Estimates and the Beginnings of Treasury Control, *Mariner's Mirror*, LIII (Feb. 1967).

Davies, C. S. L., The Administration of the Royal Navy under Henry VIII, *Eng. Hist. Rev.*, LXXX (April 1965).

Dearle, N. B., *Dictionary of Official War-Time Organizations* (1928).

Dobb, M., *Soviet Economy and the War* (New York, 1943).

Franks, O., *Central Planning and Control in War and Peace* (1947).

Gronski, P. P., L'administration civile des gouvernements russes occupés par l'armée française en 1812, *Rev. d'h. mod. contemp.*, III (1928).

The Central Government, in *The War and the Russian government* (New Haven, 1929).

Hogg, O. F. G., The Dawn of Ordnance Administration, *Journal of the Royal Artillery*, LIX (1932–3).

Hurcumb, C., The Coordination of Transport in Great Britain during the Years 1935–1944, *Journal of the Institute of Transport*, XXII (1946).

James, G. F., and Shaw, J. J. S., Admiralty Administration and Personnel, 1619–1714, *Bull. Inst. Hist. Res.*, XIV (1936–7).

Keith, A. B., *War Government of the British Dominions* (Oxford, 1921).

Kennedy, D. E., The Establishment and Settlement of Parliament's Admiralty 1642–1648, *Mariner's Mirror*, XLVIII (Nov. 1962).

Lloyd, E. M. H., *Experiments in State Control at the War Office and Ministry of Food* (Oxford, 1924).

Michaud, H., Aux origines du secrétariat de'Etat à la guerre: le règlements de 1617–1619, *Rev. d'h. mod. contemp.*, XIX (1972).

Montgomery of Alamein, Organization for War in Modern Times, *Jnl. Roy. Utd. Ser. Inst.*, C (Nov. 1955).

Newhall, R. A., *Muster and Review: A Problem of English Military Administration 1420–1440* (Cambridge, Mass., 1940).

Oppenheim, M., *The Administration of the Royal Navy, 1509–1660* (1896).

Polner, T. J., *Russian Local Government during the War and the Union of Zemstvos* (New Haven, 1930).

Pool, B., *Navy Board Contracts 1660–1832: Contract Administration under the Navy Board* (1966).
Redlich, J., *Austrian War Government* (New Haven, Conn., 1929).
Renouvin, P., *The Forms of War Government in France* (New Haven, Conn., 1927).
Roll, E., *The Combined Food Board: A Study in Wartime International Planning* (Stanford, Calif., 1956).
Slee, J. A., Control of Radio-Telegraphy in Time of War, *Jnl. Roy. Utd. Ser. Inst.*, LXXI (Feb. 1926).
Willson, F. M. G., and Chester, D. N., *The Organisation of British Central Government 1914–1956* (1957).

Finance and economic policy
Anderson, O., Loans versus Taxes: British Financial Policy in the Crimean War, *Econ. Hist. Rev.*, 2nd ser., XVI, 2 (1963–4).
Apostol, P. N., *Credit Operators of the Russian Government during the War* (1928).
Arnoult, P., Comment pour acheter notre économie les Allemands prirent nos finances, *Cahiers d'histoire de la guerre*, 4 (May 1950).
  Les finances de la France en l'occupation allemande (1940–1944) (Paris, 1951).
Artaud, D., La Grande-Bretagne en lutte contre l'inflation (1939–1945), *Revue d'histoire de la deuxième guerre mondiale*, XIX (1969).
Ashworth, W., *Contracts and Finance* (1959).
Baudhuin, F., *Le Financement des guerres* (Louvain, 1944).
  Les Finances de 1939 à 1949. III. la Belgique et la Hollande (Collections d'histoire financière) (Paris, 1951).
Baykov, A., Remarks on the Experience in the Organisation of 'War Economy' in the USSR, *Econ. Jnl.*, XXIV (1941).
Benham, F., The Taxation of War Wealth, *Economica*, VIII (1941).
Bordewijk, H. W. C., War Finances in the Netherlands 1918–1922, *The Costs of the War* (New Haven, Conn., 1928).
Brugmans, I. J., *Paardenkracht en mensenmacht, sociaal-economische geschiedenis van Nederland, 1795–1940* (Hague, 1961).
Carr, R., Two Swedish Financiers: Louis de Geer and Joel Griepenstierna, in Bell, H. E. and Ollard, R. L. (eds.), *Historical Essays Presented to David Ogg* (1963).
Cathala, P., *Face aux réalités. La direction des finances françaises sous l'occupation* (Paris, 1948).
Clapham, J. H., Loans and Subsidies in Time of War, 1793–1924, *Econ. Jnl.*, XXVII (Dec. 1917).
Clementel, E., *La France et la politique économique interallié* (Paris, 1931).
Davenport, H. J., The War-tax Paradox, *Amer. Econ. Rev.*, IX, 1 (March 1919).
Davies, E. F., *The Finances of Great Britain and Germany* (1916).
Dieterlen, P., Les finances françaises depuis l'armistice, in *Nouvel aspect des institutions françaises* (Paris, 1942).
Doucet, R., Les finances anglaises en France à la fin de la guerre de Cent Ans (1413–1435), *Le Moyen Âge*, XXXVI (1926).
Einaudi, L., *La finanza della guerra a delle opere pubbliche* (Turin, 1914).
  Il problema della finanza post bellica (Milan, 1920).
  La guerre e il sistema tributario italiono (Bari, 1927).
Einzig, P., *Economic Warfare* (1940).
  Economic Warfare, 1938–1940 (1941).
Engberg, J., Royalist Finance during the English Civil War, 1642–1646, *Scandinavian Economic History Review*, XIV (1966).

Flier, M. J., van der, *War Finances in the Netherlands up to 1918* (Oxford, 1923).

Freeman, A. Z., The King's Penny: the Headquarters Paymasters under Edward I 1295–1309, *Journal of British Studies*, VI (Nov. 1966).

Gibrin, Ch., Organisation de l'économie nationale pour les temps de guerre, *Mercure* (15 July 1939).

Goodwin, A., War Transport and 'Counter-revolution' in France in 1793: the Case of the Winter Company and the Financier Jean-Jacques de Beaune, in Foot, M. R. D. (ed.), *War and Society* (1973).

Hamilton, G. R. S., *Finance and War* (1910).

Harris, C., Finance of the Army, *Jnl. Roy. Utd. Ser. Inst.*, LXVI (May 1921).

Harris, S. E., *The Assignats* (Cambridge, Mass., 1930).

Hawtrey, R. G., The Collapse of the French Assignats, *Econ. Jnl.*, XXVIII (Sept. 1918).

Heckscher, E., Importance of the Financial Forces of a Country for Carrying on War – Possibility of Obtaining Credits Abroad, in Inter-Parliamentary Union, *What Would Be the Character of a New War?* (1933).

Henneman, J. B., *Royal Taxation in Fourteenth Century France: the Development of War Financing, 1322–1356* (Princeton, 1973).

Hirst, F. H., *Political Economy of War* (1915).

and Allan, J. E., *British War Budgets* (1926).

Hope-Jones, A., *Income Tax in the Napoleonic Wars* (Cambridge, 1939).

Hughes, J. R. F., Financing the British War Effort, *Jnl. Econ. Hist.*, XVIII, 2 (1958).

Jack, D. T., *Studies in Economic Warfare* (1940).

Jezé, G., *Les Finances de guerre de la France* (5 vols, Paris, 1915–20).

et al., *Problèmes de politique et finance de guerre* (Paris, 1915).

Johnson, A., War Economics, in *Encyclopedia of Social Sciences*, XV (New York, 1935).

Johnson, J. E., *Conscription of Wealth in Time of War* (New York, 1930).

Jones, J. H., Financial Theory and the Distribution of War Costs, *Pol. Q.*, II (Sept. 1916).

Joslin, D. M., London Bankers in Wartime 1739–84, in L. S. Pressnell (ed.), *Studies in the Industrial Revolution* (1960).

Judges, A. V., Philip Burlamachi: a Financier of the Thirty Years' War, *Economica*, VI (1926).

Kalecki, M., War Finance in 1940, 1941 and 1942, *Bull. Oxf. Inst. of Stat.*, V (26 June 1943).

Katzenbach, E. L., Liberals at War: the Economic Policies of the Government of National Defence, 1870–1871, *American Historical Review*, LVI, 4 (July 1951).

Keynes, J. H., The Income and Fiscal Potential of Great Britain, *Econ. Jnl.*, XLIX (1939).

Kirby, J. L., The Financing of Calais under Henry V, *Bull. Inst. Hist. Res.*, XXIII (Nov. 1950).

Koser, R., 'Die preussischen Finanzen im Siebenjaehrigen Kriege', in *Forschungen zur Breandenurgischen und Preussischen Geschichte*, XVI (1903).

Lachapelle, G., *Nos finances pendant la guerre* (Paris, 1915).

Langenhoven, F., van, *L'Action du governement belge en matière économique pendant la guerre* (Paris, 1927).

Laufenburger, H., La vie économique de la France au seuil de l'année, 1943, *Revue de l'economie contemporaine* (Feb. 1943).

Credit public et finances de guerre, 1914–44 (Paris, 1944).

Les Finances de 1939 à 1945 (Paris, 1947).

Lauterbach, A. T., *Economies in Uniform* (Princeton, N.J., 1943).

Lawson, W. R., *Modern Wars and War Taxes* (Edinburgh, 1912).

British War Finance, 1914–15 (1915).

Leighton, R. M., Les armes ou les armées: origines de la politique d' 'arsenal de la démocratie', *Revue d'histoire de la deuxième guerre mondiale*, XVII (1967).

Lindholm, R. W., German Finance in World War II, *Amer. Econ. Rev.*, XXXVII (1947).

Libelli, M. H., *Economia e finanze de guerre* (Florence, 1927).

Lotz, W., *Die deutsche Staatsfinanzwirtschaft im Krieg* (Stuttgart, 1927).

Madge, C., Public Opinion and Paying for the War, *Econ. Jnl.*, n.s., II (1941).

Maizels, A., Consumption, Investment and National Expenditure in Wartime, *Economica*, VIII (1941).

Michel, B., Le sabotage des emprints de guerre autrichiens par les banque tchèques, 1914–1916, *Rev. d'h. mod. contemp.*, n.s., XV (1968).

Mikhel'son, A., *Revenue and Expenditure of the Russian Government during the War* (1928).

Le Financement de la guerre et les problèmes de la reconstruction (Paris, 1945).

Mousnier, R., L'évolution des finances publiques en France et en Angleterre pendant les guerres de la Ligue d'Augsbourg et de la Succession d'Espagne, *Revue historique*, CCV (1951).

Nicholson, J. S., *War Finance* (1917).

Nogaro, B., *Le Financement de dépenses publique et la liquidation des dépenses de guerre* (Paris, 1945).

Pentlen, H., *Krieg und Finanzen* (Hamburg, 1935).

Petzina, D., La politique financière et fiscale de l'Allemagne pendant la seconde guerre mondiale, *Revue d'histoire de la deuxième guerre mondiale*, XIX (1969).

Pigou, A. C., Sources and Methods for Paying for the War, *Contemporary Review*, CVIII (1915).

Government Control in War and Peace, *Econ. Jnl.*, XXVIII (Dec. 1918).

Popovics, S., *Das Geldwesen im Kriege* (Vienna, 1925).

Prestwich, J. O., War and Finance in the Anglo-Norman State, *Proceedings of the Royal Historical Society*, IV (1954).

Radclyffe, R., *The War and Finance* (1914).

Rappard, W. E., Le financement de la guerre de l'indépendence helvétique (Guerre de Souabe, 1499), in *Mélanges d'études économiques et sociales* (Génèva, 1945).

Rasin, A., *Financial Policy of Czecho-Slovakia during the First Year of its History* (Oxford, 1923).

Rossiter, W. S., The Statistical Side of the Economic Costs of War, *Amer. Econ. Rev.*, VI (March 1916), supplt.

Sayers, R. S., *Financial Policy 1939–1945* (1956).

Scaynetti, E., La politica monetari a dell'Inghilterra durante e dopo la guerre mondiale, *Rivista di politica economica*, LVI 12 (1966).

Scott, W. R., Economics of Peace in Time of War, *Rpt. 85th Mtg. Br. Assoc. Advan. Sci. (Trans. Sect. F)* (1916).

Scherbening, E., *Wirtschaftsorganisation im Kriege* (Jena, 1938).

Sella, D., War Finance and Industry in Seventeenth Century Lombardy, *Third International Conference of Economic History* (Vienna, 1965).

Silberling, N. J., Financial and Monetary Policy of Great Britain during the Napoleonic Wars, *Quarterly Journal of Economics*, I–II (1924).

Spiegel, H. W., *The Economics of Total War* (New York, 1942).

Sprague, O. M. W., The Conscription of Income: a Sound Basis for War Finance, *Econ. Jnl.*, xxvii (March 1917).

Stamp, J. C., *Taxation during the War* (1932).

Steel, A., The Financial Background of the War of the Roses, *History*, xl (1955).

Stevenson, D., The Financing of the Cause of the Covenants, *Scottish Historical Review*, li (1972).

Truchy, H., *Les Finances de guerre de la France* (Paris, 1926).

Viner, J., Who Paid for the War?, *Journal of Political Economy*, xxviii (Jan. 1920).

Vissering, G., The Netherlands Bank and the War, *Econ. Jnl.*, xxvii (Jan. 1917).

von Willisen, F., *Begriff und Wesen des Wirtschaftskrieges* (Jena, 1919).

Wemmer, Jan. L'effort financier et militaire de la Pologne au xviie siècle, *Rev. int. d'h. milit.*, xxviii (1969).

Wilson, C., Taxation and the Decline of Empires, an Unfashionable Theme, *Bijdragen in Mededelingen van het Historisch Genootschap*, lxxvii (1963).

Wurmser, O., Organisation économique de la nation en temps de guerre, *Revue d'économie politique*, 53 (March, April 1939).

Yoshpe, H. B., Economic Mobilization Planning between the Two World Wars, *Military Affairs*, xv (1951).

British War Finance, *Round Table*, xxiv (June 1944).

Lombard Street in War, *Round Table*, iv (Sept. 1914).

Le marché noir allemand en France, *Cahiers d'histoire de la guerre*, 4 (May 1950).

War and Financial Exhaustion, *Round Table*, v (Dec. 1914).

Food Supply

Bachi, R., *L'alimentazione e la politica annonaria in Italia (con une appendice su 'Il rifornimento dei viveri dell'esercuro italiano', di G. Zingali)* (Bari, 1926).

Beveridge, W. H., *British Food Control* (1928).

Blagburn, C. H., Lessons of Wartime Control of Milk and Livestock, *Proc. Ag. Econ. Soc.*, vii (June 1946).

Burley, S. J., The Victualling of Calais 1347–1365, *Bull. Inst. Hist. Res.*, xxi (May 1958).

Campbell, H., Food Economics in Relation to the War, *Lancet*, 25 March, 1, 8 April 1916.

Clynes, J. R., Food Control in War and Peace, *Econ. Jnl.*, xxx (June 1920).

Collinet, P., et Stahl, P., *Le Revitaillement de la France occupée* (Paris, 1928).

Davies, J. L., Milk in Wartime, *Proc. Ag. Econ. Soc.*, vii (June 1946).

Galpin, W. F., *The Grain Supply of England during the Napoleonic Period* (New York, 1925).

Gide, C., *Consumers' Co-operative Societies* (Manchester, 1921).

Hammond, R. J., British Food Supplies 1914–1939, *Econ. Hist. Rev.*, xvi (1946). *Food* (3 vols, 1951–62). *Food and Agriculture in Britain, 1939–45. Aspects of wartime control* (Stanford, Calif., 1954).

Henry, A., *Le Revitaillement de la Belgique pendant l'occupation allemande* (Paris, 1924).

Kayden, E. H., *The Cooperative Movement in Russia during the War* (New Haven, 1929).

Lampett, L. H., The Development of the Home Production of Food, *Br. Med. Jnl.*, 29 June 1940.

The Function of the Food Industry, *Br. Med. Jnl.*, 6 July 1940.

Middleton, T. H., *Food Production in War* (Oxford, 1923).

Pearce, B., Elizabethan Food Policy and the Armed Forces, *Econ. Hist. Rev.*, XII (1942).

Renwick, G., Our Supply of Food Stuffs and Raw Materials in Time of War, *Jnl. Roy. Utd. Ser. Inst.*, LVI (April 1912).

Starling, E. H., The Food Supply of Germany during the War, *Jnl. Roy. Stat. Soc.*, LXXXIII (March 1920).

Stern, W. M., The Bread Crisis in Britain, 1795–1796, *Economica*, XXXI (1964).

Struve, P. B., *Food Supply in Russia during the World War* (New Haven, 1930).

Wise, E. F., The History of the Ministry of Food, *Econ. Jnl.*, XXXIX (1929).

Wood, A., Increase in the Cost of Food for Different Classes of Society since the Outbreak of War, *Jnl. Roy. Stat. Soc.*, LXXIX (July 1916).

The Problem of Food Shortage in Europe, *Round Table*, XXI (Dec. 1940).

War supplies and preparations for war

Albion, R. G., *Forests and Sea Power: the Timber Problem of the Royal Navy 1652–1862* (Cambridge, Mass., 1926).

Aylmer, G. E., The Last Years of Purveyance 1610–1699, *Econ. Hist. Rev.*, 2nd ser., X (1957–8).

Binz, G. L., *Die Erforschung der Wehrgrundlagen* (Munich, 1935).

Bovill, E. W., Queen Elizabeth's Gunpowder, *Mariner's Mirror*, XXXIII (July 1947).

Bown, R. A., Royal Castle-building in England 1154–1216, *Eng. Hist. Rev.*, LXX (1915).

Burton, I. F., The Supply of Infantry for the War in the Peninsula, 1703–1707, *Bull. Inst. Hist. Res.*, XXVIII (May 1955).

Carroll, B. A., *Design for Total War. Arms and Economics in the Third Reich* (Hague, 1968).

Chardon, J., *L'Organisation de la République pour la paix* (Paris, 1926).

Cole, G. D. H., British Capitalism and War Preparation, *Modern Quarterly* (Jan. 1939).

    The Economic Consequences of War Preparation, in Russell, B., *et al.*, *Dare We Look Ahead?* (1939).

Cooper, H. J., War and the Businessman, *Jnl. Roy. Utd. Ser. Inst.*, LXXXIV (Sept. 1940).

De Gaulle, C., Mobilization économique à l'etranger, *Revue militaire française*, CIV (Jan. 1934).

Einzig, P., *The Economics of Rearmament* (1934).

Fayle, C. E., The Supply of Raw Materials in Time of War, *Jnl. Roy. Utd. Ser. Inst.*, LXXII (Aug. 1927).

    Economic Aspects of Empire Defence, *Jnl. Roy. Utd. Ser. Inst.*, LXXIX (May 1934).

Förster, K. W., *Verkehrswirtschaft und Krieg* (Hamburg, 1937).

Green, J. F., Economic Mobilization of Great Britain, *Foreign Policy Reports*, XV, 8 (1 July 1939).

Hesse, K., *Kriegsfuhrung und Kriegswirtschaft im Feindesland* (Hamburg, 1936).

Hewitt, H. J., *The Organization of War under Edward III, 1338–1362* (Manchester, 1966).

Higham, R., Government, Companies and National Defense: British Aeronautical Experience, 1918–1945 as the Basis for a Broad Hypothesis, *Business History Review*, XXXIX (1965).

Hobson, C. K., Economic Mobilization for War, *Sociological Review*, VIII (July 1915).

Hoch, E., *Die Wehrkraft der Wirtschaft* (Hamburg, 1937).

Hodsoll, E. J., The Defense of the Population against Air Attacks, *Jnl. Roy. Utd. Ser. Inst.*, LXXX (Nov. 1935).

Hooker, J. R., Notes on the Organization and Supply of the Tudor Military under Henry VII, *Huntington Library Quarterly*, XXIII (Nov. 1959).

House, F., *Timber at War* (1965).

Hurtsfield, J., *The Control of Raw Materials* (1953).

Jenkins, R., Civil Aspects of Air Defence, *Jnl. Roy. Utd. Ser. Inst.*, LXXII (Aug. 1927).

Jusselin, M., Comment la France se preparait à la guerre de Cent ans, *Bibliothèque de l'Ecole des Chartes*, LXXIII (1912).

Klein, B. H., *Germany's Economic Preparations for War* (Cambridge, Mass., 1959).

Leslie, J. H., The Honourable the Board of Ordinance 1299–1855, *Jnl. Soc. Army Hist. Res.*, IV (July–Sept. 1925).

Macmillan, H., *Economic Aspects of Defence* (1939).

MacGregor, D. H., War and Supplies in Reference to Wool, *Pol. Q.*, II (1916).

Marriot, S. A. R., The Conscription of Wealth, *Ninteeenth Century*, LXXIX (Jan. 1916).

Payton-Smith, D. J., *Oil: A Study of War-time Policy and Administration* (1971).

Pollock, F., Influences of Preparedness on Western European Economic Life, *Amer. Econ. Rev.*, XXX, 1 (March 1940), supplt.

Rawson, S. W., Steel Supplies in War, *Jnl. Roy. Utd. Ser. Inst.*, XCVI (Aug. 1951).

Redlich, F., *The German Military Enterpriser and His Work Force: A Study of European Economic and Social History* (2 vols, Wiesbaden, 1964, 1965).

Rehfeld, P., Die preussische Ruestungindustrie unter Friedrich dem Grossen, *Forschungen zur Braendenburgischen und Preussischen Geschichte*, XVI (1903).

Reid, W., Commonwealth Supply Departments with the Tower and the Committee of London Merchants, *Guildhall Miscellany*, II (Sept. 1966).

Reuter, P., La nationalisation des usines de guerre, *Revue d'économie politique*, CIII (March, April 1939).

Richard, C. *Le Comité de Salut Public et les fabrications de guerre sous la Terreur* (Paris, 1922).

Schiff, W., The Influence of the German Armed Forces and War Industry on Argentina 1880–1914, *Hispanic American Historical Review*, LII (1972).

Schmitt, J., *Kriegsweichtige Industrie im System der Wirtschaftspolitik* (Berlin, 1937).

Scott, J. D., and Hughes, R., *Administration of War Production* (1955).

Shaw, G. C., *Supply in Modern War* (1938).

Smith, R. E., La mobilisation économique, *Revue d'histoire de la deuxième guerre mondiale*, XVII (1967).

Stafford, J., Planning for War, *Econ. Jnl.*, L (1940).

Stead, H. W., Armament and Disarmament since 1918, *Jnl. Roy. Utd. Ser. Inst.*, LXXVI (Feb. 1932).

von Blume, W., *Die Grundlagen userer Wehrkraft* (Berlin, 1899).

Ward, S. G. P., The Quartermaster-General's Department in the Peninsula 1809–1814, *Jnl. Soc. Army Hist. Res.*, XXIII (1945).

Weydert, J., L'organisation commerciale de la batellerie allemande sur le Rhin (1900–1945), *Rev. d'h. mod. contemp.*, n.s., III (1956).

Williamson, G. W., Aircraft Supply 1914–1918, *Jnl. Roy. Utd. Ser. Inst.*, LXXXIV (Feb. 1939).

Official History of the Ministry of Munitions (12 vols 1922).

Miscellaneous

Beller, E. A., *Propaganda in Germany during the Thirty Years' War* (Princeton, 1940).

Bossuet, R., Réflexions sur le deuxième cycle de la Croisade, *Le Moyen Âge*, LXIV (1958).

Crossman, R. H. S., Psychological Warfare, *Jnl. Roy. Utd. Ser. Inst.*, XCVII (Aug. 1952).

Gallup, G., How Important is Public Opinion in Time of War?, *Proc. Amer. Phil. Soc.*, LXXXV (1942).

Hale, J., War and Opinion: War and Public Opinion in the 15th and 16th Centuries, *Past & Present*, 22 (1962).

Hesse, K., *Der kriegswirtschaftliche Gedanke* (Hamburg, 1935).

Higham, R. (ed.), *A Guide to the Sources of British Military History* (1972).

Hill, A. N., *et al.*, *War and Insurance* (1927).

Huxley, J. S., The Growth of a Group-mind in Britain under the Influence of War, *Hibbert Journal*, XXXIX (July 1941).

Lasswell, H., *Propaganda Technique in the World War* (1927).

Lawson, W., Origins of the Military Road from Newcastle to Carlisle, *Archeologia Aeliana*, XLIV (1966).

Lena, F., *Macht und Wirtschaft: Die Voraussetzungen des modernen Krieges* (Berlin, 1916).

Lewis, P. S., War Propaganda and Historiography in Fifteenth-century France and England, *Trans. Roy. Hist. Soc.*, 5th ser., XV (1965).

Lockhart, R. H. B., Political Warfare, *Jnl. Roy. Utd. Ser. Inst.*, XCV (May 1950).

Lorenz, C., *Die Statistik in der Kriegswirtschaft* (Hamburg, 1936).

McKenna, J. W., Henry VI of England the Dual Monarchy: Aspects of Royal Political Propaganda 1422–1432, *Journal of the Warburg and Courtauld Institutes*, XXVIII (1965).

O'Brien, T. H., *Civil Defense* (1955).

Odinets, D. M., *Russian Schools and Universities in the World War* (New Haven, 1929).

Pirenne, J. et Vauthier, M., *La Législation et l'administration allemandes en Belgique* (Paris, 1925).

Redlich, F., *De Praeda Militari. Looting and Booty 1500–1815* (Wiesbaden, 1956).

Richardson, L. F., *Mathematical Psychology of War* (Oxford, 1919).

Rowe, B. J. H., King Henry VI's Claim to France in Picture and Poem, *The Librarian*, 4th ser., XIII (1933).

Silberner, B., *La Guerre dans la pensée économique du 16ᵉ au 18ᵉ siècle* (Paris, 1939).
 The Problem of War in Nineteenth Century Economic Thought, trans. by A. M. Krappe (Princeton, NJ, 1946).

Squires, J. D., *British Propaganda at Home and in the United States from 1914 to 1917* (Cambridge, Mass., 1935).

Stern, W. M., Wehrwirtschaft: A German Contribution to Economics, *Econ. Hist. Rev.*, 2nd ser., XIII (1960–1).

Westmoreland, H. C., Propaganda in War, *Jnl. Roy. Utd. Ser. Inst.*, LXXXVIII (Feb. 1943).

The Psychological Effect of War, *Br. Med. Jnl.*, 13 March 1916.

Index

Abbe, E., 168
Acland, A. H. D., 201
Addison, C., 156, 172
agriculture: effects of Eighty Years' War on Flemish and Dutch, 53, 59; effects of Napoleonic Wars on British, 97, 98; effects of First World War on German, 229ff.
Air Board (British), 175, 182
Albert, Archduke of Netherlands, 54
Aldis & Co., 198, 199
Alva, Duke of, 59, 64
Amersfoort, 109
Amiens, 63
Amsterdam, 59, 60, 113, 114, 127, 133, 136; effects of Eighty Years' War on economy of, 60–1, 62, 63
Amsterdam Exchange Bank, 59
Anson, G., 76
Antwerp, 51, 52, 53, 63
Appelius, J. H., 116, 120, 124, 126, 128, 134
Armstrongs Ltd, 145, 146, 147, 148, 155, 157
Army of Flanders, Spanish, 54, 55, 64
Asquith, H. H., 143, 156, 172, 197
Attlee, C., 241
Augureau, P. F. C., 116

Bacon, Sir R., 157
Baker, W., 2
Balfour Committee on Essential Industries (1917), 188, 189
Banbury, Sir F., 217
Bankes Commission (1936), 157, 158
Barr, A. J. W., 206
Barr & Stroud Ltd, 173, 176, 198, 199
Batavian Revolution, effects of on Dutch finance, 103ff.
Beaverbrook, Lord, 219, 220, 223
Beck, C., 188, 201
Beck, R. and J., 176, 195
Beit, O., 201
Bentinck van Rhoon, W., 106
Bethmann-Hollweg, T. von, 229

Bevan, E. J., 206
Beveridge, W., 4, 239ff.
Beveridge Committee on Social Insurance and Allied Services (1941–2), and Report (1942), 239ff.
Bevin, E., 241, 243
Bilbao, 57
Blaeu, J., 58
Blair, Dr Robert, 74, 80
Blair, Sir Robert, 185, 201
Blane, Sir Gilbert, 74, 77, 78, 79, 80, 81, 83, 84, 85, 86
Bleiswijk, 128
Blok, B., 113
Board of Invention and Research (British), 197
Boit, O., 201
Bolton Priory, 16, 21, 25, 26
Bonaparte, Louis, 121, 125, 128
Bontemps, G., 167, 194
Bosch, B., 113
Boswell, Prof. G., 179, 181
Brabant, 51, 58, 65, 112, 132
Brackenbury, Sir H., 144, 145, 146, 147, 155
Braudel, Prof. F., 1, 3
Brienen, W. J. van, 125
Brienne, E. C. de L. de, 104
Brinkburn, 17
British Cellulose and Chemical Manufacturing Co. Ltd, 209, 221, 223
British Cellulose Inquiry Committee (1917–18) and Report (1919), 210, 214, 220–1, 222, 223
British Optical Society, 169, 171, 195
British Potash Co., 181
British Science, Guild, 170, 171, 196, 197
Bruges, 53
Brussels, 53
Bryan, C. G., 226
Buchanan, W., 82
Bull, Sir W., 218
Burgos, 57

Caillard, Sir V., 157
Camperdown, Battle of, 114
Canneman, E., 127
Carnegie Endowment for International Peace, 3
Carson, Sir E., 245
Cattenburgh, Copes van, 127
Central Institute of Technical Optics, 169, 171, 186, 195
Chadwick, E., 86
Chance Bros. Co. Ltd, 167, 168, 169, 170–6, 182, 185, 190, 194, 195, 198
Chance, Sir H., 189, 192, 194
Chance, K., 181
Charles V, 47, 54
Charlottenburg Reichanstalt, 169
Cheshire, F. J., 172, 176, 186, 188, 201
Chester, D. N., 251
Chesterton, G. K., 219
Chilworth Gunpowder Co., 213
Churchill, Sir W., 243
City and Guilds of London Institute, 172
Clapham, Prof. J. H., 2
Clare estates, 25
Clark, Sir G. N., 2, 3
Clausewitz, C. von, 1
Clavel, A., 207, 209, 211
Coal Commission (1926), 249
Cobb, Prof. J. W., 179
Cochon de Lapparent, C., 111
Cody, S. F., 206
Colchester, 18
Cole, G. D. H., 246
Coleman, Prof. D. C., 3
Collins, G., 217
Conrady, A., 185, 186
Cook, James, 76, 80, 83
Corbridge, T. de, Archbishop of York, 24
Cornwall, Earl of, 15, 16
Courtaulds Ltd, 215, 216, 217, 222
Crawfurd, G., 103
Creagh-Osborne, F., 201
Cripps, Sir S., 245
Cromwell, Thomas, 34ff.
Crookes, Sir W., 180
Cross, C. F., 206
Crouzet, Prof. F., 6

Dallmeyer & Co., 199
Dalton, Hugh, 241
Dawson, Sir T., 145, 146, 208, 209, 210, 211, 218
Delacroix, C., 115
Delfzijl, 109
Derby Crown Glass Co., 174, 181, 190
de Smeth, T., 125
Deventer, Jacob van, 58

Dillon, J. B., 218
Dixmuide, 54
Dolland, J., 167
Dreyfus, Henry and Camille, 207, 209, 210, 211, 213, 215, 216, 217, 219, 220, 222, 223, 224
Dunkirk, 53, 64
Dunlop, Col. J., 150
Dunstable Priory, 18
Dutch East India Co., 60, 61, 64, 111
Dutch West India Co., 57, 61, 62, 64

East India Co. (British), 75
Edward I, 11, 12, 13, 14, 20, 21, 22, 23, 24
Edward II, 20, 22
Edward III, 22, 23, 24, 26
Edward IV, 33
Edward VI, 44
Eecke, 54
Ehrman, J., 6
Eichengrün, A., 206
Einaudi, L., 4
Eindhoven, 109
Elizabeth I, 44, 45, 46, 50
Esher Committee (1904), 141
Esslemont, A. D., 173, 176, 178, 181, 185, 188, 189, 198, 199, 201
Evergem, 50

Fabian Society, 251
Faraday, M., 167
Farr, W., 80
Fastolf, Sir J., 6
Fijnje, W., 115, 134
Firth-Brown Ltd, 157
Fisher, Sir J., 197
Flanders, Army of, see Army of Flanders
Framlingham, 19
Franeker, 134
Frank, J. P., 85
French, Gen. J., 144, 155
Frescobaldi, 20
Friesland, 133
Froehlich, G., 229, 230, 231, 232, 234
Froumenteau, N., 49

Gansoijen, 128
Gelderland, 110, 112, 133
Ghent, 50, 52, 53
Gide, C., 4
Girón, Don Fernando, 54
Glass Research Association, 188, 201
Glazebrook, Sir R., 169, 195, 201
Gogel, I. J. A., 107, 108, 109, 114, 115, 116, 118, 119, 120, 121, 123, 124, 125, 126, 127, 128, 129, 134, 136
Goldberg, J., 108, 122, 129

Gouda, 109
Grandisson, J., Bishop of Exeter, 25
Grant, A. J., 157
Groningen, 109, 112, 133
Guinand, P., 194

Haarlem, 109, 114, 134
Hall, C. M., 167
Hamburg, 63
Hancock, Prof. K., 4
Hankey, Sir M., 157, 158
Hanseatic League, 30, 63
Harcourt, Rev. W., 167, 168
Harlingen, 134
Hart-Dyke, Sir W., 175
Haslar Naval Hospital, 83
Heath & Co. Ltd, 176, 198
Hengelo, 109
Henry III, 12
Henry IV, 47
Henry VII, 33, 43
Henry VIII, 33, 36, 41, 43, 44, 45
Henry IV (of France), 50
Hespe, T., 114
Hilferding, R., 2
Hilger, A., 189, 199
Hobson, J. A., 2
Hodshon, J., 125
Hogendorp, G. K. van, 108, 121
Hogg, D., 219
Holt, R. D., 217–18
Hondschoote, 51, 53
Hooff, J. van, 115
Hooft, C. P., 60
Hughes, Sir S., 208, 218

Imperial College of Science and Technology, 180, 181, 186, 187, 201
Inchape, Lord, 219
industries: armaments, 5, 7, 64, 139ff., 205ff.; metal, 6, 97, 100; optical glass, 165ff.; textiles, 6, 23, 51, 53, 54, 57, 100

Jackson, Sir H., 171, 175, 179, 182, 185, 188
Jarvis, J., Earl St Vincent, 75, 83
John, Prof. A. H., 6, 92

Kasteele, L. P. van de, 113, 114
Kellaway, F., 218
Kelvin, Bottomley and Baird, 185
Kennet, 19
Keogh, Sir A., 201
Kershaw, W., 184, 198
Keuchenius, W. M., 110
Keynes, J. M., 241, 244, 245, 249, 250
Kings College London, 171, 179

Lamb, S., 174
Lamplough, F. E., 174
Lane, Prof. F. C., 1
Law, A. Bonar, 218, 219
Leiden, 59, 127
Lenin, V. I., 2
Lier, 52
Lind, J., 77, 78, 80, 83
Lloyd George, D., 143, 156, 172, 197, 201
Lockyer, Sir N., 195, 196
London County Council, 169, 185, 186, 194, 195, 201
Long, W., 210, 226
Louvain, 52
Lunge, Dr E., 224
Luxemburg, R., 2

Maassluis, 109
McFarlane, K. B., 6
McGowen, Sir H., 213
McKenna, R., 210
Magnus, Sir P., 172
Marmont, A.-F.-L., 119
Mary, Queen of Scots, 44, 47
Marx, Karl, 1
Maurice of Nassau, 51
Menin, 54
Middle Chirton, 17
Middleharnis, 109
Milward, Prof. A. S., 2
Moir, Sir E., 197
Moltke, Gen. H. von, 234
Mons, 54
Morden, W. Grant, 208, 209, 210, 211, 213, 214, 218, 219, 220, 222, 223
Morison, R., 40, 41, 42
Mowatt Committee (1900), 145, 146, 152
Munitions, Ministry of, 155, 156, 166, 172, 174, 177, 191, 197, 201, 218
Murray Committee (1906–7), 152, 153, 154, 158, 159
Muspratt, M., 158

Naples, first chair of political economy established at, 104
Napoleon I, 135
National Physical Laboratory, 169, 171, 180, 184, 201
Neck, J. van, 61
Necker, J., 104
Nef, Prof. J. U., 5, 92
Neominster, 17
Netherlands: effects of Eighty Years' War on, 49–54, 58; expenditure on defence for, 58; government borrowing during, 59; migration northwards of population during, 59, 64; fluctuations in overseas

Netherlands: (*cont.*)
  trade as a result of, 61–2, 63, 64; fiscal reform as a result of French and Napoleonic Wars, 103ff.
Nijmegen, 108, 127
Nobel's Explosives Co. Ltd, 155, 213, 215
Noble, A., 145
Noble, S., 157
Norfolk, Duke of, 36, 37, 47
Northampton Institute, 169, 172, 178, 185, 186, 195, 199, 201

Ockerse, W., 114
Olivares, Conde Duque de, 55
Ondaatje, P. Q., 127
Oostende, 53
Optical Munitions and Glassware Department, 173ff.
Osborne, F. C., 201
Overijssel, 59, 110, 112

Pakenham, F., 252
Parra-Mantois Co., 170, 173, 183, 198
Paulus, P., 112
Periscope Prism Co. Ltd, 176, 185
Philip II (of Spain), 50, 55, 56, 57, 58
Philip III, 54, 55
Philip IV, 54, 57
Phillips, Sir T., 245
Phillips Committee (1942), 245, 252
Pichegru, Gen. C., 111
Pijman, G., 133
Pinchin Johnson Co. Ltd, 208, 222
Pirenne, Prof. H., 4
Pitt, William (the younger), 94, 95
Pole, Cardinal, 39, 40
Poperinghe, 54
population, effects of Eighty Years' War on Netherlands, 50, 52, 54, 59, 64
Portugal, costs of Eighty Years' War to, 58
Postan, Prof. M. M., 5, 6, 66
Príncipe, 58
Pringle, Sir J., 78, 80, 81, 84, 85, 89
Prudential Trust Co. of Canada, 210, 218, 219

Quevedo y Villegas, F. G. de, 50, 55

Ramel, F., 111
Rathbone, E., 249
Repelaer van Driel, O., 106
Reubell, J. F., 111
Rheinburg, J., 184
Riccardi, 20
Roberts, Lord, 171
Robertson, R., 80
Robson, E., 208, 209

Rosenheim, W., 169, 180
Ross and Co. Ltd, 176, 198, 199
Rostow, Prof. W. W., 6
Rotterdam, 112, 113, 127, 134
Rowntree, Seebohm, 251
Royal Institute of Chemistry, 171
Royal Society, 167, 201

Sadler, R., 39
St Thomas's Hospital, 80, 83, 85, 89
Samuel, H., 218
Santander, 57
São Tomé, 58
Schimmelpenninck, R. J., 118, 119, 133, 135
Schmoller, Prof. G., 229, 230
Schott, O., 168, 183, 184
Schuster, Sir A., 201
science, effects of wars on, 7; 73ff.; 165ff.
Scientific and Industrial Research, Department of, 166, 172, 186, 187, 191, 202
Scientific Instruments Research Association, 187, 188, 190, 202
Sebastian, L. B., 201
Segovia, 57
Sémonville, C. H., marquis de, 116
Sering, M., 234
Sheffield University, 180, 187, 202
Shotwell, Prof. J. T., 3
Sieyes, E., 111
Skalweit, A., 236
Slinglelandt, S. van, 105, 121
Small, C. W., 214
Smith, Sir F., 219
social policy, effects of Second World War on British, 7, 239ff.
Society of Glass Technology, 187, 193, 201
Society of Instrument Makers, 199
Soetermeer, 128
Sombart, Prof. W., 3, 4
Spain, and Eighty Years' War: costs of, 54ff.; drain on economy as a result of, 55–6; government borrowing to finance, 57; industrial decline of Old Castile due to, 57; spending on defence in America, 57–8; trade with England during, 63
Spectacle Makers Co. Ltd, 175
Spiegel, L. P. van de, 104, 106, 107, 111
Spoors, J., 133
Stobart, H. J., 173, 198, 201
Stokes, Sir G., 167, 168
Sumner, Lord, 219

Tawney, Prof. R. H., 1, 247
taxation for war, 5, 7, 10ff., 33ff., 49ff., 103ff.; for purposes other than war, 33ff.
Thompson, Prof. S., 195
Thorbecke, J. R., 129

Tilburg, 109
Titmuss, Prof. R., 246
Trades Union Congress, 249
Trotter, T., 74, 75, 77, 78, 80, 83, 84, 85
Turgot, A. R. J., 104
Turner, W. E. S., 187, 202
Twyman, F., 201
Tynemouth, 17

United Alkali Co Ltd, 158
Utrecht, 107, 110, 136

Veluwe, 108
Venice, 1
Vickers Ltd, 145, 146, 147, 149, 155, 157, 208, 213
Vosmaer, J., 105
Vos van Steinwijk, J. A. de, 117
Vreede, P., 113, 114, 115

Walcheren expedition, 76, 86
Walley, Sir J., 251
Walmsley, M., 172
Wars: War of Saint-Sardos, 22; Anglo-Scottish war (14th c.), 22; Hundred Years' War, 6, 22; Anglo-Scottish war (16th c.), 43; Habsburg-Valois wars, 44; Eighty Years' War, 7, 49ff.; Thirty Years' War, 49; War of the Spanish succession, 73, 103; Seven Years' War, 140, 150;

War of American Independence, 92, 93, 104, 140; French Revolutionary and Napoleonic Wars, 6, 7, 73, 93, 94, 95ff., 103ff., 140; Crimean, 86; Franco-Prussian, 162; Boer War, 139, 141, 142, 143, 147, 159, 161, 166, 168, 193; Russo-Japanese, 139, 141; First World War, 3, 7, 139, 141, 142, 143, 148, 161, 165ff., 205ff., 229ff.; Spanish Civil War, 139; Second World War, 1, 2, 4, 7, 139, 140, 142, 143, 239ff.
Watson & Co. Ltd, 176, 184, 185, 198
Watts, E. R., 198
Webb, Beatrice and Sidney, 245, 251
Weston, Sir R., 53
William IV, Stadholder, 105
William V, Stadholder, 106
Williams, A. C., 201
Williams, F. P., 158
Willinck, W., 125
Wilson, Harold, 249
Winchester estates, 25
Winter, Adm. J. W. de, 114
Wolseley, Gen. G., 144
Wolsey, Cardinal, 34, 35, 36, 43
women, dilutees in optical industry, 177–8, 199, 200

Zeiss, C, 168, 169
Zutphen, 108